Pearson
Secondary Atlas

New Edition

Advisors

Beatrice Adimola • Charles Gahima • Joseph S Mmbando
• Samuel Owuor • Tsegay Asgele

GUIDE TO MAP PAGES

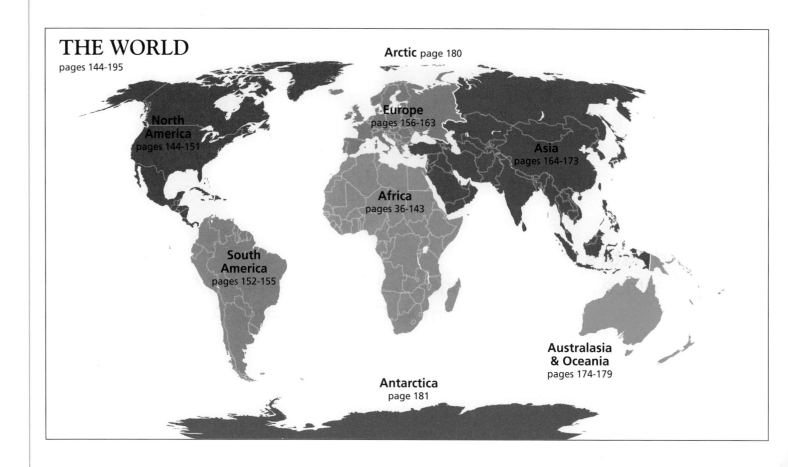

THE WORLD
pages 144-195

Arctic page 180

Europe
pages 156-163

North America
pages 144-151

Asia
pages 164-173

Africa
pages 36-143

South America
pages 152-155

Australasia & Oceania
pages 174-179

Antarctica
page 181

KEY TO REGIONAL MAP SYMBOLS

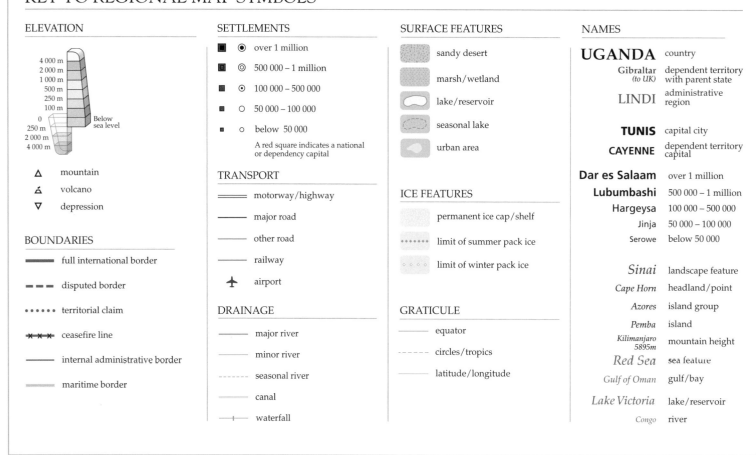

ELEVATION

4 000 m
2 000 m
1 000 m
500 m
250 m
100 m
0
250 m — Below sea level
2 000 m
4 000 m

△   mountain
⩟   volcano
▽   depression

BOUNDARIES

━━━━ full international border

━ ━ ━ disputed border

• • • • • territorial claim

✕━✕━✕ ceasefire line

━━━━ internal administrative border

━━━━ maritime border

SETTLEMENTS

■ ⊙ over 1 million

▣ ◎ 500 000 – 1 million

■ ⊙ 100 000 – 500 000

■ ○ 50 000 – 100 000

■ ○ below 50 000

A red square indicates a national or dependency capital

TRANSPORT

═══ motorway/highway

─── major road

─── other road

─── railway

✈ airport

DRAINAGE

─── major river

─── minor river

- - - - seasonal river

─── canal

──┼─ waterfall

SURFACE FEATURES

sandy desert

marsh/wetland

lake/reservoir

seasonal lake

urban area

ICE FEATURES

permanent ice cap/shelf

••••••• limit of summer pack ice

○ ○ ○ ○ limit of winter pack ice

GRATICULE

─── equator

- - - - circles/tropics

─── latitude/longitude

NAMES

UGANDA   country

Gibraltar _(to UK)_   dependent territory with parent state

LINDI   administrative region

TUNIS   capital city

CAYENNE   dependent territory capital

Dar es Salaam   over 1 million

Lubumbashi   500 000 – 1 million

Hargeysa   100 000 – 500 000

Jinja   50 000 – 100 000

Serowe   below 50 000

Sinai   landscape feature

Cape Horn   headland/point

Azores   island group

Pemba   island

Kilimanjaro 5895m   mountain height

Red Sea   sea feature

Gulf of Oman   gulf/bay

Lake Victoria   lake/reservoir

Congo   river

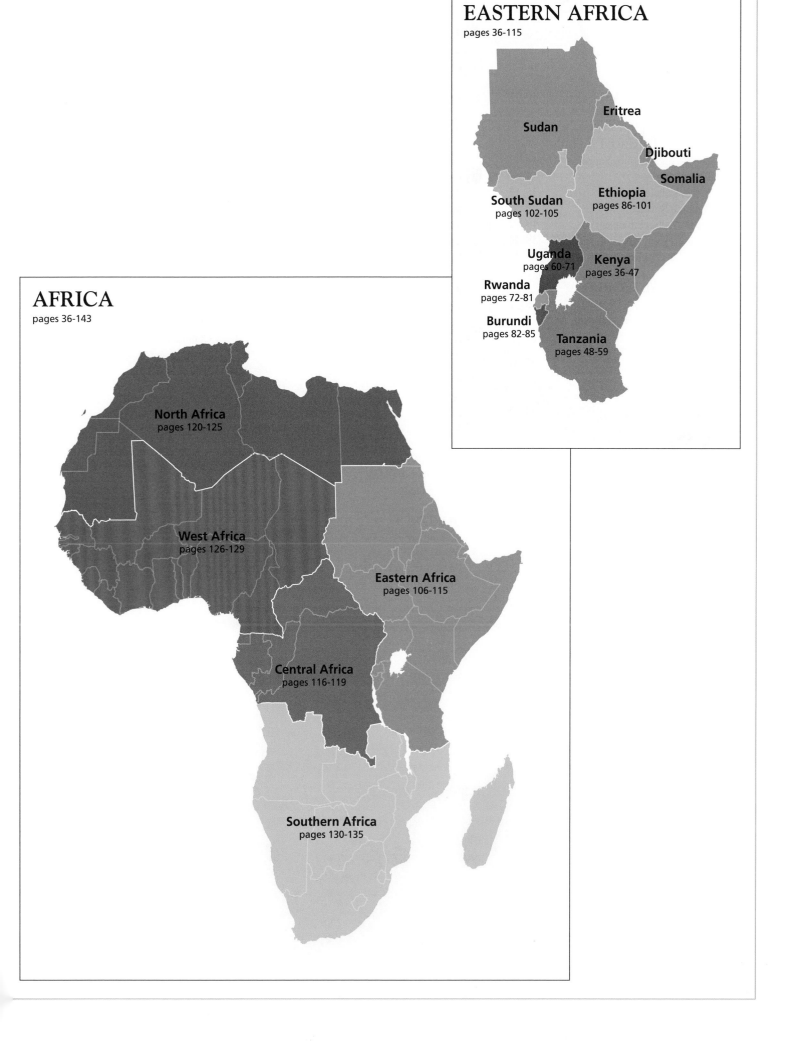

EASTERN AFRICA

Sudan

Eritrea

Djibouti

Somalia

South Sudan

Ethiopia

Uganda

Kenya

Rwanda

Burundi

Tanzania

AFRICA

North Africa

West Africa

Eastern Africa

Central Africa

Southern Africa

CONTENTS

SCALES, DISTANCE, SYMBOLS AND DIRECTION

Map reading and practical skills, such as those taught in this section, are very important to the study of Geography. In order to read maps efficiently you must learn how to use and interpret scales, distance, symbols and direction.

There are exercises on pages 11 to 21 of this atlas that have been designed to give you practical experience so that you can develop these skills.

MEASURING DISTANCE ON A MAP

The linear scale on a map is used to measure distance. You can use one of the following methods to measure the distance between two points on a map.

Method 1: Measuring straight lines

- Place a straight piece of paper between the two points.
- Mark off the distance between the two points along the edge of the paper.
- Place the marked paper along the linear scale of the map.
- Read off the distance on the linear scale.

MAP SCALES

To be able to draw a map of any part of the world, the area must be drawn to scale in order to fit onto a page, or any other size, of paper. The scale of a map can be defined as the ratio between the map distance and the ground distance. Scales on maps are used to measure distances and calculate areas. There are three main ways of showing map scales:

Representative Fraction (RF): One unit on the map represents 7 000 000 units on the ground. This means that 1 cm on the map represents 70 km on the ground.

Linear scale: The line is marked off in units that represent real distances, which are given in kilometres.

Statement of scale: In a statement, e.g. 1 cm on the map represents 70 km on the ground.

Scale 1:7 000 000

0 km	100	200	300

1 cm on the map represents 70 km on the ground

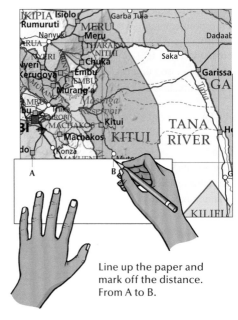

Line up the paper and mark off the distance. From A to B.

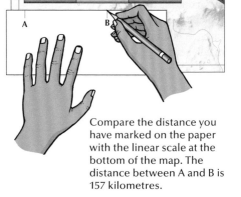

Compare the distance you have marked on the paper with the linear scale at the bottom of the map. The distance between A and B is 157 kilometres.

Method 2: Measuring curved lines

- Place a sheet of paper on the map and mark off the start point on the edge of the paper.
- Move the paper so that the edge follows the curves on the maps. (Note: Use the top of your pencil to pin the edge of the paper to the curves as you bend the paper around the curve.)
- Mark off the end point of your sheet of paper.
- Place the paper along the linear scale.
- Read off the distance on the linear scale.

Use the tip of a pencil to pin the paper to curve. This stops the paper from jumping off course.

Mark off the start point on the edge of the paper.

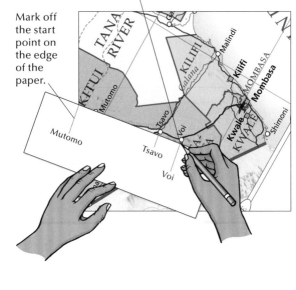

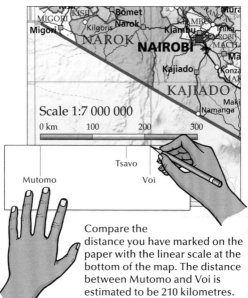

Compare the distance you have marked on the paper with the linear scale at the bottom of the map. The distance between Mutomo and Voi is estimated to be 210 kilometres.

MAP SYMBOLS

Map symbols, which are also referred to as conventional signs are used on maps to represent actual features on the land. The features include boundaries, vegetation, lakes, rivers, water bodies, built-up areas such as cities, airports, roads, railways, bridges, power transmission lines, pipelines, mines and minerals, crops, marshland or swamps.

There are **six** main types of symbols: *colours*, *figures*, *lines*, *letters* or *numbers*, *words* and *shapes*. Every map has a **key** which gives the meaning of the symbols used.

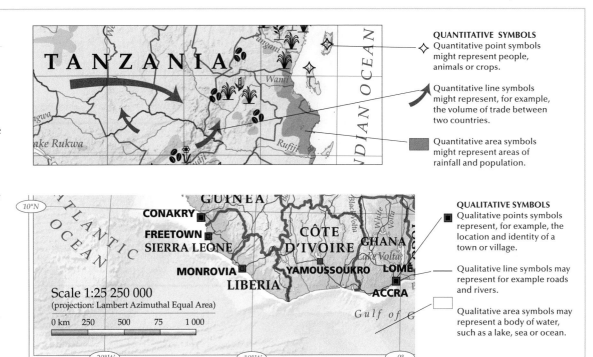

QUANTITATIVE SYMBOLS
Quantitative point symbols might represent people, animals or crops.

Quantitative line symbols might represent, for example, the volume of trade between two countries.

Quantitative area symbols might represent areas of rainfall and population.

QUALITATIVE SYMBOLS
Qualitative points symbols represent, for example, the location and identity of a town or village.

Qualitative line symbols may represent for example roads and rivers.

Qualitative area symbols may represent a body of water, such as a lake, sea or ocean.

Scale 1:25 250 000
(projection: Lambert Azimuthal Equal Area)

0 km   250   500   75   1 000

DIRECTION AND BEARING

A compass is a tool used to show direction. There are four important points on a compass: North, South, East and West. On a map, the North is at the top, South at the bottom, West to the left, and East to the right. The Earth has a North-South axis which runs from the North Pole to the South Pole. North is taken as the point of reference from which all direction is calculated.

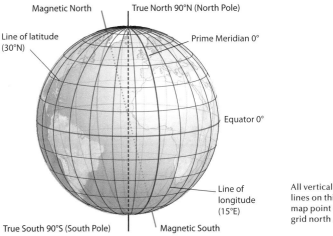

The **globe**: This represents the actual shape of the Earth. On the globe there are representations of the following geographical concepts and phenomenon:

- The **True North** or 90° degrees North, usually referred to as the North Pole.

- The **True South** or 90° degrees South, usually referred to as the South Pole.

- The **Magnetic North** and the **Magnetic South**.

- The **Grid North** which is the northward direction of all vertical parallel lines drawn on a map.

- The **Equator** cutting the globe into two equal hemispheres; the southern and northern hemisphere.

- The **Prime Meridian** is the meridian or line of longitude at which the longitude is defined to be 0°.

The Prime Meridian has its opposite, the 180th meridian (at 180° longitude).

- The **International Date Line** generally follows the Prime Meridian to form a great circle that divides the Earth into the Eastern and Western Hemispheres. The Prime Meridian passes through the Royal Observatory, at Greenwich in London, United Kingdom.

Direction can be described or measured from north by points of the compass. The full names of the points shown on the compass are written thus: north, northeast, north-northeast and so on. They may be shortened to N, NE, NNE, etc.

Direction is also described or measured accurately using a protractor and stating the measurements in degrees. There are 360° in a circle, so direction measured is through a 360° arc, beginning from north and swinging right around in a clockwise direction until north is reached again. In this measurement, the direction of north becomes 0°, east 90°, south 180° and west 270°. You can write all these measurements in groups of three figures, i.e. 000°, 090°, 180°, and so on.

The direction or bearing of one place to another is stated thus: X is east of Y, or X bears 090° from Y.

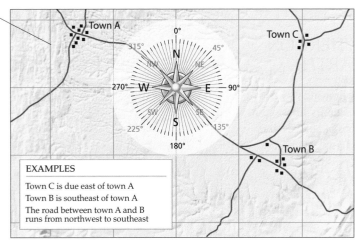

EXAMPLES

Town C is due east of town A

Town B is southeast of town A

The road between town A and B runs from northwest to southeast

The alignment trend of a feature is best described by stating both directions in which it lies, for example: The road runs from northwest to southeast; the trend of the road is 315°–135°.

MAP PROJECTIONS

The only truly accurate map of the whole world is a globe. But a globe is impractical to carry around, so cartographers produce flat maps. Changing the globe into a flat map is not simple and there is always some distortion of area, distance or direction.

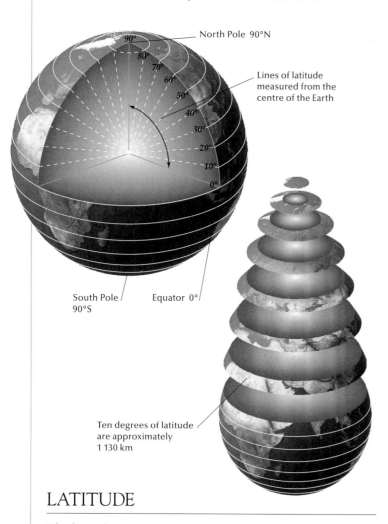

North Pole 90°N

Lines of latitude measured from the centre of the Earth

South Pole 90°S

Equator 0°

Ten degrees of latitude are approximately 1 130 km

Lines of longitude measured from the centre of the Earth

Prime Meridian

Lines of longitude are wider near the Equator and narrower at the poles – dividing the world into segments

LATITUDE

The lines that run east to west around the Earth are called the lines of latitude. Latitude is measured in degrees from 0° at the Equator. The poles are at 90° latitude. The degree of latitude indicates how far north or south a place is.

LONGITUDE

The lines that run north to south between the poles are the lines of longitude. The Prime Meridian, which runs through Greenwich, London, is numbered 0°. All other lines of longitude are numbered in degrees east or west of the Prime Meridian.

WHERE ON EARTH?

By drawing two sets of imaginary lines – the lines of latitude and longitude – around the Earth, a grid can be created. Using this grid, any place on Earth can be located by referring to the point where its line of latitude intersects with its line of longitude.

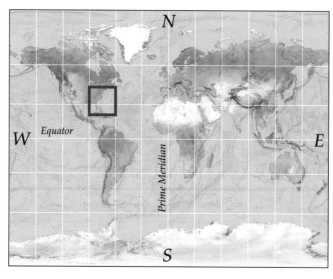

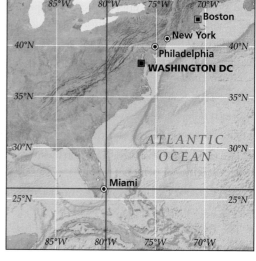

MAKING A FLAT MAP FROM A GLOBE

Cartographers use a technique called projection to show the Earth's curved surface on a flat map. There are a number of different projections, and whilst a distortion in one of these – area, distance or direction – can be minimised, another feature will become more distorted. The cartographer must choose which is most suitable for a particular purpose. There are three major types of projection:

Cylindrical projections The surface of the globe is transferred on to a surrounding cylinder. This is then cut down top to bottom and 'rolled out' to give a flat map. The Mercator projection (right) is a good example.

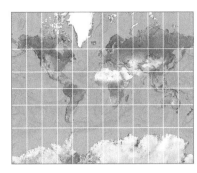

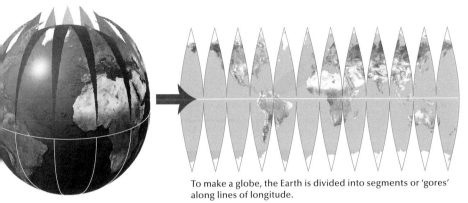

To make a globe, the Earth is divided into segments or 'gores' along lines of longitude.

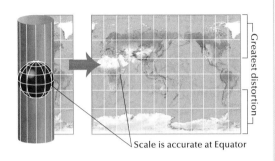

Greatest distortion

Scale is accurate at Equator

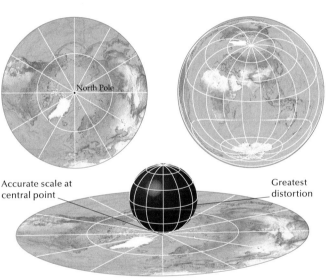

North Pole

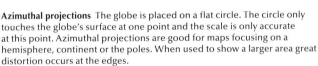

Accurate scale at central point

Greatest distortion

Azimuthal projections The globe is placed on a flat circle. The circle only touches the globe's surface at one point and the scale is only accurate at this point. Azimuthal projections are good for maps focusing on a hemisphere, continent or the poles. When used to show a larger area great distortion occurs at the edges.

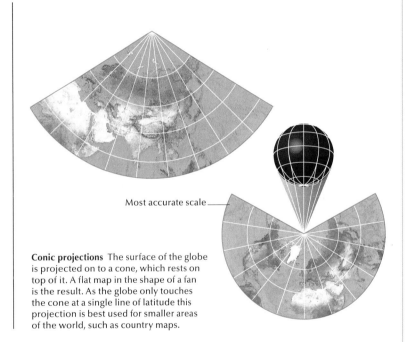

Most accurate scale

Conic projections The surface of the globe is projected on to a cone, which rests on top of it. A flat map in the shape of a fan is the result. As the globe only touches the cone at a single line of latitude this projection is best used for smaller areas of the world, such as country maps.

PROJECTIONS USED IN THIS ATLAS

The projections used have been chosen carefully to ensure very little distortion occurs. Projections appropriate for maps of world, continental or country scale are quite different.

World maps

The Eckert IV projection is used for world maps as it shows countries at their correct size relative to one another.

Continents

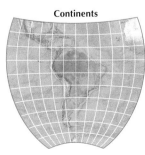

The Lambert Azimuthal Equal Area is used for continental maps. The shape distortion is relatively small and countries retain their correct sizes relative to one another.

Countries

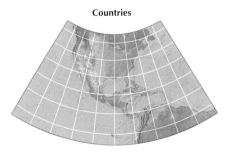

The Lambert Conformal Conic shows countries with the smallest amount of distortion possible. The angles from any point on the map are the same as they would be on the surface of the globe.

THE EARTH IN THE SOLAR SYSTEM

The planets travel in an anti-clockwise direction around the Sun, in paths known as orbits, which are oval in shape. The Earth rotates on its axis from west to east over 24 hours so at any time only half the Earth receives light from the Sun. This causes day and night.

The Solar System consists of the Sun and the astronomical objects gravitationally bound in orbit around it, all of which formed from the collapse of a giant molecular cloud approximately 4.6 billion years ago. Of the many objects that orbit the Sun, most of the mass is contained within eight relatively solitary planets whose orbits are almost circular and lie within a nearly flat disc called the ecliptic plane.

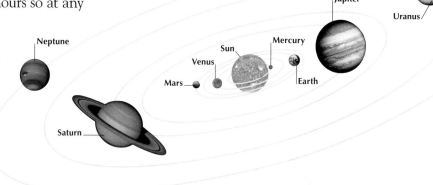

ORDER AND RELATIVE DISTANCE FROM THE SUN OF PLANETS

PLANET STATISTICS

Name of planet	Estimated distance from the Sun	Other features
Mercury	57.9 million kilometres	• Closest planet to the Sun, has no natural satellites
Venus	108.2 million kilometres	• Has a substantial atmosphere and evidence of internal geological activity • Hottest planet, with surface temperatures over 400°C
Earth	149.6 million kilometres	• The only planet known to have current geological activity • It has one natural satellite, the Moon
Mars	227.9 million kilometres	• Has a very thin atmosphere (less than 1% of the density of Earth's atmosphere) • Has two tiny natural satellites Deimos and Phobos
Jupiter	778.3 million kilometres	• Has 63 known satellites; the four largest are: Ganymede, Callisto, Io and Europa
Saturn	1431 million kilometres	• Distinguished by its extensive ring system; has 62 known satellites, two of which, Titan and Enceladus, show signs of geological activity
Uranus	2877 million kilometres	• Has 27 known satellites, the largest ones being Titania, Oberon, Umbriel, Ariel and Miranda
Neptune	4498 million kilometres	• Has 13 known satellites, the largest is Triton

PLANETS

The four smaller inner planets are: Mercury, Venus, Earth and Mars. They are also called the terrestrial planets and are primarily composed of rock and metal.

The four outer planets are substantially more massive than the terrestrials. The two largest are Jupiter and Saturn. These are composed mainly of hydrogen and helium; the two outermost planets, Uranus and Neptune are composed largely of ices, such as water, ammonia and methane and are often referred to separately as 'ice giants'.

SATELLITES, ASTEROIDS

The Solar System has a number of regions populated by smaller objects. The Asteroid belt, which lies between Mars and Jupiter, is similar to the terrestrial planets as it is composed mainly of rock and metal. Beyond Neptune's orbit lie the Kuiper belt of trans-Neptunian objects composed mostly of ices such as water, ammonia and methane.

DWARF PLANETS

There are five distinct objects; Ceres, Pluto, Haumea, Makemake and Eris that are recognised to be large enough to have been rounded by their own gravity, and are thus termed dwarf planets.

COMETS

Comets are small Solar System bodies, composed largely of volatile ice. When a comet enters the inner Solar System, its proximity to the Sun causes its icy surface to sublime and ionise, creating a long tail of gas and dust often visible to the naked eye known as a coma.

ASTEROIDS

Asteroids are small Solar System bodies composed mainly of refractory rocky and metallic minerals. They are thought to be remnants from the Solar System's formation that failed to coalesce because of the gravitational interference of Jupiter. Ceres is the largest asteroid.

ECLIPSES

An eclipse is an astronomical event that occurs when an astronomical object is temporarily obscured, either by passing into the shadow of another body or by having another body pass between it and the viewer.

Eclipse

The term eclipse is most often used to describe either a solar eclipse, when the Moon's shadow crosses the Earth's surface, or a lunar eclipse, when the Moon moves into the Earth's shadow. The region of the Earth's shadow in a solar eclipse is divided into three parts

- The umbra, in which the Moon completely covers the Sun.
- The antumbra, extending beyond the tip of the umbra, in which the Moon is completely in front of the Sun but too small to completely cover it.
- The penumbra, in which the Moon is only partially in front of the Sun.

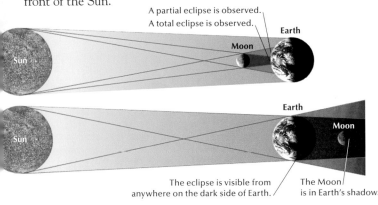

A partial eclipse is observed.
A total eclipse is observed.
Earth
Moon
Sun

Earth
Sun
Moon

The eclipse is visible from anywhere on the dark side of Earth.
The Moon is in Earth's shadow.

HEMISPHERES

The Earth is divided along two imaginary lines. One, the Equator, which runs around the Earth at the halfway point between the two poles, divides the globe into the northern and southern hemispheres. The other line, which runs from Prime Meridian (0°) to 180° longitude, creates the eastern and western hemispheres.

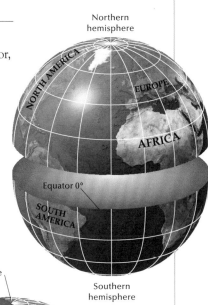

Northern hemisphere
NORTH AMERICA
EUROPE
AFRICA
Equator 0°
SOUTH AMERICA
Southern hemisphere

North Pole
Prime meridian 0°
NORTH AMERICA
EUROPE
Western hemisphere
AFRICA
Eastern hemisphere
SOUTH AMERICA

SEASONS

As the Earth orbits the Sun its axis, tilted at 23.5°, points in a fixed direction. This means that in June the northern hemisphere points towards the Sun and receives sunlight for long hours. This is the northern summer. At the same time, the southern hemisphere receives fewer hours of sunlight and this is the southern winter. As time passes, this process is reversed and by December the northern hemisphere experiences winter and the south experiences summer conditions.

Australia, 21 December: In the southern hemisphere summer is in December and winter is in June.

UK, 21 December: In winter the northern hemisphere tilts away from the sun, receiving less heat and light.

21 JUNE

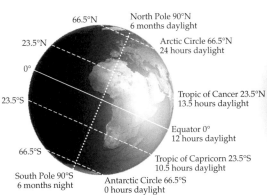

66.5°N
North Pole 90°N
6 months daylight
23.5°N
Arctic Circle 66.5°N
24 hours daylight
0°
23.5°S
Tropic of Cancer 23.5°N
13.5 hours daylight
Equator 0°
12 hours daylight
66.5°S
Tropic of Capricorn 23.5°S
10.5 hours daylight
South Pole 90°S
6 months night
Antarctic Circle 66.5°S
0 hours daylight

21 DECEMBER

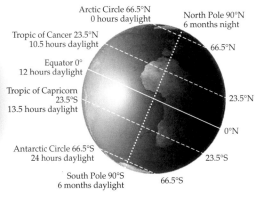

Arctic Circle 66.5°N
0 hours daylight
North Pole 90°N
6 months night
Tropic of Cancer 23.5°N
10.5 hours daylight
66.5°N
Equator 0°
12 hours daylight
Tropic of Capricorn 23.5°S
13.5 hours daylight
23.5°N
0°N
Antarctic Circle 66.5°S
24 hours daylight
23.5°S
South Pole 90°S
6 months daylight
66.5°S

On 21 June the northern hemisphere receives most direct light from the Sun and has its longest day.

Places between the tropics are hot all year round. Here, the Sun's rays strike the Earth almost vertically, so are more intense. Places near the poles have the coldest climate. At high latitudes the Sun's rays hit the Earth at an angle so are less intense.

On 21 December the southern hemisphere receives the most direct heat and light.

MAP SKILLS: ORDNANCE MAP INTERPRETATION

A map is a drawing, usually on a flat surface, of all or part of the Earth's surface, ordinarily showing countries, water features, cities and mountains. Maps of the world are often either 'political' or 'physical'. The most important purpose of the political map is to show territorial borders; the purpose of a physical map is to show features of geography such as mountains, soil type or land use, including infrastructure such as roads, railroads and settlements.

TYPES OF MAPS

Topographic maps show elevation and relief using contour lines or shades of colour, and are also called ordnance maps. **Geological** maps show not only the physical surface, but characteristics of the underlying rock, fault lines and sub-surface structures.

MAP KEY

A **map key** is a list of words or phrases, colours, lines, letters, numbers and shapes, explaining the meaning as used on the particular map. The key is usually in a box in one corner of the map. It is also referred to as a **legend**.

MAP INTERPRETATION

There are many types of maps that people use. Ordnance maps are maps that contain a lot of information. Ordnance maps are produced at different scales and the scale determines the amount of detail a map can have. It is therefore important to develop map reading skills to be able to read such maps. Refer to pages 6–9 to remind you about scale, symbols, direction, latitude and longitude.

CONTOURS AND RELIEF

Relief is an important feature of the Earth's surface. Cartographers or map makers use various methods to show landforms, height or altitude. One method is by using **contours**, which are lines drawn on a map which join all places with the same height or altitude above sea level. Contours on a map have a fixed height interval between them. The height of each contour is shown on the map and, although not all contour heights are marked, it is possible to work out the height by identifying the marked contours. After doing some exercises you will see that where contours are far apart they represent a gentle slope and where they are close to one another, they represent a steep slope.

A CROSS SECTION

A **cross section** is a plane cutting through an object at right angles to an axis. A cross section on an ordnance map is as if one is cutting through the piece of land thus showing the shape of the surface.

HOW TO DRAW A CROSS SECTION

Study the ordnance maps of Songea and Arusha. On the Map of Songea choose two points **A** and **B**; and on the map of Arusha choose two points marked **C** and **D**. By using the steps below, draw a cross section of the area between points A and B on the map of Songea.

Step one: Take a pencil and a ruler and draw a line joining, **A** to **B**.

Step two: Take a piece of paper that has a straight edge and place the straight edge between point **A** and **B** (see example right).

Step three: Put a mark on the paper wherever a contour line touches the edge of the paper; and write the height of the contour at each mark.

Step four: On a graph paper, draw a horizontal line representing the distance between **A** and **B**, write down the height of each contour (see example right).

Step five: Draw a vertical line that represents the contour heights found between point **A** and **B**.

Step six: Transfer the contour heights information onto the vertical line.

Step seven: Put a mark **x** where the two corresponding heights on the vertical axis and horizontal axis meet.

Step eight: Join the points marked **x** with a line and what you see is the cross section of the land between points **A** and **B**.

EXERCISE 1

Study the maps of Songea and Arusha then do the following exercises.

1. What is the contour interval on the map of Songea?
2. Describe the landforms as shown in the cross section.
3. What is the most characteristic land use on the map of Arusha?
4. What types of vegetation are found in the map of Songea?
5. What is the scale of these maps?

SONGEA AND ARUSHA, TANZANIA

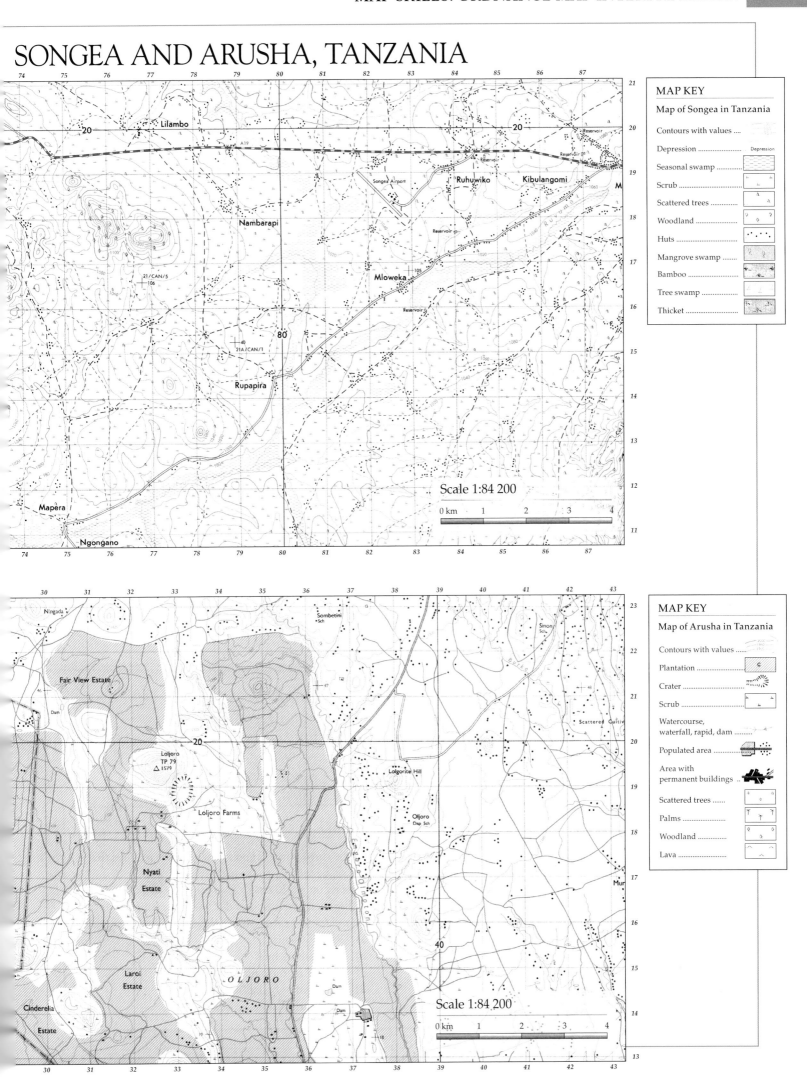

MAP KEY

Map of Songea in Tanzania

Contours with values ....

Depression ....

Seasonal swamp ....

Scrub ....

Scattered trees ....

Woodland ....

Huts ....

Mangrove swamp ....

Bamboo ....

Tree swamp ....

Thicket ....

Scale 1:84 200

0 km   1   2   3   4

MAP KEY

Map of Arusha in Tanzania

Contours with values ......

Plantation ....

Crater ....

Scrub ....

Watercourse,
waterfall, rapid, dam ....

Populated area ....

Area with
permanent buildings ..

Scattered trees ....

Palms ....

Woodland ....

Lava ....

Scale 1:84 200

0 km   1   2   3   4

ELDORET, KENYA

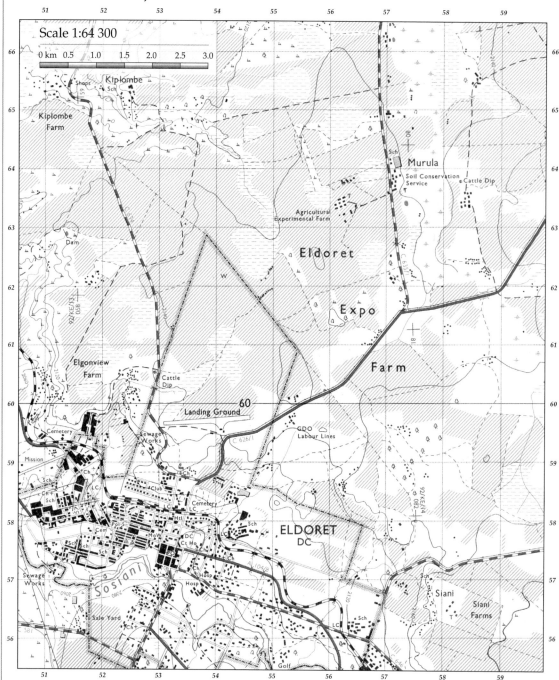

Scale 1:64 300

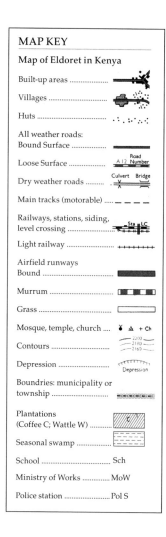

MAP KEY

Map of Eldoret in Kenya

Built-up areas	
Villages	
Huts	
All weather roads: Bound Surface	
Loose Surface	Road A 12 Number
Dry weather roads	Culvert Bridge
Main tracks (motorable)	– – – –
Railways, stations, siding, level crossing	Sta LC
Light railway	+++++++
Airfield runways Bound	
Murrum	
Grass	
Mosque, temple, church	
Contours	
Depression	Depression
Boundries: municipality or township	
Plantations (Coffee C; Wattle W)	
Seasonal swamp	
School .... Sch	
Ministry of Works .... MoW	
Police station .... Pol S	

EXERCISE 2

Study the map of Eldoret and answer these questions.

1. Measure the distance covered by the following:
   a) River Sosiani
   b) All weather bound surface road from grid reference 536 587 to the bridge at grid reference 587 618.

2. Use evidence from the map to do the following.
   a) List eight principal functions of Eldoret town.
   b) Give five reasons why agriculture is a dominant activity in the area.
   c) Identify two major settlement patterns in the area.

3. Describe three physical and five man-made features that can be seen on the map.

4. Draw a rectangle 20 cm by 15 cm to represent the area between eastings 51 and 60, and northings 55.5 and 66. On the rectangle show the following:
   a) River Sosiani
   b) The railway line
   c) Eldoret municipality boundary
   d) All weather bound surface roads
   e) All weather loose surface roads.

NSIKA, UGANDA

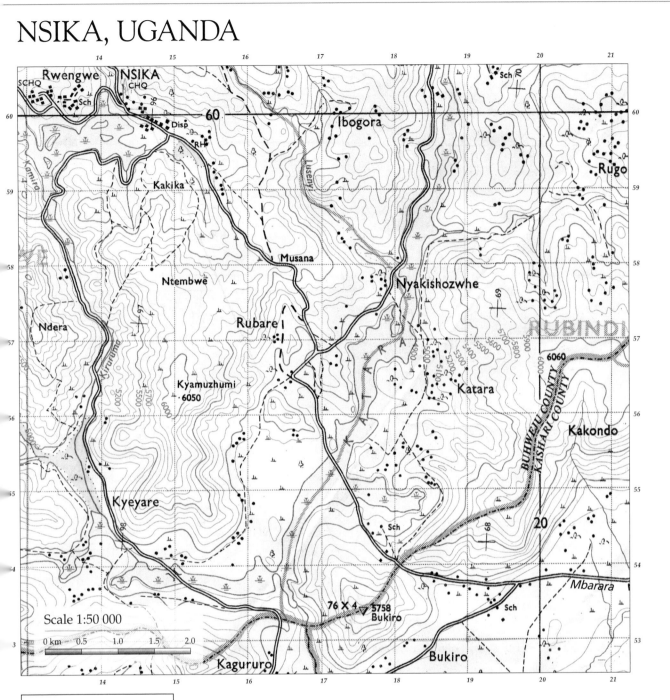

Scale 1:50 000

0 km   0.5   1.0   1.5   2.0

MAP KEY

Map of Nsika in Uganda

School	Sch
Sub-County headquarters .	SCHQ
Rest House	RH
County Headquarters	CHQ
Mosque, church	☾ + Ch
Trignometrical point	▽
Scattered trees	
Papyrus swamp, marsh, bog	
Seasonal swamp	
Woodland	
Scrub	
Populated area/huts	
Thicket	
Forest	

EXERCISE 3

Study the map of Nsika and answer these questions.

1. State the grid reference for the following features:
   a) The school between Bukiro and Mbarara Road.
   b) Rwengwe sub-county headquarters and name:
      i) Man-made feature at 150 539.
      ii) Natural feature at 188 600.
2. State the direction of the flow of River Kiruruma.
3. Describe the landforms in the area shown on the map.
4. Explain the settlement pattern in the area.
5. Giving examples describe the influence of relief on land use.
6. Draw an annotated sketch map of the map showing the physiographic regions.
7. Draw a sketch section from Bukiro secondary trigonometrical station to Kamira wetland at 138 598. Mark and label:
   a) Relief features   c) Settlement
   b) Drainage features

RUHUHA, RWANDA

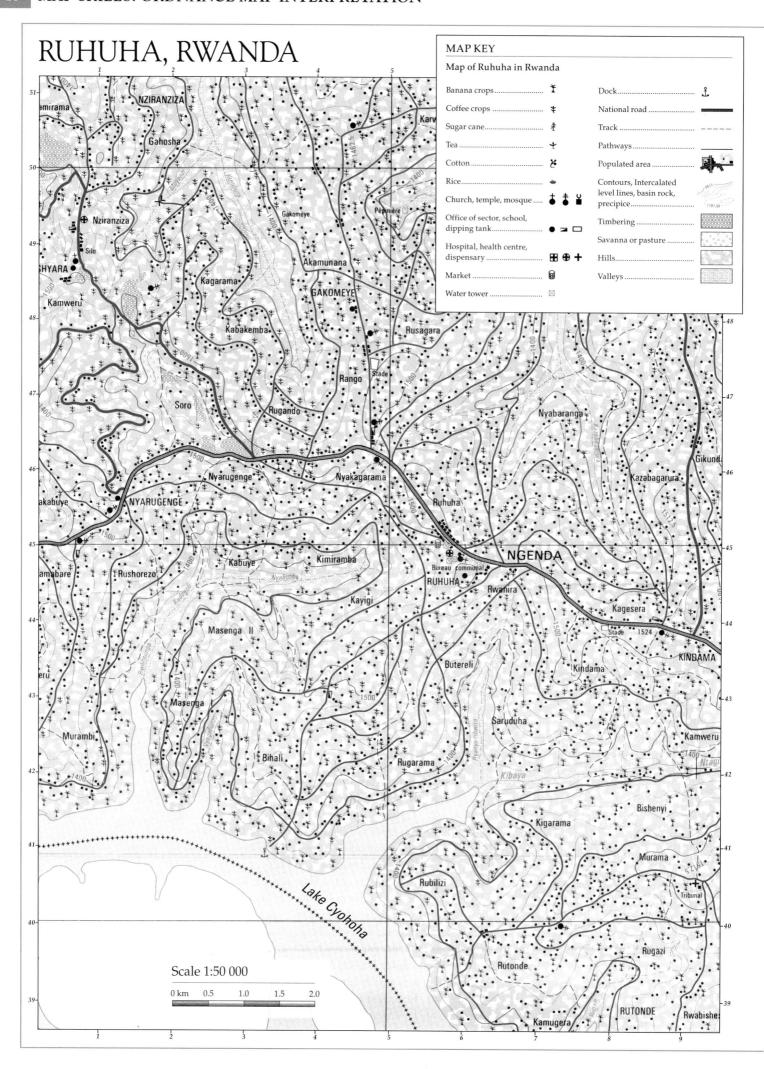

MAP KEY

Map of Ruhuha in Rwanda

Banana crops		Dock	
Coffee crops		National road	
Sugar cane		Track	
Tea		Pathways	
Cotton		Populated area	
Rice		Contours, Intercalated level lines, basin rock, precipice	
Church, temple, mosque			
Office of sector, school, dipping tank		Timbering	
Hospital, health centre, dispensary		Savanna or pasture	
Market		Hills	
Water tower		Valleys	

Scale 1:50 000

0 km   0.5   1.0   1.5   2.0

KABALE, UGANDA

MAP KEY

Map of Kabale in Uganda

Built-up areas

Villages

Huts

All weather roads bound surface

All weather roads loose surface

Dry weather roads

Railways, station, siding, level crossing

Sub-county or location

National park, game reserve or nature reserve

Forest

Plantation (coffee C, sisal S, sugar su, palm I, wattle W, paw paw pa)

Mangrove swamp

Papyrus swamp, march, bog

Seasonal swamp

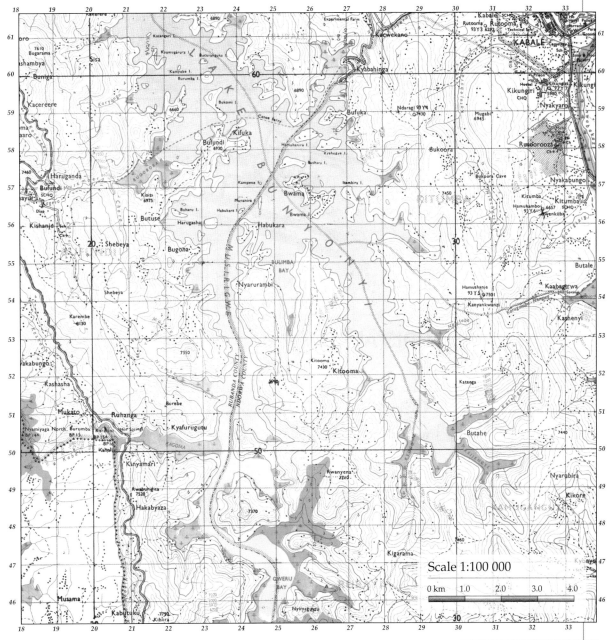

Scale 1:100 000

0 km   1.0   2.0   3.0   4.0

EXERCISE 4

Study the map of Ruhuha (page 16) and answer these questions.

1. With evidence from the map, identify any four economic activities carried out in the area shown.

2. a) Give any four uses of Lake Cyohoha to the people of Ngenda.

   b) State any three disadvantages of Lake Cyohoha to the people living near it.

3. Describe
   a) the road system in the area shown;
   b) the type of vegetation found in the area shown.

4. a) Measure the distance of the road from grid reference 020 465 to 090 438.

   b) What is the direction of Ruhuha from Kagarama?

   c) Identify the man-made feature at grid reference 049 475.

EXERCISE 5

Study the map of Kabale provided (above) and answer the questions that follow.

1. Reduce the area of the Kabale map by 2 times between Eastings 26 and 33 Northings 50 and 61. On the sketch drawn, mark and name the following.
   a) Lake Bunyonyi
   b) Swamps
   c) Plateaux
   d) River systems
   e) Transport network

2. State the new scale of the new sketch map.

3. Name the features found at the following grid references.
   a) 307 542
   b) 288 588

4. Describe the relief of the area as it is shown on the map extract.

5. Describe the relationship between relief and the following.
   a) Settlement
   b) Transport network
   c) Drainage

6. Identify two problems likely to be faced by the people living in the area based on evidence from the map.

7. Give reasons for the answers given in question 6.

SOUTHEASTERN PART OF ADDIS ABABA, ETHIOPIA

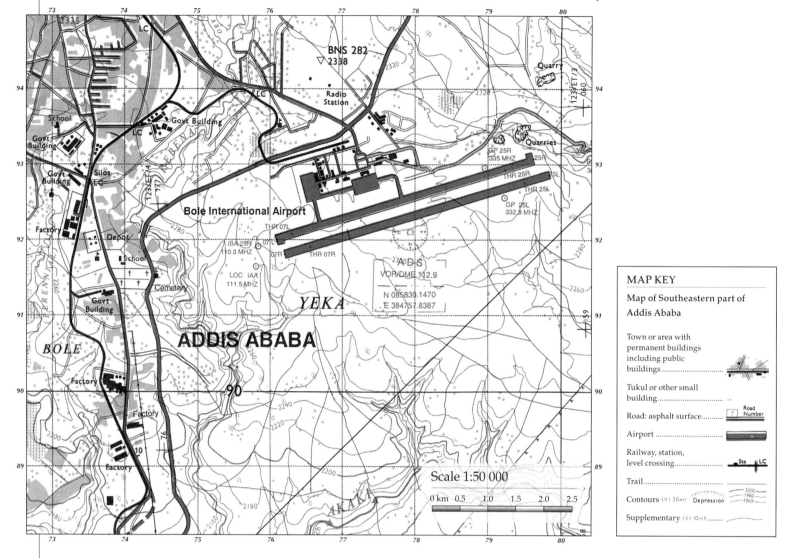

EXERCISE 6

Study the ordnance/topographic map of a section of Addis Ababa above and do the exercises that follow.

PART 1 Drawing a cross-section profile from a topographic map

Draw a cross section between two points of your own choice on the 1:50 000 topographic map above of a section of Addis Ababa to show the topographic profile between the selected places.

1. Identify two points on the map representing the highest and lowest parts of the area and mark them H and L.
2. Draw a line connecting these two points by using a sharp, soft pencil.
3. Place the edge of a blank piece of white paper along the line and mark the two end points (H and L) as well as all the points of the contour lines crossed by the edge of the paper.
4. Mark the elevation readings of each contour line on to the marked points along the edge of the white paper.
5. Transfer the marked readings on the edge of the white paper to another horizontal line drawn on a separate graph paper.

6. Choose a suitable vertical scale on the graph paper and plot the marked elevations of each contour line along the vertical scale.
7. Join the plotted points to see the topographic profile between points H and L.

PART 2 Measuring distance, area and direction on a map

1. Mark any two points (A and B) along a road of your choice on the ordnance map and measure the ground distance between them.
2. Explain the general direction of flow of the major streams shown in the map.
3. Draw a 5 cm square on the map and calculate the actual area on the ground.

TANZANIA

EXERCISE 7

To interpret or read a photograph, use the following guidelines. Imagine that the photograph above is divided in nine parts as shown in the plan below.

Left background	Central background	Right background
Left middle ground	Central middle ground	Right middle Ground
Left foreground	Central foreground	Right foreground

Use the plan left to identify and describe the various features you see on the photograph. Now do the following exercises.

1. Write a short description of what you see in the photograph.
2. Describe what you see in the background of the photograph.
3. Describe the vegetation in the foreground.
4. What is the name of the animals in the photograph?
5. What is the white space seen in the photograph?
6. What part of Tanzania is shown in the photograph?

KENYA

Satellite image of Nairobi taken in 2011

EXERCISE 8

Use the maps and image provided to answer the following questions.

1. You have been provided with a satellite image of Nairobi and a corresponding topographical map for 2011. An area of the image has been marked with a red circle. Identify this area on the topographical map.
2. Identify the developments that have taken place in Nairobi between 1975 and 2011.
3. Use evidence from the image to outline the challenges that may be affecting Nairobi as a city.

Map of Nairobi, 1975

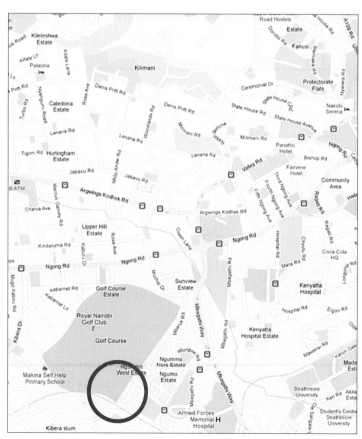

Map of Nairobi, 2011

UGANDA

EXERCISE 9

Study the images and answer these questions.

1. Using evidence from photographs A, B and C, name the economic activities in the area.
2. Describe the influence of relief on the land use in photograph A.
3. What product is being exploited in photograph B.
4. What is the impact of economic activity in photograph B on the environment?
5. Using evidence from the photograph, how is the product in photograph C transported?
6. Draw a sketch of photograph A and label:
   a) Relief features
   b) Vegetation
   c) Settlement

A

Banana plantation, Kabale, Uganda

B

Oil rig, Uganda

C

Nakinogo, Uganda

RWANDA

Gisovu, Karongi District, Rwanda

EXERCISE 10

Study the photograph (left) and answer these questions using evidence from the photograph.

1. Describe the landscape of the area.
2. Describe the economic activities shown in the foreground and background of the photograph.
3. What is the type of farming shown in the foreground and middle ground of the photograph?
4. What crop is grown in both the foreground and middle ground of the photograph?
5. What are the climatic conditions that favour the growing of the crop in the area?
6. State the method used to control soil erosion in the area.

Environmental degradation, Gicumbi district

EXERCISE 11

Study the photograph (left) and answer these questions using evidence from the photograph.

1. What economic activity(ies) can you identify in the photograph on the left?
2. Describe the landscape seen in the photograph.
3. Describe any environmental degradation shown in the photograph.
4. Explain ways in which the environmental degradation identified above can be mitigated.

BURUNDI

Bujumbura, Burundi

EXERCISE 12

Study the photograph (above) and answer these questions using evidence from the photograph.

1. Describe the relief of the place you see in the photograph.
2. What kind of rainfall is likely to dominate in this area? Give reasons for your answer.
3. Describe the kind of settlement depicted in the mid-background of the photograph.
4. What are the likely economic activities in the area where this photograph was taken?
5. Describe the weather conditions depicted in the area where the photograph was taken.

ETHIOPIA

Blue Nile Falls (locally called Tis-Isat)

EXERCISE 13

Study the photograph (left) and answer these questions using evidence from the photograph.

1. The river is flowing on a very shallow course before the water falls over the cliff. What type of rock/s do you think the area is made of?

2. In which season do you think the photograph was taken? Why?

3. Describe the possible economic importance of the river.

Dungeta Shet Canyon, Ethiopia

EXERCISE 14

Study the photograph (left) and answer these questions using evidence from the photograph.

1. Explain the general landform of the area.

2. In which part of Ethiopia do you think such landforms are commonly found?

3. In which season do you think the photograph was taken?

4. Identify the major streams and the direction of their flow, assuming that the upper part of the photograph is north.

EARTH'S ATMOSPHERE AND STRUCTURE

The Earth is one of the eight planets orbiting the Sun. (Pluto, originally considered to be the ninth planet, was downgraded to the status of dwarf planet in 2006.) Earth is a dense, rocky spheroid with a diameter 12 750 km across. The atmosphere is a collection of gases including nitrogen, oxygen and water vapour that surrounds the Earth.

The Earth and the universe

THE ATMOSPHERE

The atmosphere is divided into layers as the result of major changes in temperature. Gravity pushes the layers of air down on the Earth's surface. This push is called air pressure. 99% of the total mass of the atmosphere is below 32 kilometres from sea level. The layers are as follows.

Troposphere (0 to 12 km) This contains 75% of the gases in the atmosphere. This is where we live and where weather occurs. As height increases, temperature decreases; for every kilometre above the Earth's surface, temperature drops about 6.5°C. The tropopause is found at the top of the troposphere. Here the temperature remains fairly constant with the increase in height. The tropopause separates the troposphere from the stratosphere above it.

Stratosphere (12 to 50 km) In the lower part of the stratosphere the temperature is about -60°C. The stratosphere contains the ozone layer that absorbs ultraviolet radiation from the Sun and thereby acts as a shield for the Earth's surface from the effects of direct sunlight.

Mesosphere (50 to 80 km) The temperature drops in this layer to about -100°C. This is the coldest region of the atmosphere.

Thermosphere (80 km and up) The air is very thin here. Thermosphere means 'heat sphere'. The temperature is very high in this layer because ultraviolet radiation is turned into heat. Temperatures often reach 2000°C. There are three regions in this layer:

- **Ionosphere** This is the lower part of the thermosphere. It extends from about 80 to 550 km.

- **Exosphere** The upper part of the thermosphere. It extends from about 550 km for thousands of kilometres. Air is very thin here. This is the area where satellites orbit the Earth.

- **Magnetosphere** The area around the Earth that extends beyond the atmosphere. The Earth's magnetic field operates here.

EARTH'S INTERNAL STRUCTURE

If we could cut through the Earth, we would see the main layers as described below.

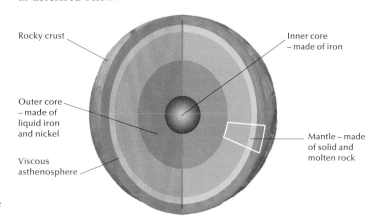

Crust: There are two different types of crust: thin oceanic crust that underlies the ocean basins and thicker continental crust that underlies the continents. These two different types of crust are made up of different types of rock.

Mantle: The Earth's mantle is thought to be composed mainly of olivine-rich rock. It has different temperatures at different depths. The temperature is lowest immediately beneath the crust and increases with depth.

Core: The Earth's core is thought to be composed of an iron and nickel alloy. The core is the Earth's source of internal heat because it contains radioactive materials which release heat as they break down into more stable substances. The core is divided into two different zones. The outer core is a liquid because the temperatures there are high enough to melt the iron-nickel alloy. The inner core is a solid, even though its temperature is higher than the outer core. Here, tremendous pressure, produced by the weight of the overlying rocks, is strong enough to crowd the atoms tightly together so that the material stays as a solid.

TECTONIC PLATES

The Earth's crust is not a continuous unbroken shell. It is divided into several major, and a number of smaller, slabs of rock called tectonic plates. These move in different ways on the liquid rock of the mantle below the Earth's surface. The majority of the world's volcanoes and fault lines are found at or near the plate boundaries.

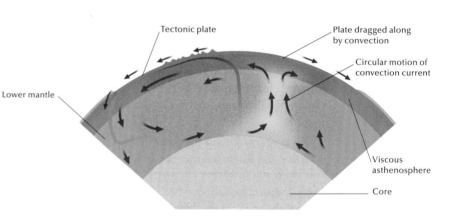

- Continental plate
- Plate boundary or margin
- Oceanic plate

The Earth's plates
The crust is relatively thin and is made up of a series of 'plates' which fit closely together. Movement of the molten rock deep within the mantle causes the plates to move, creating changes in the surface features of the Earth.

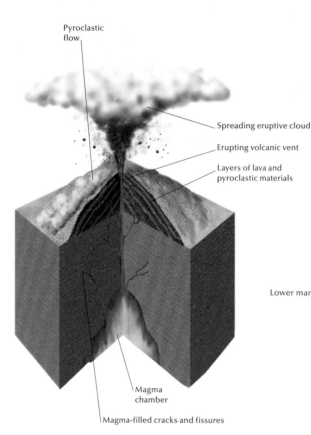

Pyroclastic flow

- Spreading eruptive cloud
- Erupting volcanic vent
- Layers of lava and pyroclastic materials

Magma chamber

Magma-filled cracks and fissures

Volcanoes
A volcano is formed when molten rock (magma) from the core of the Earth forces its way up to the surface. When volcanic activity takes place under the ocean huge tidal waves, or tsunamis, can be formed.

Tectonic plate

Plate dragged along by convection

Circular motion of convection current

Lower mantle

Viscous asthenosphere

Core

Inside the Earth
The heart of the Earth is a solid core of iron surrounded by several layers of very hot, sometimes liquid, rock.

JAPANESE TSUNAMI, 2011

In March 2011 a powerful earthquake of 8.4 magnitude struck near the northeast coast of Japan. This triggered off a tsunami that killed over 25 000 people and caused a lot of destruction along the east coast. The tsunami rolled across the Pacific at 800 km per hour. It was the most powerful earthquake to have hit Japan.

Destruction by tsunami in Japan

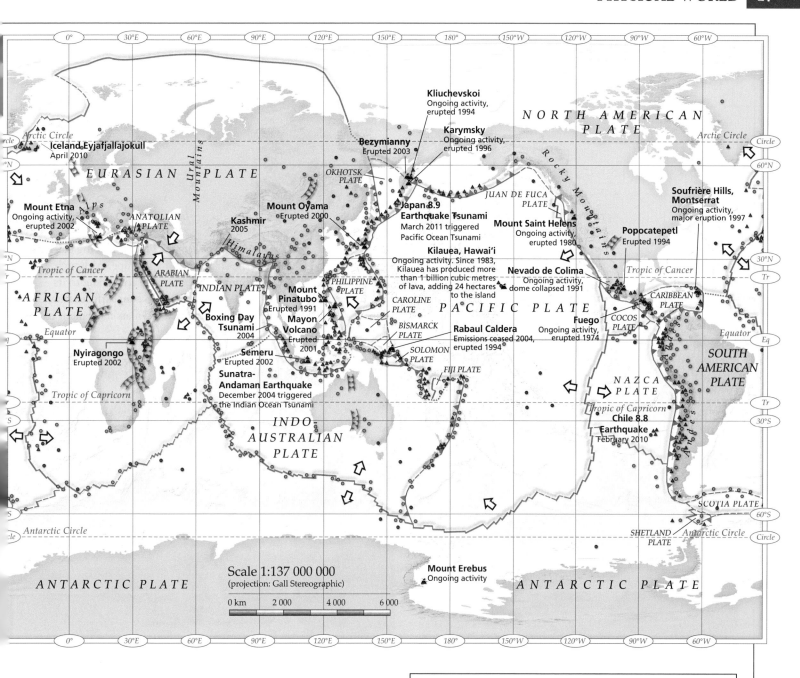

Kliuchevskoi
Ongoing activity,
erupted 1994

Karymsky
Ongoing activity,
erupted 1996

Bezymianny
Erupted 2003

NORTH AMERICAN PLATE

Arctic Circle

Iceland Eyjafjallajokull
April 2010

EURASIAN PLATE

Ural Mountains

OKHOTSK PLATE

JUAN DE FUCA PLATE

Soufrière Hills, Montserrat
Ongoing activity,
major eruption 1997

Mount Etna
Ongoing activity,
erupted 2002

Alps

ANATOLIAN PLATE

Kashmir
2005

Mount Oyama
Erupted 2000

Japan 8.9
Earthquake Tsunami
March 2011 triggered
Pacific Ocean Tsunami

Mount Saint Helens
Ongoing activity,
erupted 1980

Popocatepetl
Erupted 1994

Tropic of Cancer

ARABIAN PLATE

Himalayas

INDIAN PLATE

Mount Pinatubo
Erupted 1991

PHILIPPINE PLATE

Kilauea, Hawai'i
Ongoing activity. Since 1983,
Kilauea has produced more
than 1 billion cubic metres
of lava, adding 24 hectares
to the island

Nevado de Colima
Ongoing activity,
dome collapsed 1991

AFRICAN PLATE

Equator

Boxing Day
Tsunami
2004

Mayon
Volcano
Erupted
2001

CAROLINE PLATE

PACIFIC PLATE

CARIBBEAN PLATE

COCOS PLATE

Nyiragongo
Erupted 2002

Semeru
Erupted 2002

BISMARCK PLATE

Rabaul Caldera
Emissions ceased 2004,
erupted 1994

SOLOMON PLATE

Fuego
Ongoing activity,
erupted 1974

Sunatra-
Andaman Earthquake
December 2004 triggered
the Indian Ocean Tsunami

FIJI PLATE

SOUTH AMERICAN PLATE

Tropic of Capricorn

INDO-
AUSTRALIAN PLATE

NAZCA PLATE

Andes

Chile 8.8
Earthquake
February 2010

SCOTIA PLATE

SHETLAND PLATE

Antarctic Circle

ANTARCTIC PLATE

Mount Erebus
Ongoing activity

ANTARCTIC PLATE

Scale 1:137 000 000
(projection: Gall Stereographic)

0 km   2 000   4 000   6 000

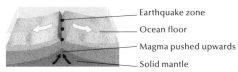

Diverging (Constructive) plates
As plates move apart, magma rises
through the outer mantle. When it
cools, it forms new crust. The Mid-
Atlantic Ridge and East African Rift
Valley are caused by diverging plates.

Earthquake zone
Ocean floor
Magma pushed upwards
Solid mantle

MAP KEY

Plate boundaries
—— constructive
▲▲ destructive
- - - conservative
········ uncertain

Tectonic features
 major volcanic events since 1980
▲ volcanic zone
● hot spot
○ major earthquake

 direction of plate movement
rift valley

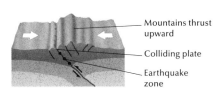

Colliding plates
When two plates bearing
landmasses collide with one
another, the land is crumpled
upwards into high mountain
peaks such as the Alps and
the Himalayas.

Mountains thrust upward
Colliding plate
Earthquake zone

Subducting (Destructive) plates
When an ocean-bearing plate collides
with a continental plate, it is forced
downwards under the other plate and into
the mantle. Volcanoes occur along these
boundaries and they were also the cause
of the Indian Ocean Tsunami 2004.

Ocean plate
Mountains
Earthquake zone
Continental plate

Conservative (Sliding) plates
As two plates slide past each
other, great friction occurs along
the fault line that lies between
them. This can lead to powerful
earthquakes.

Plate
Fault line
Earthquake zone

WEATHERING AND DEPOSITIONAL FEATURES

Rocks on the Earth's surface are subjected to physical, chemical and biological processes, which are known collectively as weathering. Over long periods of time, weathering can lead to the breakdown or disintegration of rocks to create smaller soluble and insoluble particles. These particles or sediments are further subjected to erosion, transportation and deposition.

A branch of the Blue Nile River splits the rock in the Nile Gorge, Ethiopia

EROSION

Erosion is the movement of products of weathering. Erosion may be caused by fast-flowing water, waves, strong winds and moving glaciers. Erosion constantly changes the shape of the landscape. Although erosion is a natural process, human practices also contribute to its occurrence. Erosion takes place more quickly on bare surfaces that are not protected by vegetation, and may lead to mass movement of weathered particles and soil.

Wind and water erosion

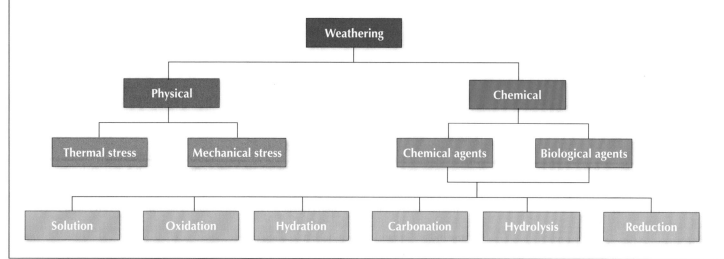

Speke glacier bounded by steep scarps in the Rwenzori Mountains, Uganda

GLACIATION

A glacier is a large mass of ice and snow that forms in areas where the rate of snowfall exceeds the melting rate. A glacier moves slowly down a mountain or along a valley until it melts. There are two types of glaciers: valley glaciers and lowland glaciers. Valley glaciers form on highland peaks and on the upper valleys of mountain ranges. They are best experienced in mountain ranges such as the Rockies of North America, the Andes, the Himalayas and the Alps (especially in Switzerland). In Africa, small ice caps and glaciers exist on higher mountains, in particular on Mount Kilimanjaro, Mount Rwenzori and Mount Kenya.

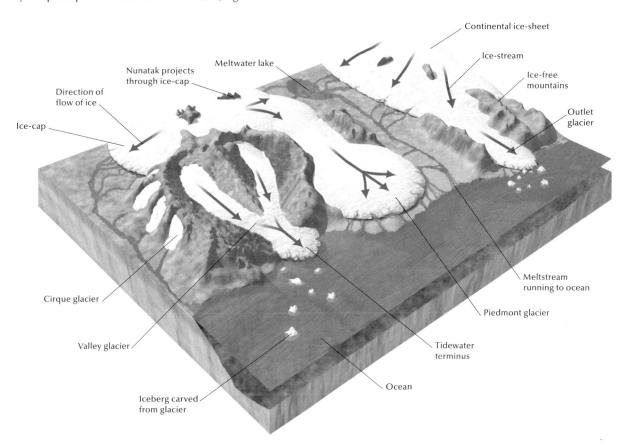

DEPOSITION

Deposition is the laying down of sediments in water or on the ground, normally after the process of erosion and transportation. Sediments are deposited when water, wind, waves and glaciers cannot transport them any further.

Beach sand dunes in Mambrui, Kenya

THE HYDROLOGICAL CYCLE AND RIVER SYSTEMS

The circulation of water around the Earth is known as the hydrological cycle or water cycle. The process is driven by the Sun, which evaporates water from the atmosphere produced by the transpiration of plants and by the respiration of animals. As water vapour rises in the atmosphere, it condenses to form clouds, which may then release water back to the Earth in form of precipitation (rain and snow). More water may enter the water cycle when the ice stored in glaciers is melted by the Sun. When water reaches the surface of the Earth, it drains into streams and rivers or percolates into underlying rock to become ground water. The water then flows downhill, either over or underground until it reaches the sea. Some of the water will be absorbed by plants or animals before it reaches the end of its journey to the ocean.

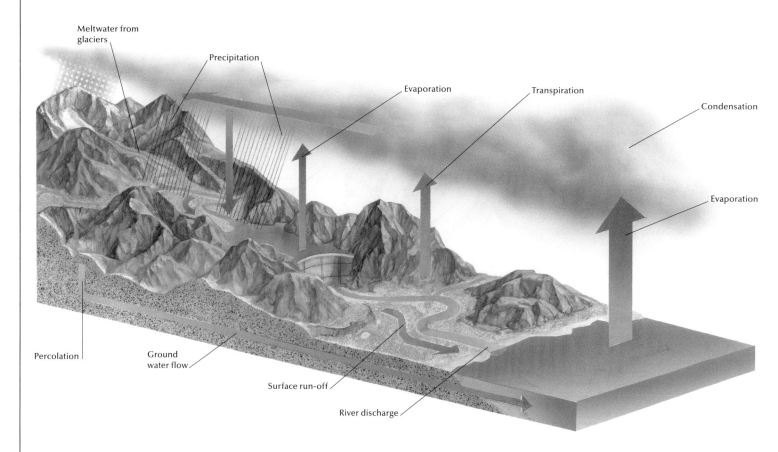

Meltwater from glaciers

Precipitation

Evaporation

Transpiration

Condensation

Evaporation

Percolation

Ground water flow

Surface run-off

River discharge

RIVERS

The source of a river is the place where it begins, or rises. The place where it flows into the sea is called the mouth. A river that joins a larger river is called a tributary and the place where the two rivers join is a confluence. A drainage basin is the entire area of land drained by one river. Drainage basins are separated from one another by areas of high land called watersheds.

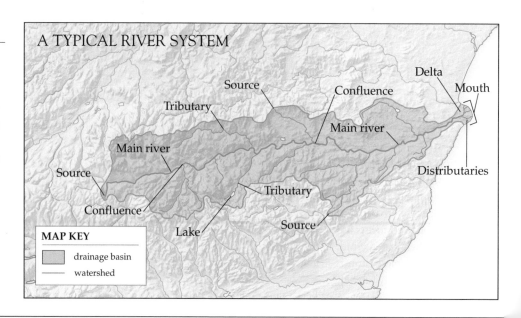

A TYPICAL RIVER SYSTEM

Delta

Source

Confluence

Mouth

Tributary

Main river

Main river

Source

Distributaries

Confluence

Tributary

Lake

Source

MAP KEY

drainage basin

watershed

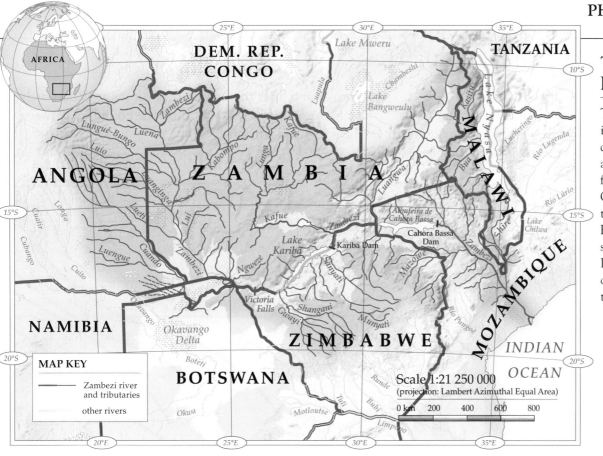

THE ZAMBEZI RIVER, ZAMBIA

The fourth-largest river in Africa, the Zambezi, drains 1 300 000 km^2 and is 3540 km long. It flows eastwards from the Central African plateau to the Indian Ocean. River Zambezi is the main source of water for Kariba Dam, which is the source of hydroelectricity for the region.

One of the world's most spectacular waterfalls, Victoria Falls, is situated along the Zambezi. The waterfall is 1708 m wide and drops 110 m into the Zambezi Gorge. Around 550 000 m^3 of water pass over the edge of the falls every minute.

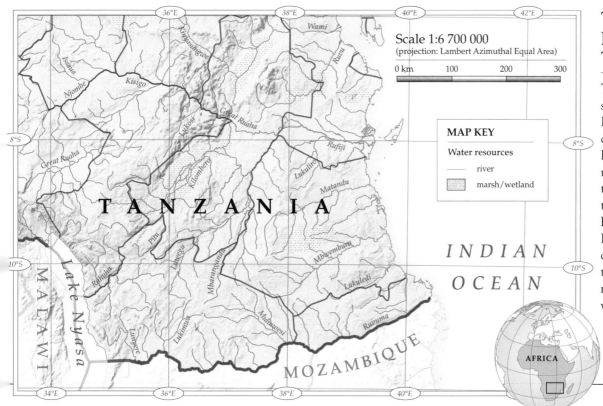

THE RUFIJI RIVER, TANZANIA

The Rufiji River is in southeastern Tanzania. It is formed by the convergence of the Kilombero and Luwegu rivers. It is mainly fed by the Great Ruaha River tributary. The Rufiji River's mouth enters the Indian ocean at Mafia channel, forming a delta that contains the largest mangrove forest in the world.

AIR MASSES

An air mass is a body of air with uniform characteristics. It would normally cover most of a continent or ocean and acquires its characteristics from the surface below it. A continental air mass will be warmer and drier than a maritime air mass. When such air masses meet they do not mix; the boundary between them is called a front.

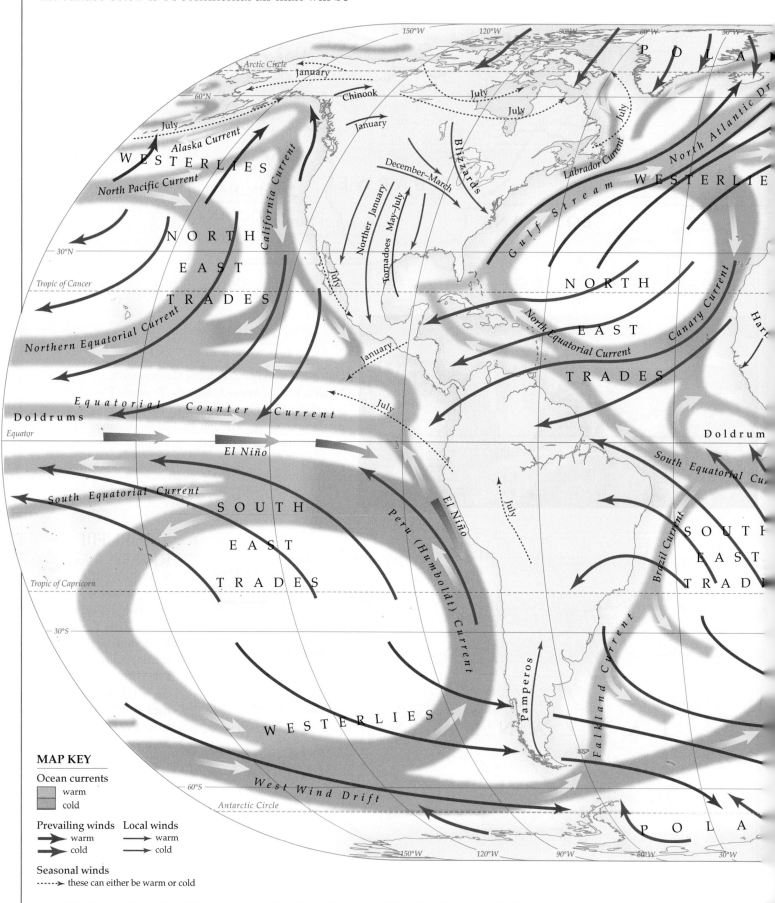

MAP KEY

Ocean currents

warm

cold

Prevailing winds   Local winds

→ warm   → warm

➔ cold   → cold

Seasonal winds

······▶ these can either be warm or cold

OCEAN CURRENTS

There is continuous circulation of water at the surface and at different depths of the sea. Winds, the rotation of the Earth and several processes of solar heating maintain the movement of ocean currents.

Surface movement or circulation is driven by winds that move from the warm equatorial to cold temperate areas, transporting warmth from equatorial areas to cold latitudes and returning cooler air to the tropics.

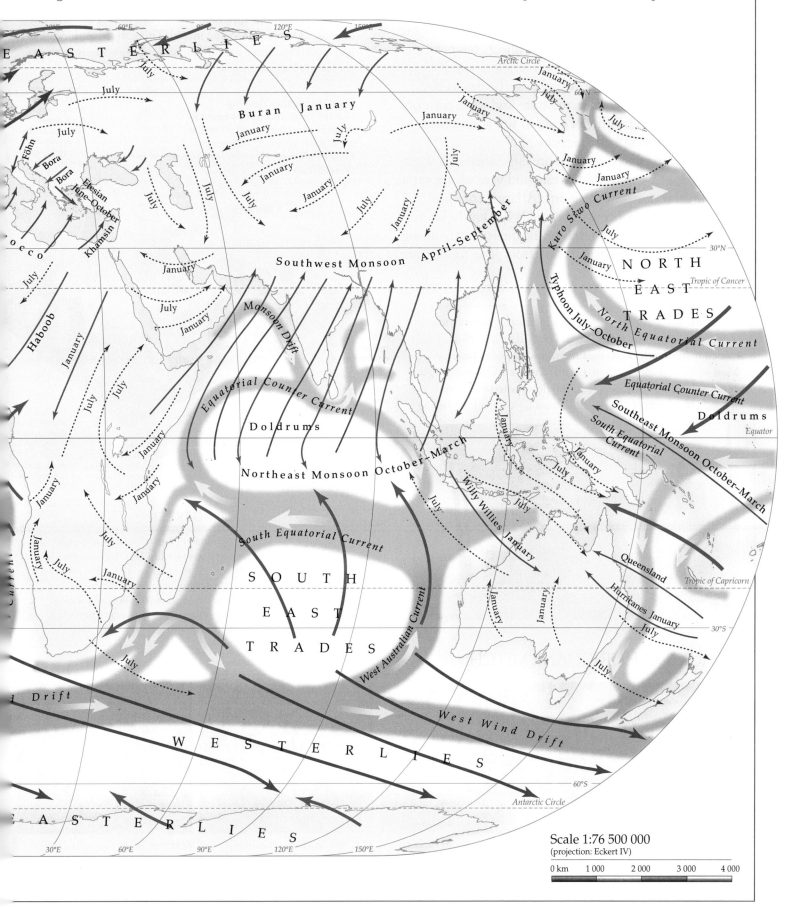

Scale 1:76 500 000
(projection: Eckert IV)

0 km   1 000   2 000   3 000   4 000

WEATHER SYSTEMS

As a result of the movements of wind in the atmosphere, which is driven by the energy from the Sun, weather occurs. Without wind there would be no weather. Wind has interdependent relationships with other Earth cycles like ocean currents, which is the main source of water vapour and also contributes to weather variations. Wind direction affects temperature and air movement affects weather. Cyclones and hurricanes affect weather. Weather is the day-to-day fluctuation of temperature, moisture and wind currents. The cooling and heating of gases in the atmosphere gives rise to atmospheric pressure.

Tropical storms or cyclones are large areas of low air pressure that bring torrential rain and very strong winds to tropical regions. In the North Atlantic they are called hurricanes once wind exceeds 120 km/h. Up to 20 tropical storms may reach hurricane strength during the hurricane season, which runs from June to October.

HURRICANE KATRINA

In August 2005, America was hit by Hurricane Katrina, which first formed over The Bahamas and crossed over to Florida and caused many deaths and flooding in the state of Louisiana. Most significant devastation occurred in New Orleans. 80 per cent of the city was flooded and the flood lasted for several weeks. The effects of Hurricane Katrina have been long lasting.

The effects of Hurricane Katrina

IMPACT OF HURRICANES

Tropical storms or hurricanes last an average of ten days but the biggest can last for up to four weeks. They cause damage in three main ways: winds, storm surges (in coastal areas) and floods. Winds can destroy crops, buildings, power, and communications infrastructure. Storm surges along coastal areas can be devastating. Torrential rainfall can last for hours or days, causing widespread flooding inland. This can trigger landslides and mudslides. Some countries have warning systems to prepare people to evacuate in time.

How Hurricanes develop
North Atlantic hurricanes begin as tropical depressions and storms in warm waters (over 27 degrees Celsius) off the West African coast.

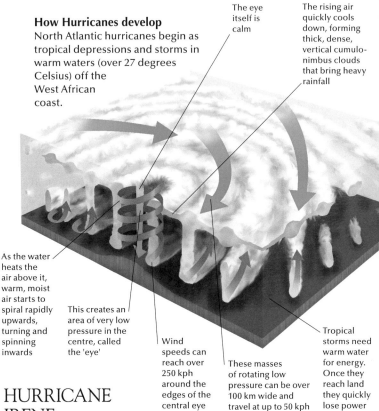

The eye itself is calm

The rising air quickly cools down, forming thick, dense, vertical cumulo-nimbus clouds that bring heavy rainfall

As the water heats the air above it, warm, moist air starts to spiral rapidly upwards, turning and spinning inwards

This creates an area of very low pressure in the centre, called the 'eye'

Wind speeds can reach over 250 kph around the edges of the central eye

These masses of rotating low pressure can be over 100 km wide and travel at up to 50 kph

Tropical storms need warm water for energy. Once they reach land they quickly lose power

HURRICANE IRENE

In August 2011, Hurricane Irene originated from the Atlantic and caused extensive damage and floods along the eastern coast of the USA and Canada.

KEEPING TRACK

To help identify and track hurricanes especially as there may be more than one happening at a time, meteorologists use alternative male and female names from agreed alphabetical lists, rotated over a six-year cycle. If a hurricane has been particularly destructive its name is retired and replaced.

TRACKING HURRICANE MITCH

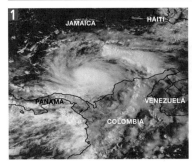

21.10.1998 Mitch began as a tropical depression south of the Caribbean. The next day it was upgraded to a tropical storm, then a hurricane as wind speeds increased.

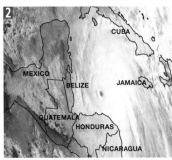

27.10.1998 Meteorologists tracked Mitch via satellite, but could not predict which direction it would take or where it would make landfall.

02.11.1998 Mitch turned northeast across the Gulf of Mexico, regaining strength.

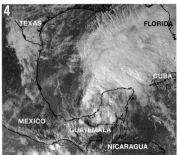

03.11.1998 Mitch reaches the coast of Florida in the USA before dying out.

All satellite images supplied by the National Oceanic and Atmospheric Association (NOAA)

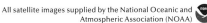

THE SAFFIR-SIMPSON CLASSIFICATION

Category	Wind speed (kph)	Pressure (mb)	Storm surge (m)	Damage
1	120–153	> 980	1.0–1.7	Minor: trees; mobile homes
2	154–177	979–965	1.8–2.6	Moderate: roof; windows; small boats ripped from moorings; flooding
3	178–209	964–945	2.7–3.8	Extensive: structural damage to buildings; flooding on land less than 1.7 metres above sea level to 10 km inland
4	210–249	944–920	3.9–5.6	Extreme: destroys buildings; beaches; flooding on land less than 3.3 metres above sea level to 5 km inland
5	> 250	< 920	over 5.7	Catastrophic: destruction on land less than 5 metres above sea level; mass evacuation needed

MAP KEY

Storm strength
(Saffir-Simpson classification)

- category five
- category four
- category three
- category two
- category one
- tropical storm
- tropical depression

— international border

1 numbers correspond to satellite images below

Scale 1:20 400 000
(projection: Lambert Conformal Conic)

0 km 200 400 600 800

EL NIÑO

El Niño is a reversal in the normal flow of the South Equatorial Current in the Pacific that brings dramatic changes in the weather at intervals of between two and seven years. The effects of El Niño become evident in late December, and are associated with a change in the distribution of air pressure over the South Pacific. This change is known as the Southern Oscillation. The full cycle is called an El Niño–Southern Oscillation (ENSO) event and includes La Niña, the opposite of El Niño. Ordinarily, pressure is high over the eastern South Pacific and low in the west. This produces the trade winds that drive the South Equatorial Current, carrying warm water away from South America and towards Indonesia. This pattern produces heavy rain over Indonesia and extremely arid conditions along the coast of Peru and northern Chile. During and ENSO event, the pressure difference weakens or reverses, as do the trade winds. Heavy rain falls over Peru and Chile, causing deserts to bloom, while Indonesia experiences drought, sometimes leading to serious forest fires.

El Niño also has an effect on East Africa. It brings rainy conditions and flooding. This has become very frequent. Some of the most severe cases are the 2007 Teso floods in Uganda. The floods also lead to destruction, landslides, outbreak of diseases and bridges are destroyed. La Niña contributes to prolonged drought in East Africa, for example the 2011 drought in the Horn of East Africa. Drought has had a negative impact on the livestock industry in Kenya. The rise in temperature has affected coffee production in Uganda and tea in Kenya. There are early warning systems in place, but the level of preparedness to mitigate the effects on droughts and floods is still weak.

Teso floods in Uganda

Normal climatic conditions

Ordinarily, a low-pressure system over Australia draws the southeast trade winds across the eastern Pacific from a high-pressure system over South America. These winds drive the warm South Equatorial Current towards the coast of Australia. Off the coast of South America, the warm water layer is only 100 m (300 ft) deep, so upwellings of cold water bring nutrients to the surface.

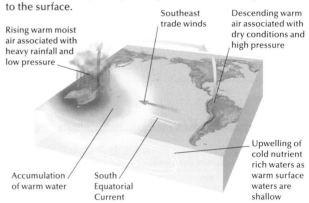

Rising warm moist air associated with heavy rainfall and low pressure

Southeast trade winds

Descending warm air associated with dry conditions and high pressure

Accumulation of warm water

South Equatorial Current

Upwelling of cold nutrient rich waters as warm surface waters are shallow

El Niño effect

During El Niño, the pressure systems that normally develop over Australia and South America are much weaker or reversed, which is reflected by the flow of the trade winds and ocean currents. Warm water to a depth of about 152 m (500 ft) flows eastward, blocking the normal upwelling of nutrients along the west coast of the Americas, and devastating fish stocks.

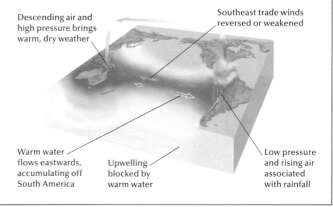

Descending air and high pressure brings warm, dry weather

Southeast trade winds reversed or weakened

Warm water flows eastwards, accumulating off South America

Upwelling blocked by warm water

Low pressure and rising air associated with rainfall

ADMINISTRATION

Kenya is located on the east coast of Africa, and shares borders with Somalia to the east, Uganda to the west, Tanzania to the south, Ethiopia to the north and South Sudan to the northwest. It extends from meridian 34° east to 42° east and from latitude 5° north to 4° 30' south. The equator divides the country into two, almost equal, parts. With the new constitution that came into effect on 27 August 2010, Kenya is currently divided into 47 semi-autonomous counties. Under the old constitution, Kenya was divided into eight administrative provinces, which were further subdivided into districts, divisions, locations and sub-locations.

Official name: REPUBLIC OF KENYA	
Surface area	582 646 km²
Population	43 million (in 2012)
Capital city	Nairobi
Official languages	English and Kiswahili
Currency	Kenyan shilling

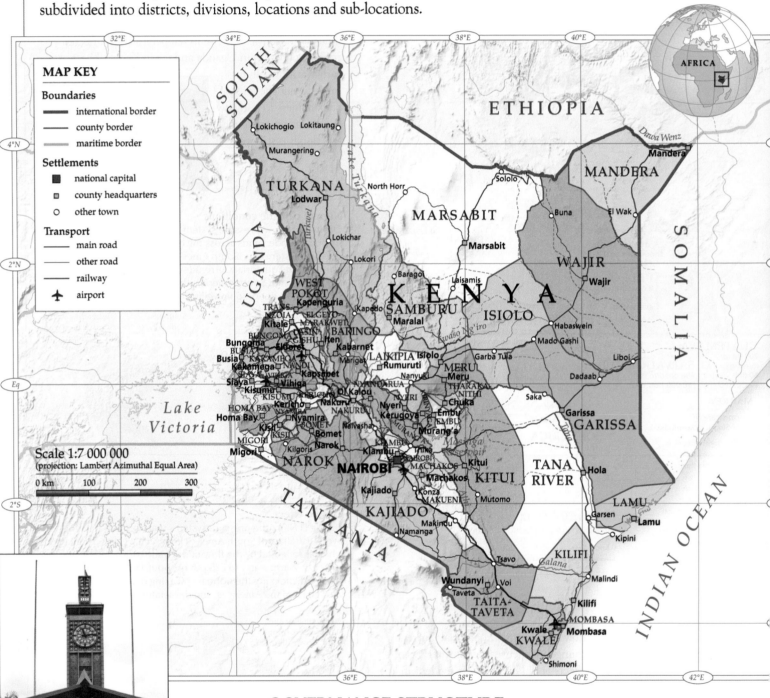

MAP KEY

Boundaries
- international border
- county border
- maritime border

Settlements
- national capital
- county headquarters
- other town

Transport
- main road
- other road
- railway
- airport

Scale 1:7 000 000
(projection: Lambert Azimuthal Equal Area)
0 km   100   200   300

Parliament Building

GOVERNANCE STRUCTURE

The new constitution has established two levels of governance: the national government and county governments. Each county will have a county government consisting of a County Assembly and a County Executive, and shall decentralise its functions and the provision of its services.

RELIEF AND LANDFORMS

Kenya's landscape is unique and varied. From the Indian Ocean to Batian Peak, 5199 m above sea level on Mount Kenya, a variety of physical features can be observed. There are six distinctive physical regions in Kenya: the coastal belt and plains; the Duruma–Wajir low belt; the low foreland belt; the northern plain lands; the central highlands dissected by the Great East African Rift Valley; and the Nyanza Western plateau.

The summit of Mount Elgon

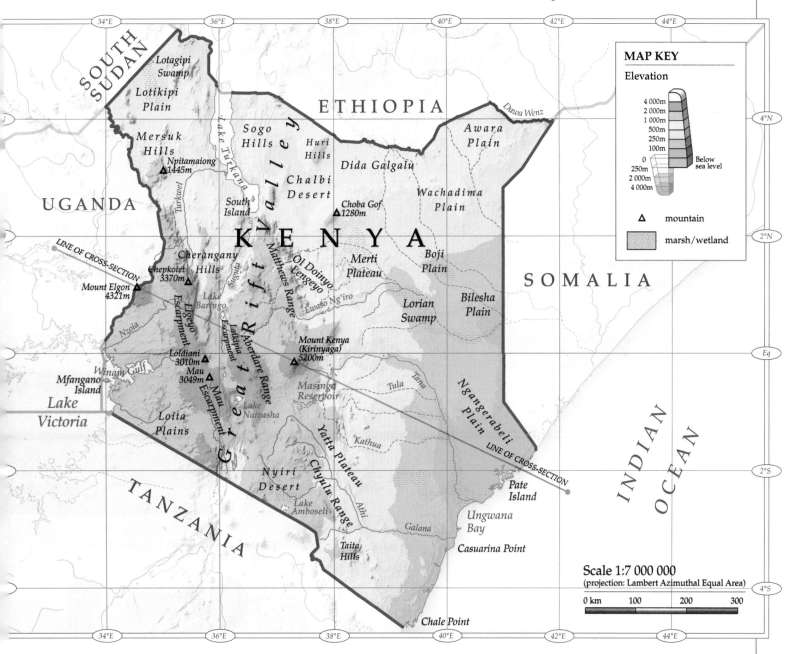

MAP KEY

Elevation

4 000m
2 000m
1 000m
500m
250m
100m
0
250m
2 000m
4 000m

Below sea level

△ mountain

marsh/wetland

Scale 1:7 000 000
(projection: Lambert Azimuthal Equal Area)

0 km   100   200   300

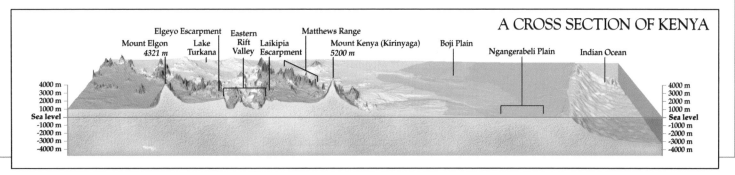

A CROSS SECTION OF KENYA

Mount Elgon 4321 m
Elgeyo Escarpment
Eastern Rift Valley
Laikipia Escarpment
Lake Turkana
Matthews Range
Mount Kenya (Kirinyaga) 5200 m
Boji Plain
Ngangerabeli Plain
Indian Ocean

4000 m
3000 m
2000 m
1000 m
Sea level
-1000 m
-2000 m
-3000 m
-4000 m

IRRIGATION AND LAND RECLAMATION

Irrigation is when, due to a lack of sufficient rainfall, crops are grown using artificial water resources. About 87 per cent of Kenya is arid and semi-arid with rich alluvial deposits and non-acid soils. Irrigated crops include rice, sugar cane, cotton, chillies and onions. Reclamation is the process of recovering land that was previously underwater, for example, swamp or tsetse fly invaded areas. Two areas are currently earmarked for reclamation: Yalla swamp for paddy rice/cotton and the Tana river delta for sugar cane/paddy rice.

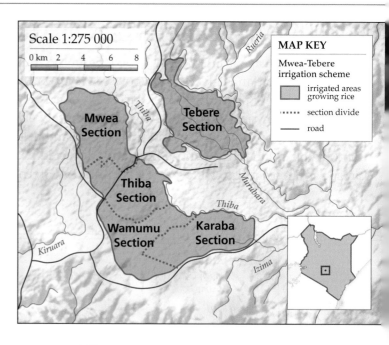

Scale 1:275 000

0 km 2 4 6 8

MAP KEY
Mwea-Tebere irrigation scheme

▨ irrigated areas growing rice
⋯⋯ section divide
— road

Mwea Section

Tebere Section

Thiba Section

Wamumu Section

Karaba Section

MWEA-TEBERE IRRIGATION SCHEME

The Mwea-Tebere irrigation scheme is one of the major schemes in Kenya. It had 6145 hectares under crops by 1997, the major crop being rice paddy. It is the biggest single supplier of rice to Kenyans. It is run on a tenant scheme with each tenant farming 1.6 hectares.

Crops growing as part of the Mwea-Tebere irrigation scheme.

MAP KEY
Irrigation
● major town
△ irrigation scheme

SOUTH SUDAN
ETHIOPIA
UGANDA
SOMALIA
TANZANIA
INDIAN OCEAN
Lake Victoria

K E N Y A

Lake Turkana
Turkwel
Lake Baringo
Ewaso Ng'iro
Dawa Wenz
Tana
Galana

Perkerra △
213
150
Bunyala △ ● Kakamega
Ahero △
Kisumu
827 △
Lake Nakuru
Nakuru
● Nyeri
West Kano △
449
Mwea-Tebere △ Embu ●
Musinga Reservoir
● Garissa
2454 △ Bura
△ Tana
878
Lake Naivasha
Nairobi ●
5818

Mombasa ●

Scale 1:8 000 000
(projection: Lambert Azimuthal Equal Area)

0 km 100 200 300

MAP KEY
Hectares of irrigated land
(symbols proportional to area of irrigated land)

5000
2000
500

FOCUS ON

IRRIGATION AND LAND RECLAMATION

Currently, Kenya imports food to supplement the ever-receding food budget.

Irrigation and land reclamation are two possible solutions to raise food production in the country in order to feed the rapidly growing population, reduce landlessness, create job opportunities and even increase exports. Countries that have succeeded in this regard include Egypt and Israel.

AGRICULTURE

Kenya is largely an agricultural economy with both small scale and large scale agriculture. About 75 per cent of the population depends on agriculture, directly or indirectly. The agricultural sector is a source of food, employment, raw materials for agro-industries, and foreign exchange earnings from exports. Large scale agriculture is practised for commercial purposes while small scale agriculture produces food crops and livestock products for local consumption. The type of crops cultivated and livestock kept vary with climatic conditions and soil type, among other factors.

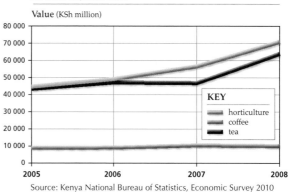

VALUE OF PRINCIPAL AGRICULTURAL EXPORTS IN KENYA, 2005–2008

Value (KSh million)

KEY
horticulture
coffee
tea

Source: Kenya National Bureau of Statistics, Economic Survey 2010

HORTICULTURE

Horticulture is the production of flowers, fruits and vegetables mainly for export. In Kenya, horticultural crops are grown seasonally or in greenhouses and their production has increased rapidly over time. Horticultural crops grown in Kenya include cut flowers, fruits and French beans. The cut flower industry is the third most important foreign exchange earner after tea and tourism in Kenya. Main cut flower growing areas include Lake Naivasha, Thika and Kiambu/Limuru regions.

FOOD SECURITY IN KENYA

Food security is defined as existing when all people at all times have access to sufficient, safe and nutritious food to maintain a healthy and active life. It is a function of food availability, accessibility and quality. Most parts of Kenya suffer from food insecurity due to climate change and unpredictable weather patterns, poor agricultural practices and policies, poverty and inadequate infrastructure.

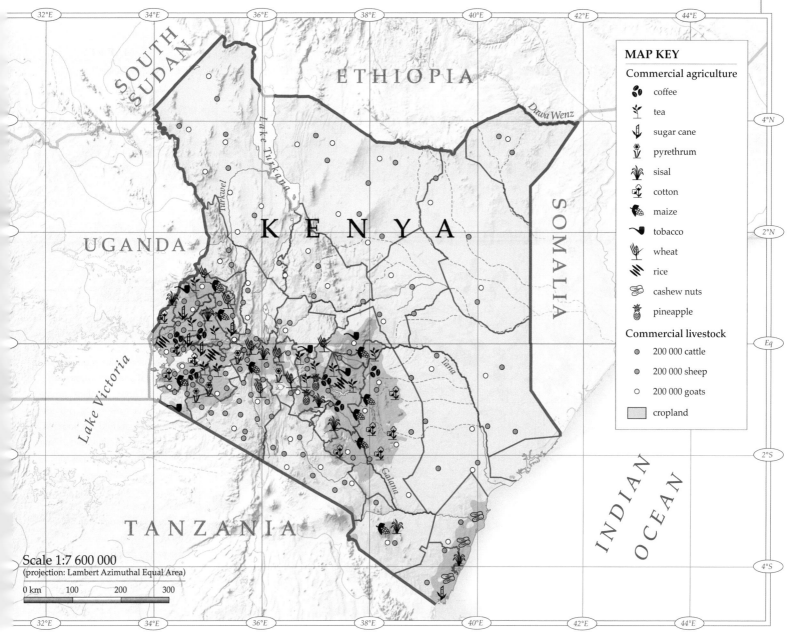

MAP KEY

Commercial agriculture
- coffee
- tea
- sugar cane
- pyrethrum
- sisal
- cotton
- maize
- tobacco
- wheat
- rice
- cashew nuts
- pineapple

Commercial livestock
- 200 000 cattle
- 200 000 sheep
- 200 000 goats
- cropland

Scale 1:7 600 000
(projection: Lambert Azimuthal Equal Area)

0 km   100   200   300

FORESTRY, LIVESTOCK AND FISHING

Kenyan forests are an important source for water catchment, pasture preservation and wood. Wood is the main fuel for cooking in Kenya, especially in rural areas. Where forests are destroyed, pastures for livestock and rivers, which are sources for fishing, are badly affected. This has a negative impact on the economy.

FORESTRY

It is estimated that 3 per cent of Kenyan land is forested with both exotic and indigenous tree species. This is equivalent to 2 200 000 hectares, of which 1 697 000 hectares have been formally gazetted. Most of the forests are found on the Kenya highlands, around Mount Kenya and along the Rift Valley highlands. Forest cover in Kenya is well below the international minimum level of 10 per cent. Kenyan forests have been severely threatened by deforestation brought about by excision to pave way for agriculture and human settlement, illegal encroachment, clearance and cutting.

RE-AFFORESTATION INITIATIVES IN KENYA

After experiencing the impacts of deforestation, Kenya has initiated nationwide campaigns to restore its forest cover to the recommended international standards. The most successful campaign is the restoration of the Mau Forest Complex. The Mau Forest Complex, Mount Kenya, Aberdares Range, Cheranganyi Hills and Mount Elgon are the five most important water towers in Kenya.

Restoration of the Mau Complex

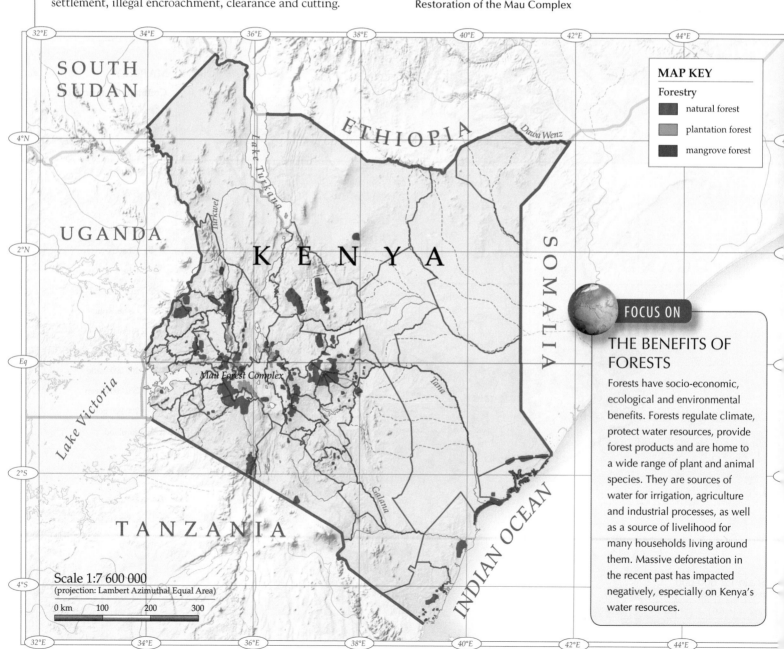

MAP KEY

Forestry

- natural forest
- plantation forest
- mangrove forest

Scale 1:7 600 000
(projection: Lambert Azimuthal Equal Area)

0 km   100   200   300

FOCUS ON

THE BENEFITS OF FORESTS

Forests have socio-economic, ecological and environmental benefits. Forests regulate climate, protect water resources, provide forest products and are home to a wide range of plant and animal species. They are sources of water for irrigation, agriculture and industrial processes, as well as a source of livelihood for many households living around them. Massive deforestation in the recent past has impacted negatively, especially on Kenya's water resources.

Fish sellers

FISHING

Kenya has a long coastline with potential for the development of a strong fishing industry. There are also 14 789 km² of inland lakes and several rivers where fishing occurs. However, about 92 per cent of fish comes from Lake Victoria, 4 per cent from the Indian Ocean and 3 per cent from inland lakes and rivers.

While artisanal fishing is the most common in Kenya, there are institutions and farmers who practice fish farming or aquaculture. Fishing and fish farming is a potential source of food, income, foreign exchange and employment.

Pastoralist leads cattle

PASTORALISM

Pastoralism is concerned with keeping of livestock. However, pastoralists traditionally move from one area to another in search of pasture and water for their animals in response to drought. Livestock production is common in the pastoral areas, where it sustains up to 80 per cent of the population. In Kenya, pastoralists are concentrated in northern Kenya and in the Rift Valley area. They keep relatively large herds and local breeds of cattle, goats and camels.

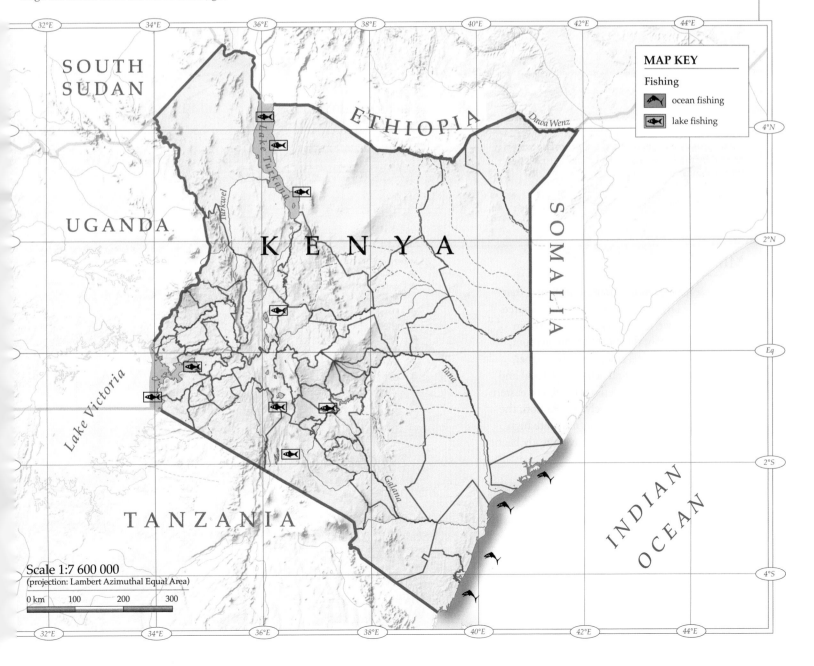

MAP KEY

Fishing

ocean fishing

lake fishing

Scale 1:7 600 000
(projection: Lambert Azimuthal Equal Area)

0 km   100   200   300

ENERGY, MINING AND INDUSTRY

Kenya is dependent on three major sources of energy: wood fuel, petroleum and electricity. These sources account for 70 per cent, 21 per cent and 9 per cent, respectively, of the total energy consumed in the country.

Much attention is being given to production of geothermal energy and hydroelectricity. The major hydroelectric plants in Kenya are Gitaru, Masinga, Kiambere, Kindaruma, Kamburu and Turkwel Gorge. Geothermal energy comes from Olkaria Geothermal Plant. The government is gradually exploiting the potential of other sources of energy such as solar, wind and biomass.

ELECTRICITY GENERATION (2010)

Type	Capacity in Megawatts
Hydro	719
Thermal	419
Geothermal	128

A geothermal power station. Geothermal power comes from steam made from underground water heated by the Earth's core, which is in turn used to turn turbines.

MINING

Available geological information indicates that Kenya has a large unexploited mineral resource base. The known minerals being exploited in Kenya are soda ash, fluorspar, kaolin, gypsum, salt, silica, manganese, zinc, graphite, copper, diatomite, gold, nickel and gemstones. Coal and titanium deposits have been discovered in eastern and coastal Kenya, respectively. In addition, the prospects for oil and natural gas are quite high. In fact, significant oil deposits have already been discovered in Turkana.

MINERAL PRODUCTION (2010)

Type	Value of sales (in Ksh millions)
Soda Ash	8882
Fluorspar	1949
Diatomite	4
Gold	593

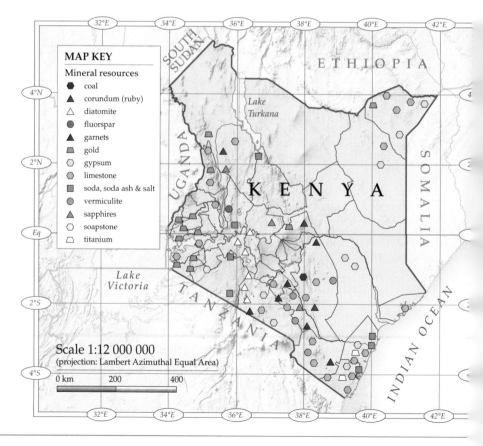

MAP KEY

Energy
- ▲ hydroelectric power station
- △ planned hydroelectric power station
- ▲ thermal power station
- ▲ geothermal power station
- ▢ oil booster station
- ⊛ wind turbine
- — major power transmission line
- ···· projected power transmission line
- ····· oil pipeline

Scale 1:12 000 000
(projection: Lambert Azimuthal Equal Area)

0 km   200   400

MAP KEY

Mineral resources
- ⬟ coal
- ▲ corundum (ruby)
- △ diatomite
- ● fluorspar
- ▲ garnets
- ○ gold
- ⬡ gypsum
- ⬡ limestone
- ▪ soda, soda ash & salt
- ● vermiculite
- ▲ sapphires
- ⬡ soapstone
- ▢ titanium

Scale 1:12 000 000
(projection: Lambert Azimuthal Equal Area)

0 km   200   400

INDUSTRY

There are several industries in Kenya with varied location factors. Industries tend to be located where raw materials, market, labour, transport, communication and energy sources are available, including favourable government policy. Kenya has primary (extractive) industries; secondary (processing) industries; tertiary (service) industries; and quaternary (high-technology) industries. Export Processing Zones have been set up to encourage industrial production for export purposes.

TRADE

Kenya's domestic and international trade is dominated by agro-based goods and products from the industrial and manufacturing sector. Wholesale, retail and international trade has expanded rapidly since the introduction of trade liberalisation in the 1990s. Kenya's trade strategy aims at ensuring that Kenyan business enterprises get the necessary support to be able to sell in the domestic market and penetrate the international markets. Kenya is a member of the World Trade Organization.

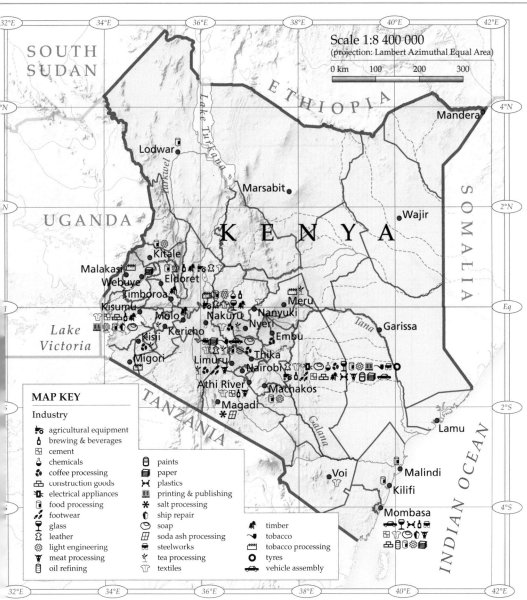

Scale 1:8 400 000
(projection: Lambert Azimuthal Equal Area)

0 km   100   200   300

MAP KEY

Industry

- agricultural equipment
- brewing & beverages
- cement
- chemicals
- coffee processing
- construction goods
- electrical appliances
- food processing
- footwear
- glass
- leather
- light engineering
- meat processing
- oil refining
- paints
- paper
- plastics
- printing & publishing
- salt processing
- ship repair
- soap
- soda ash processing
- steelworks
- tea processing
- textiles
- timber
- tobacco
- tobacco processing
- tyres
- vehicle assembly

TRANSPORT AND COMMUNICATION

A well-developed and efficient transport and communication infrastructure is important to any development. Kenya is connected with varied degrees and spatial concentration of road, rail, water and air transport networks. Internationally, the country is well connected through Jomo Kenyatta International Airport in Nairobi. There is also an oil pipeline that runs from Mombasa, Nairobi, Kisumu to Eldoret. The communications sector, previously dominated by postal and telecommunications services, has undergone a major transformation with mobile phone technology, the internet and freedom of press.

The modern highway between Nairobi and Thika

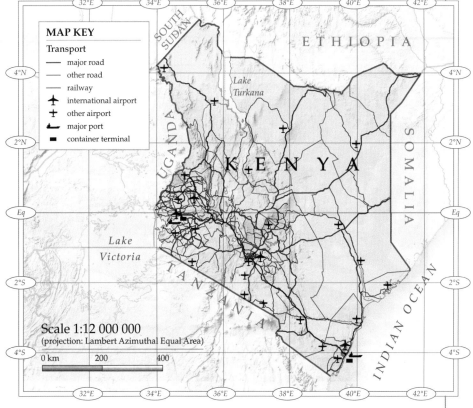

MAP KEY

Transport

- major road
- other road
- railway
- ✈ international airport
- ✛ other airport
- ⚓ major port
- ■ container terminal

Scale 1:12 000 000
(projection: Lambert Azimuthal Equal Area)

0 km   200   400

POPULATION

In Kenya, a population census is conducted every ten years by the Kenya National Bureau of Statistics. A population census provides vital information on the country's demographic, social and economic characteristics. According to the Mundi Index 2012, the country has an estimated total population of 43 million people.

POPULATION GROWTH TRENDS IN KENYA

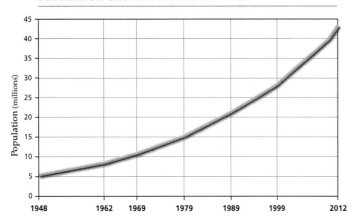

KENYA POPULATION PROFILE

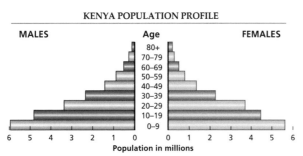

Source: Kenya National Bureau of Statistics, 2009 Population Census Data

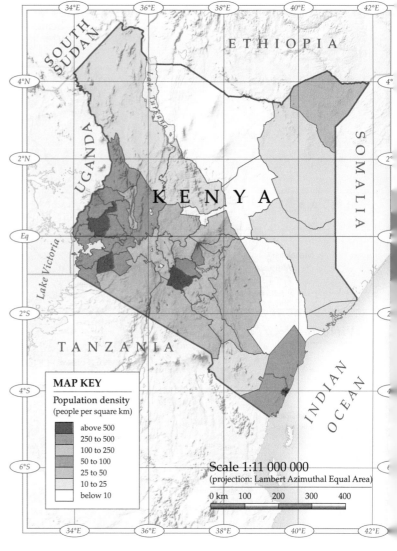

MAP KEY

Population density
(people per square km)

- above 500
- 250 to 500
- 100 to 250
- 50 to 100
- 25 to 50
- 10 to 25
- below 10

Scale 1:11 000 000
(projection: Lambert Azimuthal Equal Area)

0 km 100 200 300 400

A market in Kenya

URBANISATION

Kenya's urban population growth has been increasing since independence. Rural-to-urban migration has been the major contributor to urban population growth. However, other growth factors are urban natural increase (more urban births than deaths) and the absorption of peri-urban areas into town boundaries. The five largest towns in Kenya are Nairobi (the capital city), Mombasa, Kisumu, Nakuru and Eldoret.

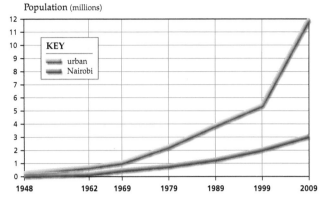

URBAN POPULATION GROWTH TRENDS IN KENYA

Population (millions)

KEY
— urban
— Nairobi

Source: Kenya National Bureau of Statistics, Various Census Reports

THE CITY OF NAIROBI

Nairobi was first established in June 1899 as a transportation and administrative centre, which later grew to become the capital of Kenya (in 1905), a municipality (1919) and a city (1950). In the 2009 census, Nairobi had a population of 3.1 million people on an area of 695 km², with a population density of 4515 people per km². Nairobi is an important regional hub in Eastern and Central Africa, as well as the headquarters for many international and regional organisations, institutions and companies.

Part of Nairobi

CHALLENGES OF URBAN GROWTH

The high rate of urbanisation in Kenya brings with it challenges such as: poor provision of urban services; considerable strain on existing urban infrastructural facilities; transportation problems; unemployment; crime and socially related problems; urban environmental degradation; proliferation of informal (slum) settlements; and urban poverty. These challenges call for sustainable urban development, planning, management and effective governance.

Slum settlement

LANGUAGES AND HISTORICAL MIGRATION ROUTES

Although Kenya has only two official languages: Kiswahili and English, it is a linguistically diverse country with over 60 indigenous languages spoken in different regions.

LANGUAGES

Kenyan indigenous languages can be divided into three main language groups. A language group is a set of languages with similar words and sounds, largely because of common historical origins. The three main language groups in Kenya are:

Bantu: Aembu, Pokomo, Wataveta, Abakuria, Agikuyu, Abagusii, Mbeere, Abaluyia, Wadawida (Taita), Ameru, Mijikenda, Akamba.

Nilotes: Luo, Maasai, Iteso, Samburu, Turkana, Njemps, Elmolo, Kipsigis, Okiek, Sabaot/Sebei, Nandi, Pokot, Marakwet, Terik, Keiyo, Tugen.

Cushites: Somali, Borana, Galla/Oromo, Gabbra, Rendille, Sanyeor, Dahalo.

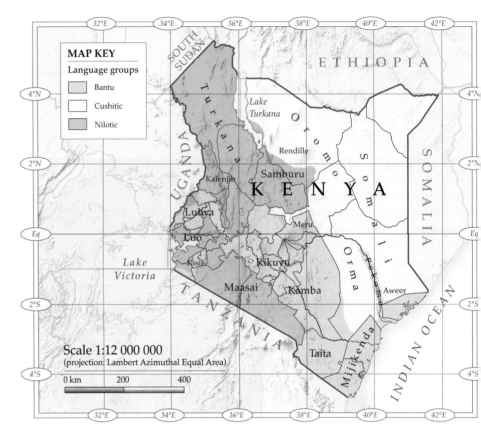

MAP KEY
Language groups
Bantu
Cushitic
Nilotic

Scale 1:12 000 000
(projection: Lambert Azimuthal Equal Area)

0 km   200   400

WHERE DID THESE GROUPS ORIGINATE?

Historically, the Bantu, Nilotic and Cushitic ethnic groups migrated from different regions of Africa to settle in Kenya (and other countries in Eastern Africa). The main migration routes taken by each group are shown separately on the maps below.

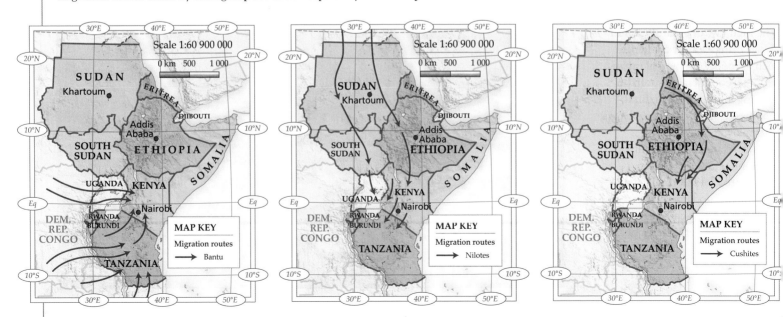

HISTORY

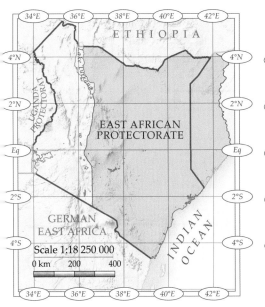

KENYA IN 1895

Before the 1900s, the boundaries of countries were not clearly defined and groups of people moved freely throughout the region. This changed with the arrival of foreigners and in 1895, the British established the East African Protectorate in order to safeguard trade routes. Much of present day Kenya fell under the Protectorate.

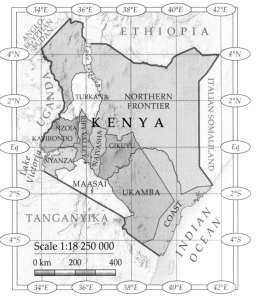

KENYA IN 1929

In 1920, the Protectorate became a British colony named Kenya. By 1929, the British had established internal regions to allow for more decentralised local government. These internal boundaries were established on racial and tribal bases but the inhabitants were not consulted and were largely unsatisfied with the division.

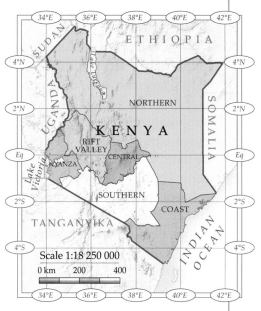

KENYA IN 1961, JUST BEFORE INDEPENDENCE

In 1952, the British declared a state of emergency to quell unrest over land ownership and self-governance (a movement known as the Mau-Mau). In 1961, the British made some changes to the internal regions both in order to keep control while Kenya pushed towards independence.

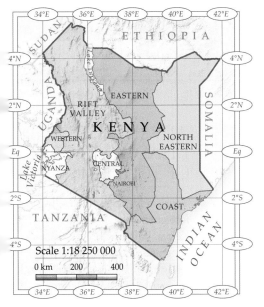

KENYA IN 1964, JUST AFTER INDEPENDENCE

In December 1963 Kenya was granted independence from Britain. In 1964, Kenya became an independent republic under the leadership of President Jomo Kenyatta. The Republic was divided into seven provinces which remained more or less unchanged until 2010.

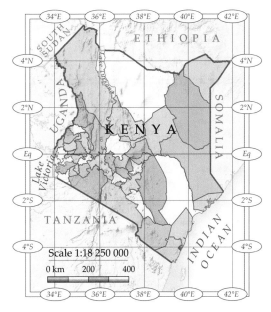

PRESENT-DAY KENYA

In 2010, the Constitution of Kenya was changed and the provinces were replaced by 47 counties, some of which were further divided into districts. The new divisions aim to make administration easier and to make it easier for local authorities to provide services to the people in each county.

TOURISM AND WILDLIFE

Kenya is known all over the world for its tourist attractions. The words *safari* (game drives) and *big five* (wildlife) have been, for a long time, synonymous with tourism in Kenya. A wide range of tourist attractions exist in Kenya. These are national parks and reserves, wildlife, scenic landforms, bird sanctuaries, archaeological and historical sites, warm climate, coastal beaches, and the rich historical and cultural heritage.

Maasai warriors

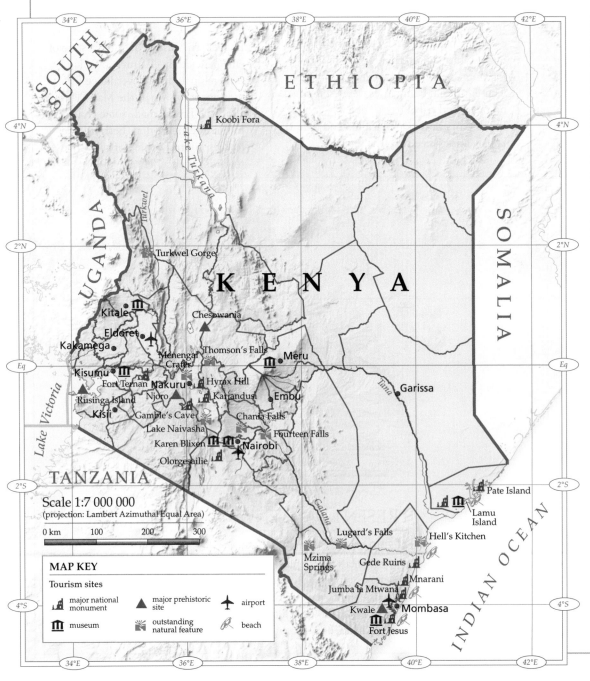

Many Kenyan animals, such as these white-bearded gnu, migrate seasonally and may stray outside the boundaries of protected areas.

ADVANTAGES AND DISADVANTAGES OF TOURISM

Tourism is one of the leading foreign exchange earners in Kenya. Furthermore, tourism generates many jobs locally, leads to improvement of physical infrastructure, and encourages national integration and conservation of natural resources related to tourism. Some of the disadvantages of tourism include environmental degradation, human-wildlife conflicts, socio-cultural changes and uneven distribution of tourism benefits locally and nationally.

Scale 1:7 000 000
(projection: Lambert Azimuthal Equal Area)

0 km   100   200   300

MAP KEY

Tourism sites

- 🏛 major national monument
- 🏛 museum
- ▲ major prehistoric site
- 🎐 outstanding natural feature
- ✈ airport
- 🐚 beach

WILDLIFE CONSERVATION

Kenya's conservation area is 44 359 km², accounting for 7.5 per cent of its total land area. This comprises 21 national game parks, four national marine parks, 23 national reserves, five national marine reserves and one local sanctuary. In addition, there are several private and community-based conservation areas.

Flamingos flock in the shallow lakes of Kenya's Great Rift Valley.

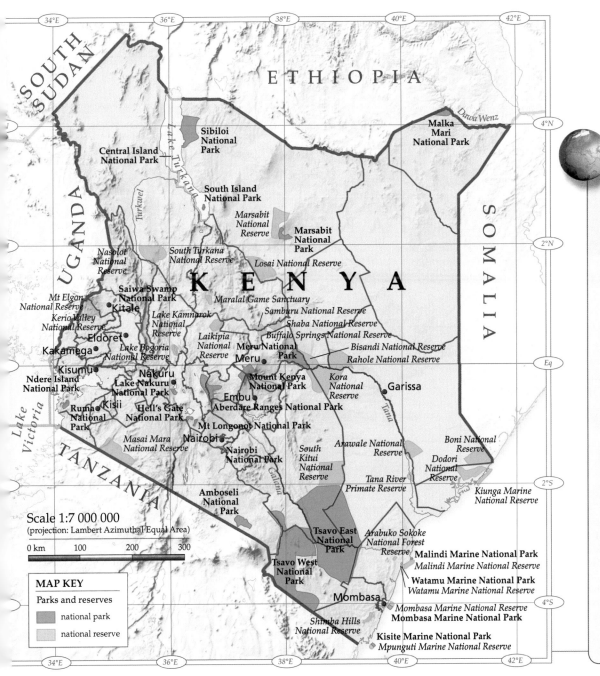

Scale 1:7 000 000
(projection: Lambert Azimuthal Equal Area)

0 km   100   200   300

MAP KEY

Parks and reserves

national park

national reserve

FOCUS ON

WILDLIFE CONSERVATION CHALLENGES

Wildlife conservation and management in Kenya is faced with a number of challenges such as poaching; human-wildlife conflicts; pressure of existing wildlife habitats due to increased human population; climate change and prolonged droughts; fire outbreaks; urban development; animal diseases; environmental and wildlife habitat degradation; and the migratory habits of some wildlife species. Some of these challenges can be reduced through:

- community-based wildlife conservation efforts
- promotion of eco-tourism protecting endangered species of fauna and flora
- diversification of tourism products and markets
- revenue sharing programmes with the local community
- sustainable wildlife conservation policies and programmes.

ADMINISTRATION

The United Republic of Tanzania was formed by the union of Tanganyika and Zanzibar. The Union Government is headed by the Union President and the Zanzibar President heads the Revolutionary Government of Zanzibar.

Tanzania is divided into 26 regions, 21 on the mainland and five in Zanzibar (three in Unguja, two in Pemba). There are one hundred and seventeen (117) Local Government Authorities, which have been created to further devolve power to the localities. The Local Government Authorities (LGAs) are administered by an Executive team of professionals under the political leadership of elected Councillors.

Parliament Building – Dodoma

Official name:	THE UNITED REPUBLIC OF TANZANIA
Surface area	945 203 km²
Population	46.3 million
Capital city	Dodoma
Official languages	Kiswahili and English
Currency	Tanzanian Shilling

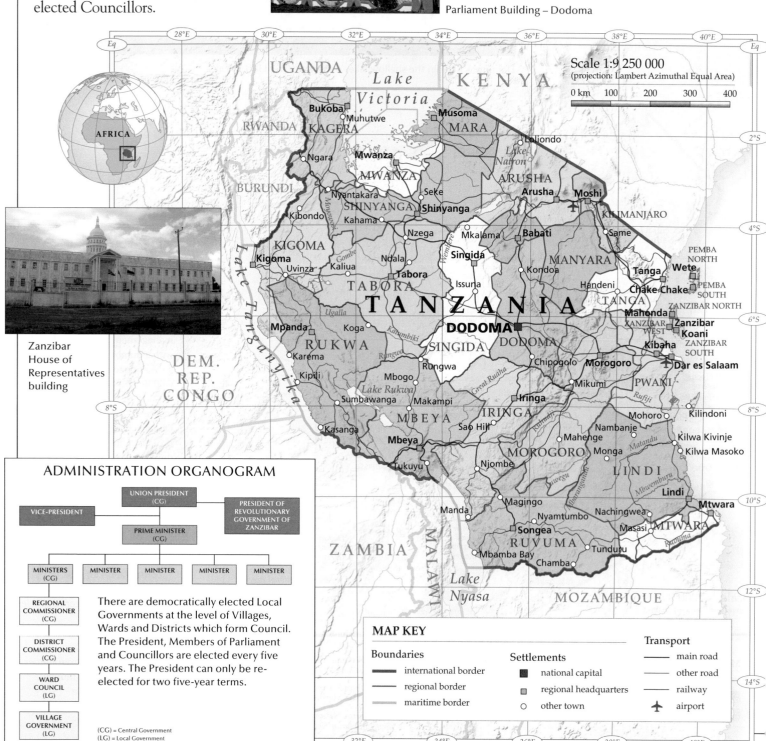

Zanzibar House of Representatives building

ADMINISTRATION ORGANOGRAM

- UNION PRESIDENT (CG)
  - VICE-PRESIDENT
  - PRESIDENT OF REVOLUTIONARY GOVERNMENT OF ZANZIBAR
  - PRIME MINISTER (CG)
    - MINISTERS (CG)
    - MINISTER
    - MINISTER
    - MINISTER
    - MINISTER
- REGIONAL COMMISSIONER (CG)
- DISTRICT COMMISSIONER (CG)
- WARD COUNCIL (LG)
- VILLAGE GOVERNMENT (LG)

(CG) = Central Government
(LG) = Local Government

There are democratically elected Local Governments at the level of Villages, Wards and Districts which form Council. The President, Members of Parliament and Councillors are elected every five years. The President can only be re-elected for two five-year terms.

Scale 1:9 250 000
(projection: Lambert Azimuthal Equal Area)

0 km   100   200   300   400

MAP KEY

Boundaries
— international border
— regional border
— maritime border

Settlements
■ national capital
▪ regional headquarters
○ other town

Transport
— main road
— other road
— railway
✈ airport

RELIEF AND LANDFORMS

Tanzania has coastal lowlands but the land rises to the central plateau with mountain ranges of Usambara and Uluguru on the east and the Kipengere range in the south west. Tanzania contains part of the Great Rift Valley, which splits into two branches forming the Eastern Rift Valley, which has Lakes Manyara and Natron, and the Western Rift Valley, which has Lakes Tanganyika and Nyasa. The volcanic Mount Kilimanjaro is 5895 m above sea level. There are the large water bodies of Lake Victoria (the largest in Africa, with an area of 69 500 sq km) and Lakes Nyasa, Manyara and Tanganyika (the second deepest lake in the world with a maximum depth of 1471 m).

Lake Tanganyika is one of the African Great Lakes. It is the second largest fresh water lake in the world by volume, and the second deepest (1470 m), after Lake Baikal in Siberia. It is also the world's longest freshwater lake (670 km). The lake is divided among four countries – Burundi, Democratic Republic of Congo, Zambia and Tanzania.

The Ngorongoro Crater is a National Conservation area that occupies 8300 km². It has a variety of habitats and landscapes, including grassland plains, savanna woodlands, forests, mountains, volcanic crater lakes, rivers and swampland.

NGORONGORO CONSERVATION AREA

Ngorongoro Conservation Area was added to the UNESCO World Heritage list in 1979 – it is host to more than 400 species of birds and some of the largest animal herds in the world, including wildebeests, plains zebras, and Thomson's and Grant's gazelles. Predatory animals include lions, spotted hyenas, leopards and cheetahs. The endangered black rhinoceros and African hunting dog can also be found there. Although cultivation is not permitted within the area, some 25 000 to 40 000 Maasai are allowed to graze their livestock there. Current issues of concern are the damage to the ecosystem caused by overgrazing and tourism, where hotels and vehicles contribute to the damage. There are diminishing numbers of the black rhinoceros, leopard and elephant populations because of poaching.

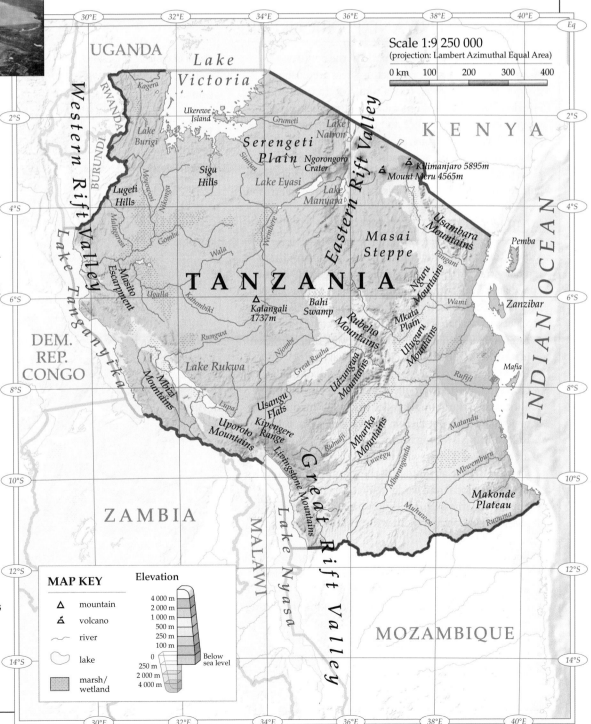

Scale 1:9 250 000
(projection: Lambert Azimuthal Equal Area)

0 km   100   200   300   400

MAP KEY

△ mountain
⏃ volcano
～ river
⬭ lake
▨ marsh/wetland

Elevation

4 000 m
2 000 m
1 000 m
500 m
250 m
100 m
0
250 m
2 000 m
4 000 m
Below sea level

AGRICULTURE, FORESTRY AND FISHING

Agriculture is the foundation of the economy of Tanzania. It accounts for about half of the national income, three quarters of merchandise exports and is the source of food and provides employment opportunities to about 80 per cent of Tanzanians.

Agriculture is dominated by smallholder farmers (peasants) cultivating an average farm size of between 0.9 and 3.0 hectares each. About 70 per cent of crop area is cultivated by hand hoe, 20 per cent by ox plough and 10 per cent by tractor. It is rain-fed agriculture. There are about 1.0 million hectares of irrigable land available, but currently only 150 000 hectares are under irrigation.

Low levels of mehanisation, such as the use of the hand hoe, and rain dependency contribute to low yields. An increased adoption of modern farm technologies, including improved seeds and greater use of fertilisers, pesticides and herbicides is needed in order to improve agricultural productivity.

The major staple food crops that are produced include maize, sorghum, millet, rice, wheat, beans, cassava, potatoes, bananas and cassava.

The bulk of the country's export crops are coffee, cotton, cashew nuts, tobacco, sisal, pyrethrum, tea, cloves, horticultural crops, oil seeds, spices and flowers.

HORTICULTURE AND FLORICULTURE

Horticulture is found in most parts of the country. However, the dominant production areas are Lushoto district, Morogoro rural, Iringa rural, Moshi rural and Arusha. Vegetables such as cabbages, tomatoes, sweet pepper, cauliflower, lettuce and indigenous vegetables are grown. A variety of fruits, such as pears, apples, plums, passion fruits, peaches, avocado, oranges, mangoes, pineapples, pawpaw and grapes, are produced. Flowers are cultivated mainly in Moshi rural and Arumeru in Arusha.

AGRICULTURE FIRST STRATEGY

Kilimo Kwanza, literally translated as '**agriculture first**' is a new strategy that was launched in August 2009. It is aimed at spearheading government efforts to bring about agricultural revolution in the country. Under this strategy, productivity and growth in agriculture is to be boosted by:

- Improvements to the rural road network and irrigation infrastructure, including rain water harvesting.
- Improvements to storage facilities for agricultural crops and livestock products and giving priority in the allocation of farm implements, and other inputs, to the major food crop production regions of Mbeya, Ruvuma, Rukwa, Iringa, Morogoro and Kigoma.
- Identifying and surveying land for large-scale food crop farming to take advantage of the existing opportunities in terms of local and world market demand.
- Supporting research institutions to develop improved seeds and encouraging other institutions to scale-up seed production.
- Reduction of unsustainable forest harvesting.
- Establishing and reviving agro-processing industries, with private sector participation.
- Improving access to credit, and fast-tracking the setting up of a special window for lending to agricultural ventures at the Tanzania Investment Bank (TIB).
- Establishment of an Agricultural Development Bank.
- VAT and customs duty changes to promote the sector.

VALUE OF MAJOR AGRICULTURAL EXPORT CROPS

Name of crop	Value of agricultural exports (TZS bn)				
	2005	**2006**	**2007**	**2008**	**2009**
Coffee	83.6	92.8	143.3	124.1	150.0
Cotton	127.2	56.8	49.8	95.6	115.2
Sisal	8.2	9.3	7.4	18.5	
Tea	28.8	41.7	48.3	50.3	88.1
Tobacco	91.4	129.1	116.9	210.2	116.9
Cashew nuts	54.2	62.7	33.8	82.0	88.43
Cloves	9.6	10.0	10.6	16	18.5

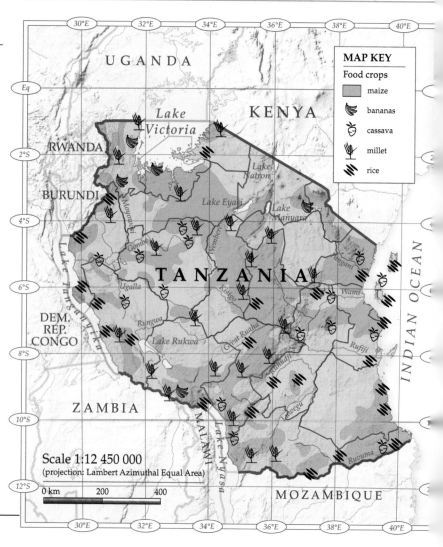

Scale 1:12 450 000
(projection: Lambert Azimuthal Equal Area)

0 km   200   400

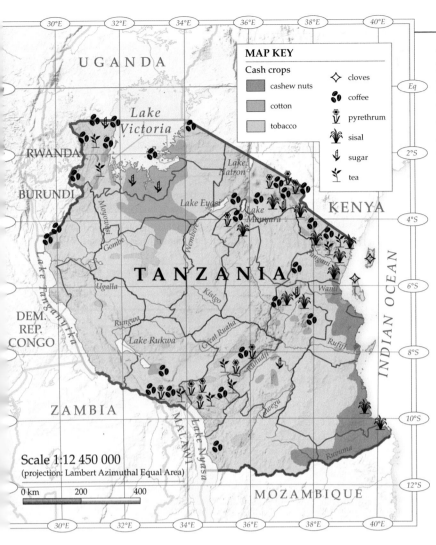

MAP KEY

Cash crops
- cashew nuts
- cotton
- tobacco

- ◇ cloves
- ⬥ coffee
- ⚘ pyrethrum
- ⚘ sisal
- ↓ sugar
- ⚘ tea

Scale 1:12 450 000
(projection: Lambert Azimuthal Equal Area)

0 km   200   400

LIVESTOCK

Livestock production is one of the major agricultural activities in Tanzania. The sub-sector contributes to national food supply, converts rangeland resources into products suitable for human consumption and is a source of cash incomes and inflation – a free store of value. Out of the sub-sector's contribution to GDP, about 40 per cent originates from beef production, 30 per cent from milk production and another 30 per cent from poultry and small stock production. Three livestock production systems are commonly distinguished in the rangeland areas: commercial ranching, pastoralism and agro-pastoralism.

The 2008 National Livestock Census shows livestock population at 21.3 million cattle, 53.8 million goats, 6.4 million sheep, 1.6 million pigs and 43 million poultry.

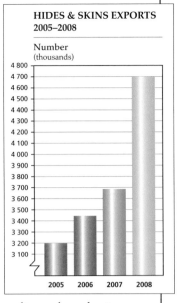

HIDES & SKINS EXPORTS
2005–2008

Number
(thousands)

FISHING

Tanzania is abundantly rich in fishery resources. The marine water covers 64 300 km² and fresh water covers 58 000 km². The fisheries contribute 30 per cent of food consumption in the country. Over 60 000 people are involved in artisan fishing, out of whom 46 670 operate in fresh water while 15 153 operate in marine waters. The total catch has continued to rise steadily to 3.1 mi. tons in 2008.

FORESTRY

Tanzania has about 38.8 million hectares of forests and woodlands. Out of this area, almost two thirds consists of woodlands on public lands that lack proper management. About 13 million hectares of this total forest area have been gazetted as forest reserves. Over 80 000 hectares of the gazetted area is under plantation forestry and about 1.6 million hectares are under water catchment management. The forests offer habitat for wildlife and beekeeping; unique natural ecosystems and genetic resources. Bio-energy is the main source of fuel for the rural population and accounts for 92 per cent of the total energy consumption in the country. The current problems include, among others, deforestation, inadequate forestry extension services and poor infrastructural facilities for wood-based industries.

BEEKEEPING

The estimated potential of bee products is about 138 000 tons of honey and 9200 tons of beeswax per annum from an estimated potential of 9.2 million honey bee colonies. Traditional beekeepers are the main producers of these products.

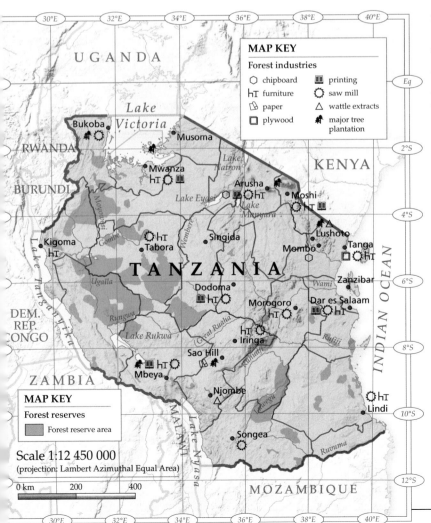

MAP KEY

Forest industries
- ⬡ chipboard
- hT furniture
- 🗋 paper
- ▱ plywood
- 🕮 printing
- ⚙ saw mill
- △ wattle extracts
- 🌲 major tree plantation

MAP KEY

Forest reserves
- Forest reserve area

Scale 1:12 450 000
(projection: Lambert Azimuthal Equal Area)

0 km   200   400

WATER RESOURCES AND ENERGY

There is a great variation of water availability in different parts of the country. The variation is explained by differences in topography and rainfall patterns. Despite this, Tanzania has sufficient surface and underground water resources to meet most of its present needs. Tanzania has 61.5 km^2 of inland water resources, which include the major lakes of Victoria, Tanganyika, Nyasa, Rukwa, Eyasi, Manyara, Natron and rivers, springs, swamps and man-made reservoirs and natural ponds. Underground water is an important source of water and it is the most viable alternative water supplement in the drier central and northern parts of the country.

This water processing plant is on the Wami River along the Chalinze to Segera road.

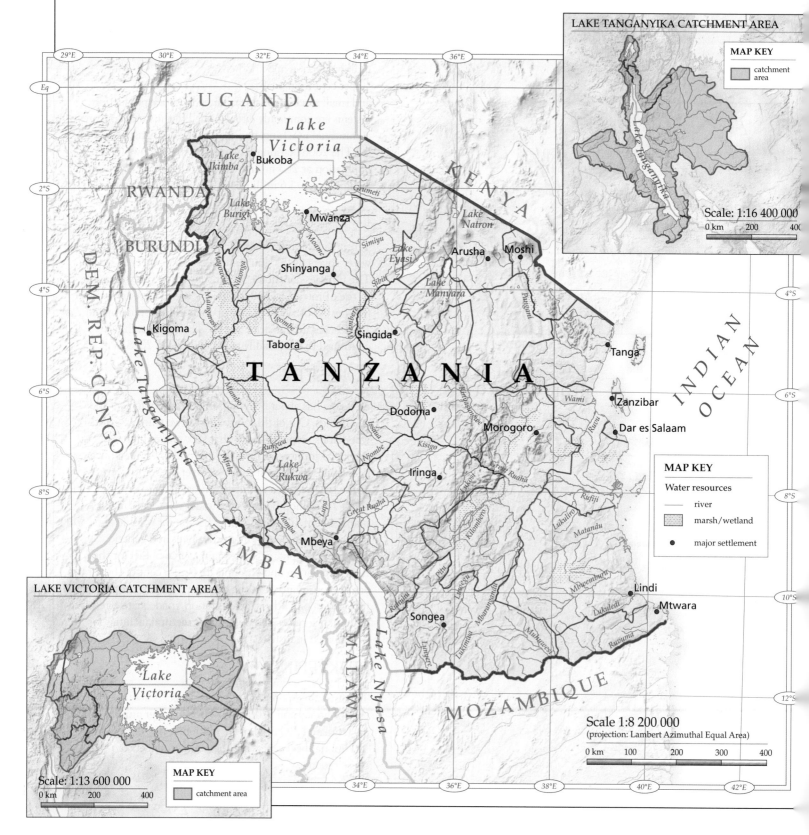

LAKE TANGANYIKA CATCHMENT AREA

MAP KEY

catchment area

Scale: 1:16 400 000

0 km   200   400

LAKE VICTORIA CATCHMENT AREA

MAP KEY

catchment area

Scale: 1:13 600 000

0 km   200   400

MAP KEY

Water resources

river

marsh/wetland

● major settlement

Scale 1:8 200 000
(projection: Lambert Azimuthal Equal Area)

0 km   100   200   300   400

WATER FOR DOMESTIC USE

The largest use of water is domestic. Access to safe water is essential for addressing poverty and health problems. The poor, most of whom live in rural areas, have limited access to clean water. Ongoing sector reform stipulates the following:

- Water development and supply is liberalised by involving all potential stakeholders, such as the government, local communities, private sector and NGOs.
- The national aim is achieving equitable access to an adequate, sustainable supply of clean, safe water both in rural and urban areas, and ensuring universal access to clean, safe water supply within a distance of 400 metres from people's homes.

ENERGY

Petroleum, hydropower and coal are the major sources of commercial energy in the country. Biomass, which comprises fuel-wood and charcoal, accounts for 93 per cent of total energy consumption.

Petroleum is imported. However, there are a number of companies exploring for oil, and so far positive results have yielded in some coastal areas. Natural gas is available, and is being used to produce electricity as a substitute for oil.

HYDROPOWER DAM FACILITIES

Name of dam	Capacity MW
Kidatu	204
Kihansi	180
Mtera	80
Pangani	68
Hale	21
Nyumba ya Mungu	8

Hydroelectric dams, such as the Kihansi River dam, could provide the answer to more sustainable energy production.

THERMAL POWER FACILITIES

Name of facility	Capacity MW
Tegeta	100
Ubungo	112
Other	30

The country's power generation system encompasses the use of hydro, thermal and gas power. Electricity is mainly generated from hydropower, which is prone to drought effects. Some thermal power stations have been installed. Three quarters of the country, mainly urban areas, is connected to the national electricity grid. It is intended that the rest of the country, including an estimated 8200 villages, would be supplied with electricity to curb deforestation.

There are other indigenous alternative sources of energy which include coal. Tanzania has 1200 million metric tons, which could provide energy for paper mills, cement factories, agriculture and household consumption and for generation of power.

Wind and solar energy are alternative sources of energy, although currently very little solar energy is used as an alternative source of energy.

Tanzania also imports 10 MW of electric power for Kagera Region from Masaka substation in Uganda while Sumbawanga, Tunduma and Mbozi districts receive about 3 MW from neighbouring Zambia.

Tanzania faces a major challenge of providing reliable electricity supply throughout the year to sustain economic activities.

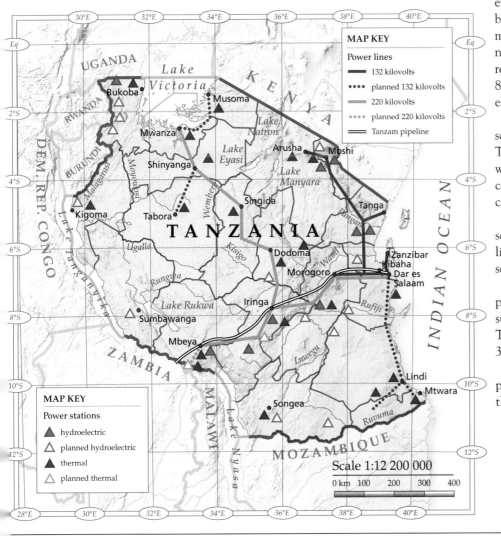

MAP KEY

Power lines
- —— 132 kilovolts
- •••• planned 132 kilovolts
- —— 220 kilovolts
- •••• planned 220 kilovolts
- —— Tanzam pipeline

MAP KEY

Power stations
- ▲ hydroelectric
- △ planned hydroelectric
- ▲ thermal
- △ planned thermal

Scale 1:12 200 000

0 km 100 200 300 400

MINING, INDUSTRY AND TRADE

Tanzania has a great number of mineral resources, particularly gold, base metals, diamonds, ferrous minerals and a wide variety of gemstones such as tanzanite, which is unique to Tanzania. Coal, uranium and various industrial minerals such as soda, kaolin, tin, gypsum, phosphate and dimension stones are available in economic quantities.

MAP KEY

Mineral resources

●	coal field	●	iron
●	gas field	●	kaolin
◻	copper	◼	magnetite
△	diamonds	▲	meerschaum
▲	gem stones	●	mica
◻	gold	●	salts
◼	gypsum	◼	tanzanite

Scale 1:12 200 000

0 km   100   200   300   400

This huge conveyor belt at Meremeta mine is carrying gold ore up from a mine to be processed into pure gold.

MINERAL RESOURCES

The following are minerals that have attracted most interest in the recent years:

- Gold, which is found in greenstone belts located in the east and south of Lake Victoria, and rock formations in the south and south-west of the country.
- Base metals, which are found in a belt running from Kagera through Kigoma to Mbeya, Ruvuma and Mtwara regions.
- Gemstones, which are found in eastern and western belts running from the Kenyan border in the north, to Mozambique in the south, and Mbeya and Rukwa regions.

Gold and diamonds are the mainstay of the country's mineral production.

The mining of Tanzanite in Mererani, Arusha was spearheaded by small-scale miners. Recently, big mining companies have acquired mining rights. The extraction process begins with machine force, but ends with the utmost care to avoid damaging the gems. Tanzanite is trichroic, meaning it shows different colours when viewed in different directions.

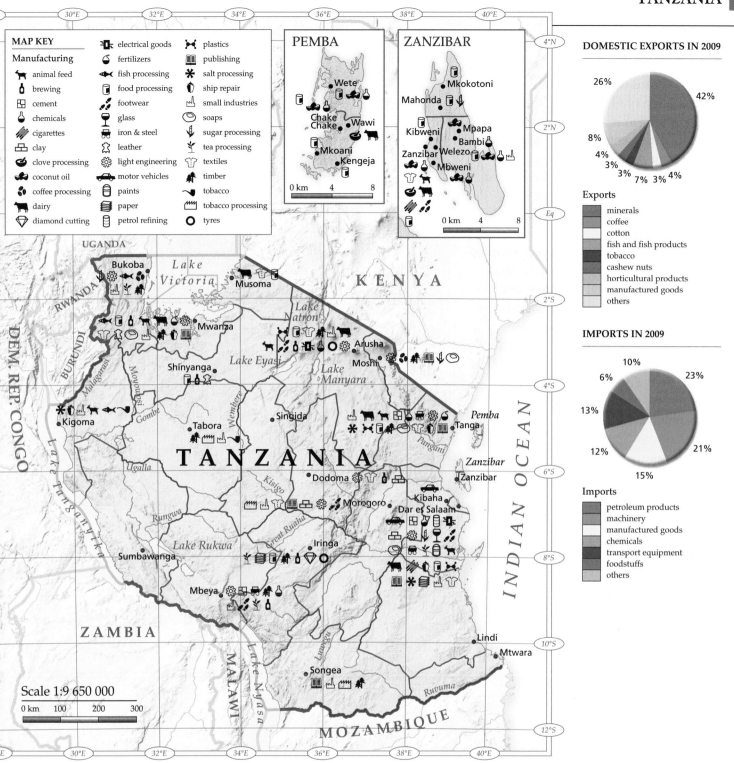

MAP KEY

Manufacturing

- animal feed
- brewing
- cement
- chemicals
- cigarettes
- clay
- clove processing
- coconut oil
- coffee processing
- dairy
- diamond cutting

- electrical goods
- fertilizers
- fish processing
- food processing
- footwear
- glass
- iron & steel
- leather
- light engineering
- motor vehicles
- paints
- paper
- petrol refining

- plastics
- publishing
- salt processing
- ship repair
- small industries
- soaps
- sugar processing
- tea processing
- textiles
- timber
- tobacco
- tobacco processing
- tyres

PEMBA

Wete, Chake Chake, Wawi, Mkoani, Kengeja

0 km 4 8

ZANZIBAR

Mkokotoni, Mahonda, Kibweni, Mpapa, Bambi, Zanzibar, Welezo, Mbweni

0 km 4 8

Scale 1:9 650 000

0 km 100 200 300

DOMESTIC EXPORTS IN 2009

- 42%
- 26%
- 8%
- 4%
- 3%
- 3%
- 7%
- 3%
- 4%

Exports

- minerals
- coffee
- cotton
- fish and fish products
- tobacco
- cashew nuts
- horticultural products
- manufactured goods
- others

IMPORTS IN 2009

- 23%
- 10%
- 6%
- 13%
- 12%
- 15%
- 21%

Imports

- petroleum products
- machinery
- manufactured goods
- chemicals
- transport equipment
- foodstuffs
- others

VALUE OF DIRECT IMPORTS, TOTAL EXPORTS AND THE DEFICIT ON THE BALANCE OF TRADE

	2003	2009	% increase
Direct imports	Tshs 2 277 171 m	Tshs 8 446 727 m	271%
Total exports	Tshs 1 267 349 m	Tshs 4 108 282 m	224%
The balance of trade deficit	Tshs 1 009 822 m	Tshs 4 338 445 m	330%

Tea processing

POPULATION

In the census of 2009, Tanzania had a population of 41 916 000. Estimated 2012 population is about 45 million. Human settlement followed a scattered pattern, but population density varied from one region to another; the highest was in Dar es Salaam (1931 per km^2) and the lowest density was in Lindi (12 people per km^2).

The next population census is planned for 2012 and apart from updating data on the country's social and economic progress, will also enable the government to evaluate the stage Tanzania has reached in implementing the globally agreed Millenium Development Goals. For the first time since independence 50 years ago, it will count its citizens living abroad.

TOTAL FERTILITY RATE IN TANZANIA, 2010

Total fertility rate (number of children per woman)

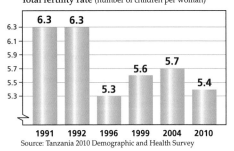

Source: Tanzania 2010 Demographic and Health Survey

RURAL POPULATION STRUCTURE IN TANZANIA, 2002

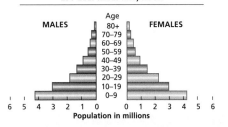

Kilimanjaro Hotel

Scale 1:6 550 000
(projection: Lambert Azimuthal Equal Area)

0 km   100   200   300

HISTORY OF POPULATION CENSUSES IN TANZANIA

Location	1978 Census	1988 Census	2002 Census	2009 Census
Tanzania mainland	17 036 000	22 584 000	33 462 000	40 683 000
Tanzania Zanzibar	476 000	641 000	982 000	1 233 000
Tanzania total	17 512 000	23 225 000	34 444 000	41 916 000

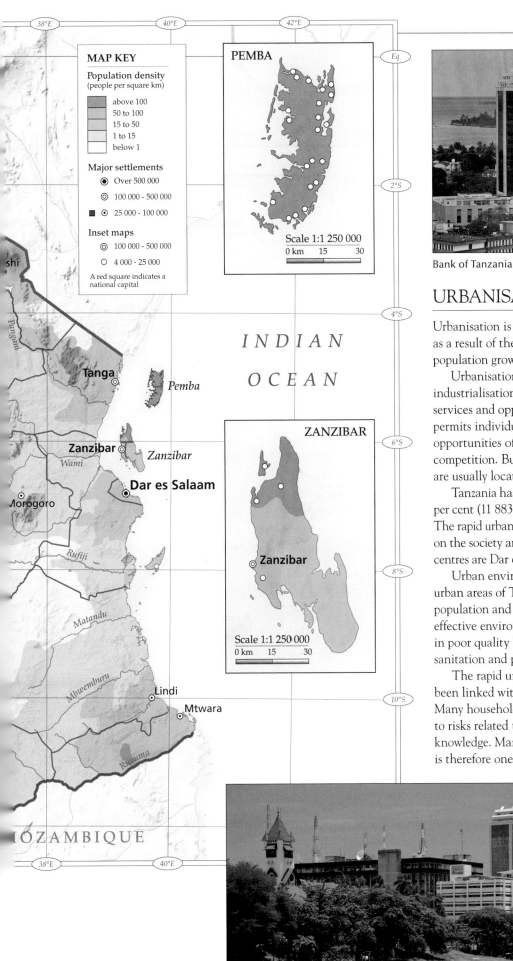

MAP KEY

Population density
(people per square km)

	above 100
	50 to 100
	15 to 50
	1 to 15
	below 1

Major settlements

◉ Over 500 000

◎ 100 000 - 500 000

■ ◉ 25 000 - 100 000

Inset maps

◎ 100 000 - 500 000

○ 4 000 - 25 000

A red square indicates a
national capital

PEMBA

Scale 1:1 250 000

0 km   15   30

INDIAN

OCEAN

Tanga

Pemba

Zanzibar

Zanzibar

Wami

Dar es Salaam

Morogoro

Rufiji

ZANZIBAR

Zanzibar

Scale 1:1 250 000

0 km   15   30

Matandu

Mbwemburu

Lindi

Mtwara

Ruvuma

MOZAMBIQUE

Bank of Tanzania

URBANISATION IN TANZANIA

Urbanisation is defined as the physical growth of towns as a result of the movement of people from rural areas and population growth within the urban settlement.

Urbanisation is closely linked to modernisation and industrialisation, and people being attracted by the services and opportunities available. Living in cities permits individuals and families to take advantage of the opportunities of proximity, diversity and marketplace competition. Businesses, which generate jobs and capital, are usually located in urban areas.

Tanzania has a relatively low level of urbanisation with 24 per cent (11 883 000) of its population living in urban areas. The rapid urbanisation in Tanzania has had a great impact on the society and the environment. The four main urban centres are Dar es Salaam, Mwanza, Mbeya and Arusha.

Urban environmental degradation is evident in the urban areas of Tanzania. The very rapid growth in urban population and industrialisation has occurred without effective environmental management. This has resulted in poor quality housing, inadequate infrastructure, poor sanitation and public transport, and industrial pollution.

The rapid urbanisation trends in many towns have been linked with widespread poverty and unemployment. Many households are increasingly becoming vulnerable to risks related to disease, food shortage and lack of knowledge. Managing the urban environment sustainably is therefore one of the major challenges for the future.

Dar es Salaam

WILDLIFE, TOURISM AND ENVIRONMENT

Tanzania has 19 per cent of its surface area devoted to wildlife in protected areas, where no human settlement is allowed, and 9 per cent of its wildlife co-exists with humans.

Tanzania has a rich and diverse spectrum of flora and fauna, including a wide variety of endemic species. The biological diversity includes 34 species of antelopes, many species of fish in Lake Victoria, Tanganyika and Nyasa and other small lakes and rivers, and 290 species of reptiles, amphibians, and invertebrates. Tanzania possesses important populations of species that are threatened, such as the black rhinoceros. Wildlife is a unique natural heritage and resource of Tanzania that is of great importance both nationally and globally.

Wildebeest in the Serengeti

Giraffe

TOURISM

Tanzania's tourism mission is 'to develop sustainable quality tourism that is ecologically friendly to the conservation and restoration of the environment and its people's culture'.

Tanzania's tourism sector has great economic growth potential. It provides a substantial amount of foreign exchange earnings, employment for 30 000 people and stimulates other sectors like agriculture, thereby contributing to the economic growth. Its contribution to the Gross Domestic Product is about 14 per cent, but this is very minimal compared to country's tourism potential. Tanzania is endowed with numerous tourist attractions:

- The abundant and diverse wildlife promotes game viewing, game hunting and photographic safaris.
- The spectacular landscape, environment and scenery promote sightseeing, photographic safaris, beach holiday activities and mountain climbing.

Tanzania's unique tourist attractions are:

- Kilimanjaro, the highest permanently snow-capped mountain in Africa.
- The exotic islands of Zanzibar and Pemba.
- The game sanctuaries of Serengeti, Tarangire, Lake Manyara, Ngorongoro Crater, Ruaha and Selous.,
- The 14th–16th Century ruins of Kilwa Kisiwani, Songomnara and Bagamoyo.
- The Olduvai George and Laetoli footprints.
- The Marine Park of Mafia Island.

The tourism industry provides excellent opportunities in construction and management of hotels, lodges and restaurants, road infrastructure ventures, aviation projects, training institutions, tour operations and travel agencies and marketing organisations.

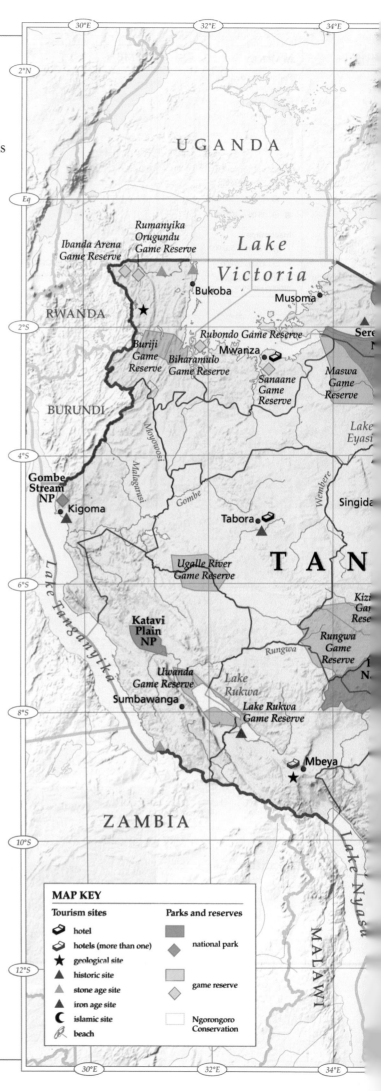

MAP KEY

Tourism sites

- hotel
- hotels (more than one)
- ★ geological site
- ▲ historic site
- ▲ stone age site
- ▲ iron age site
- ☾ islamic site
- beach

Parks and reserves

- national park
- game reserve
- Ngorongoro Conservation

MAP KEY

Zanzibar tourism

- hotel
- hotels
- historic site
- building of interest
- beach
- forest

Scale 1:1 500 000

0 km   20   40

Scale 1:6 550 000
(projection: Lambert Azimuthal Equal Area)

0 km   100   200   300

ENVIRONMENT

The number of people, where they live and how they live, all affect the condition of the environment. People alter the environment by clearing land for agriculture, mining or industries; using natural resources such as forests, and producing liquid and solid wastes.

Changes in environmental conditions, in turn, affect human health and well-being. Rural poverty, a high population growth rate, deforestation, and scarcity of fresh water are the outcomes of poor environmental management.

Tanzania is a globally recognised natural heritage site. Its diverse terrestrial, marine and freshwater ecosystems provide a habitat for a wide array of plant and animal species. Fifteen per cent of its area is set aside for biodiversity conservation. About 50 per cent of the total land is covered by forests and woodland and 40 per cent by grassland and scrub.

Resource degradation and pollution are becoming major problems, due in part to the failure to implement environmental policy recommendations and mandates. Moreover, the failure to engage communities adequately in the planning and implementation of development schemes has hampered efforts to reverse environmental degradation and improve health status at the local level.

Deforestation on this hillside in the Gombe National Park has destabilised the soil and resulted in a landslide.

The government has adopted sector policies related to forests, minerals, wildlife, fisheries, agriculture, livestock and land use, which give priority to conservation and management of the environment. Examples of environment protection projects are:

- Lake Tanganyika Catchment Reforestation and Education (TACARE) Program
- Sustainable Coastal Communities and Ecosystems (SUCCESS-Tanzania) Project,
- Tanzania Coastal Management Partnership (TCMP)
- Lake Victoria Environmental Management Project (LVEMP)
- The Usambara Mountains is an example of a well-managed environment – see the trees and plant cover in the photograph.

Usambara Mountains

ADMINISTRATION

Uganda has promoted a policy of decentralisation and the country is currently made of 112 districts with 30 more districts being established in the next three years. The Uganda Local Authorities Association has divided the districts into four regions, namely Central, Western, Northern and Eastern.

MPs in session

Under the decentralisation policy, authority has been transferred from Central Government to the local governments, communities, civil societies and the private sector.

The local government has authority to recruit, control, assign

and discharge without interference. The Capital City is now managed by the Kampala Capital City Authority headed by the Director and the Mayor is ceremonial head of the council.

Official name: REPUBLIC OF UGANDA	
Surface area	236 040 km²
Population	34.509 million (in 2011)
Capital city	Kampala
Official languages	English and Ganda
Currency	Ugandan shillings

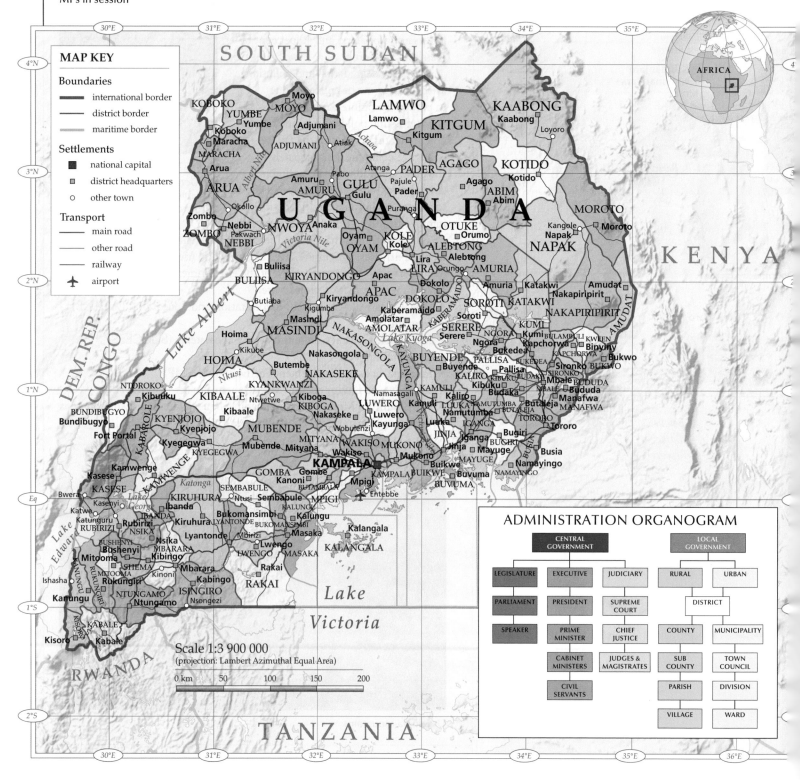

MAP KEY

Boundaries
— international border
— district border
— maritime border

Settlements
■ national capital
□ district headquarters
○ other town

Transport
— main road
— other road
— railway
✈ airport

Scale 1:3 900 000
(projection: Lambert Azimuthal Equal Area)

0 km   50   100   150   200

ADMINISTRATION ORGANOGRAM

- CENTRAL GOVERNMENT
  - LEGISLATURE → PARLIAMENT → SPEAKER
  - EXECUTIVE → PRESIDENT → PRIME MINISTER → CABINET MINISTERS → CIVIL SERVANTS
  - JUDICIARY → SUPREME COURT → CHIEF JUSTICE → JUDGES & MAGISTRATES
- LOCAL GOVERNMENT
  - RURAL → DISTRICT → COUNTY → SUB COUNTY → PARISH → VILLAGE
  - URBAN → DISTRICT → MUNICIPALITY → TOWN COUNCIL → DIVISION → WARD

RELIEF AND LANDFORMS

Most of Uganda is situated on the interior high plateau of the African continent, characterised by flat-topped hills. The hills are separated by uniform valley slopes that descend into extensive papyrus wetlands.

The northern region is an undulating plain whilst to the west lie the Mufumbiro volcanoes and Ruwenzori mountains. Eastwards lie Mount Elgon and the plug of Tororo Rock. To the north are Mounts Moroto and Kadam and the western rift valley stretches from Nimule to the south-western border.

The top of Mount Ruwenzori is permanently covered with ice and snow

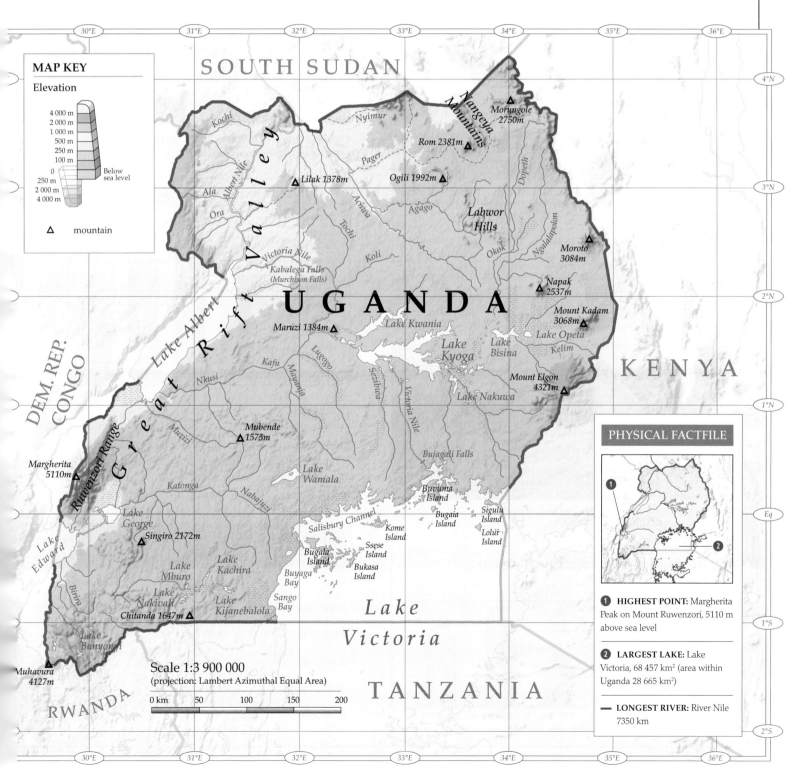

MAP KEY

Elevation

4 000 m
2 000 m
1 000 m
500 m
250 m
100 m
0
250 m   Below
2 000 m   sea level
4 000 m

△   mountain

SOUTH SUDAN

SOUTH SUDAN

Kochi

Nyimur

Nangeya Mountains

Morungole 2750m △

Albert Nile

Ala

Ora

Pager

Rom 2381m △

Lilak 1378m △

Ogili 1992m △

Achwa

Agago

Labwor Hills

Dopeth

Tochi

Koli

Okok

Ngalalapolon

Moroto 3084m △

Victoria Nile

Kabalega Falls
(Murchison Falls)

Great Rift Valley

Napak 2537m △

U G A N D A

Mount Kadam 3068m △

Maruzi 1384m △

Lake Kwania

Lake Opeta

Kelim

Lake Albert

Lake Kyoga

Lake Bisina

K E N Y A

Kafu

Mayanja

Lugogo

Ssezibwa

Nkusi

Victoria Nile

Mount Elgon 4321m △

Lake Nakuwa

Muzizi

Ruwenzori Range

Mubende 1573m △

Bujagali Falls

Margherita 5110m △

Lake Wamala

Buvuma Island

Katonga

Nabajuzi

Salisbury Channel

Bugaia Island

Sigulu Island

PHYSICAL FACTFILE

Lake George

Singiro 2172m △

Kome Island

Bugala Island

Ssese Island

Bukasa Island

Lolui Island

Lake Edward

Lake Mburo

Lake Kachira

Buyaga Bay

Sango Bay

Lake Nakivali

Lake Kijanebalola

Chitanda 1647m △

Lake Victoria

Lake Bunyonyi

Birira

Muhavura 4127m △

Scale 1:3 900 000
(projection: Lambert Azimuthal Equal Area)

0 km   50   100   150   200

R W A N D A

T A N Z A N I A

DEM. REP. CONGO

① HIGHEST POINT: Margherita Peak on Mount Ruwenzori, 5110 m above sea level

② LARGEST LAKE: Lake Victoria, 68 457 km² (area within Uganda 28 665 km²)

— **LONGEST RIVER:** River Nile 7350 km

AGRICULTURE, LIVESTOCK AND FISHING

Uganda's favourable climate and relatively fertile soils allow production of a variety of cash and food crops and the Ugandan economy is highly dependent on agriculture. In the drier areas of the country, agricultural activity is centred around cattle rearing and other livestock enterprises. Common food crops include bananas, millet, cassava and sorghum. The market for cash crops, such as coffee and tobacco, suffered a brief decline in the latter part of the last century and so new cash crops including horticulture, vanilla and aloe were developed. Initiatives are being made to adapt agriculture to climate change through the growth of resistant varieties. The National Agricultural Research Organisation has developed and introduced improved varieties for maize, sweet potatoes, groundnuts, sorghum, bananas, cassava, coffee and solanum potashes, along with new technology in livestock management such as fodder bank.

Coffee is typical of the 'cash crops' that are grown in Uganda and exported worldwide

EXPORTS FROM AGRICULTURAL PRODUCTS, 2006-2010 (000' tonnes)

Year	Coffee	Tea	Tobacco	Maize	Fishing	Cotton
2005/2006	133 110	34 334	15 793	2124	542	73
2006/2007	175 346	44 923	26 383	2315	625	132
2007/2008	218 781	45 680	29 040	2362	740	65
2008/2009	195 871	48 663	18 846	2355	787	145
2009/2010	167 952	49 182	27 615	2374	1030	97

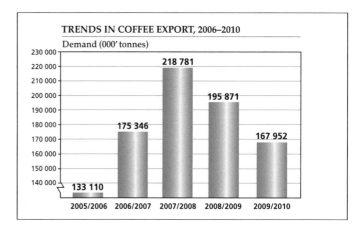

TRENDS IN COFFEE EXPORT, 2006–2010

Demand (000' tonnes)

- 2005/2006: 133 110
- 2006/2007: 175 346
- 2007/2008: 218 781
- 2008/2009: 195 871
- 2009/2010: 167 952

The small scale of this farming enterprise is typical of much of the agriculture in Uganda

FISHING

Fishing is carried out on the major lakes and in 2004 fish and fish product exports earned nearly US$ 15 million. Promotion of aquaculture has led to an increase in production from 500 metric tonne in 2000 to 20 000 metric tonne in 2007.

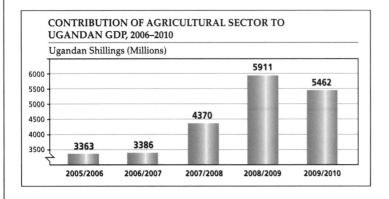

CONTRIBUTION OF AGRICULTURAL SECTOR TO UGANDAN GDP, 2006–2010

Ugandan Shillings (Millions)

- 2005/2006: 3363
- 2006/2007: 3386
- 2007/2008: 4370
- 2008/2009: 5911
- 2009/2010: 5462

ANNUAL GDP GROWTH FOR FOOD AND CASH CROPS, 2006-2010 (Ugandan Shillings Millions)

Year	Cash crops	Food crops
2005/2006	350	2708
2006/2007	476	2564
2007/2008	559	3350
2008/2009	539	4800
2009/2010	358	4498

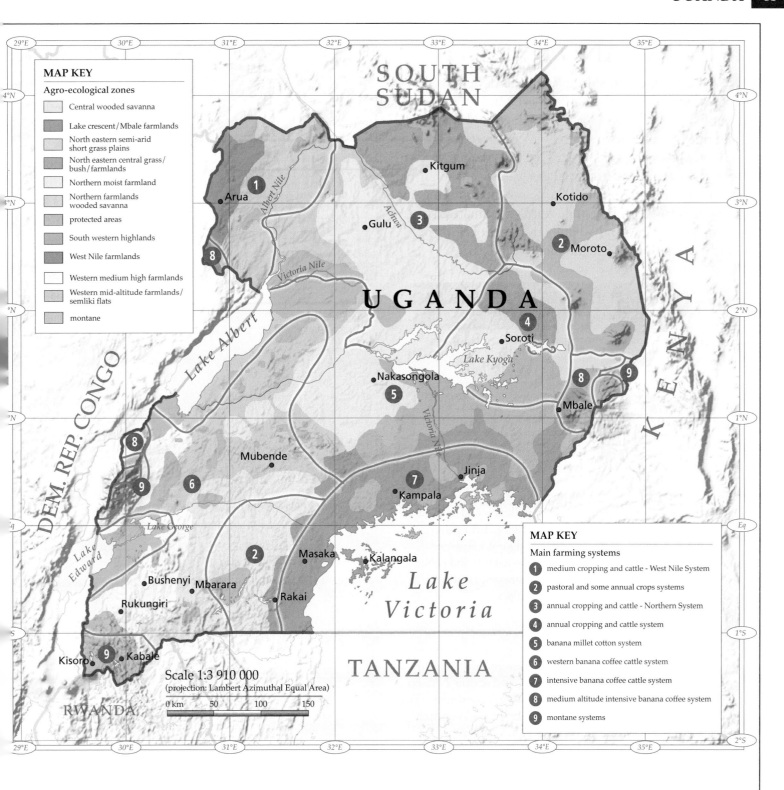

MAP KEY

Agro-ecological zones

- Central wooded savanna
- Lake crescent/Mbale farmlands
- North eastern semi-arid short grass plains
- North eastern central grass/bush/farmlands
- Northern moist farmland
- Northern farmlands wooded savanna
- protected areas
- South western highlands
- West Nile farmlands
- Western medium high farmlands
- Western mid-altitude farmlands/semliki flats
- montane

MAP KEY

Main farming systems

1. medium cropping and cattle - West Nile System
2. pastoral and some annual crops systems
3. annual cropping and cattle - Northern System
4. annual cropping and cattle system
5. banana millet cotton system
6. western banana coffee cattle system
7. intensive banana coffee cattle system
8. medium altitude intensive banana coffee system
9. montane systems

Scale 1:3 910 000
(projection: Lambert Azimuthal Equal Area)
0 km   50   100   150

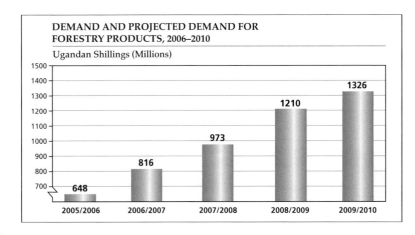

DEMAND AND PROJECTED DEMAND FOR FORESTRY PRODUCTS, 2006–2010

Ugandan Shillings (Millions)

Year	Value
2005/2006	648
2006/2007	816
2007/2008	973
2008/2009	1210
2009/2010	1326

FORESTRY

About 24 per cent of Uganda's land area is made up of forest, of which 80 per cent is woodland and 20 per cent is moist highland forest. Two thirds of the total forest area is on private land, the rest is government owned – protected areas. Forestry contributes about 6 per cent of Uganda's GDP. Forest and tree resources provide energy for approximately 90 per cent of the population and the industry employs around one million people.

MINING AND ENERGY

Minerals and mineral exploration today play only a small part in the national economy, unlike in past years. Aggregate, gravel and small quantities of gold, tin and tungsten concentrates are currently produced and exported. There are many areas of high mineral potential in Uganda that remain inadequately explored. The potential mining industry is based on limestone reserves estimated at 200 million tonnes and 50 million tonnes of iron ore, which could support cement and iron industries.

PRODUCTION OF SELECTED MINERALS IN UGANDA 2009 AND 2010		
Mineral	**2009**	**2010**
Limestone (tonnes)	588.9	634.7
Wolfram (tonnes)	8.83	55.2
Cobalt (tonnes)	389.2	568.3

ENVIRONMENTAL IMPACTS

Mining activities in Uganda have contributed to the degradation of the environment through pollution and damage to the landscape. The multitudes of open ditches left behind by small-scale mining of gold, lime, clay and sand, constitute landscape damage. They are also a hazard to wildlife and public health as they interfere with water flow to streams, creating pools of water in which disease vectors multiply.

OIL EXTRACTION

Oil and gas have been discovered in the Western Rift Valley in Uganda. The oil reserves are currently estimated at over 2 billion barrels equivalent with the exploration phase still continuing. The development phase has started in some of the areas so hopefully oil revenue will enhance Uganda's economic development.

Solar harnessing at a holiday resort

MAP KEY

Minerals
- gold
- copper
- lead
- chromite
- iron
- cassiterite
- tungsten
- bismuth
- beryl
- cobalt
- columbite, pyrochlore
- diatomite
- graphite
- gypsum
- kaolin
- kyanite
- phosphate
- salt
- mica
- limestone
- oil

SOUTH SUDAN

DEM. REP. CONGO

Arua

Buliisa

Lake Albert

Albert Nile

Victoria Nile

Lake George

Lake Edward

Mubende

Kasese

Bushenyi

Masaka

Kalai

Rukunguri

Mbarara

Rakai

Kisoro

Kabale

RWANDA

Scale 1:3 520 000
(projection: Lambert Azimuthal Equal Area)

0 km   50   100   150

Oil extraction in Uganda

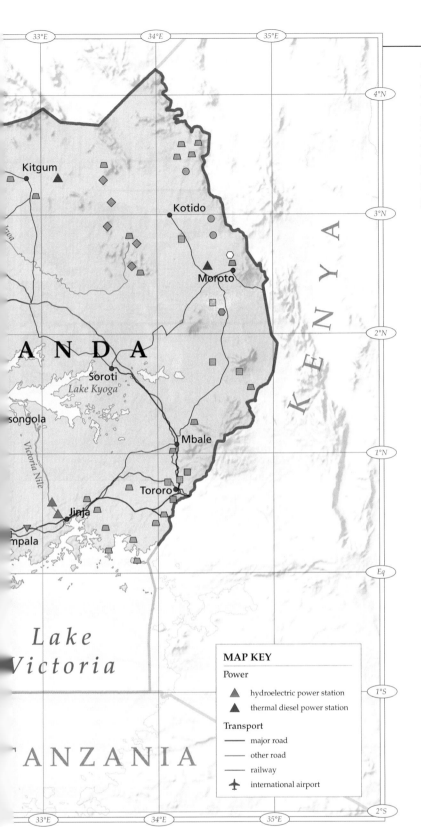

ENERGY

Hydro-power is the main source of energy in Uganda. Its production even permits export of energy to other countries. However, only an estimated 6 per cent of Uganda's population has access to electricity. The government is encouraging private investment in the power sector, particularly in rural areas where a high percentage of the population live. Ninety per cent of Uganda' population use woodfuel for energy.

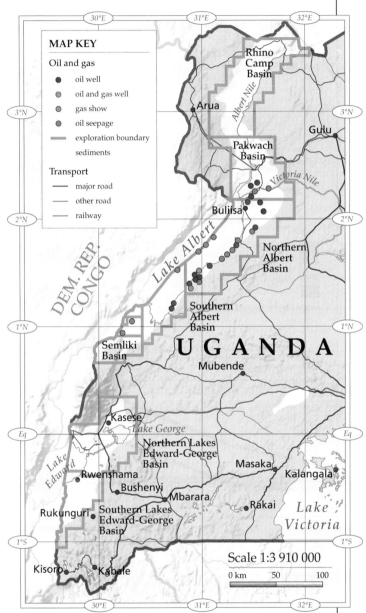

MAP KEY

Oil and gas
- ● oil well
- ○ oil and gas well
- ◐ gas show
- ● oil seepage
- exploration boundary
- sediments

Transport
- major road
- other road
- railway

MAP KEY

Power
- ▲ hydroelectric power station
- ▲ thermal diesel power station

Transport
- major road
- other road
- railway
- ✈ international airport

Scale 1:3 910 000

0 km   50   100

Hydro-electric power makes 99 per cent of generation capacity

The hydro-electric power station at Owen Falls Dam, Jinja

INDUSTRY AND TRADE

Manufacturing industries are growing, but largely producing agricultural products. Markets are available within the COMESA region, of which Uganda is a member. Currently, the manufacturing sector contributes 7.4 per cent of the GDP.

The COMESA region takes the largest share of 70.7 per cent of Uganda's trade with traditional export commodities declining.

The Asian continent is the leading source of Uganda's imports with a share of 37.2 per cent.

CONTRIBUTION OF DIFFERENT INDUSTRIAL SECTORS TO THE UGANDAN GDP, 2001–2003

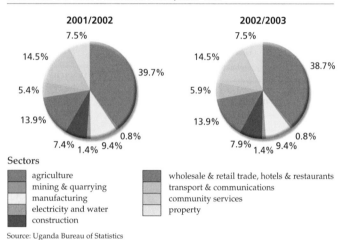

2001/2002
7.5%
14.5%
39.7%
5.4%
13.9%
0.8%
7.4% 1.4% 9.4%

2002/2003
7.5%
14.5%
38.7%
5.9%
13.9%
0.8%
7.9% 1.4% 9.4%

Sectors

agriculture	wholesale & retail trade, hotels & restaurants
mining & quarrying	transport & communications
manufacturing	community services
electricity and water	property
construction	

Source: Uganda Bureau of Statistics

Construction site

IMPORTS AND EXPORTS 2005–2009

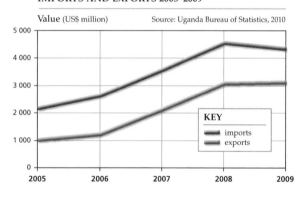

Value (US$ million)   Source: Uganda Bureau of Statistics, 2010

KEY
imports
exports

GROWTH IN GDP FOR SELECTED INDUSTRY SECTORS 2005–2009

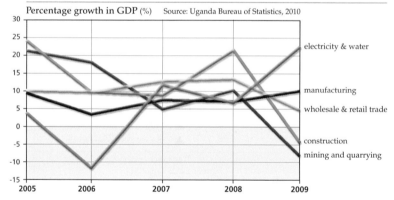

Percentage growth in GDP (%)   Source: Uganda Bureau of Statistics, 2010

electricity & water
manufacturing
wholesale & retail trade
construction
mining and quarrying

TRANSPORT AND COMMUNICATION

Uganda is a landlocked country. The major forms of transport include road, railway, water and air. Lake Victoria is the largest water body.

Telecommunication is one of the fast growing sectors in Uganda. This has been made easier through mobile phones and availability of the Internet. The country used to rely on satellites until recently when it became connected through a nationwide fibre optic cable network extending to its borders. To date, there are five mobile phone companies and more than nine million people own mobile phones.

Mobile phone mast

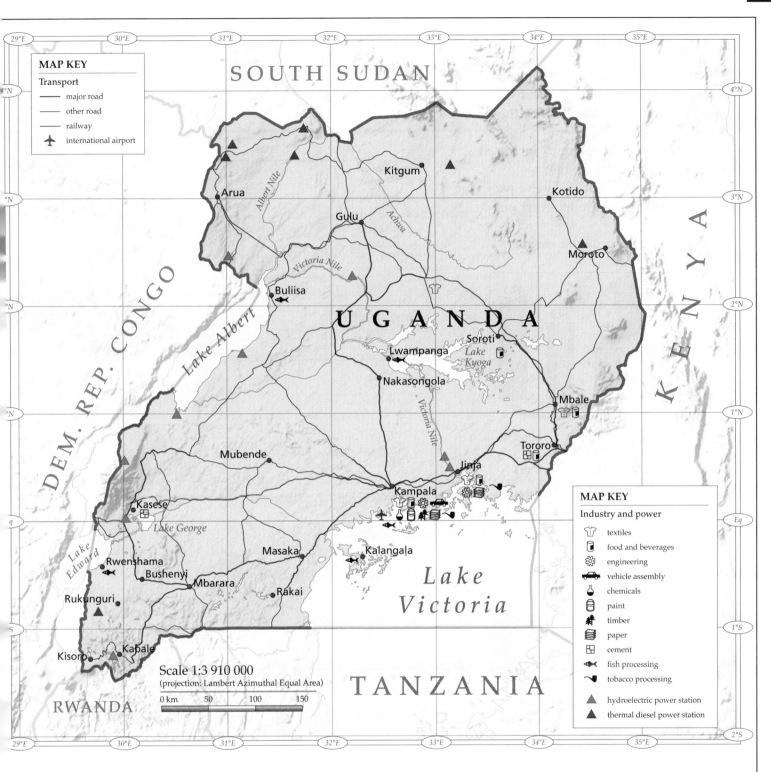

MAP KEY

Transport

— major road
— other road
— railway
✈ international airport

SOUTH SUDAN

DEM. REP. CONGO

KENYA

Arua

Kitgum

Kotido

Gulu

Moroto

Buliisa

U G A N D A

Albert Nile

Achwa

Victoria Nile

Lake Albert

Soroti

Lwampanga

Lake Kyoga

Nakasongola

Victoria Nile

Mbale

Mubende

Tororo

Jinja

Kampala

Kasese

Lake George

Masaka

Kalangala

Lake Edward

Rwenshama

Bushenyi

Mbarara

Rakai

Lake Victoria

Rukunguri

Kisoro

Kabale

RWANDA

TANZANIA

Scale 1:3 910 000
(projection: Lambert Azimuthal Equal Area)

0 km   50   100   150

MAP KEY

Industry and power

👕 textiles
🥫 food and beverages
⚙ engineering
🚗 vehicle assembly
🧪 chemicals
🛢 paint
🌲 timber
📚 paper
⊞ cement
🐟 fish processing
🌿 tobacco processing
▲ hydroelectric power station
▲ thermal diesel power station

TELEPHONE AND INTERNET USERS 2005-2009

Number of subscribers   Source: Uganda Bureau of Statistics, 2010

100 000 000
10 000 000
1 000 000
100 000
10 000
1 000
100
10
0

Logarithmic Scale

KEY
— mobile phone
— mobile wireless internet
— fixed telephone
— fixed internet

2005   2006   2007   2008   2009

Entebbe airport

POPULATION

The 2006 census showed that Uganda had a total population of 28 196 000 people. The annual population growth rate between 1991 and 2006 was 3.3 per cent. The population density increased from 25 persons per km² in 1948 to 124 persons per km² in 2006. Twelve per cent of the population live in urban areas.

POPULATION TREND IN UGANDA, 1969–2011

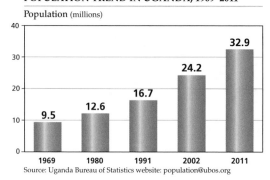

Source: Uganda Bureau of Statistics website: population@ubos.org

UGANDA POPULATION AGE BREAKDOWN 2012

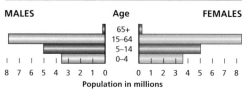

Source: Uganda Bureau of Statistics

UGANDA POPULATION BY GENDER

Year	Male	Female	Total
2008	14 383 200	15 209 400	29 592 600
2009	14 933 900	15 727 400	30 661 300
2010	15 516 600	16 268 000	31 784 600
2011	16 118 600	16 821 200	32 939 800
2012	16 741 400	17 390 000	34 131 400

STRUCTURE

Children below 18 years constitute 56 per cent of the population. Children of primary school age make up 22 per cent of the population and most of them are now able to go to school, as a result of the Universal Primary Education programme. Secondary school children make up 16 per cent of the population and the ratio of dependents is still high. The male population is 11 929 803 and the female population is 12 512 281.

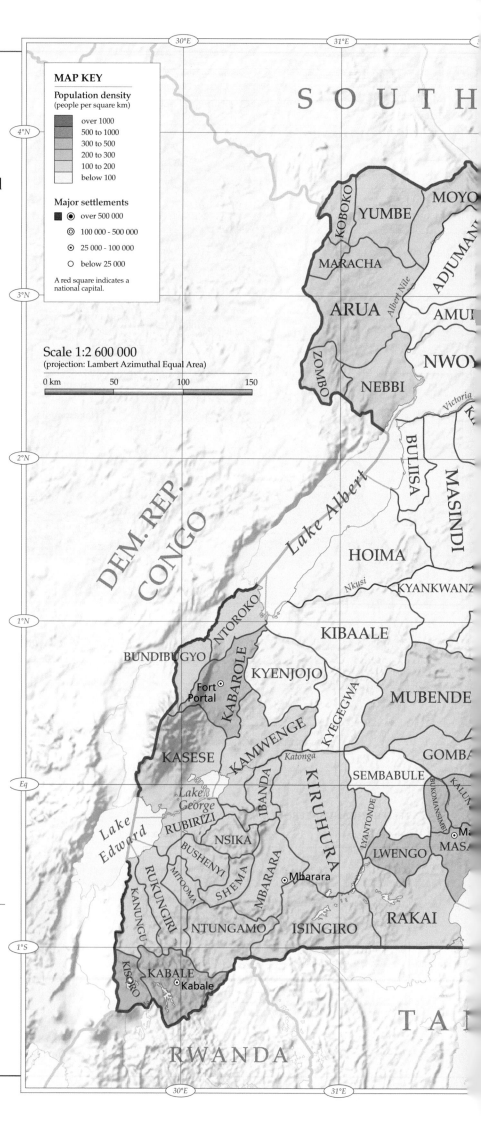

MAP KEY

Population density
(people per square km)

- over 1000
- 500 to 1000
- 300 to 500
- 200 to 300
- 100 to 200
- below 100

Major settlements

- ■ ◉ over 500 000
- ◎ 100 000 – 500 000
- ⊙ 25 000 - 100 000
- ○ below 25 000

A red square indicates a national capital.

Scale 1:2 600 000
(projection: Lambert Azimuthal Equal Area)

0 km   50   100   150

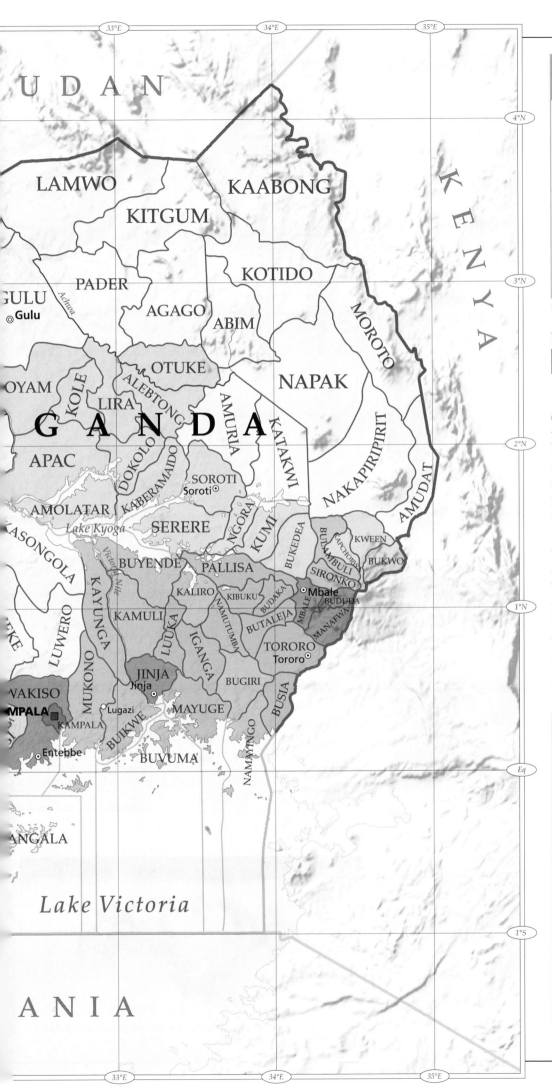

UGANDA POPULATION BY REGION (000's)

Region	Census figures		Projection mid year	
	1991	2002	2011	2012
Central	4844	6575	8466	8716
Eastern	4128	6205	8624	8956
Northern	3152	5149	7621	7972
Western	4548	6298	8230	8487
Total	16 672	24 227	32 940	34 131

Source: Uganda Bureau of Statistics

URBAN/RURAL POPULATION SPLIT

12%   88%

GROWTH RATE

Uganda's population growth rate is among the highest in the world at 3.3 per cent. The projected population for 2011 was 32.9 million people.

YOUTH

The challenges of the growing population is the rising number of unemployed youth, many of whom are being trained in entrepreneurial skills to engage in business. The next census will be conducted in 2013.

Youths in Uganda

TOURISM, WILDLIFE AND ENVIRONMENT

Uganda's tourism is mainly carved around a network of 10 national parks, wildlife conservation areas, sanctuaries and commercial wildlife areas. There are also cultural sites as well as a growing ecotourism industry centred around the forest reserves and wetlands. Tourism contributes to the enhancement of environmental quality and protection of wildlife and habitats and it makes a significant contribution to the economy. Another development in the tourism industry is 'Landscape of Peace' which is an international cross border tourism management. This is between Rwanda and the Democratic Republic of Congo in the South and with South Sudan in the North.

NON-RESIDENT TOURIST ARRIVALS BY PURPOSE OF VISIT

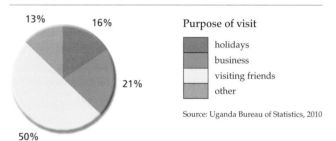

13%
16%
21%
50%

Purpose of visit
- holidays
- business
- visiting friends
- other

Source: Uganda Bureau of Statistics, 2010

Mountain gorillas

MOUNTAIN GORILLA TOURISM PER YEAR, 2005–2010

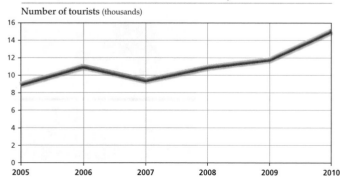

Number of tourists (thousands)

16					
14					
12					
10					
8					
6					
4					
2					
0					
2005	2006	2007	2008	2009	2010

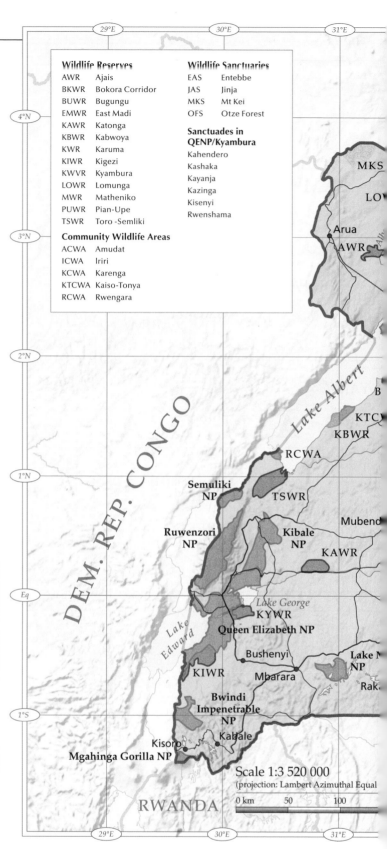

Wildlife Reserves
AWR Ajais
BKWR Bokora Corridor
BUWR Bugungu
EMWR East Madi
KAWR Katonga
KBWR Kabwoya
KWR Karuma
KIWR Kigezi
KWVR Kyambura
LOWR Lomunga
MWR Matheniko
PUWR Pian-Upe
TSWR Toro -Semliki

Community Wildlife Areas
ACWA Amudat
ICWA Iriri
KCWA Karenga
KTCWA Kaiso-Tonya
RCWA Rwengara

Wildlife Sanctuaries
EAS Entebbe
JAS Jinja
MKS Mt Kei
OFS Otze Forest

Sanctuades in QENP/Kyambura
Kahendero
Kashaka
Kayanja
Kazinga
Kisenyi
Rwenshama

Scale 1:3 520 000
(projection: Lambert Azimuthal Equal

0 km   50   100

European tourists enjoy an exhilarating white-water rafting trip down the River Nile at Bujagali Falls

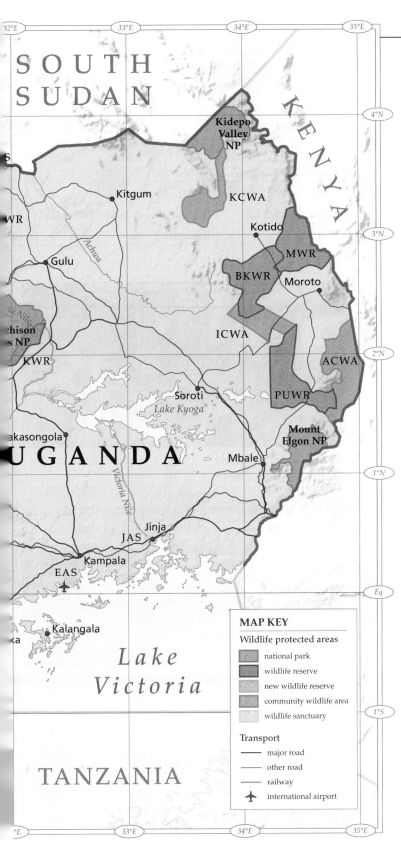

Local crafts

ENVIRONMENT

Uganda is endowed with abundant natural resources. There are many biodiversity hot spots such as the Albertine Rift Valley, which is very spectacular. Other biodiverse areas include the Sango Bay ecosystem and the dry montane forests of Karamoja.

Uganda's biodiversity is threatened by different human activities such as agriculture, charcoal burning settlements in wetlands and the clearing of land for economic activities. There are several programmes and initiatives to conserve the biodiversity in the forests, parks and outside protected areas. Some of the programmes include the National Wetlands Management and Conservation Programme, Protected Areas Management and Sustainable Utilisation Programme and the National Forest Management and Conservation Project. Uganda has also ratified regional and international conventions relating to biodiversity.

Regional programmes include the Lake Victoria Environment Management Project which includes all the countries in the Lake Victoria Watershed, the Nile Basin Initiative and its subsidiary projects in the Nile Basin countries. Cross border biodiversity projects have been set up along the East African borders and include the Virunga Massif transboundary tourism plan, which aims at protecting and jointly managing the mountain gorillas and their habitats.

Areas such as Lake Bunyonyi provide both important habitats for wildlife and popular tourist attractions

PROTECTED AREAS, 2005	
Protected area	**Area (km²)**
Queen Elizabeth National Park	2056
Kidepo Valley National Park	1431
Mount Elgon National Park	1110
Murchison Falls National Park	3877
Pian Upe Wildlife Reserve	2304
Bokora Corridor Wildlife Reserve	1816
Matheniko Wildlife Reserve	1757

MAP KEY

Wildlife protected areas

- national park
- wildlife reserve
- new wildlife reserve
- community wildlife area
- wildlife sanctuary

Transport

- —— major road
- —— other road
- —— railway
- ✈ international airport

ADMINISTRATION, RELIEF AND LANDFORMS

Rwanda is located and landlocked in east-central Africa. It lies 270 km south of the Equator, 970 km inland from the Indian ocean and 2000 km east of the Atlantic Ocean - literally in the heart of Africa. The country is located between latitudes 1°04' and 2°15' south and longitudes 28°45' and 30°45' with a surface area of 26 338 km². Rwanda is bordered by Uganda to the north, Tanzania to the east, Burundi to the south and the Democratic Republic of Congo to the west. Rwanda is comprised of five provinces namely: Eastern Province, Western Province, South and Northern Provinces and the Municipality of Kigali City. It comprises 30 Districts, 416 Sectors, 2148 Cells and 14 842 villages locally known as Imidugudu.

Rwanda is governed through three branches of Government namely the Executive, Legislature, and Judiciary. While separate and independent, the work of these three branches is complementary. Executive authority in Rwanda is vested in the President and Cabinet. The President has the direct electoral mandate. The Cabinet's role is that of decision making. It has the final say in all propositions. The term of office of the President is limited to two terms of seven years each. The Legislature is composed of the Senate and Chamber of Deputies in charge of passing laws and overseeing the functions of the executive in accordance with procedures stipulated by the Constitution. What is unique in Rwanda is that there are more women than men in the Legislature. The Supreme Court and other courts exercise judicial powers and are independent in their execution of duties.

RELIEF AND LANDFORMS

The Rwandan relief is hilly and mountainous; it is part of the East Africa plateau and, in general, rises from east to west. Elevations vary from 1000 m to 4500 m above sea level. The highest elevations are located in the Virunga, a range of volcanoes along the north west border the DRC, where Mount Karisimbi is the highest (4507 m above sea level). There are also volcanoes between Rwanda and Uganda. These are Muhabura, Gahinga and Sabyinyo. A narrow band on the west is part of the Great Rift Valley, a series of deep, steep-sided trenches crossing Eastern Africa, while the lowlands of the south west in Bugarama Plain, with an altitude of 900 m, are part of the tectonic depression of the East African Rift Valley.

The relief pattern gives Rwanda a mild, cool and moderate climate which is temperate due to altitude variation. Average temperatures are near 21°C (70°F) all year round, except in the highlands where they are lower. Total annual rainfall averages between 760 to 1780 mm, depending on location, though there are occasional droughts to the east.

Also known as 'the land of a thousand hills', Rwanda has five volcanic mountains, many lakes and numerous rivers, the largest body of water being Lake Kivu which is partly within Rwanda's and partly within DRC's borders. Most of Rwanda's rivers flow east to the Akagera River, the main headstream of the famous Nile River.

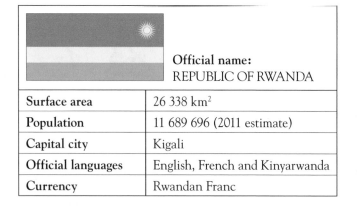

Official name:	REPUBLIC OF RWANDA
Surface area	26 338 km²
Population	11 689 696 (2011 estimate)
Capital city	Kigali
Official languages	English, French and Kinyarwanda
Currency	Rwandan Franc

Inside Rwandan parliament

Rwandan parliament building at Kimihurura-Kigali

Mount Muhabura, extinct volcano

Mist over a valley in
Kigali, Rwanda

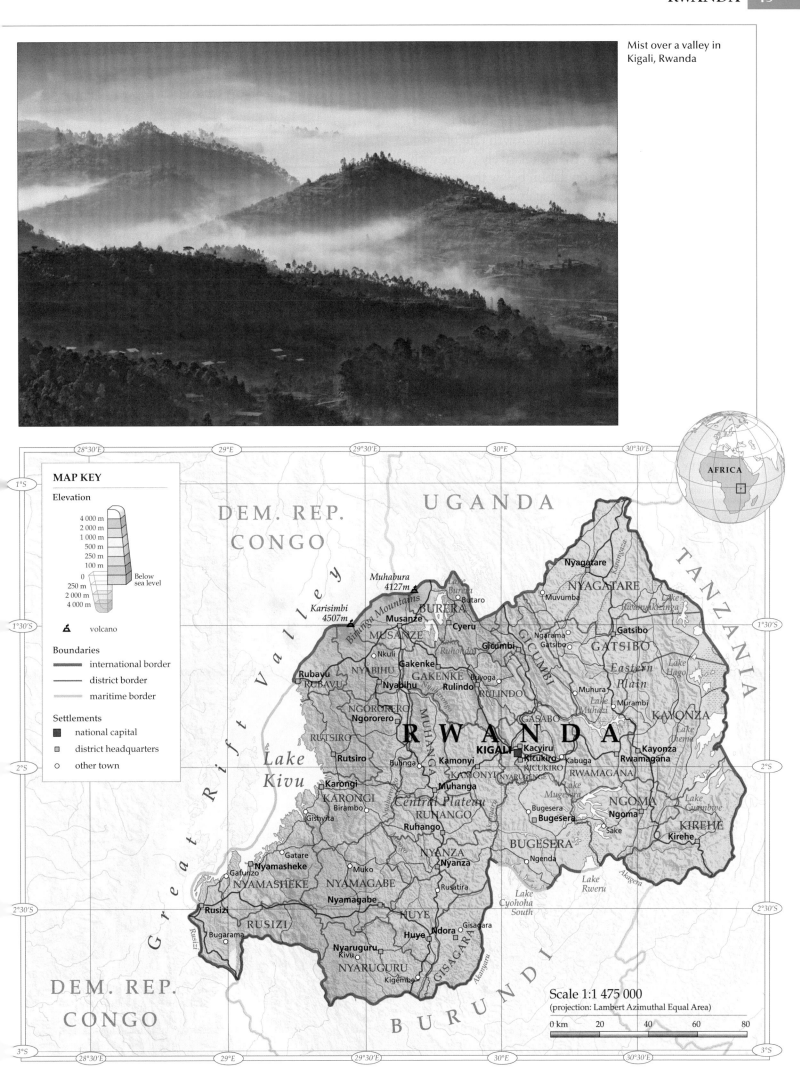

AFRICA

MAP KEY

Elevation

4 000 m
2 000 m
1 000 m
500 m
250 m
100 m
0
250 m
2 000 m
4 000 m
Below
sea level

⌃ volcano

Boundaries

international border
district border
maritime border

Settlements

■ national capital
□ district headquarters
○ other town

DEM. REP.
CONGO

UGANDA

TANZANIA

Great Rift Valley

Muhabura
4127m ⌃

Birunga Mountains

Karisimbi
4507m ⌃

Lake
Burera

Nyagatare ■

NYAGATARE

Muvumba ○

Butaro ○

BURERA

Musanze ■

MUSANZE

Cyeru ■

Ngarama ○

Gatsibo ○

Gatsibo ■

GATSIBO

Nkuli ○

*Lake
Ruhondo*

Gicumbi ■

*Eastern
Plain*

*Lake
Hago*

Gakenke ■

GAKENKE

Buyoga ○

Muhura ○

Murambi ○

KAYONZA

Rubavu ■
RUBAVU

NYABIHU

Nyabihu ■

Rulindo ■

RULINDO

Nduba River

*Lake
Muhazi*

NGORORERO

Ngororero ■

MUHANGA

GASABO

R W A N D A

RUTSIRO

*Lake
Kivu*

Rutsiro ■

Bulinga ○

Kamonyi ■

KIGALI ■ Kacyiru ■
Kicukiro ■

KICUKIRO

NYARUGENGE

Kabuga ○

RWAMAGANA

Kayonza ■

Rwamagana ■

Karongi ■
KARONGI

Birambo ○

KAMONYI

Muhanga ■

Central Plateau

RUHANGO

*Lake
Mugesera*

Bugesera ○

NGOMA

*Lake
Gisambwe*

Gishyita ○

Ruhango ■

Bugesera ■

Ngoma ■

Sake ○

KIREHE

Gatare ○

NYANZA

Ngenda ○

Kirehe ■

Nyamasheke ■

Muko ○

Nyanza ■

Rusatira ○

*Lake
Rweru*

Gafunzo ○

NYAMASHEKE

NYAMAGABE

Nyamagabe ■

Akagera River

Rusizi ■
RUSIZI

HUYE

*Lake
Cyohoha
South*

Bugarama ○

Huye ■
Ndora ■
Gisagara ○

Nyaruguru ■
Kivu ○

GISAGARA

NYARUGURU

Kigembe ○

DEM. REP.
CONGO

BURUNDI

Scale 1:1 475 000
(projection: Lambert Azimuthal Equal Area)

0 km   20   40   60   80

POPULATION

Rwanda is one of the most densely populated countries in Africa, with about 397 inhabitants per km². Birth rates are high; according to 2011 estimates, Rwanda has an annual growth rate of 2.8 per cent, a population that is relatively young with 67 per cent of the total population below the age of 25. The population is currently estimated at 11 689 696.

POPULATION PYRAMID

Rwanda's population pyramid has a broader base of younger age groups due to high birth rates and reduced infant mortality. The progressive narrowing towards the apex results from low life expectancy, where the number of older people is reduced by death.

RWANDA POPULATION AGE BREAKDOWN
2011

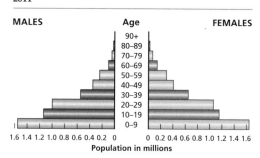

RWANDA POPULATION AGE BREAKDOWN
2015 (Predicted)

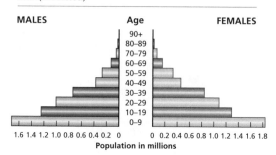

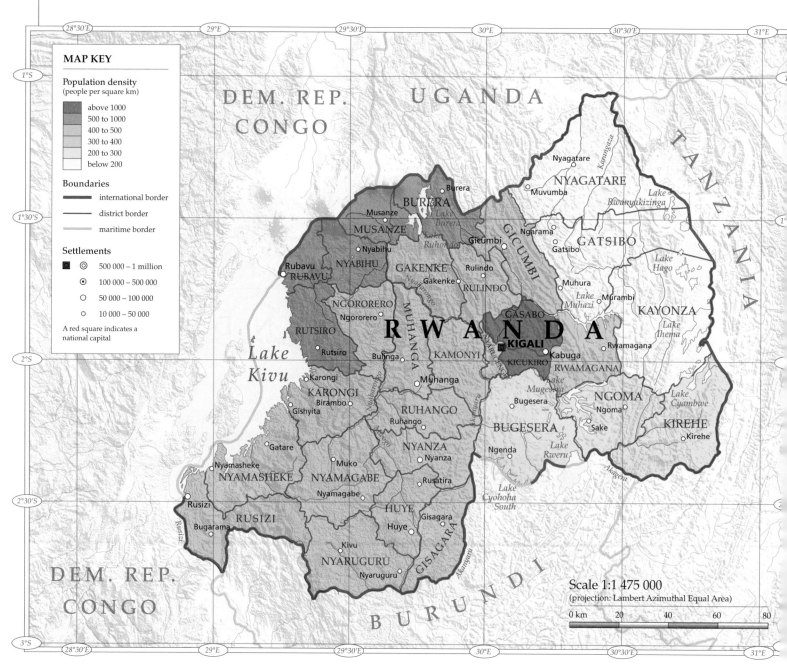

AGRICULTURE, LIVESTOCK, FORESTRY AND FISHING

The agriculture sector is very important to the economy of Rwanda, as the total area of arable land is about 1.4 million hectares, which is 52 per cent of the total 26 336 km² of the country, with 80 per cent of the population involved in the sector. Substantial traditional crops include bananas, maize, beans, sorghum, wheat, rice, peas, groundnuts, soyabeans, Irish potatoes, sweet potatoes, cassava, roots and tubers, yams, fruit and vegetables. Non-traditional products like coffee, tea, flowers and pyrethrum are the major export crops.

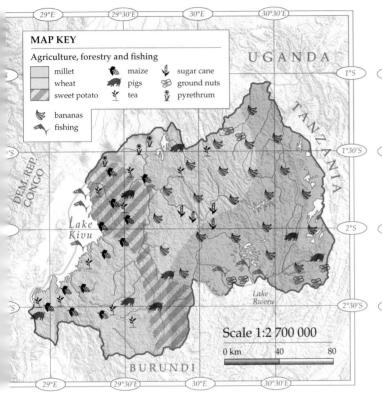

MAP KEY

Agriculture, forestry and fishing

millet
wheat
sweet potato

maize
pigs
tea

sugar cane
ground nuts
pyrethrum

bananas
fishing

Scale 1:2 700 000

0 km   40   80

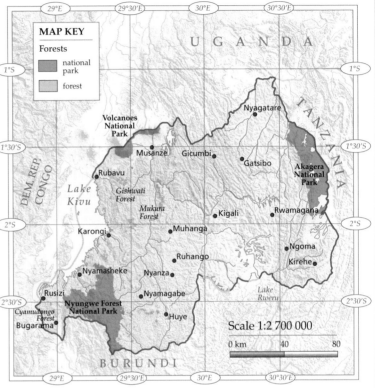

MAP KEY

Forests

national park

forest

Scale 1:2 700 000

0 km   40   80

LIVESTOCK

Livestock rearing is also important in Rwanda because it contributes to income generation and nutrition for farm and non-farm families. Most reared livestock are cattle, goats, sheep, pigs, poultry and rabbits. Livestock products are meat, milk, eggs and skins. The increase in dairy cattle numbers through 'one cow per family' and other agricultural policies resulted in a significant increase in milk products.

FISHING

Rwanda's wetlands and aquatic lands are generally lakes and rivers, and marshes associated with these lakes and rivers. These constitute an important fish habitat as they support a large population of fish. Water bodies such as Lake Kivu, Lake Muhazi, Lake Ihema, Lake Cyohoha, Lake Burera and Lake Ruhondo are among the major sources of fish. Although the fishing industry is not well-developed in Rwanda, many local communities depend on these fish sources for their livelihood. There is an ever increasing demand for fish that cannot be met by the national fish industry. As such, the shortage is covered by imports from Uganda and Burundi.

FORESTRY

Forest ecosystems are essential to human life, as they provide water catchment protection, resources for eco-tourism, water purification, wood for fuel and construction, medicinal plants, honey and other various handcraft materials. Rwanda's forests cover almost 10 per cent of the land surface.

The forests and woodland are categorized in the following classes:
• Forest plantations dominated by exotic species (Eucalyptus sp. Pinus sp. Grevellea robusta) and trees scattered on farmlands and along anti-erosion ditches.
• Natural forests of the Cong Nile Ridge in Gishwati, Mukura and Nyungwe National Parks.
• Natural forests of the Volcanoes National Park.
• Natural forests in the savannah and gallery-forests of the Akagera National Park and remnants of gallery-forests and savannahs of most of present Eastern Province. The institute responsible for forest preservation and management is the National Forestry Authority (NAFA).

Gisakura tea plantation at the edge of Nyungwe forest – Rusizi District

MINING AND ENERGY

Mining started in Rwanda in the 1930s and, since then, it has always been one of the major export earners. The biggest part of Rwanda is underlain by the Kibaran Belt rocks, which extend from north Tanzania, through south west Uganda, underlying almost the whole of Rwanda and Burundi, then through south east DRC up to Angola. These rocks are known to be mineralised.

The key mineral ores currently being mined and traded in Rwanda are cassiterite, wolframite, colombo-tantalite and gold. There are 268 prospecting, exploration and exploitation mining licences in the country.

Rwanda Geology and Mines Authority (RGMA) was established in 2007. The major responsibility of RGMA is to strengthen the manpower base and to develop the institutions' capacity to deliver data and regulate the sector.

Tungsten mining in Rwanda

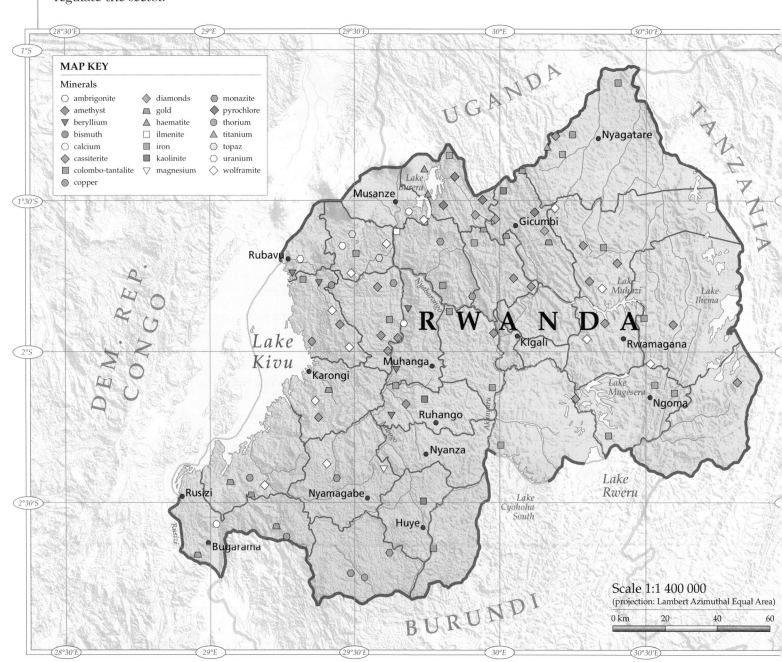

MAP KEY

Minerals

- ○ ambrigonite
- ◆ amethyst
- ▼ beryllium
- ● bismuth
- ○ calcium
- ◇ cassiterite
- ▪ colombo-tantalite
- ● copper
- ◆ diamonds
- ▲ gold
- ▲ haematite
- □ ilmenite
- ▪ iron
- ▪ kaolinite
- ▽ magnesium
- ⬠ monazite
- ◆ pyrochlore
- ▲ thorium
- ▲ titanium
- ○ topaz
- ○ uranium
- ◇ wolframite

Scale 1:1 400 000
(projection: Lambert Azimuthal Equal Area)

0 km   20   40   60

ENERGY

Rwanda has considerable opportunities for energy development from hydro sources, methane gas, solar power and peat deposits. However, most of these energy sources have not been fully exploited. Therefore the major part of the energy consumed in Rwanda today still comes from wood (80.4 per cent). Rwanda's energy sector comprises three sub-sectors: power, hydrocarbon and renewable sources such as biomass, solar, peat, wind, geothermal and hydropower. Biomass is used in the form of charcoal, agricultural residues or firewood, and dominates both the demand and supply sides of the Rwandan economy. Rwanda's electricity comes through cross-border joint interconnections from RUSIZI I and RUSIZI II. There are also other hydro-electricity stations in the country for example Ntaruka between lake Burera and lake Ruhondo as well as Mukungwa power station on river Mukungwa. However, these imports are not sufficient and are supplemented by the hydrocarbon sub-sector where imported petroleum fuel diesel is used in power generators. The Lake Kivu methane gas project is expected to provide a long-term solution to the power deficit in Rwanda, because Lake Kivu has a big reserve containing more than 50 billion cubic metres of dissolved methane gas. This project is expected to increase Rwanda's energy generation capability.

Methane gas pilot plant on Lake Kivu

Hydro-electric plant in Lake Ruhondo

INDUSTRY, TRADE, TRANSPORT AND COMMUNICATIONS

Industrial development is part of the government's strategy for achieving the Rwanda Vision 2020. Rwanda's industrial base remains generally weak. However, there has been an increase in the establishment of a wide variety of small scale commercial and industrial operations in recent years. The large industrial establishments are primarily engaged in production and/or processing of wood, beer, soft drinks, tobacco, cement, textiles, tea and coffee. Others include chemicals, construction, printing, paper, engineering and methane gas. The economy is therefore heavily dependent on the primary sector, with industry strongly tied to the processing of primary products. Challenges facing the industrial sector are mainly inadequate energy supply and inadequate pollution control. Distribution of industries by sector is shown on the map and industrial contribution to domestic product is also shown in the two tables.

GROSS DOMESTIC PRODUCT BY KIND OF ACTIVITY AT CONSTANT 2001 PRICES GROWTH RATES

Sector/Activity	2001	2002	2003	2004	2005	2006	2007
Agriculture	9	15	-5	0	5	1	1
Industry	13	5	3	13	8	11	10
Mining and quarrying	172	-24	-21	49	30	-14	38
Manufacturing of which: Food	25	-3	-1	23	2	7	7
Beverages and tobacco	1	18	-10	2	11	7	1
Textiles and clothing	4	0	-3	6	-1	5	14
Wood, paper and printing	6	22	22	1	25	13	27
Chemicals, rubber, plastics	7	11	10	4	3	13	-2
Non-metallic minerals	24	15	5	0	-2	4	-3
Furniture and others	6	10	23	0	-11	33	24
Electricity, gas and water	-10	15	8	-16	17	28	4
Construction	10	3	8	20	9	13	12
Services	7	9	5	8	9	11	13
Adjustments	9	16	-4	1	6	6	2

Source: NISR 2008

GROSS DOMESTIC PRODUCT BY KIND OF ACTIVITY AT CONSTANT 2001 PRICES PERCENTAGES

Sector	2001	2002	2003	2004	2005	2006	200
Agriculture	37	35	38	39	39	39	36
Industry	14	14	13	14	14	14	14
Mining and quarrying	1	0	0	1	1	1	1
Manufacturing of which: food	7	7	6	6	6	6	5
Beverages and tobacco	2	2	2	2	2	2	2
Textiles and clothing	0	0	0	0	0	0	0
Wood, paper and printing	0	0	0	0	0	0	0
Chemicals, rubber, plastics	0	0	0	0	0	0	0
Non-metallic minerals	1	1	1	1	1	1	1
Furniture and others	1	1	1	1	1	1	1
Electricity, gas and water	0	1	0	0	0	1	1

Source: NISR 2008

MAP KEY

Industry

animal feed	electrical goods	matches	plastics
bakery/ confectionery	metal products	rice mill	
brewing	flour mill	paints	soft drinks/ fruit preserves
bricks/ tiles	food processing	mining and quarrying	sugar factory
cement/ limeworks	furniture	pharmaceuticals	tea
chemicals/ gas processing	leather/ textiles	printing and publishing	tobacco
coffee	meat processing		tyres
cosmetics/ toiletries	dairy products		

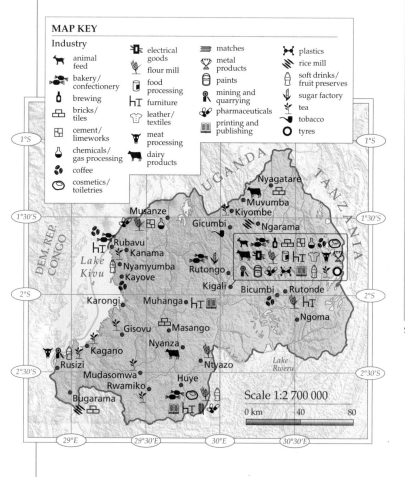

Scale 1:2 700 000

0 km   40   80

DISTRIBUTION OF INDUSTRIES PER SECTOR

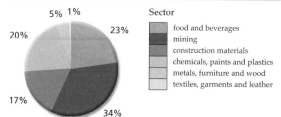

Sector
- food and beverages
- mining
- construction materials
- chemicals, paints and plastics
- metals, furniture and wood
- textiles, garments and leather

5% 1%
20%
23%
17%
34%

TRADE

Rwanda's most important exports are coffee, tea and minerals (mainly tin ore, niobium and tantalum). However, Rwandan businesses have been exploring other agro-based exports that would be equally suited to the country's small farms, steep slopes and cool climates. Rwanda's main imports include commodities like motor vehicles, petroleum oils, computers and other machinery, electrical machinery, plastics, medical appliances, salt, cement, cooking oils, sugar, textile articles and articles of iron and steel.

Rwanda imports and exports worldwide. Its main trading partners are EU, USA, Brazil, Pakistan, Uganda, Tanzania and Kenya. Most of Rwanda's coffee and tea are shipped to Germany and other European countries. Rwanda's main import partners are Kenya, Tanzania, Uganda, the United States, the Benelux countries, France and China.

TRANSPORT

Rwanda's transport infrastructure is mainly dominated by road transport for both passengers and cargo; with a road network of 14 000 km (with 4698 km of this being classified road network). Rwanda has one international airport at Kigali, the capital of Rwanda, and has six other airfields across the country. Kigali Airport is the main air gateway for all destinations in and out of the country and RwandAir is a national carrier.

COMMUNICATION

In a fast technologically changing world, Rwanda recognises Information and Communications Technology (ICT) as a key instrument for economic growth. The ICT sector, as a social-economic development backbone in Rwanda, has witnessed tremendous growth in terms of subscriptions, investments and network coverage. There are three licensed operators (MTN Rwanda cell S.A.R.L, TIGO Rwanda S.A and AIRTEL) that currently provide telecommunications services in Rwanda using both fixed and mobile service technologies. Twelve licensed operators provide Internet services across the country. More than 20 national and international radio stations are available and a state-owned television station is supplemented by Tele 10 Rwanda and Star Africa Media services.

Mobile phone service in Rwanda

Kigali International Airport

TOURISM AND WILDLIFE

Rwanda, which is widely known as 'the land of a thousand hills', with its rich biodiversity, surprising natural beauty and temperate climate, is becoming an increasingly popular tourist destination. Tourist attractions include:

- gorilla tracking in the Volcanoes National Park
- the unique savannah plains
- wildlife (such as antelopes, buffaloes, giraffes, zebras, baboons) in Akagera National Park
- the incredible biodiversity of the extensive Nyungwe National Park
- multiple terraced hills and lakeshore beaches and hotels around the beautiful Lake Kivu.

Rwanda is also recognised as one of the safest countries in the world and honoured in recognition of its cleanliness and greenness. Sources from RDB (Rwanda Development Board) and Directorate General of Immigration and Emigration indicate that visitors to Rwanda were estimated at 405 801 in January–June, 2011 and generated 115.6 million USD, a 28 per cent increase compared to 2010 at the same period.

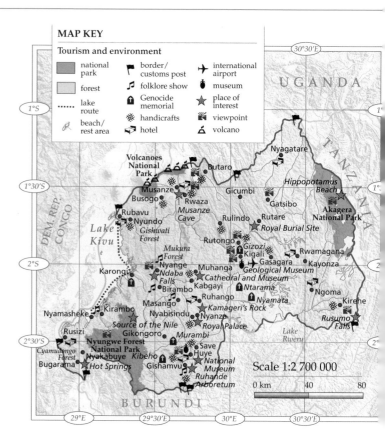

MAP KEY

Tourism and environment

- national park
- forest
- lake route
- beach/ rest area
- border/ customs post
- folklore show
- Genocide memorial
- handicrafts
- hotel
- international airport
- museum
- place of interest
- viewpoint
- volcano

Scale 1:2 700 000

0 km 40 80

Akagera National Park antelopes

Gorilla tracking in Mt Muhabura

Canopy walking

Waterfall, Nyungwe Forest National Park, Rwanda

VISITOR ARRIVALS BY REGION JAN-JUN 2010 VS JAN-JUN 2011

Number of visitors (thousands)

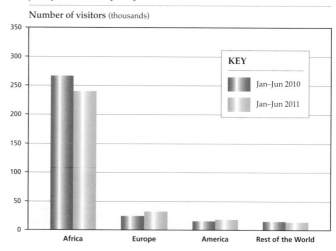

KEY
- Jan–Jun 2010
- Jan–Jun 2011

VISITOR ARRIVALS BY PURPOSE OF VISIT JAN-JUN 2010 VS JAN-JUN 2011

Number of visitors (thousands)

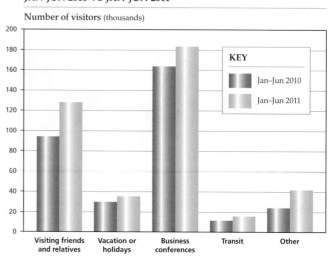

KEY
- Jan–Jun 2010
- Jan–Jun 2011

ENVIRONMENT

Environment refers to the sum total of all surroundings and living things, including all the physical nature and associated effects, which provide conditions for development and growth, as well as of danger and damage. The people of Rwanda, like those of many other countries, depend much on natural resources for their livelihoods. This has exerted pressure on natural resources, which has resulted in environmental degradation. Rwanda faces the challenge of utilising natural resources to develop the economy whilst conserving the environment.

ENVIRONMENT CONSERVATION MEASURES

As such, Rwanda has invested much effort and funds in the implementation of various environmental protection policies such as:
- reforestation
- use of locally made energy saving cook stoves
- slopes terracing and digging ditches
- indoor cattle rearing
- grouped settlements and storeyed apartments to reduce population density pressure
- use of biogas to reduce firewood consumption
- land consolidation
- monthly national-wide environment cleaning (umuganda)
- demarcation of protected areas
- ban of rampant burning of charcoal
- controlled tree harvesting
- ban on the use of plastic bags.

Despite clear regulations against human habitat close to water bodies, human encroachment continues: (human settlement at the shores of Lake Kivu in the Western Province) Terracing against soil erosion in Gicumbi

ENVIRONMENTAL CHALLENGES

In Rwanda, the implementation of environmental policies, and conservation, is the responsibility of Rwanda Environment Management Authority (REMA). Major environmental challenges include loss of genetic resources, especially through agriculture and animal husbandry intensification and bamboo cutting in Nyungwe and Volcanoes National Parks which affects the natural habitats of species. Another environmental threat is the invasion of alien species such as the water hyacinth (*Eichhornea crassipes*) that has invaded lakes in Rwanda from Muhazi to Rweru, from the River Nyabarongo to Akagera River and on to Lake Victoria. Lantana camara has also become a dangerous weed and, in some areas, a habitat for tsetse flies. Most of these alien species were introduced as ornamental plants, but have since become a menace to the environment.

How human activities impacts on environment

Dry lands

Storeyed apartments, Kigali

Despite clear regulations against human habitat close to water bodies, human encroachment continues.

Terracing against soil erosion in Gicumbi

Flooded farmland

Charcoal being taken to market

Conserved environment

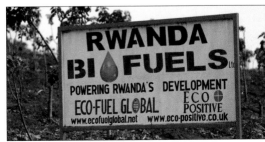
Rwanda uses biofuels

Energy saving cook stoves.

ADMINISTRATION, RELIEF AND LANDFORMS

Burundi occupies an area of 27 830 km², of which 2180 km² is water. The country is located in east-central Africa and lies between Tanzania to the west and south, the Democratic Republic of the Congo to the east, and Rwanda to the north. Burundi, like any other democratic country, is governed through three universally known powers namely the Executive, the Legislative and the Judiciary. The President and the Cabinet assume executive power while the Senate and the Chamber of Parliamentarians exercise legislative power that deals with passing laws. The Supreme Court and affiliated judicial institutions supervise the implementation of the law and sanctions where necessary. The president serves a five-year term which is renewable only once if he/she is re-elected, while parliamentarians and senators serve a five-year term with unlimited renewal as long as they are re-elected by the population. The country comprises 17 provinces, 129 districts (communes) divided into zones and cells (collines).

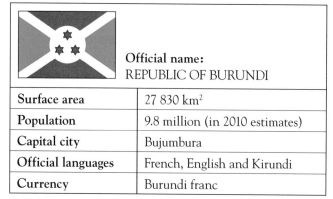

Official name:
REPUBLIC OF BURUNDI

Surface area	27 830 km²
Population	9.8 million (in 2010 estimates)
Capital city	Bujumbura
Official languages	French, English and Kirundi
Currency	Burundi franc

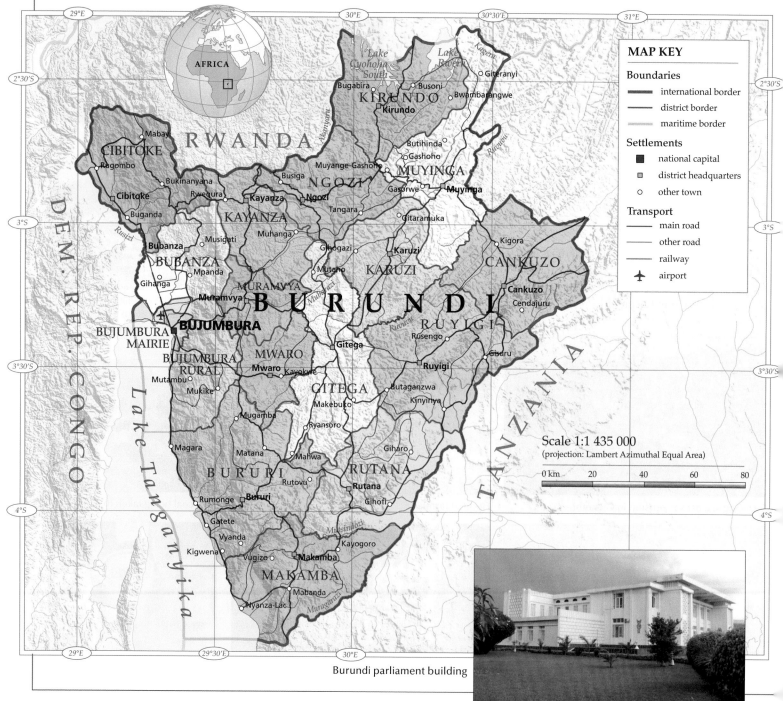

Burundi parliament building

Scale 1:1 435 000
(projection: Lambert Azimuthal Equal Area)

0 km   20   40   60   80

MAP KEY

Boundaries
- international border
- district border
- maritime border

Settlements
- national capital
- district headquarters
- other town

Transport
- main road
- other road
- railway
- airport

RELIEF AND LANDFORMS

The terrain of Burundi is hilly and mountainous, and is characterised by five eco-climatic zones: Imbo lower Plains, Mumirwa hilly region, the mountainous Congo-Nile crest zone, central plateaus zone, and the depressions of Bugesera and Kumoso zone. The highest point is on Mount Heha (2684 m) while the lowest point is on Lake Tanganyika (722 m). Burundi generally has a tropical highland climate where temperature and rainfall vary from one region to another because of altitude differences. Areas around Lake Tanganyika, including Bujumbura, are warmer and have an average annual temperature of 23°C. The central plateau enjoys cool weather, with an average temperature of 20°C, while the highest areas are cooler, averaging 16°C. Rain is irregular, falling most heavily in the northwest. The following four seasons can be distinguished:

Long dry season: June–August
Short wet season: September–November
Short dry season: December–January
Long wet season: February–May.

Teza high altitude tea plantation in Mugamba mountains

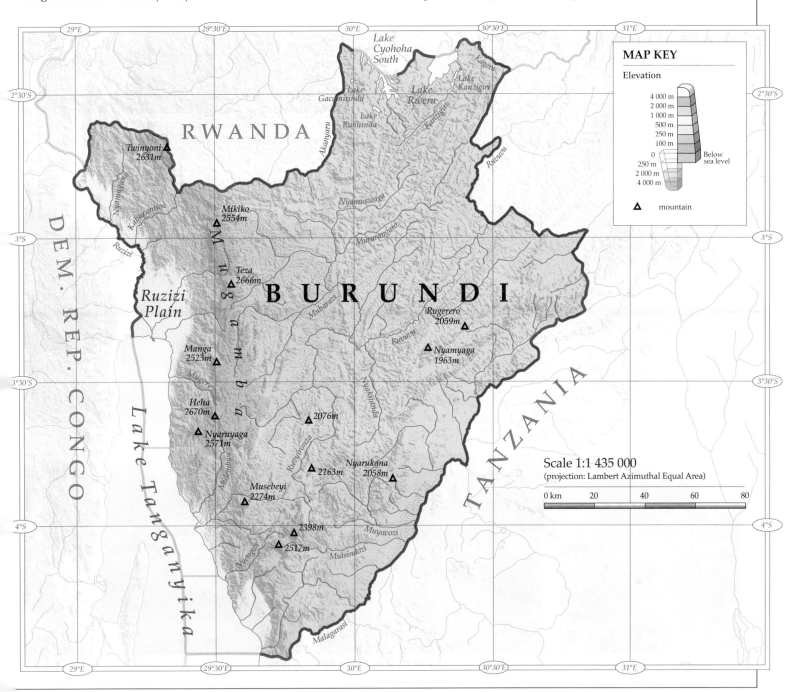

MAP KEY

Elevation

4 000 m
2 000 m
1 000 m
500 m
250 m
100 m
0
250 m
2 000 m
4 000 m
Below sea level

△ mountain

Scale 1:1 435 000
(projection: Lambert Azimuthal Equal Area)

0 km   20   40   60   80

POPULATION AND TOURISM

In 1993, Burundi was hit by a social-political crisis that has left the country with numerous socio-economic and structural problems from which it is gradually recovering. One of these problems is the lack of population statistics per age group so population pyramids are difficult to construct. However, according to the population census of August 2008, the population of Burundi was estimated at 8 038 618, of which 51.1 per cent are females and 48.9 per cent are males. Burundi is one of the most densely populated countries in Africa, with an estimated 310 inhabitants per km^2 with 89.9 per cent of its population in rural areas. Burundi has a young population, with 50 per cent below 21 years old.

BURUNDI POPULATION % PER GENDER

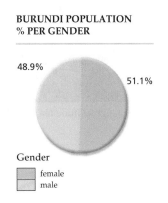

48.9%

51.1%

Gender
- female
- male

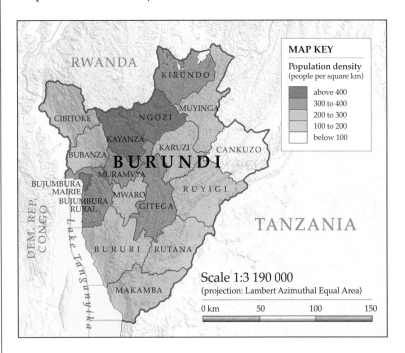

MAP KEY

Population density (people per square km)

- above 400
- 300 to 400
- 200 to 300
- 100 to 200
- below 100

RWANDA

KIRUNDO

CIBITOKE
MUYINGA
NGOZI
KAYANZA
KARUZI
CANKUZO
BUBANZA
BURUNDI
MURAMVYA
BUJUMBURA MAIRIE
BUJUMBURA RURAL
MWARO
GITEGA
RUYIGI
DEM. REP. CONGO
Lake Tanganyika
BURURI
RUTANA
MAKAMBA

TANZANIA

Scale 1:3 190 000
(projection: Lambert Azimuthal Equal Area)

0 km   50   100   150

TOURISM

Burundi has great potential for tourism. However, tourism, like many other sectors, is less developed when compared to neighbouring countries because of the socio-political crisis that has characterized Burundi since 1993. With the current political stability and the efforts of the National Tourism Office, the tourism sector is recovering. The country boasts national reserves and protected areas such as Lake Tanganyika beaches, the thermal water reserves of Munini, Muhweza, Cibitoke, Mugara, the natural forests reserves of Rumonge, Kigwena Bururi and Kibira. Ruvubu and Rusizi national parks are home to a variety of wild animals.

Rutovu, source of the River Nile. It is also believed that the source of River Nile could be in Nyungwe forest in Rwanda or at Jinja in Uganda.

Lake Tanganyika beaches

Livingstone and Stanley monument

Village of Masango, Cibitoke province, Burundi

Muhweza thermal waters

AGRICULTURE AND INDUSTRY

Burundi is essentially an agricultural country and the sector is a cornerstone of the country's economy. Agriculture occupies 94 per cent of the country's active population, and currently contributes 46 per cent of the GDP. Subsistence farming (bananas, cassava and potatoes, vegetables, fruit and cereals) occupies 90 per cent of arable land while commercial farming (coffee, tea, cotton, tobacco, sugarcane, and palm oil) occupies 10 per cent of the arable land and contributes up to 90 per cent of exports. The industrial sector in Burundi is very weak; it contributes only 15.5 per cent to the GDP. Industrial products are less competitive because of the high cost of production, which is a result of expensive raw materials and transport costs because Burundi is landlocked. However, Burundi possesses large reserves of nickel, uranium, rare earth oxides, peat, cobalt, platinum and vanadium, which are not fully exploited.

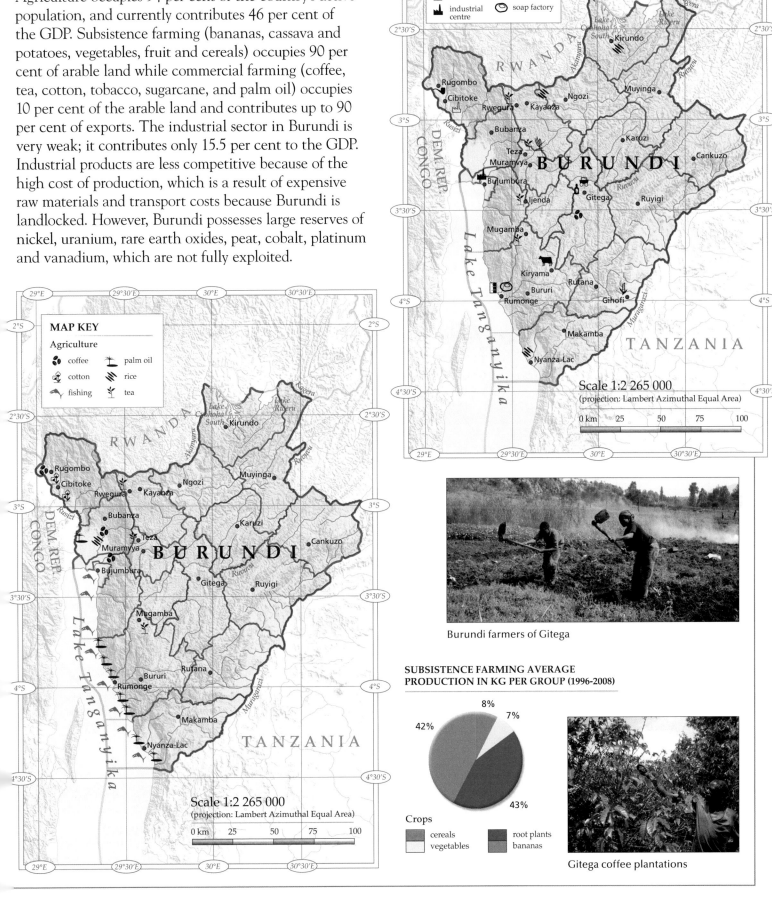

MAP KEY

Industry

- brewery
- coffee processing
- dairy
- flour mill
- industrial centre
- lime kiln
- oil refinery
- rice mill
- sheet metal works
- soap factory
- sugar processing
- tea processing
- tobacco processing

Scale 1:2 265 000
(projection: Lambert Azimuthal Equal Area)

0 km 25 50 75 100

MAP KEY

Agriculture

- coffee
- cotton
- fishing
- palm oil
- rice
- tea

Scale 1:2 265 000
(projection: Lambert Azimuthal Equal Area)

0 km 25 50 75 100

Burundi farmers of Gitega

SUBSISTENCE FARMING AVERAGE PRODUCTION IN KG PER GROUP (1996-2008)

8%
7%
42%
43%

Crops

- cereals
- vegetables
- root plants
- bananas

Gitega coffee plantations

ADMINISTRATION

Ethiopia is the oldest and tenth largest country in Africa, with the second highest population. It extends between latitudes 3° and 15° north and longitudes 33° and 48° east. It is a landlocked country, occupying a prominent position in the Horn of Africa. Ethiopia became a Federal Democratic Republic in 1995. The government is a two-tier parliamentary system, namely the House of People's Representatives, whose members are directly elected by the people for five years and the House of Federation, whose members are elected by the state councils to represent their respective nations, nationalities and peoples. The House of People's Representatives is the highest authority of the Federal Government, and the House of Federation has the power to interpret the constitution.

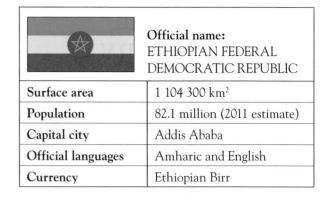

Official name:	ETHIOPIAN FEDERAL DEMOCRATIC REPUBLIC
Surface area	1 104 300 km²
Population	82.1 million (2011 estimate)
Capital city	Addis Ababa
Official languages	Amharic and English
Currency	Ethiopian Birr

ADMINISTRATION ORGANOGRAM

ETHIOPIA FEDERAL DEMOCRATIC REPUBLIC

LEGISLATIVE — EXECUTIVE — JUDICIARY

HOUSE OF PEOPLES REPRESENTATIVES | HOUSE OF FEDERATION | COUNCIL OF MINISTERS (PRIME MINISTER) | SUPREME COURT / HIGH COURT / FEDERAL FIRST INSTANCE COURT

REGIONAL STATES

LEGISLATIVE | EXECUTIVE | JUDICIARY

LEGISLATIVE	EXECUTIVE	JUDICIARY
STATE COUNCIL	REGIONAL ADMINISTRATION	SUPREME COURT
ZONAL COUNCIL	ZONAL ADMINISTRATION	HIGH COURT
WOREDA COUNCIL	WOREDA ADMINISTRATION	WOREDA COURT
KEBELE COUNCIL	KEBELE ADMINISTRATION	KEBELE SOCIAL COURT

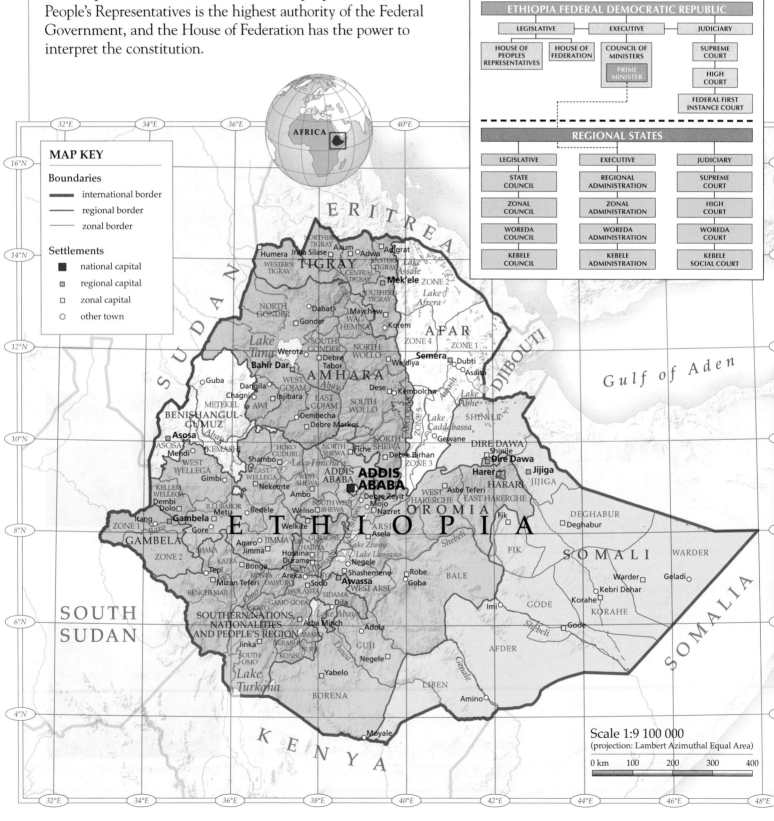

MAP KEY

Boundaries
- ━━━ international border
- ─── regional border
- ─── zonal border

Settlements
- ■ national capital
- ▪ regional capital
- □ zonal capital
- ○ other town

Scale 1:9 100 000
(projection: Lambert Azimuthal Equal Area)

0 km 100 200 300 400

RELIEF AND LANDFORMS

Ethiopia has diverse topography, ranging from around 156 m below sea level in the Dalol area of the Afar Depression to the 4550 m high Mount Ras Dejen in the Semien Mountains, the highest peak in Ethiopia and the fourth highest in Africa. It has heavily dissected rugged plateaus and mountain massifs, deep river valleys and gorges, and vast rolling outlying plains and depressions. Among the prominent mountain massifs are the Semien, Chokie and Arsi-Bale Mountains, with many towering peaks rising over 4000 m above sea level. In general, Ethiopia has the highest proportion of elevated landmass in Africa, which is why it is often referred as the Roof of East Africa. Based on altitude, the country is classified into five major agro-ecological zones, traditionally known as (from cold to hot) Wourch, Dega, Woina Dega, Qolla and Bereha, each with its conspicuous fauna and flora, soil composition and settlement patterns.

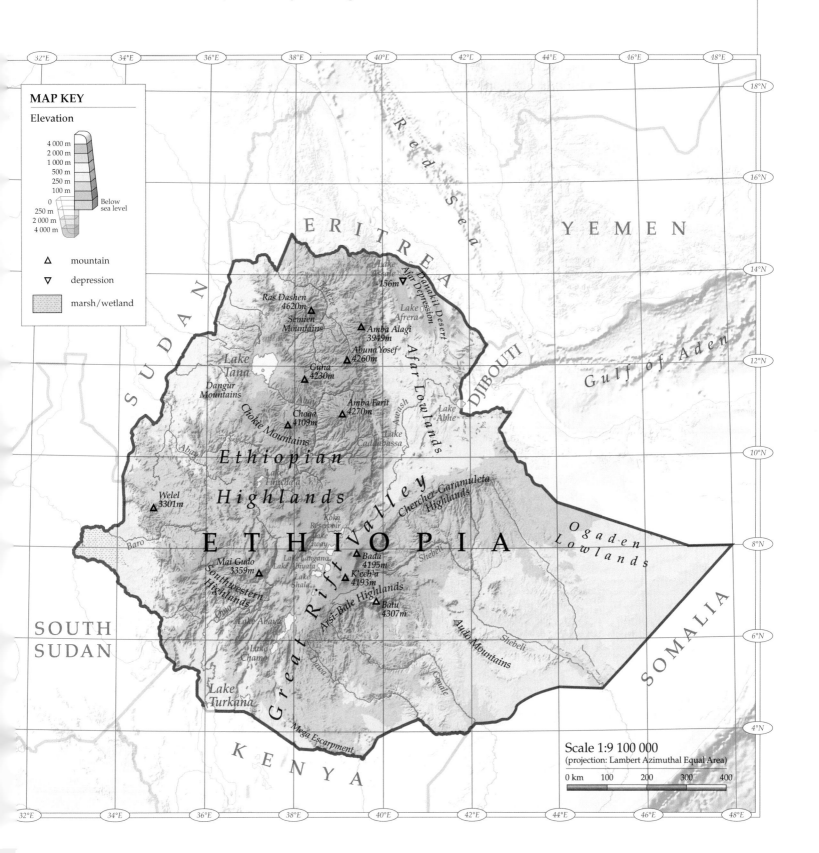

MAP KEY

Elevation

4 000 m
2 000 m
1 000 m
500 m
250 m
100 m
0
250 m
2 000 m   Below
4 000 m   sea level

△ mountain

▽ depression

marsh/wetland

Scale 1:9 100 000
(projection: Lambert Azimuthal Equal Area)

0 km   100   200   300   400

AGRICULTURE, LIVESTOCK, AND FISHING

In the last ten years, agricultural productivity in Ethiopia has increased by around 10 per cent, largely as a result of the focus given to the sector under successive development plans following the Agricultural Development-Led Industrialisation (ADLI) umbrella strategy (1994). All these subsequent plans have given focus to: crop production and agricultural diversification; conservation-based agricultural practices; establishment of an agricultural marketing system; expansion of agricultural research and extension services; increasing the supply of agricultural inputs; expansion of local level credit facilities; and expansion of small and medium scale irrigation schemes.

Small-scale farming on the Ethiopian plateau

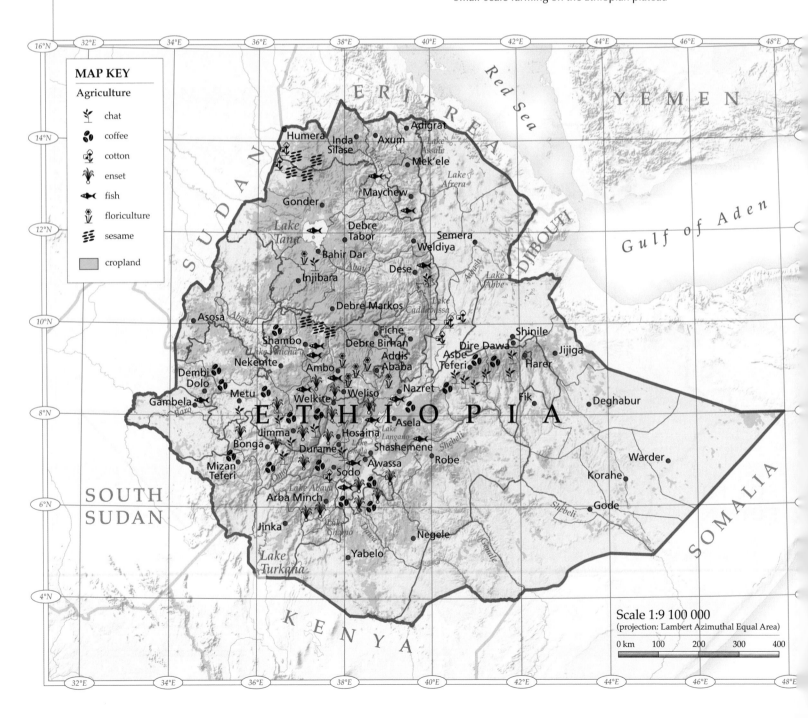

MAP KEY

Agriculture

- chat
- coffee
- cotton
- enset
- fish
- floriculture
- sesame
- cropland

Scale 1:9 100 000
(projection: Lambert Azimuthal Equal Area)

0 km   100   200   300   400

AGRICULTURE

Ethiopia's economy is heavily dependent on the agricultural sector, which is mainly small-scale traditional rain-fed subsistence farming. The sector accounts for most of the country's food supply: about 41.1 per cent of the GDP, 70 per cent of the industrial raw material supply, 80 per cent of the export earnings and about 83 per cent of the total employment. The small-holding peasant farming consists of three sub-sectors: about 60 per cent crop, 30 per cent livestock and 10 per cent forestry, of which the crop sub-sector covers over 93 per cent of the cultivated land and over 90 per cent of the major crops produced in the country per year.

Ethiopia grows different varieties of food and cash crops including cereals, pulses, oil seeds, root crops, fruits, vegetables, spices and stimulants in its wide range of agro-ecological zones. The major food crops in the warm temperate (*Woina Dega*), temperate (*Dega*) and cool temperate parts of the central plateau include *teff*, wheat, barley, *inset*, and a variety of pulses and oil seeds, while maize, sorghum and millet predominate in the warm temperate (*Woina Dega*), and tropical or *Qolla* areas. The major cash crops are coffee, chat, sugarcane, tea, cotton, oil seeds, citrus fruits, and flowers, most of which are grown in the tropical (*Kola*) and warm temperate (*Woina Dega*) areas.

A boy in charge of threshing grain

LIVESTOCK

Animal husbandry is an integral part of the Ethiopian small-scale traditional mixed-farming system. It provides draught animals, animal food products and social and economic security to the farmers. Ethiopia's livestock population is first in Africa and tenth in the world. Nowadays, the rising demand for animal food products in the country's big urban centres, as well as for export, have encouraged the development of small and medium scale commercial livestock farming, including dairy, fattening and poultry. Exports of live animals, meat, hides and skins are becoming an important source of external earnings to the country.

PERCENTAGE OF LIVESTOCK BY TYPE, 2009

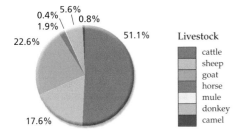

0.4% 5.6%
1.9%   0.8%
22.6%   51.1%

17.6%

Livestock
- cattle
- sheep
- goat
- horse
- mule
- donkey
- camel

HORTICULTURE

Ethiopia produces a variety of horticultural products, including tropical citrus fruits and vegetables. These are produced for the local market and for export in small and medium-size farms in many of its warm and warm temperate areas, such as in the Rift Valley and some other suitable basins using irrigation. Floriculture, which was introduced in the early 2000s, has now shown a remarkable rate of growth in both the area it covers and the export earning it generates. Among the globally competitive advantages for quality flowers to be grown in Ethiopia are its altitude-moderated highland temperatures, the low cost of production, tax exemption, and easy access to international markets. Ethiopia's export earnings from cut flowers has steadily increased from US$ 660 000 in 2001 to US$ 12.7 million in 2005; US$ 65 million in 2007 to US$ 86 million in 2010. Recent forecasts indicate that the country will soon become one of the leading flower exporting countries in Africa.

IRRIGATION

Ethiopia has around 3.5 to 4.25 million hectares of irrigable land, but only around 9 per cent has been irrigated up to now, mostly by small holding farmers. Currently, large and medium scale irrigation schemes are being established, both by government enterprises and private investors, to grow sugar cane, cotton, rice, citrus fruits and flowers on a commercial basis. These would be for export and domestic consumption, in accordance with the country's new irrigation policy.

FISHING

Ethiopia has many lakes, rivers and dams, inhabited by more than 200 freshwater fish species. The country's annual fish harvest potential is around 50 000 tons but only around 13 000 is harvested every year. The taste for fish food is not well developed among many Ethiopians, especially in the rural areas. A fishery research centre has been established to conduct research on how to develop the fishing sector, to promote fish and to organise and train traditional fishers.

POPULATION

Ethiopia has a fast-growing population of approximately 82 million people, which includes more than 80 nations, nationalities and peoples (CSA, 2011). It is the second most populated country in Africa after Nigeria. The 1984, 1994 and 2007 population and housing censuses demonstrate that the national population is increasing steadily at an annual average rate of 2.6 per cent (2.1 per cent rural and 3.9 per cent urban)and it takes around 26.9 years to double in size. Out of the total population, about 50.46 per cent are males and the male to female ratio is 1.02:1. About 83 per cent of the population is classified as rural, making Ethiopia one of the least urbanised countries in Africa.

The average life expectancy is around 56 years, which is strongly influenced by occasional droughts and HIV/AIDS.

DENSITY

The average population density of Ethiopia is around 74 persons per km². However, this varies from region to region, due to the impacts of physical and human factors such as topography, climate, soils, historical patterns of population movement and types of economic activities. In general, the densest concentrations of people are found in the humid and sub-humid central highlands, while the arid and semi-arid outlying lowlands are sparsely populated.

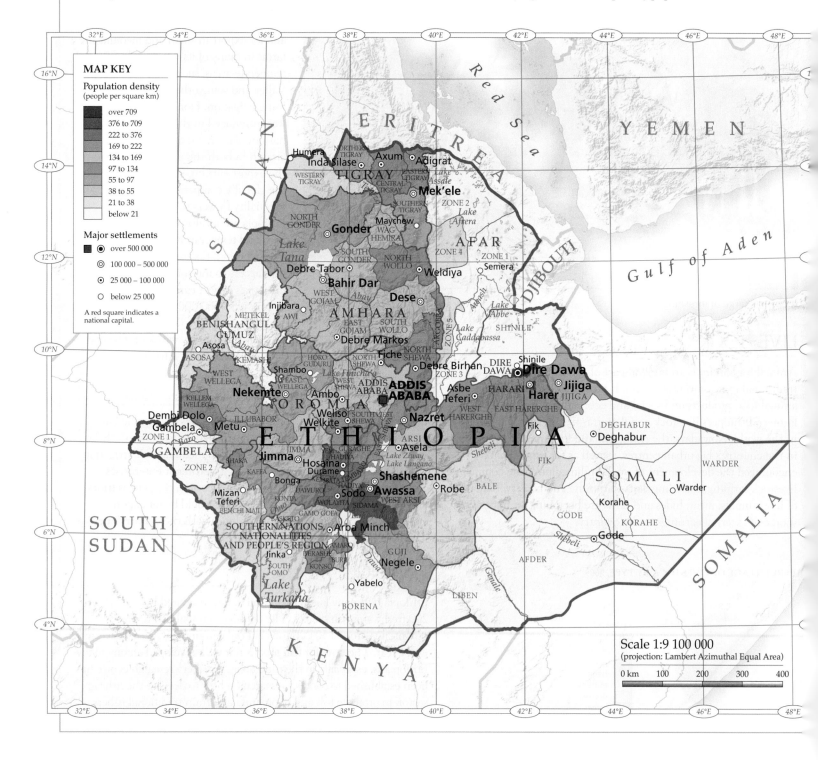

MAP KEY

Population density
(people per square km)

- over 709
- 376 to 709
- 222 to 376
- 169 to 222
- 134 to 169
- 97 to 134
- 55 to 97
- 38 to 55
- 21 to 38
- below 21

Major settlements

- ◉ over 500 000
- ◎ 100 000 – 500 000
- ⊙ 25 000 – 100 000
- ○ below 25 000

A red square indicates a national capital.

Scale 1:9 100 000
(projection: Lambert Azimuthal Equal Area)

0 km   100   200   300   400

POPULATION PYRAMID

The age-gender population pyramid of Ethiopia is generally broader at the base and tapers sharply at the apex. This demonstrates the dominance of the younger generation, particularly the 0–4 age group, which accounts for 45 per cent of the total population. This is partly due to the prevalence of early marriage and high crude birth rate. The young age dependency ratio is therefore high (96:100) with negative implications on family savings and national budget allocation. In the urban areas the dominance of the 0–14 age group has shown a tendency to decline, largely due to the expansion of modern education and declining rate of early marriage.

POPULATION BY REGION AND GENDER, 2011

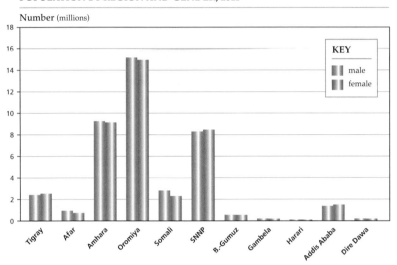

ETHIOPIA POPULATION AGE BREAKDOWN 2011

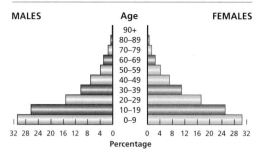

ETHIOPIA RURAL POPULATION AGE BREAKDOWN 2011

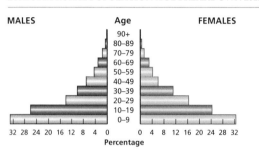

ETHIOPIA URBAN POPULATION AGE BREAKDOWN 2011

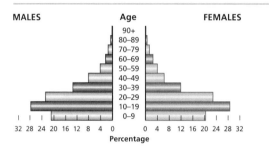

URBANISATION

About 17 per cent of the Ethiopian population are urban dwellers. The percentage varies from region to region, ranging from 11.3 per cent in the SNNP region in the southwest to 21.3 per cent in the Tigray Region in the north. Currently there are 973 small, medium and large towns and cities in the country with populations ranging from 2000 to 3 million people. The urban population is growing at an average rate of 3.9 per cent per year due to both natural increase and immigration. The number of urban centres is increasing relatively fast as a result of the opening up of many rural areas by all-weather roads and the growing scarcity of agricultural land. However, most of the rural migrants come to the urban areas with little or no work skills, and many of them are less readily accommodated. As a result, there is high unemployment and poor housing and sanitation conditions in the towns, for which the government has come up with an ambitious plan to overcome.

A section of Merkato in Addis Ababa, the largest market place in Africa

ENERGY AND MINING

Ethiopia has huge hydropower, wind power and geothermal energy potential, but the primary source of energy in the country has long been biomass (fuelwood, charcoal, animal dung and crop residue), followed by petroleum and electricity generated from hydropower and thermal. The heavy dependence on biomass energy over a long period of time has contributed to the widespread destruction to the country's natural forest, resulting in severe soil degradation and subsequent decline in agricultural productivity.

Tekeze Hydroelectric Dam

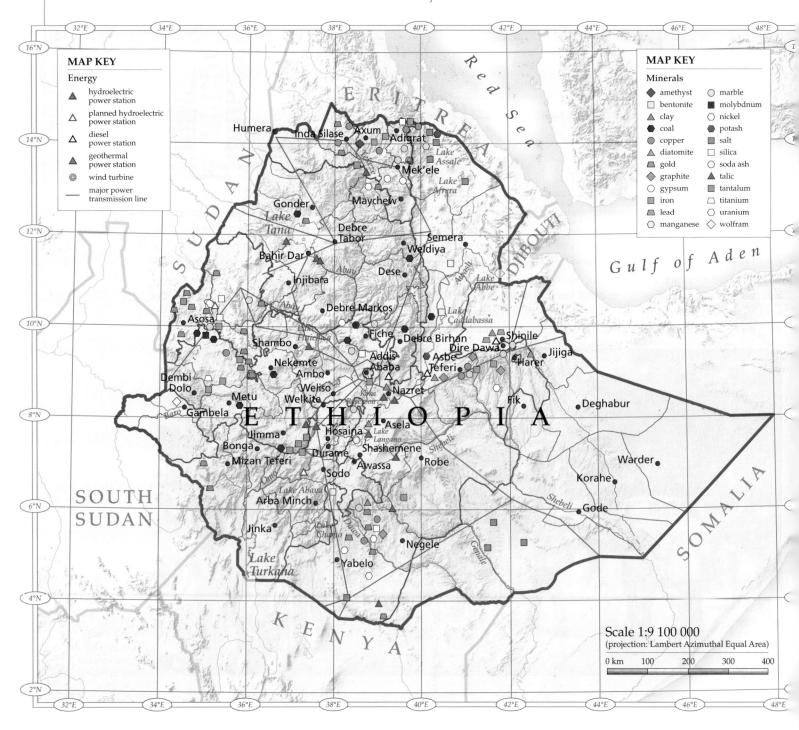

MAP KEY

Energy

▲ hydroelectric power station
△ planned hydroelectric power station
△ diesel power station
▲ geothermal power station
⊛ wind turbine
— major power transmission line

MAP KEY

Minerals

◆ amethyst
□ bentonite
▲ clay
⬣ coal
⬤ copper
▲ diatomite
⬢ gold
◇ graphite
○ gypsum
⬜ iron
⬓ lead
⬡ manganese

○ marble
■ molybdnum
○ nickel
⬣ potash
⬛ salt
□ silica
○ soda ash
▲ talic
⬜ tantalum
⬗ titanium
○ uranium
◇ wolfram

Scale 1:9 100 000
(projection: Lambert Azimuthal Equal Area)

0 km   100   200   300   400

YEARLY GROWTH IN DEMAND OF ELECTRICITY, 1999–2009

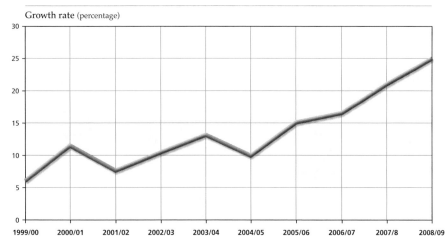

ACCESS TO ELECTRICITY, 2005–2011

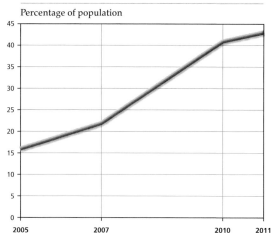

ENERGY

Prior to 1992, the amount of electricity produced in the country was around 420 MW, which was generated from four small hydropower stations and several small diesel generators. Since then, however, Ethiopia has had a new hydropower policy aimed at effectively and sustainably developing its available water resources to meet the fast-growing national energy demand, and for export to earn foreign exchange. By 2010, an additional six hydropower stations had become operational, raising the country's installed capacity to 2112 MW, of which 88 per cent was produced from hydropower, 11 per cent from diesel and 1 per cent through geothermal. In accordance with the Universal Electricity Access Program (UEAP) of the Ethiopian Electric Power Corporation (EEPCo), the number of electrified towns and villages has increased from 320 in 1992 to 1620 in 2007 and to 5163 in 2011, with the number of customers increasing to 1 896 265. A recent report of the Ministry of Water and Energy also shows that access to electricity in the country has steadily increased from 16 per cent in 2005 to 22 per cent in 2007, 41 per cent in 2010 and 47 per cent in 2011.

Currently, an additional three hydropower and three wind power projects, with a combined capacity of 7433 MW, are under construction, and this will enable Ethiopia to increase its electric power generation capacity to about 10 000 MW by 2015.

The EEPCo has announced a plan to construct 17 additional hydropower plants, four new wind farms and six new geothermal energy projects, with a combined capacity of 12 655 MW to be commissioned during the period from 2011 to 2020. Upon their completion, the country's installed capacity will be raised to more than 20 000 MW. About 10 000 MW of this will be used to meet the demand from the country's growing domestic, commercial and industrial sectors, which will raise access to electricity to 75 per cent. The rest will be exported to neighbouring countries, including Djibouti, Somalia, Kenya, Eritrea, South Sudan, North Sudan and even beyond to Egypt and Yemen, to diversify Ethiopia's export earning and to spur regional economic growth. The export of 30 MW electricity to Djibouti has been going on since around mid 2011 and similar agreements are underway with Kenya.

MINING

Ethiopia is rich in different varieties of metallic and non-metallic minerals. The old Precambrian basement rocks, which are widely exposed to the surface along the western and southwestern parts of the country, contain a variety of economic metallic mineral deposits. These include primary and placer gold, platinum, nickel and tantalum, base metals like copper, lead and zinc, industrial minerals like phosphate and iron ore, gemstones including ruby, emerald, sapphire and garnet, as well as decorative and dimension stones like marble, granite and other coloured stones. A significant amount of coal and phosphates, signs of oil, natural gas and oil shale, some other metallic ores like malachite, manganese, gypsiferous minerals and enormous construction and cement raw materials have also been identified in several areas. These are found in Mesozoic rocks such as in the Ogden, the Afar areas and around the southwest lowlands. Industrial minerals including potash, rock salt, sulfur, bentonite, soda ash, diatomite, opalised stones and numerous types of construction and cement raw materials have been found in Cenozoic sedimentary and volcanic rocks.

A significant amount of local and foreign private capital and expertise has been attracted to the mineral sector. Its contribution to the country's economy (GDP) has grown from less than 1 per cent before the 1990s to about 6 per cent now. Up to 2009, about US$ 1.1 billion was invested to mine precious and industrial minerals, out of which 95 per cent was foreign investment.

Currently, several minerals such as gold, platinum, tantalum, marble and gemstones are being mined, generating foreign currency earnings of around US$ 135 million per year, which is about 7-10 per cent of the country's total annual export earnings. In 2008 alone, the country earned more than 922 million Birr from the export of gold. A large number of individual and formally established traditional miners in the western, southwestern, southern and northern parts of the country are also producing about 3 tons of gold every year, which is significantly reducing the poverty of millions of the rural people in these areas.

QUANTITY OF MINED GOLD, 1998–2008

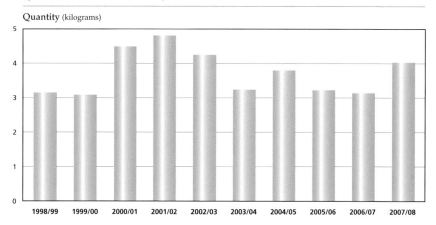

WATER RESOURCES

Ethiopia has an estimated potential resource of annually renewable 122 billion m³ surface water and 2.6 billion m³ ground water resource potential, making it second in Africa after the Democratic Republic of Congo. The surface water resources are contained in the 12 major river basins, 22 lakes and more than eight man-made reservoirs. However, despite the repeated occurrences of drought and food shortages that the country has faced for decades, only about 2 per cent of this resource has been used for irrigation.

Blue Nile River source

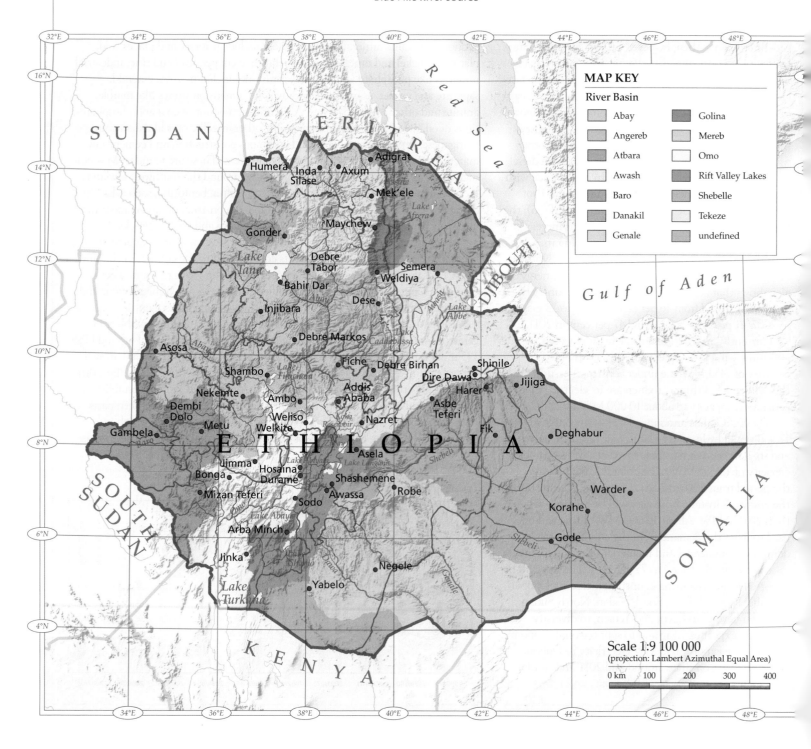

MAP KEY

River Basin

	Abay		Golina
	Angereb		Mereb
	Atbara		Omo
	Awash		Rift Valley Lakes
	Baro		Shebelle
	Danakil		Tekeze
	Genale		undefined

Scale 1:9 100 000
(projection: Lambert Azimuthal Equal Area)

0 km   100   200   300   400

HARNESSING THE WATER

Most of the rivers are cross-border, and drain over 75 per cent of their waters into neighbouring countries. The Awash River is the most used river, along which about 15 to 20 thousand hectares of land is developed to grow cotton, sugar and various types of fruits on a commercial basis, together with other tropical food crops like maize which is grown by native Afar pastoralists for food and forage.

In the past ten years several dams have been constructed for the generation of hydroelectricity along several of the major rivers in the country, including the Blue Nile (Abay), Tekeze, Fincha, Wabishebelle, Ghibe and several other small streams.

Blue Nile River in Ethiopia

Woman pumping water from a borehole in Dalocha

ACCESS TO SAFE WATER

While substantial financial assistance from external aid organisations has enabled access to clean water and sanitation, coverage has to be increased significantly as this is still among the lowest in the world and much remains to be done. National figures show that access to safe water in 2010 was 68.5 per cent, with 91.5 per cent and 66.8 per cent for urban and rural areas respectively. By the end of the current Growth and Transformation Plan (GTP) in 2015, this figure is expected to rise to 98.5 per cent.

Great white pelicans in Chano Lake

INDUSTRY, TRADE, TOURISM AND WILDLIFE

Recent policy changes have stimulated the industrial sector. The number of medium and large scale manufacturing industries has increased from 796 in 2002 to 2172 in 2010, which is a 172.9 per cent increase during the period. The sector's contribution to employment has therefore increased by 67.8 per cent and its share of the total GDP has reached 13.4 per cent.

Most of the country's industries are classified as light and labour intensive. More than 26 per cent of the industries fall within the category of food products and beverages, 22 per cent non-metallic mineral products (glass, cement, concrete, clay products) and 13 per cent furniture industries. Of the 2172 industrial establishments registered in the country, more than 40 per cent of them are located in and around Addis Ababa, 21 per cent in Oromia and 13 per cent in Southern Nations, Nationalities, and People's Region (SNNPR).

END-USE CLASSIFICATION OF IMPORTS, 2010

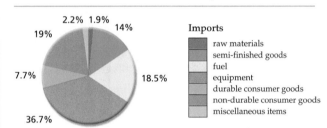

Imports
- raw materials
- semi-finished goods
- fuel
- equipment
- durable consumer goods
- non-durable consumer goods
- miscellaneous items

14%
1.9%
2.2%
19%
7.7%
36.7%
18.5%

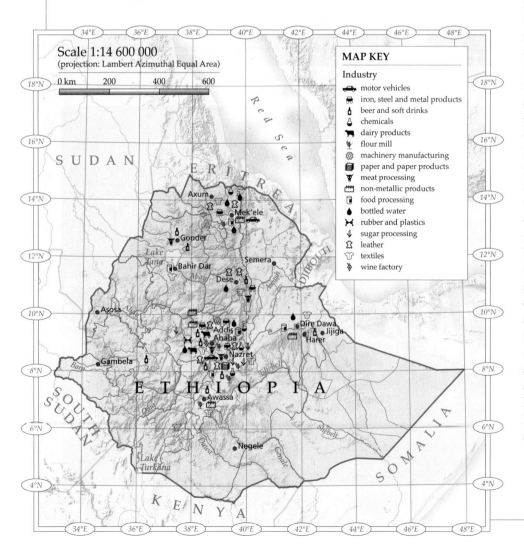

Scale 1:14 600 000
(projection: Lambert Azimuthal Equal Area)

0 km   200   400   600

MAP KEY

Industry
- motor vehicles
- iron, steel and metal products
- beer and soft drinks
- chemicals
- dairy products
- flour mill
- machinery manufacturing
- paper and paper products
- meat processing
- non-metallic products
- food processing
- bottled water
- rubber and plastics
- sugar processing
- leather
- textiles
- wine factory

VALUE OF IMPORT AND EXPORT GOODS, 1976–2010

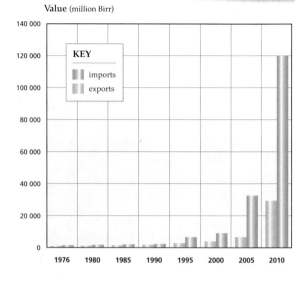

Value (million Birr)

KEY
- imports
- exports

TRADE

Ethiopia has a large population which has the potential to grow into a huge internal market for agricultural and domestic industrial products. However, it might take some time for the buying power of the people to be improved. Currently, foreign trade is playing a vital role in stimulating the country's economic development. The major objectives of the country's foreign trade policy focus on ensuring broad international markets for the country's agricultural products, generating sufficient foreign exchange (which is essential for importing capital goods, intermediate inputs and other goods and services that are necessary for the growth and development of the economy), and improving the efficiency and international competitiveness of domestic producers through participation in the international market. The volumes and values of Ethiopia's exports and imports have increased tremendously throughout the past two decades. The value of exports during the period from 1990 to 2009 grew 28.9 times, while the corresponding increase of imported commodities was 40.5 times. The value of exports reached US $2.7 billion by 2011, which is greater by 24 per cent than that of the preceding year (2010). The exported items have been diversified and increased to 35 per cent, of which the major ones are coffee, gold, chat, oil seeds, live animals and animal products. However, the balance of trade deficit is still high, which is explained by the fact that the major exports are predominantly agricultural commodities, and the imports are predominantly high value capital goods. Ethiopia's major trading partners are Western Europe, East and Southeast Asia, Africa and America.

TOURISM POTENTIAL IN ETHIOPIA

Ethiopia has a diverse altitude-moderated climate and rich natural, historical, cultural and pre-historic heritages that have high potential for tourist attraction. Things of interest to tourists include the uniquely diverse topography, the varied wildlife and birds, many of them sheltered in more than 13 national parks, and the remains of the country's ancient history, such as the amazingly curved towering stales and many ruins of imperial palaces and tombs in Aksum. There are also many magnificent rock-hewn churches in Lalibela and Eastern Tigray. The beautiful palaces of Gondar and many museums in Addis Ababa, Aksum, Gondar and several other towns are stocked with priceless historical artifacts. A number of world-known archaeological sites, such as Hadar in the Afar region, where the 3.5 million-year-old Lucy was discovered, are also spectacular. Finally, the diversely unique cultures, traditions and colourfully celebrated religious festivals of the various nations, nationalities and peoples in the country add value to tourism in Ethiopia.

TOURIST ARRIVALS BY YEAR, 1997–2010

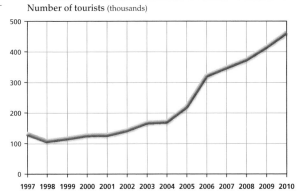

TOURIST ARRIVALS BY CONTINENT OF RESIDENCE, 2006–2008

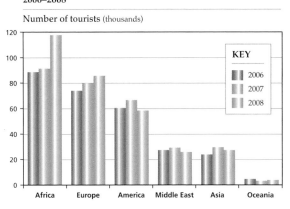

TOURIST ARRIVAL BY PURPOSE OF VISIT, 2008

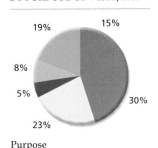

Purpose

- business
- vacation
- transit
- conference
- visiting relatives
- not stated

TOURIST ARRIVALS AND TOURIST RECEIPTS

A large number of tourists come to Ethiopia every year. The charts show the number per year, where they come from and the reasons for visiting. The annual number of visitors and the income earned from tourism has increased due to improvements in infrastructural facilities like transport and hotel accommodation. The number of visitors increased from 139 000 in 1997 to 468 305 in 2010, growing at a rate of 18 300 tourists every year. The income received from tourists has grown from US$ 43 million to US$ 240.2 million during the same period. Ethiopia has adopted a new tourism policy to help it develop its tourism industry to be one of the top five countries in Africa.

WILDLIFE

Ethiopia's diverse climate and topography mean that it has a wide variety of flora and fauna. Recent studies have shown that the country has 277 species of mammals (35 of them endemic), 862 species of birds (16 endemic), 201 species of reptiles (10 endemic), 63 species of amphibians (34 endemic), and more than 200 species of fresh water fishes. Among the well-known endangered endemic mammals are Walia Ibex, Semien Fox/Red Fox and Gelada Baboon (Chilada) in the Semien Mountains and Mountain Nyala in the Bale highlands. There are a number of National Parks and Wildlife Sanctuaries in the country hosting different varieties of wildlife.

Gelada baboons

Scale 1:14 600 000
(projection: Lambert Azimuthal Equal Area)

0 km   200   400   600

MAP KEY

National parks and sanctuaries
- national park
- wildlife sanctuary

FORESTRY AND ENVIRONMENT

About a century and a half ago, different varieties of forests used to cover around 40 per cent of the land area in Ethiopia. Forests have been destroyed to meet the growing demand of the fast growing population for cultivation and grazing lands, construction and fuelwood, agricultural tools and domestic utensils, and for other forest products. The result has been severe land degradation and a subsequent decline in agricultural productivity. Most of the remaining forest is concentrated in the humid southwest highlands and some other less accessible areas such as the Harenna Forest, which is part of the preserved National Parks in the Bale Mountains of Ethiopia. Eucalyptus trees are widely planted, especially around the urban areas, to fill the acute shortage of fuel wood and light timber and for the chip-wood factories.

Harenna Forest, Bale Mountains National Park, Ethiopia

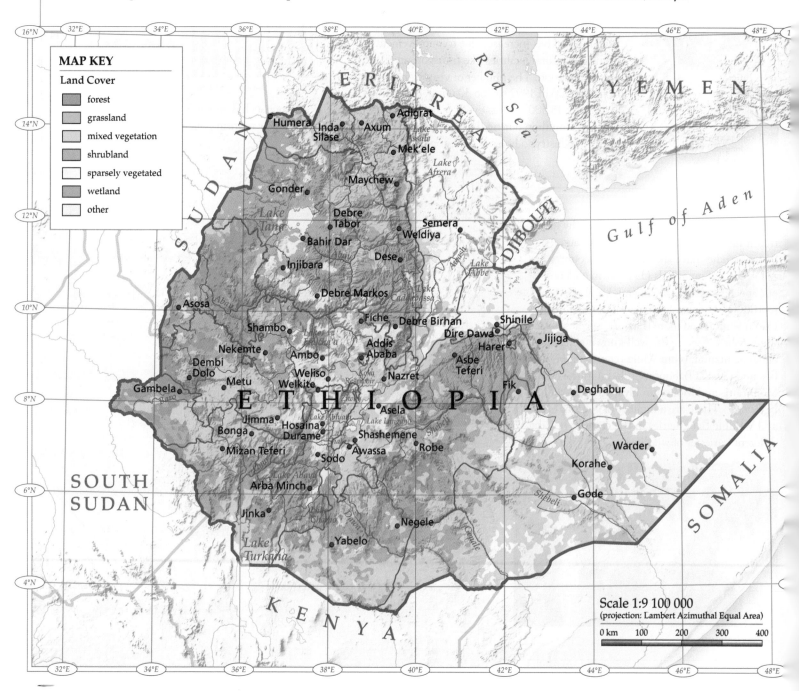

MAP KEY

Land Cover

- forest
- grassland
- mixed vegetation
- shrubland
- sparsely vegetated
- wetland
- other

Scale 1:9 100 000
(projection: Lambert Azimuthal Equal Area)

0 km   100   200   300   400

REFORESTATION EFFORTS

Since the late 1990s, efforts have been made by the government, in collaboration with several donors and local communities, to revitalise the country's forest cover until it reaches its optimum forest potential. A new forest policy was developed, and the Ethiopian Forest Action Plan adopted, with the major objectives to improve woodland conservation, increase public participation in reforestation projects, and to prevent further depletion of existing forest resources. The target of the new policy is to increase the forest area to 9 per cent by 2015. In 2007 alone, 700 million tree seedlings were planted throughout the country under a massive awareness *"raising and tree planting campaign"*, which is still being practised every year.

ENVIRONMENT

Many natural and human factors have led to severe environmental degradation in Ethiopia. These include widespread clearing of the natural vegetation cover by the fast growing population, overgrazing, frequent droughts, wild fire and the rugged nature of the topography. Ethiopia loses an estimated 2 billion metric tons of fertile soil every year by running water, largely from cultivated lands. The average soil depth in the country has decreased to around 50 cm, causing agricultural productivity to decline. Local communities in many of these hard-hit regions have adopted their own indigenous environmental protection and rehabilitation practices and, in many areas, have achieved impressive outcomes. For instance, the Konso people in southern Ethiopia have well planned and effective hillside terraces, built more than a century ago.

The government has long given strong emphasis to environmental rehabilitation and agricultural management practices in support of the country's Agricultural Development Led Industrialization (ADLI) strategy. It has been involved in various environmental rehabilitation activities, such as the construction of various soil and water conservation structures, expansion of closure areas and distributing energy-saving stoves. It has also introduced alternative energy sources like biogas digesters in cooperation with many NGOs. Up to mid 2011 more than 4 420 000 improved stoves have been distributed and around 1740 biogas digesters have been introduced in several rural villages in a pilot programme. Through massive community awareness raising programmes, hundreds of thousands of hectares have been rehabilitated and become agriculturally productive in many of the severely affected areas. In Tigray alone, about 32 per cent of the degraded area of the region has been rehabilitated. The photographs show the same area before and after the rehabilitation.

Degraded area in Tigray region

Terraced fields of the Konso tribe, Ethiopia

ADMINISTRATION

South Sudan (the Republic of South Sudan) officially attained its independence from Sudan on 11 July 2011. South Sudan is composed of ten states, which are sub-divided into 86 counties. The capital city is Juba, but there are plans to move it to a central place. Salva Kiir Mayardit is the first elected President of South Sudan. The 2008 census report puts the population of South Sudan at 8.26 million people.

South Sudan aerial view of capital Juba at river White Nile

Official name: REPUBLIC OF SOUTH SUDAN	
Surface area	644 329 km²
Population	8.26 million (in 2008)
Capital city	Juba
Official language	English
Currency	South Sudan Pounds

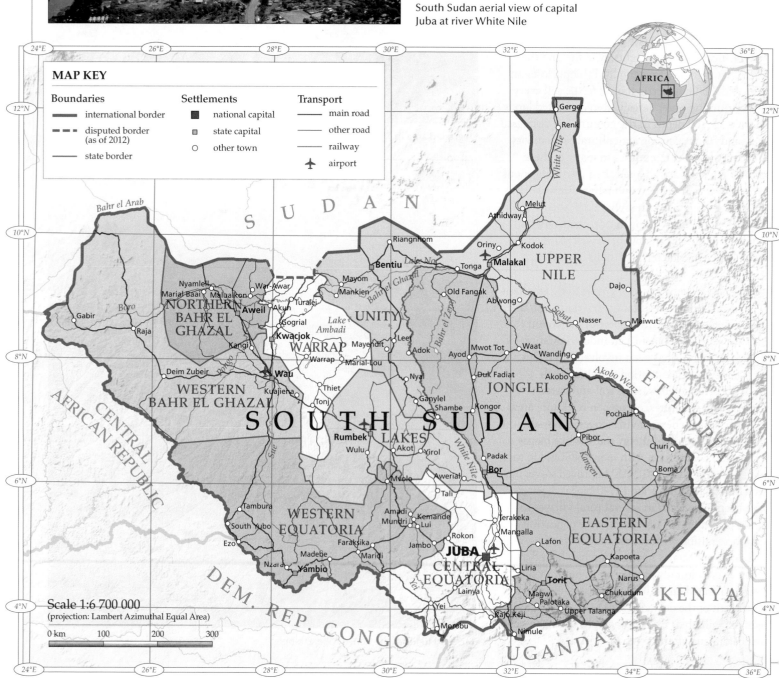

MAP KEY

Boundaries
— international border
- - - disputed border (as of 2012)
— state border

Settlements
■ national capital
▪ state capital
○ other town

Transport
— main road
— other road
— railway
✈ airport

Scale 1:6 700 000
(projection: Lambert Azimuthal Equal Area)

0 km   100   200   300

RELIEF AND LANDFORMS

Most of South Sudan is a flat land. The Imatong Mountains, of which the highest point is 3189 metres, lie on the southern border with Uganda and Kenya. To the western border is the Ironstone plateau and the White Nile flows through the country from south to north. The centre and the north are characterised by flood plains and marshes.

Juba South Sudan from the air

The White Nile flows through the country

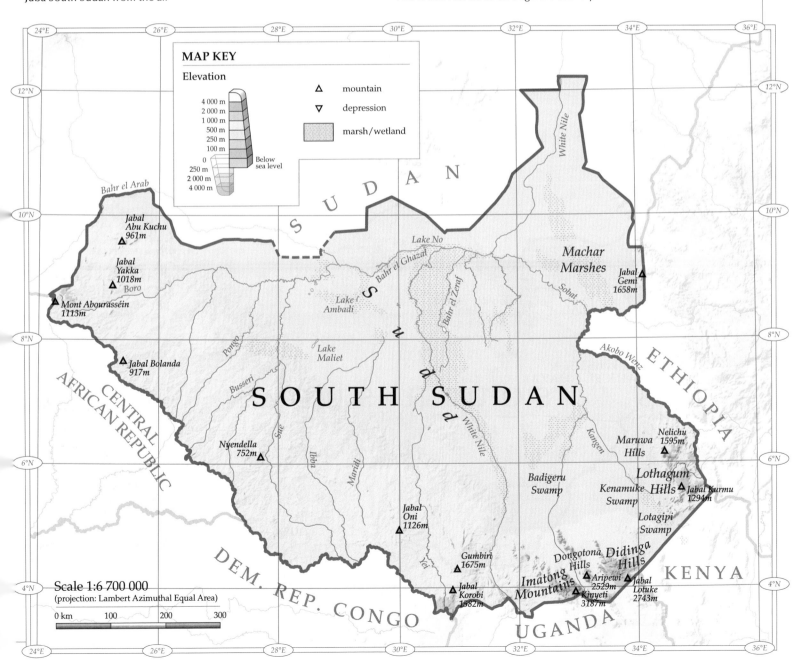

MAP KEY

Elevation

4 000 m
2 000 m
1 000 m
500 m
250 m
100 m
0
250 m
2 000 m
4 000 m
Below sea level

△ mountain

▽ depression

marsh/wetland

Scale 1:6 700 000
(projection: Lambert Azimuthal Equal Area)

0 km   100   200   300

POPULATION

The Population and Housing census from 2008 puts the population at 8 260 000 people.

Most of the population had been displaced during the war. After gaining independence in 2011, two million people returned and more are still returning. The population is denser in the central parts of the country, urban areas and along the southern borders. A number of people are still internally displaced. Some of the people are nomadic and a bit difficult to account for. Major tribes include the Bari, Nuer, Azande and Shilluk, while the largest is the Dinka.

South Sudan people watching wrestlers

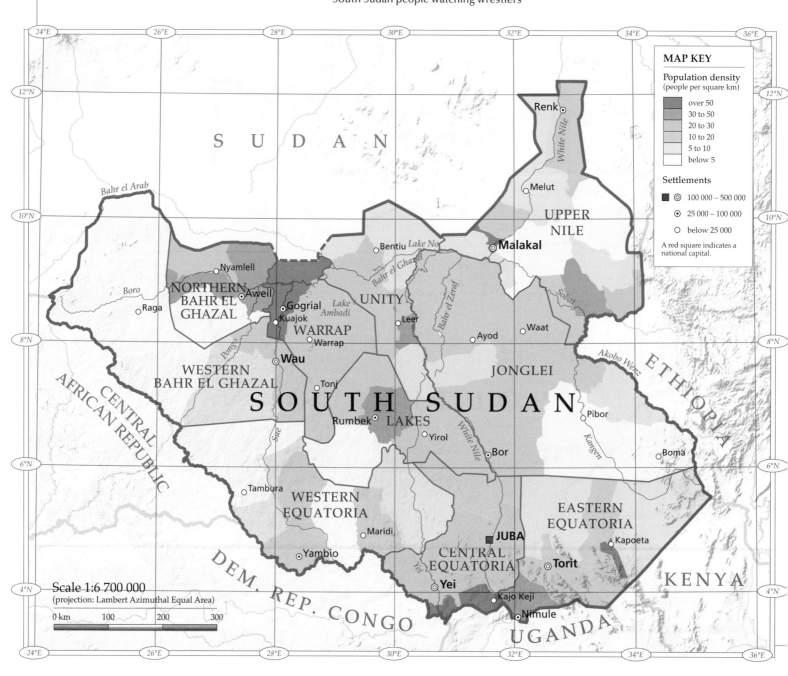

MAP KEY

Population density
(people per square km)

- over 50
- 30 to 50
- 20 to 30
- 10 to 20
- 5 to 10
- below 5

Settlements

- ■ ◎ 100 000 – 500 000
- ◉ 25 000 – 100 000
- ○ below 25 000

A red square indicates a national capital.

Scale 1:6 700 000
(projection: Lambert Azimuthal Equal Area)

0 km   100   200   300

AGRICULTURE, INDUSTRY, AND TOURISM

AGRICULTURE

Most of the agriculture in South Sudan is subsistence. 80 per cent of the population are employed in agriculture, which contributes to 35 per cent of the GDP. South Sudan has large tracts of arable land so livestock and cattle rearing are a very important part of the farming system. Some of the agricultural produce includes cotton, ground nuts, sorghum, millet, wheat, gum Arabic, sugarcane, cassava, mangoes, sesame, bananas and sweet potatoes. The government of South Sudan plans to develop extension and veterinary services.

Cattle rearing in South Sudan

INDUSTRY

The main industry in South Sudan is the oil refinery. There is a large potential for agro processing industries such as dairy, leather tanning and sugar cane processing In contrast, the industrial sector is not yet developed, with the lack of sustainable energy sources hindering such types of development.

Oil refinery

TOURISM

South Sudan has great potential for tourism development. There are a wide variety of tourist attractions, including, spectacular wildlife migrations, a large wildlife population and around 1.3 million antelopes. Wildlife is in abundance. This includes white-eared kob, bushbuck, red duiker, colobus monkeys, elephants, chimpanzees and other attractions in the National Parks. The Sudd wetlands and the White Nile offer a scenic attraction. The challenges being addressed in the region are poaching and accessibility. Improvements in infrastructures, such as roads, hotels and National Parks are now in progress.

Savanna elephants

COUNTRIES AND RELIEF

Geographically, Eastern Africa is famous for its contrasting areas of highland and rift valley. It is home to Africa's two highest mountains; Mount Kilimanjaro and Mount Kenya, and Africa's largest lake; Lake Victoria. Eastern Africa is composed of 11 countries; most are members of the Intergovernmental Authority on Development (IGAD). The seven countries that make up the Nile Basin are also members of the Nile Basin Initiative.

DECENTRALISATION

There are four forms of decentralisation:

Devolution: The complete transfer of authority from the central government to the local government and community.

Delegation: An assignment of certain functions by the local government to its agencies or statutory authority and the local government.

Deconcentration: Dispersal of central authority to its representative office at regional and local government levels.

Privatisation: Divesture of certain specific functions from government to private sector.

IGAD MEMBERSHIP

Intergovernmental Authority on Development (IGAD)

MAP KEY

Elevation

4 000 m
2 000 m
1 000 m
500 m
250 m
100 m
0
250 m
2 000 m
4 000 m
Below sea level

△ mountain
▽ depression
sandy desert
marsh/wetland

Boundaries

— international border
--- disputed border
— maritime border

Settlements

■ ⊙ over 1 million
■ ◉ 500 000 – 1 million
■ ⊙ 100 000 – 500 000
■ ○ 50 000 – 100 000

Scale 1:23 360 000
(projection: Lambert Azimuthal Equal Area)

0 km   250   500   750   1 000

RIFT VALLEY

The East African Rift Valley forms the lower part of the African Rift System that extends from Jordan and Syria in the north to Malawi in the south. In Eastern Africa there are two rift valleys – the eastern and western rifts. The western rift contains Lakes Albert and Tanganyika while the eastern rift contains Lakes Turkana, Baringo, Nakuru, Naivasha, Natron and Manyara.

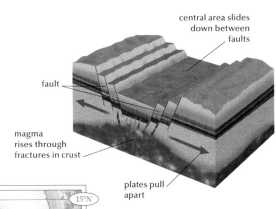

central area slides down between faults

fault

magma rises through fractures in crust

plates pull apart

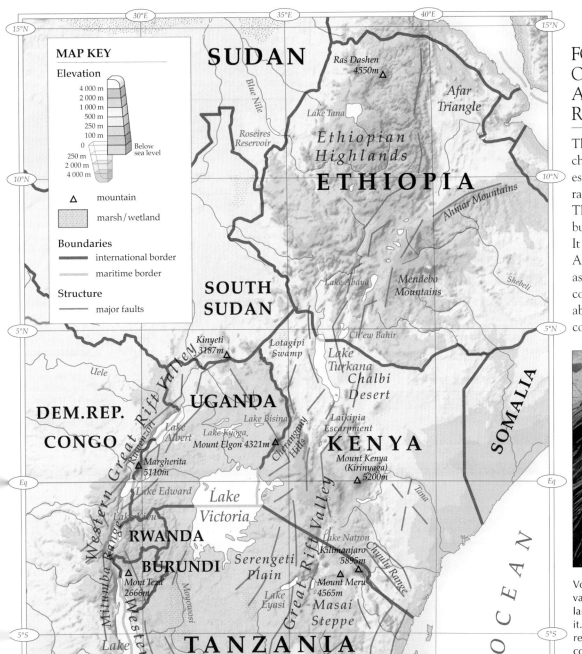

MAP KEY

Elevation

4 000 m
2 000 m
1 000 m
500 m
250 m
100 m
0
250 m — Below sea level
2 000 m
4 000 m

△ mountain

marsh/wetland

Boundaries

—— international border
—— maritime border

Structure

—— major faults

SUDAN

Ras Dashen 4550m △

Blue Nile

Lake Tana

Afar Triangle

Roseires Reservoir

Ethiopian Highlands

ETHIOPIA

Ahmar Mountains

SOUTH SUDAN

Lake Abaya

Mendebo Mountains

Shebeli

Kinyeti 3187m △

Lotagipi Swamp

Ch'ew Bahir

Lake Turkana

Chalbi Desert

Uele

UGANDA

Lake Bisina

Laikipia Escarpment

DEM.REP. CONGO

Lake Albert

Lake Kyoga

Mount Elgon 4321m △

Cherangany Hills

KENYA

Mount Kenya (Kirinyaga) 5200m △

Margherita 5110m △

Lake Edward

Lake Victoria

Tana

Lake Kivu

RWANDA

BURUNDI

Mont Teza 2666m △

Serengeti Plain

Lake Natron

Kilimanjaro 5895m △

Mount Meru 4565m △

Masai Steppe

Lake Eyasi

Monyovosi

Chunly Range

TANZANIA

Wami

Lake Tanganyika

Rubeho Mountains

Rufiji

Lake Rukwa

Usangu Flats

Kipengere Range

Luwegu

ZAMBIA

Livingstone Mountains

Ruvuma

MALAWI

Lake Nyasa

INDIAN OCEAN

Western Great Rift Valley

Mitumba Range

Western Great Rift Valley

Great Rift Valley

Eastern Great Rift Valley

Scale 1:13 700 000
(projection: Lambert Azimuthal Equal Area)

0 km   200   400   600

FORMATION OF THE EAST AFRICAN RIFT VALLEY

The East African Rift Valley is characterised by step faults and escarpments with steep walls ranging from 900 m to 2700 m. The average width is 50 km, but is wider in some places. It is believed that the East African Rift Valley was formed as a result of tensional and compressional forces brought about by the movement of continental plates.

Volcanic eruptions along the rift valley have further complicated the landscape features associated with it. The East African Rift Valley still remains unstable, with some active cones like Lengai in Tanzania.

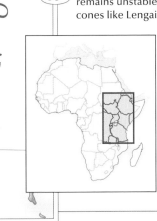

CLIMATE AND LAND USE

Much of Eastern Africa lies between 10° S and 20° N and thus experiences tropical climate. The climate varies from hot desert to modified tropical. The climate in some parts is greatly modified by altitude, prevailing winds and distance from water bodies. Most parts of Sudan (north), Somalia, Ethiopia and Kenya have a desert climate. The Ethiopian Highlands and most of South Sudan experience moderate temperatures. Rainfall occurs from two months to eight months of the year. Severe droughts occur in the arid and semi-arid areas. Other Eastern African countries – Kenya, Uganda, Rwanda, Tanzania and Burundi – experience humid equatorial and mountain climates, mainly influenced by south-easterly tropical winds, north-easterly trade winds and westerly winds. Lake Victoria has a direct influence on climate especially in areas surrounding it.

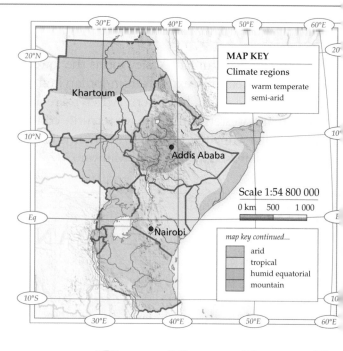

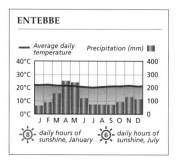

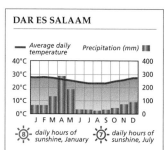

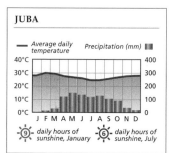

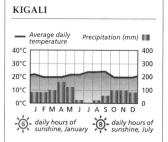

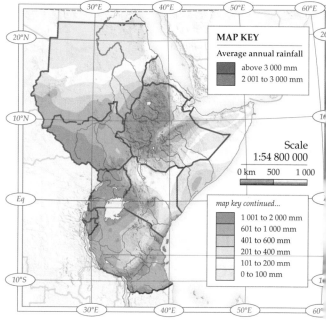

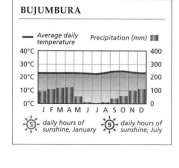

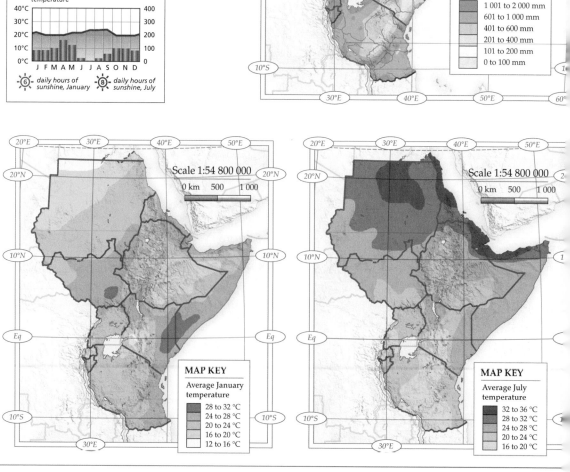

ENVIRONMENTAL ISSUES IN EASTERN AFRICA

The livelihoods and food security of the Eastern African people, and indeed the whole world, depend directly on ecosystems. The diversity of goods and services derived from these ecosystems plays a very important role. Ecosystems provide a range of inputs that are essential for sustainable economic development.

Most of the Eastern African National States are faced with diverse environmental degradation that is threatening the basic livelihoods of their people. As such, most of the Eastern Africa National States are grappling with strategies to address different threats that endanger their environment. The threats include, but are not limited to, soil erosion and nutrient loss control, population explosion control and farming methods, pollution control, solid and liquid waste management, land and urban planning and implementing and mainstreaming environmental legislation.

Water is a scarce resource in most of the East African semi-arid areas, and providing clean water is a big challenge to East African governments.

Dumping of rubbish represents a major crisis in many cities around the world.

During the dry season, grass and other vegetation in the Ngorongoro Crater, Tanzania, dies off, and Lake Magadi dries out to leave only a white crust of salt on the lake bed.

VEGETATION, SOILS AND GEOLOGY

The vegetation of Eastern Africa is closely related to the climate. It is a product of a combination of factors such as relief and altitude. Major vegetation types in Eastern Africa include: evergreen forests (confined to a few areas in the South Sudan and Lake Victoria basin) the Savanna grassland (found in most low-altitude areas of the region) and mountain vegetation. There is also the semi-desert and desert vegetation in Ethiopia, Somalia, South Sudan and Eastern parts of Kenya. Natural vegetation is dwindling as a result of destruction caused by human activities.

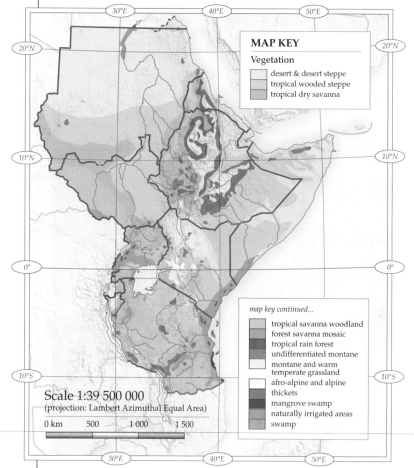

MAP KEY

Vegetation

- desert & desert steppe
- tropical wooded steppe
- tropical dry savanna

map key continued...

- tropical savanna woodland
- forest savanna mosaic
- tropical rain forest
- undifferentiated montane
- montane and warm temperate grassland
- afro-alpine and alpine
- thickets
- mangrove swamp
- naturally irrigated areas
- swamp

Scale 1:39 500 000
(projection: Lambert Azimuthal Equal Area)

0 km   500   1 000   1 500

The baobab tree is able to store water in its vast trunk for up to nine months, which enables it to survive in areas of dry scrubland such as this.

High-altitude rainforest in Rwanda

Tropical savanna in the Serengeti, Tanzania

SOILS

Eastern Africa has many types of soils, each with its specific characteristics that are related to climate, vegetation, the nature of the slopes and the underlying rocks and time. The specific soils are referred to as zonal soils. Examples include the lateritic soils found in many parts, and desert soils mainly found in Ethiopia, Sudan, north east Kenya and Somalia. Other soils include peat soils which are found in poorly drained areas, alluvial soils, found along river valleys and terra rossa soils found in limestone areas of Eastern Africa.

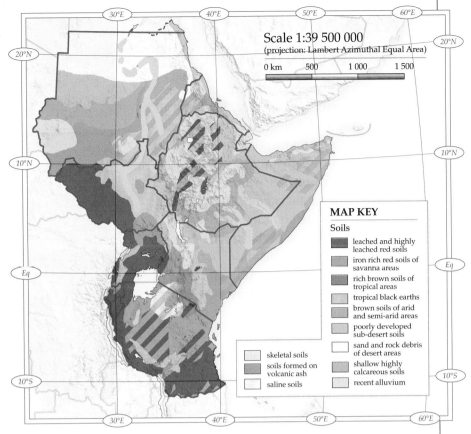

Scale 1:39 500 000
(projection: Lambert Azimuthal Equal Area)

0 km   500   1 000   1 500

MAP KEY

Soils

- leached and highly leached red soils
- iron rich red soils of savanna areas
- rich brown soils of tropical areas
- tropical black earths
- brown soils of arid and semi-arid areas
- poorly developed sub-desert soils
- sand and rock debris of desert areas
- shallow highly calcareous soils
- recent alluvium
- skeletal soils
- soils formed on volcanic ash
- saline soils

Lateritic soils usually have a distinctive red colour.

GEOLOGY

Eastern Africa has rocks that are more than 3000 million years old. These rocks were formed mainly during Pre-Cambrian, Mesozoic and Quaternary periods. Tectonic and volcanic movements that followed led to the formation of the igneous and volcanic rocks that characterise most of the Eastern Africa region. Sedimentary rocks have covered most of the original rocks as a result of soil erosion.

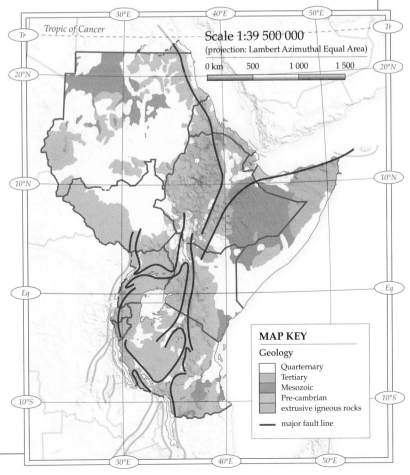

Tropic of Cancer

Scale 1:39 500 000
(projection: Lambert Azimuthal Equal Area)

0 km   500   1 000   1 500

MAP KEY

Geology

- Quaternary
- Tertiary
- Mesozoic
- Pre-cambrian
- extrusive igneous rocks
- major fault line

Lion-shaped mountain rocks in Yeha

TRANSPORT AND COMMUNICATIONS

Transport involves carriage of goods and people from place to place. With advances in science and technology, new modes of transport and communication networks have been developed. There are four main methods of transport in Eastern Africa:

- Human and animal portage (walking and riding), which are common in areas that are not accessible, especially in desert and mountainous environments.
- Land transport via road and rail.
- Water transport by inland rivers, lakes and the Indian Ocean.
- Air transport.

Although all the four major forms of transport are commonly used in Eastern Africa, they are not well developed. This is especially so in rugged terrain and inaccessible rural areas.

Communication involves transmission of words and messages. Communication has improved tremendously in most of the Eastern African National States. New technologies have led to the development of landline and mobile telephones, radios, televisions and, most recently, satellite communication. These developments have led to increased dissemination of ideas and information and have had a positive influence on trade, and economic development in general.

Rugged terrain like this makes developing transport networks difficult.

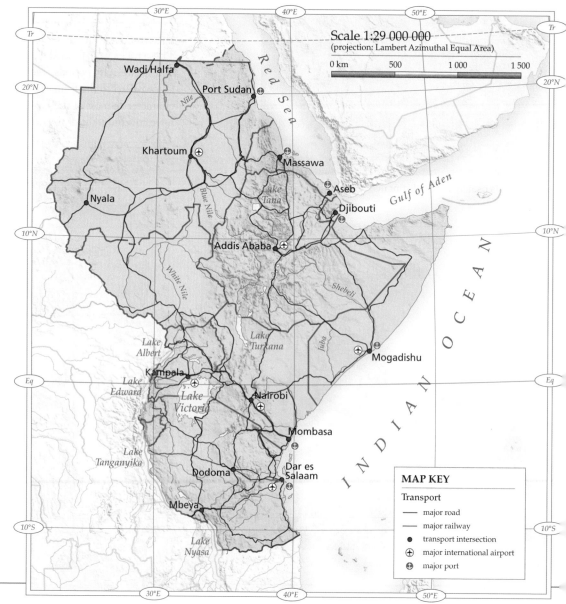

Scale 1:29 000 000
(projection: Lambert Azimuthal Equal Area)

0 km   500   1 000   1 500

MAP KEY

Transport

— major road

— major railway

● transport intersection

⊕ major international airport

⊕ major port

INDUSTRY AND TRADE

The Eastern Africa region has a population of 122.1 million. This is a huge market for products manufactured within the five Partner States of the East African Community. Plans are underway to:
- rationalise investments and make full use of established industries
- harmonise investment incentives to make the Community into a single investment area.

MEASURES TO ENHANCE EAST AFRICAN TRADE

Measures have been taken by the E. A. Community to enhance trade. The Customs Union that became effective on 1 January 2005 was formed in order to promote:
- intra-regional trade
- production efficiency
- economic development
- industrial diversification, standardisation and harmonization of information and documentation.

Admission to the Customs Union is based on the following criteria:
- Acceptance of the Community as set out in the Treaty.
- Adherence to universally acceptable principles of good governance, democracy, the rule of law, observance of human rights and social justice.
- Potential contribution to the strengthening of integration within the East African region.
- Geographical proximity to and inter-dependence between it and the EAC Partner States.
- Establishment and maintenance of a market driven economy.
- Social and economic policies being compatible with those of the Community.

Non-traditional exports (NTEs) from the East African Community include horticultural products such as these statice flowers, growing in the Great Rift Valley in Kenya. In Uganda, NTEs make up 62.7 per cent of total export earnings.

EAST AFRICAN MAJOR EXPORTS
Goods
Coffee
Tea
Cotton
Horticultural products
Fish
Gold

EAST AFRICAN MAJOR IMPORTERS
Country
China
Germany
India
Japan
Saudi Arabia
South Africa
UAE

EXPORTS IN MILLIONS, USD		
Country	**2007**	**2008**
Burundi	63.3	74.3
Rwanda	183.2	201.4
Uganda	920.5	1724
Tanzania	1472.5	2947
Kenya	748.6	912.1

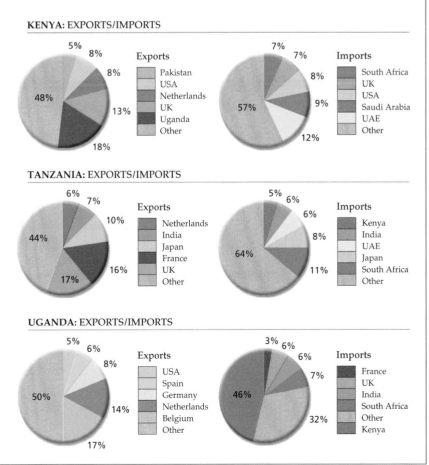

KENYA: EXPORTS/IMPORTS

Exports: 5%, 8%, 8%, 13%, 18%, 48%
Pakistan, USA, Netherlands, UK, Uganda, Other

Imports: 7%, 7%, 8%, 9%, 12%, 57%
South Africa, UK, USA, Saudi Arabia, UAE, Other

TANZANIA: EXPORTS/IMPORTS

Exports: 6%, 7%, 10%, 16%, 17%, 44%
Netherlands, India, Japan, France, UK, Other

Imports: 5%, 6%, 6%, 8%, 11%, 64%
Kenya, India, UAE, Japan, South Africa, Other

UGANDA: EXPORTS/IMPORTS

Exports: 5%, 6%, 8%, 14%, 17%, 50%
USA, Spain, Germany, Netherlands, Belgium, Other

Imports: 3%, 6%, 6%, 7%, 32%, 46%
France, UK, India, South Africa, Other, Kenya

POPULATION

The population of Eastern Africa is dense in Ethiopia, Tanzania, Kenya, Uganda and Somalia. There are increasing numbers of refugees and internally displaced people. Civil wars in Rwanda, Burundi and Somalia have resulted in refugees in the neighbouring countries. Refugees are concentrated in a number of camps in the region. The largest refugee camp is Dadaab in northern Kenya, which accommodates thousands of Somali refugees. Political and ethnic violence has also led to internally displaced persons. For example, thousands of people were internally displaced in Kenya following the 2007 post-election violence.

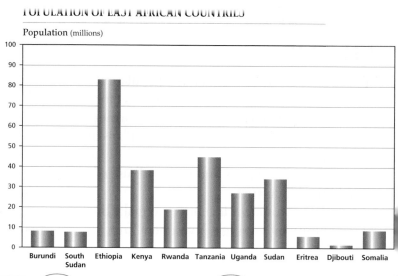

POPULATION OF EAST AFRICAN COUNTRIES

Population (millions)

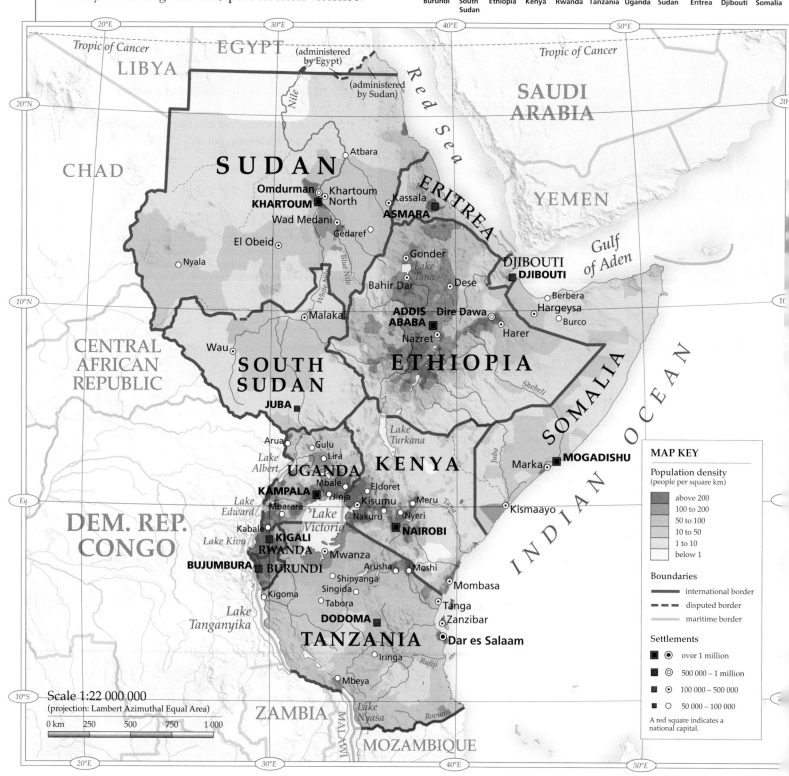

Scale 1:22 000 000
(projection: Lambert Azimuthal Equal Area)

0 km   250   500   750   1 000

MAP KEY

Population density
(people per square km)

- above 200
- 100 to 200
- 50 to 100
- 10 to 50
- 1 to 10
- below 1

Boundaries

——— international border
- - - disputed border
——— maritime border

Settlements

■ ◉ over 1 million
■ ◎ 500 000 – 1 million
■ ⊙ 100 000 – 500 000
■ ○ 50 000 – 100 000

A red square indicates a national capital.

POPULATION AND LAND AREA

Country	Area (in thousands km²)	Population (in millions)
Burundi	27.8	9.9
South Sudan	619.7	8.2
Ethiopia	1104.3	82.1
Kenya	582.6	38.6
Rwanda	26.3	11.6
Tanzania	945.2	46.3
Uganda	236.0	28.2
Sudan	250.6	34.3
Eritrea	101.0	5.4
Djibouti	23.2	0.9
Somalia	627.3	9.5

UN Conference Centre, Addis Ababa

Newly arrived refugees in Kenya's Dadaab Refugee Camp

Kenya's Dadaab Refugee Camp

COUNTRIES AND RELIEF

Central Africa as a region is characterised by a tropical, wet, equatorial climate, with dense rain forests distributed in low lying basins, some as low as 200 m above sea level, with numerous rivers. It is composed of six countries: the Democratic Republic of Congo (DRC), The Central African Republic (CAR), Congo, Gabon, São Tomé and Príncipe and Equatorial Guinea. The Central African Republic (CAR) is the only country in the region that is landlocked.

Dense rain forests, Congo basin, Central Africa

Scale 1:14 800 000
(projection: Lambert Azimuthal Equal Area)

0 km   250   500   750

AFRICA

MAP KEY

Elevation

4 000 m
2 000 m
1 000 m
500 m
250 m
100 m
Below sea level
250 m
2 000 m
4 000 m

△ mountain

marsh/wetland

Boundaries

━━━ international border
━━━ maritime border

Capital Cities

▣ ⊙ over 1 million
▣ ◎ 500 000 – 1 million
▪ ⊙ 100 000 – 500 000
▪ ○ 50 000 – 100 000
▪ ∘ below 50 000

A red square indicates a national capital.

CHAD
SUDAN
NIGERIA
CAMEROON
SOUTH SUDAN

CENTRAL AFRICAN REPUBLIC

Birao
Ndélé
Markounda
Kaga Bandoro
Bossangoa
Bria
Djéma
Bouar
Sibut
Bambari
Obo
Berbérati
BANGUI
Bangassou
Zongo
Nola
Bondo
Dungu
Aba
Bétou
Gemena
Buta
Titule
Isiro
Mungbere
Dongou
Lisala
Bumba
Aburo 2449m
Lake Albert
Ouésso
Nia-Nia
Beni
UGANDA
Epéna
Yangambi
Kisangani

EQUATORIAL GUINEA
MALABO
Bico
Príncipe
Bata
Bitam
Sembé
Congo Basin
Mbini
Oyem
Mongomo
Bélinga
Ngoko
Ouésso
SÃO TOMÉ & PRÍNCIPE
SÃO TOMÉ
Makokou
CONGO
Makoua
Mbandaka
Boende
Tshuapa
Ikela
Goma
São Tomé
LIBREVILLE
GABON
Lac Ntomba
RWANDA
Port-Gentil
Ogooué
Lambaréné
Owando
Lomela
Bukavu
Lake Kivu
Koulamoutou
Gamboma
Lac Mai-Ndombe
DEM. REP. CONGO
Kalima
Omboué
Moanda
Franc_ville
Kindu
Mouila
Ndendé
Mossendjo
Djambala
Bandundu
Lukenie
Lodja
Kibombo
BURUNDI
Sibíti
Kwa
Kasai
Sankuru
Kasongo
Setté Cama
Ndindi
Dolisie
Nkayi
BRAZZAVILLE
Mangai
Ilebo
Lomami
Lulimba
Pointe-Noire
KINSHASA
Kikwit
Mweka
Kongolo
Kalemie
Lake Tanganyika
Tshela
Kwango
Demba
Mbuji-Mayi
Kabinda
CABINDA (to Angola)
Mbanza-Ngungu
Kananga
Manono
Moba
Matadi
Boma
Kasongo-Lunda
Tshikapa
Gandajika
Mitumba Range
ATLANTIC OCEAN
Mwene-Ditu
Lac Upemba
Lake Mweru
ANGOLA
Kamina
Kasaji
ZAMBIA
Dilolo
Kolwezi
Likasi
Lubumbashi

Great Rift Valley
Lake Edward
TANZANIA
Oubangui
Ubangi
Uele
Bomu
Kotto
Bahr Aouk
Congo
Lulonga
Lualaba
Mbomou

CLIMATE AND LAND USE

The Central African region is a low-lying region, mainly characterised by tropical climate, with heavy rainfall throughout the year. The wet climate supports dense, impenetrable forests and numerous rivers.

LAND USE

Land use is influenced by topography, climate and levels of development, accessibility, population density and distribution. Land use in the Central African region is dominated by traditional farming and subsistence food production. Mining, forestry and fishing form an important component of land use in the Central African region.

Traditional methods are used to catch fish in the Congo River and other areas in Central Africa

Aeriel view of the farmlands in highlands of eastern Democratic Republic of Congo

MINING AND ENERGY

Mining in Central Africa is dominated by the Democratic Republic of Congo, although other countries have a significant share in the region's mining production. However, most of the mines were used by rebel groups to fuel civil wars, which have hampered economic growth of the Central African countries. A typical example is the second DRC war notoriously known as the Coltan War and the greatest war of Africa. Most of the countries in the region have adhered to the Kimberley Process in order to avoid illegal trade from mines, which funds rebel groups. Minerals like coltan are very important raw materials for communication devices such as mobile telephones.

Scale 1:23 400 000

MAP KEY

Minerals
- coltan
- copper
- diamonds
- gold
- manganese
- oil
- tin
- uranium

Nuclear power plant

ENERGY

In 2006, the world generated a total of 18 930 Terawatt-hour (TWh) of electricity (excluding pumped storage) from mainly coal/peat (41.0 per cent), gas (20.1 per cent), hydro (16.0 per cent), nuclear (14.8 per cent) and oil (5.8 per cent) fuels. Other sources (2.3 per cent) included geothermal, solar, wind, combustible renewable and waste, and heat. Of this total, Africa was responsible for only 3.1 per cent. In Central Africa, a significant amount of consumption is by industry and, in some central African countries; industrial growth has outstripped the installed power capacity. Almost all of the Central African nations face electricity shortages and unprecedented power crises.

Nuclear power is only a small part of African energy supply. There are more than 440 nuclear power plants in operation worldwide and, of these, only two are in Africa: Koeberg-1 and Koeberg-2 in South Africa, which started operating in 1984. Both of these are of 900 MW capacity.

TRANSPORT AND COMMUNICATION

Central African countries in general have very poorly-developed road and communication networks, partly as a result of the wet tropical climate and also partly as a result of the negative impact of wars and civil strife that has afflicted the region for the last two decades. Roads and railways have been damaged and not adequately repaired. The situation has been worsened by heavy tropical rains that make the few available roads unusable. The most common means of transport is via water along the numerous rivers that characterise the equatorial basin. Air transport is well developed and is ranked the second most commonly used means of transport. The east part of DRC can be considered to be landlocked, because it is very far from the sea ports in the west. Goods to the eastern DRC are ferried through either Mombasa or Das es Salaam.

Central African roads are frequently made impassable by heavy rains.

Scale 1:16 500 000
(projection: Lambert Azimuthal Equal Area)

0 km   250   500   750

SUDAN

CHAD

SOUTH SUDAN

NIGERIA

CENTRAL

Birao

Bahr Aouk

Kotto

CAMEROON

AFRICAN REPUBLIC

Kaga Bandoro

BANGUI

Oubangui

Ubangi

Uele

Bomu

MALABO

EQUATORIAL GUINEA

Bata

Ngoko

Congo

Lulonga

Bumba

Mungbere

Lake Albert

UGANDA

SÃO TOMÉ & PRÍNCIPE

Kisangani

SÃO TOMÉ

LIBREVILLE

CONGO

Mbandaka

Lualaba

Lake Edward

GABON

Port-Gentil

Ogooué

Alima

Congo

Lac Ntomba

Tshuapa

Ikela

DEM. REP.

Lake Kivu

RWANDA

Bukavu

Franceville

Lac Mai-Ndombe

CONGO

Kindu

BURUNDI

Ndendé

Kwa

Kasai

Sankuru

Lomami

TANZANIA

BRAZZAVILLE

KINSHASA

Pointe-Noire

Kalemie

Lake Tanganyika

CABINDA
(to Angola)

Matadi

Kananga

ATLANTIC OCEAN

Kwango

Kasai

Lac Upemba

Kamina

Lulua

Lake Mweru

ANGOLA

Kolwezi

Lubumbashi

MAP KEY

Communications

── major road

── minor road

── railway

⊕ international airport

⊙ major port

Settlements

■ capital city

○ other town

ZAMBIA

COUNTRIES AND RELIEF

The countries that cover the North Africa Region are Egypt, Libya, Algeria, Morocco, Western Sahara, Mauritania and Tunisia. The north is bordered by the Atlantic Ocean and the Mediterranean Sea, with a narrow coastal plain in Mauritania, Western Sahara, Morocco, Algeria and Tunisia that becomes wider in Libya and Egypt. The Atlas Mountains in Morocco and Algeria have an altitude of between 2000 and 3000 m above sea level. Otherwise, most of the land is between 1000 and 2000 m above sea level.

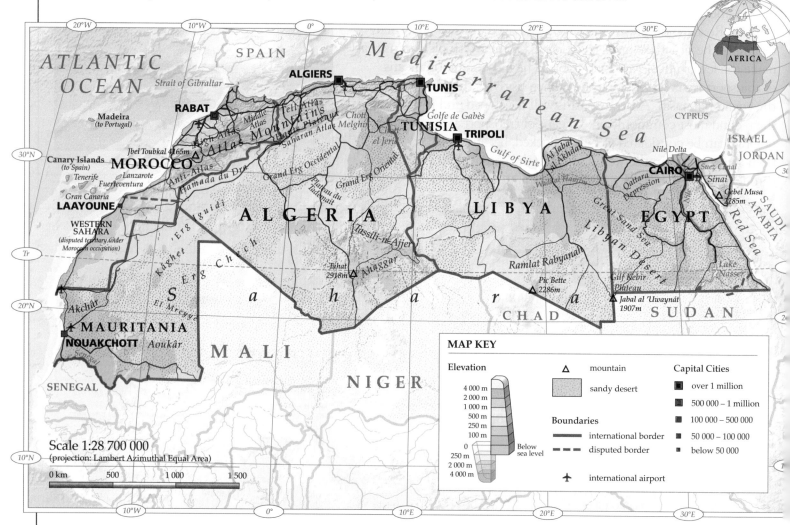

MAP KEY

Elevation

4 000 m
2 000 m
1 000 m
500 m
250 m
100 m
0
250 m
2 000 m
4 000 m
Below sea level

△ mountain

sandy desert

Boundaries

—— international border
----- disputed border
✈ international airport

Capital Cities

■ over 1 million
▣ 500 000 – 1 million
▪ 100 000 – 500 000
▫ 50 000 – 100 000
· below 50 000

Scale 1:28 700 000
(projection: Lambert Azimuthal Equal Area)

0 km   500   1 000   1 500

Left: Cairo, the capital of Egypt, is situated alongside the River Nile. Settlements were recorded in the area as long ago as 3500 BCE, although the current city was founded officially in 969 AD.

Right: A Berber village in the Atlas Mountains, Morocco. It is estimated that there are between 14 and 25 million speakers of Berber across North Africa.

CLIMATE, WATER ISSUES AND VEGETATION

CLIMATE

Along the Mediterranean coast, rain falls in the cool winter but the summers are dry and hot. In other parts, rainfall is scarce and unreliable. The Atlas Mountains experience cool conditions throughout the year. In the interior, there are the semi-arid to desert conditions of the Sahara. Due to these arid conditions, this region suffers from chronic shortages of water. For Egypt, the main source of water is the Nile River; other countries depend on wells in the oases and artesian wells in the plains.

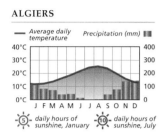

ALGIERS

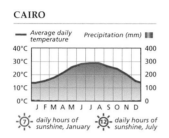

CAIRO

DESERTIFICATION

This process is the continuous spread of desert-like conditions as a result of unsustainable human activities. Desertification has been an issue of great concern because the phenomenon is spreading fast. More than a quarter of the Earth is affected by it. Overexploitation of natural resources may lead to desertification as well as climate change. Desertification can lead to soil depletion, leading to food shortages due to poor yields.

In semi-arid deserts, conditions are dry but there is enough moisture to support some vegetation.

WATER ISSUES: OASES

Most human activities in deserts have traditionally depended upon a reliable water supply that guarantees plant growth for grazing livestock, planting food crops and drinking water. Deserts do contain large reserves of ground water that sometimes come to the surface as springs. Oases are places that have permanent springs: rich plant cover, particularly palm trees, grows around them. Such springs provide vital water supplies to the local communities that travel long distances to collect water.

VEGETATION

Vegetation in this region is sparse due to the dry conditions. It is mainly made up of wild plants and short grass. Most of the vegetation has been used as firewood and, in many places, soils have been exposed to water and wind erosion. Planting drought-resistant trees and shrubs has been adopted in the fringes of the Sahara desert to combat its spread.

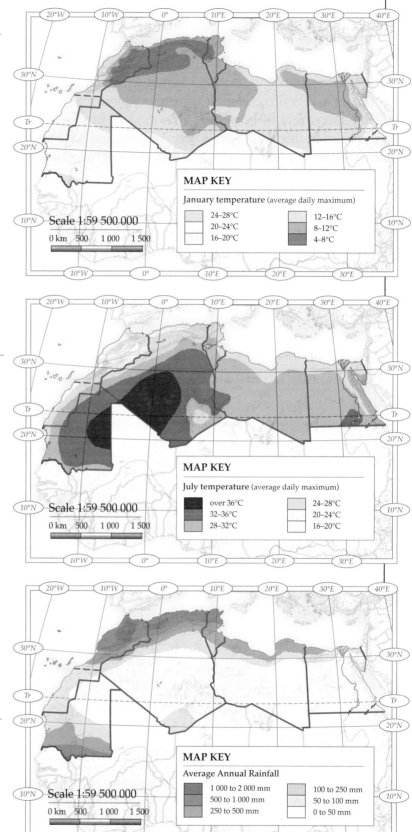

Scale 1:59 500 000
0 km 500 1 000 1 500

MAP KEY

January temperature (average daily maximum)

24–28°C 12–16°C
20–24°C 8–12°C
16–20°C 4–8°C

Scale 1:59 500 000
0 km 500 1 000 1 500

MAP KEY

July temperature (average daily maximum)

over 36°C 24–28°C
32–36°C 20–24°C
28–32°C 16–20°C

Scale 1:59 500 000
0 km 500 1 000 1 500

MAP KEY

Average Annual Rainfall

1 000 to 2 000 mm 100 to 250 mm
500 to 1 000 mm 50 to 100 mm
250 to 500 mm 0 to 50 mm

NILE BASIN

The Nile River, which has four major tributaries – the White Nile, the Blue Nile, Sobat and Atbara – is the world's longest river and flows 6700 kilometres through eleven countries in North Eastern Africa: Rwanda, Burundi, Democratic Republic of Congo, Tanzania, Kenya, Uganda, Ethiopia, Eritrea, Sudan, Egypt and South Sudan. It is therefore subject to political interactions or hydro politics. The modern history of hydro politics in the Nile Basin is very complex and has had wide ramifications both for regional and global developments.

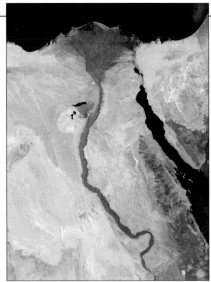

Satellite image of the River Nile

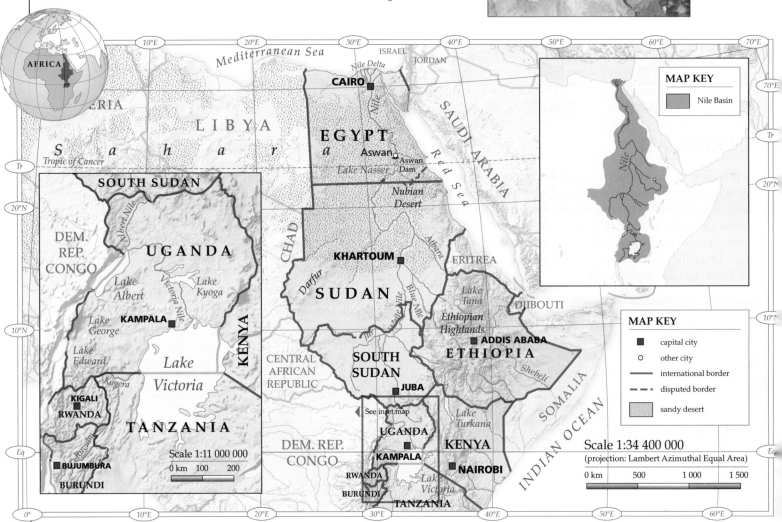

THE NILE BASIN INITIATIVE (NBI)

The Nile Basin Initiative (NBI), established in 1999 in Dar es Salaam, is an inter-governmental organisation dedicated to equitable and sustainable management and development of the shared water resources of the Nile Basin. NBI Member States include Burundi, Democratic Republic of Congo, Egypt, Ethiopia, Kenya, Rwanda, Sudan, Tanzania and Uganda. Eritrea is an observer.

The NBI has a Shared Vision that states: 'to achieve sustainable socio-economic development through the equitable utilisation of, and benefit from, the common Nile Basin water resources'.

The 'Strategic Action Program' (SAP) is comprised of two complementary programmes – the 'Shared Vision Program'

(SVP) and the 'Subsidiary Action Program' (SAP) – to guide Nile cooperation. The SVP is comprised of eight basin-wide projects whose major focus is:

- building trust, confidence and capacity in member countries
- creating an enabling environment for trans-boundary investments.

The Shared Vision Program was largely completed during 2009. The overriding goal of the investment agenda is to contribute to poverty alleviation, reverse environmental degradation and promote socio-economic growth in the countries.

MINING AND ENERGY

The minerals found in the North Africa region are: oil, natural gas, iron ore, phosphates, lead, zinc, silver, manganese, uranium, copper, diamonds, gypsum and salt. Mauritania has the world's largest deposits of gypsum. However, in economic terms, oil and natural gas are the most valuable in this region.

North Africa is the continent's most developed oil region. It has proven oil reserves and refining capacity.

Three countries, Egypt, Algeria, and Libya, dominate the region's oil sector. Egypt's oil and gas are in the Gulf of Suez and the Nile Delta. Algeria has 11.8 billion barrels of proven oil reserves, the eighth largest in the world. Libya, a member of OPEC, holds the largest oil reserves and is the largest producer in Africa. Morocco and Tunisia are actively pursuing the expansion of their upstream oil sectors.

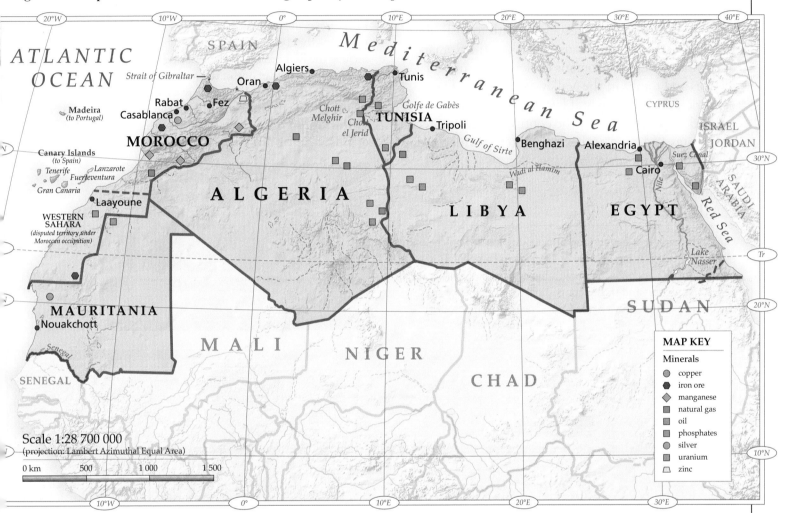

Scale 1:28 700 000
(projection: Lambert Azimuthal Equal Area)

0 km   500   1 000   1 500

MAP KEY

Minerals

- copper
- iron ore
- manganese
- natural gas
- oil
- phosphates
- silver
- uranium
- zinc

ENERGY

North Africa has oil and a huge potential of renewable energy. The region has an abundance of solar resources together with wind resources.

Algeria has in place a legislative framework for the renewable energy sector. However, delays in implementation have delayed the growth of renewable energy's proportion of the country's energy supply. Algeria remains committed to its ambitious targets of 20 per cent of energy supply from renewable energy sources. By 2030 it will be investing US$120 billion into renewable energy projects. Wind energy potential is relatively low, yet several small-scale wind projects with capacities of 10 MW to 20 MW are planned to be constructed over the next three years, mostly in the northern coastline

Egypt is seeking to derive 20 per cent of its energy from renewable sources by 2020 mostly through wind (12 per cent) and hydro and solar photovoltaics (PV) (8 per cent).

Morocco has no domestic coal or oil reserves, but energy demand is expected to double by 2020; and it has targeted to generate 42 per cent of electricity from renewable energy sources by 2020. Morocco has privatised the energy sector, which has encouraged private and foreign investment in renewable energy. Further reforms are planned with the breakup of the former monopoly enjoyed by the state utility, Office National de l'Electricité (ONE). Morocco is the only North African country connected to the European grid. It has a great opportunity to transform from a net energy importer to a net energy exporter by exploiting solar and significant wind resources.

Tunisia has ambitious targets in the renewable energy sector, although there is currently no feed in tariff or renewable energy certificate incentive scheme in place. Tax incentives and subsidies are used to encourage development and construction. Investment and expansion are required to develop and increase the grid to meet solar and wind targets.

TOURISM

North African countries provide fascinating insights into the ways of life of the local people, their customs and culture. The countries in North Africa provide tourists with a deeper appreciation of Africa's history and culture than they could ever obtain from movies and textbooks.

The unique climate of North Africa supports a variety of indigenous wildlife species, such as foxes and desert cats, desert monitors and horned vipers.

Some of the activities associated with tourist safaris in North Africa date back as far back as the Roman occupation of Egypt. Romans explored the ruins of Thebes and tombs in the Valley of the Kings. For centuries, Arab, Asian and later European travellers trekked across portions of the continent, keeping records of the sites and peoples they encountered, which today is useful tourist information.

CAIRO

Cairo, the capital of Egypt, is an ancient city located on the banks of the Nile River. It has an area of 453 km² and a population of 19.9 million. Its rapid population growth has created problems of urban poverty, pollution and traffic congestion. At Giza, in the southwest, the Great Pyramids have made Cairo one of the great tourist destinations.

COUNTRY PROFILES

Morocco is a country where diversity thrives. There the main focus is on the country's coast, culture and history.

Tunisia is a hospitable land of colours and contrasts, spices and scents. Its natural beauty lies with its ancient cities, lively festivals and the warm friendliness of its people. Among Tunisia's tourist attractions, there is the capital city of Tunis. This is situated on the large Mediterranean Sea gulf, the Gulf of Tunis. The town is popular for its golden beaches, affordable luxuries and sunny weather. Other tourist attractions include the ancient ruins of Carthage, the Muslim and Jewish quarters of Jerba and coastal resorts in the outskirts of Monastir.

Egypt is a country of diversity, yet full of all the history and traditions that typifies this great country. Major tourist attractions include the Red Sea coast, the amazing desert landscapes, the fantastic remnants of one of the greatest civilisations known to mankind – the pyramids, and Egypt's lifeline, the River Nile.

Libya's tourist attractions include, the archaeological ruins of areas such as Leptis Magna, Cyrene and Sabratha, the desert landscapes of Tadrart Acacus and the oasis of Ghadames.

A visitor rides a camel across the sands to see the Great Pyramids, Egypt

The Nile proper rises at Lake Victoria, and flows north through much of Eastern Africa. Heavy rainfalls cause the Nile to flood each summer, while the river reaches its lowest volumes between January and May. Here we can see the river flowing through central Cairo.

INDUSTRY, TRADE, TRANSPORT AND COMMUNICATION

The processing of minerals such as oil, natural gas, iron ore, phosphates, lead, zinc, silver, manganese, uranium, copper, diamonds, gypsum and salt, form a major base for industrial development in the North Africa region. The main industrial activities are oil and gas refining, petrochemicals, steel, textiles, light engineering and salt production.

Industrial plant, heavy metal industry, near Rosetta, Delta area, Egypt

TRADE

North African countries dominate the oil sector and are known to the major traders in the product. Trade performance is hampered by the poorly developed exporting structures in these countries. Despite the countless regional integration initiatives, intra-regional trade flows remain extremely low.

Exports: North African countries, such as Libya, Tunisia, Morocco, Algeria, and Egypt, export between about 40 and 80 per cent of their product to Europe, mainly the European Union market. Studies have shown the following degree of exports for North African countries: Libya (83%), Tunisia (80%), Morocco (69%), Algeria (55%) Mauritania (53%) and Egypt (42%). The American and Canadian markets are poorly explored by North Africa exports, except for Algeria (30%) and Egypt (13%).

Imports: North African countries depend highly on European imports. According to statistics, imports from European markets range from 4 per cent in Libya to 75 per cent in Tunisia. Morocco, Egypt and Algeria respectively are supplied with 65 per cent, 38 per cent and 63 per cent from Europe. The most noticeable change in the importing structure of North African countries is the reinforcement of imports from emerging Asian countries.

Intra-regional Trade: North Africa is not as strong in intra-regional trade and lacks regional integration. Overall, the share of intra North Africa exports stands at around 2.7 per cent. This trade integration level is quite below the performances achieved by other regional communities on the African continent.

TRANSPORT AND COMMUNICATION

Transport and communication facilities are vital infrastructures of any modern economy. A transport system comprises several modes including roads, railways and waterways and a communication system includes post offices, courier services and wireless and electronic media.

The development of a country's transport system is a prerequisite to its economic growth. There is a close relationship between transport, communication and the level of economic activity. Economic development requires a highly organised system of transport and communications. A planned and organised system of transport and communication is one of the indications of country's development.

Highway in Morocco

A camel trip in the Sahara Desert

COUNTRIES AND RELIEF

West Africa, with 16 countries, has a colonial history. Anglo-colonies were Nigeria, Ghana, Gambia and Sierra Leone, and Franco-colonies were Côte d'Ivoire, Togo, Benin, Mali, Niger, Burkina Faso and Chad. Cameroon was initially a German territory but was later ceded to Britain, and then to France. Guinea Bissau was a Portuguese colony. Liberia was a colony created for freed slaves from the United States.

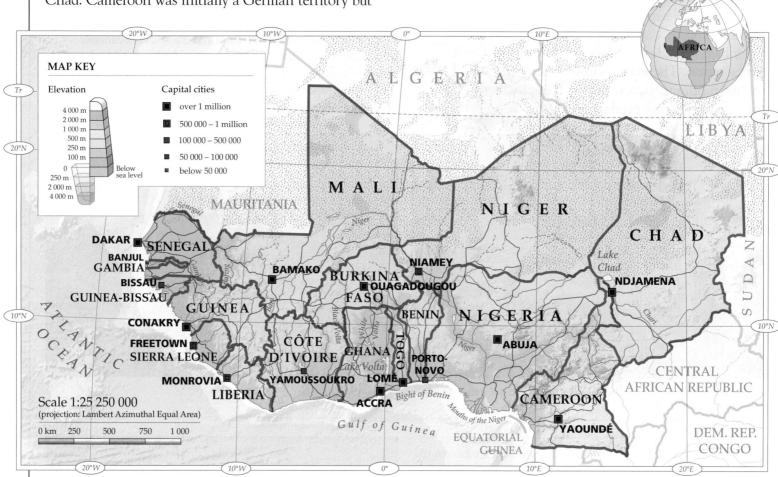

MAP KEY

Elevation

4 000 m
2 000 m
1 000 m
500 m
250 m
100 m
0
250 m
2 000 m
4 000 m
Below sea level

Capital cities

■ over 1 million
▪ 500 000 – 1 million
▪ 100 000 – 500 000
▪ 50 000 – 100 000
▪ below 50 000

Scale 1:25 250 000
(projection: Lambert Azimuthal Equal Area)

0 km   250   500   750   1 000

RELIEF

Most of West Africa consists of an undulating low plateau below 500 m above the sea level, fringed on the west and south by a coastal plain. There are some isolated highland areas above 500 m and some peaks exceed 1000 m. The most important are Fouta Djallon (1537 m), Guinea Highlands (1656 m), Sierra Leone Mountains (1948 m), Nimba Mountains (1752 m), Jos Plateau (1690 m), Mandara Mountains (1142 m), Adamawa Highlands (2042 m), the Saharan Uplands of Air (1850 m) and the Plateau of Djado (1120 m) in northern Niger.

Women paddling skiff canoes in Benin

CLIMATE AND VEGETATION

The interaction of two migrating air masses gives West Africa wet and dry seasons. The first is the hot, dry tropical continental air mass of the northern high pressure system, which gives rise to the dry, dusty, Harmattan winds that blow from the Sahara over most of West Africa from November to February. The second is the moisture-laden, tropical maritime, or equatorial air mass, which produces southwest winds. Where these two air masses meet is a belt of variable width and stability called the Inter-Tropical Convergence Zone (ITCZ). The north and south migration of this ITCZ, which follows the apparent movement of the Sun, controls the climate of the region. Temperatures are greatly modified by altitude. The general rainfall pattern is modified by ocean currents and physiographic features. Generally, West Africa experiences equatorial, tropical, semi-desert and desert climates.

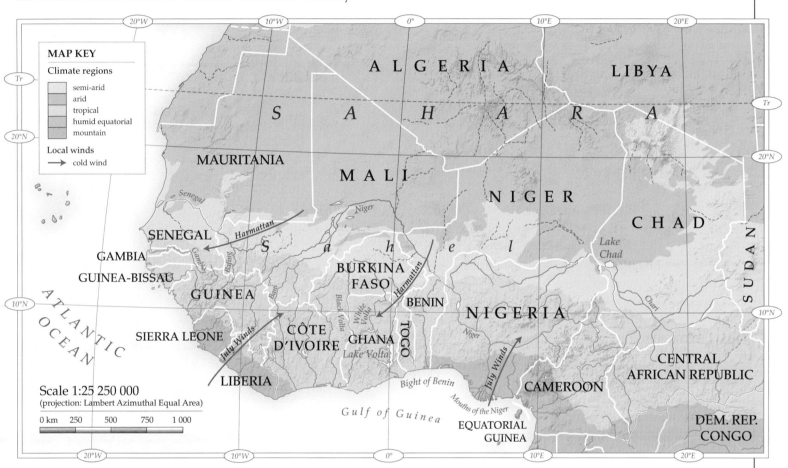

MAP KEY

Climate regions
- semi-arid
- arid
- tropical
- humid equatorial
- mountain

Local winds
- → cold wind

Scale 1:25 250 000
(projection: Lambert Azimuthal Equal Area)

0 km 250 500 750 1 000

VEGETATION

Vegetation is determined, to a large extent, by rainfall. The dominant vegetation in West Africa is of tropical rainforest, savannah, semi-desert and desert types. However, human activities are constantly modifying the species diversity of these vegetation types, especially in the tropical rainforest and savannah.

Aerial view of the tropical rainforest near Konimbo in Liberia

AGRICULTURE

The location of major agricultural activities in West Africa is closely related to climatic conditions. The northern zone, which consists mostly of tropical savanna land, is known for livestock keeping and irrigated agriculture. The southern zone is a rich equatorial rainforest region, where commercial agriculture thrives. The Atlantic coast is famous for fishing. West Africa is famous for cocoa, palm oil and rubber production.

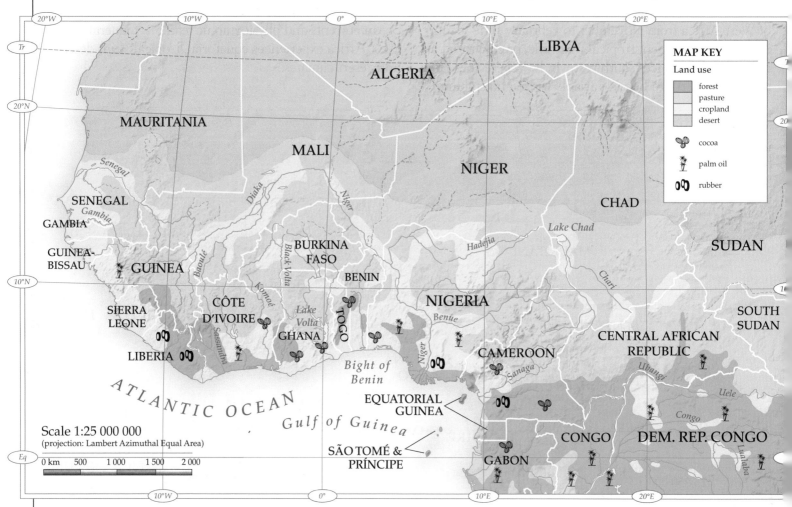

MAP KEY

Land use
- forest
- pasture
- cropland
- desert

🌱 cocoa
🌴 palm oil
👣 rubber

Scale 1:25 000 000
(projection: Lambert Azimuthal Equal Area)

0 km   500   1 000   1 500   2 000

PALM OIL

Palm, a foodstuff, is grown throughout the lowlands of equatorial Africa. In West Africa, it is grown on the coastal plains regions of Guinea and Guinea-Bissau. Palm oil is grown both for subsistence and commercial purposes. It is used for cooking and as a source protein.

RUBBER

Rubber is a tree-crop that is best suited to plantation agriculture and is mainly grown in Liberia. Rubber is processed locally and is used for products like motor vehicles tyres and shoe soles. Rubber is also grown in Nigeria, Côte d'Ivoire, Cameroon and Chad.

COCOA

The major producers of cocoa are Ghana and Côte d'Ivoire, followed by Nigeria and Cameroon. Globally, Ghana and Côte d'Ivoire are the world's leading cocoa producers. Cocoa grows in the southern region, where rainfall is heavy and altitude is high.

In Ghana, women play a large part in cocoa production and are involved from planting right through to harvesting and processing the beans.

MINING AND ENERGY

Existing evidence indicates that most West African countries have oil and natural gas deposits. Many of the oil deposits are in Nigeria. There are moderate deposits of gold, bauxite, iron, salt, diamond, lime, zinc, silver, uranium, phosphates, manganese, copper, marble and limestone all over the West African region. However, civil strife and military coups in the region have hindered the full exploitation of these mineral resources, sometimes leading to more conflicts.

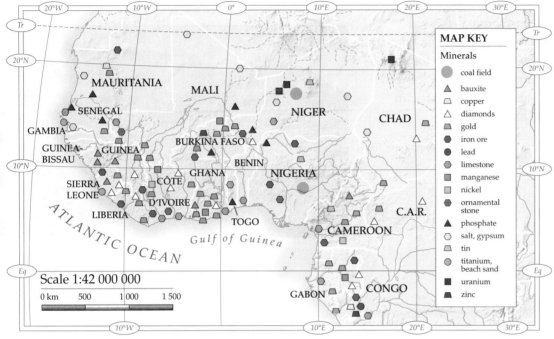

MAP KEY

Minerals
- coal field
- bauxite
- copper
- diamonds
- gold
- iron ore
- lead
- limestone
- manganese
- nickel
- ornamental stone
- phosphate
- salt, gypsum
- tin
- titanium, beach sand
- uranium
- zinc

Scale 1:42 000 000

0 km 500 1 000 1 500

OIL IN NIGERIA

Oil in Nigeria is found both on land and offshore in southern states. Oil exploitation in Nigeria began in 1957. Ten per cent of the oil is refined and used locally in Nigeria. The rest is exported as crude oil to Europe, North America and South America. The challenges facing the oil industry in Nigeria include civil war, overdependence on oil at the expense of other sectors of the economy, competition from other oil producing regions such as the Middle East, and serious environmental degradation.

ENERGY

West Africa has abundant energy resources. For example, there is thermal power in Nigeria, the Akosombo hydro-electric power plant in the Volta River, and wood fuel in regions within the equatorial rainforest and savannah.

Akosombo Dam, Volta River, Ghana

VOLTA BASIN

The Akosombo Dam, on the Volta River in Ghana, was constructed in 1963. The dam is 134 m long and 426 m wide. Currently, it produces hydropower for Ghana's industrial areas such as Tema. The dam also serves as source of fish and water for irrigation, and is a north-south shipping route which connects the ports of Keter Krachi, Kpanda and Akosombo.

COUNTRIES AND RELIEF

The Southern African region lies between latitude 10°
S to 35° S and longitude 10° E to 40° E. The region
is very diverse and is crossed by the Tropic of Capricorn.
The countries comprising Southern Africa include Angola,
Botswana, Lesotho, Malawi, Mozambique, Namibia,
Swaziland, Republic of South Africa, Zambia and Zimbabwe.
Over the past 20 years, the governments and people have
worked together in different areas and formed regional
organisations. Regional organisations comprise more countries
outside the region. These are the New Partnership for Africa's
Development (NEPAD), The Common Market for Eastern
and Southern Africa (COMESA) and Southern African
Development Community (SADC).

RELIEF

Southern Africa is made up of three main physiographic
regions. The eastern coastal plain is flat and gently rolling.
The Drakensberg Mountains rise from the coastal plains and
run along the east coast to the south. Most of the central part
is dominated by the high plateau also known as the High Veld.
The plateau used to be a mountain but has been eroded by
wind, rain and heat. The western coastal plain is mostly desert.

Table Mountain, Cape Town

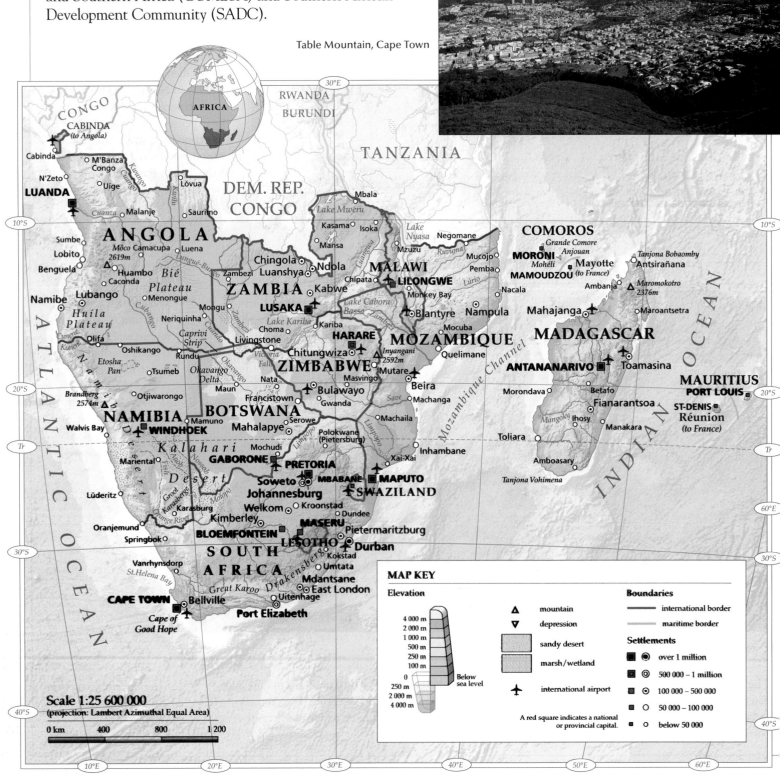

MAP KEY

Elevation

4 000 m
2 000 m
1 000 m
500 m
250 m
100 m
0
250 m
2 000 m
4 000 m
Below sea level

△ mountain
▽ depression

sandy desert

marsh/wetland

✈ international airport

A red square indicates a national
or provincial capital.

Boundaries

—— international border
—— maritime border

Settlements

■ ◉ over 1 million
▣ ◎ 500 000 – 1 million
◩ ◉ 100 000 – 500 000
▪ ◦ 50 000 – 100 000
▪ ○ below 50 000

Scale 1:25 600 000
(projection: Lambert Azimuthal Equal Area)

0 km   400   800   1 200

CLIMATE AND VEGETATION

Southern Africa has a climate that ranges from tropical, Mediterranean to temperate. Rainfall is almost entirely from evaporation over the Indian Ocean. During winter and drought periods, the Botswana Upper High, along with the eastern mountain belt stretching from the Drakensberg in South Africa right across Tanzania, blocks the moist air from entering the region. Its establishment reduces rain across Southern Africa.

The rainfall patterns are highly variable. In most of the past years, the region has experienced recurrent droughts of varying severity. Droughts intensify land degradation. Along the western coast, the cold Benguela currents greatly affect the rainfall, creating semi-arid and desert like conditions.

The vegetation ranges from desert type in the semi-arid areas to grassland in the plateau. Vegetation is influenced by the climate and relief. Much of the vegetation has been altered by human activities, especially agriculture.

Lush forests and tropical savanna vegetation occur along the eastern coast, fynboss vegetation around the Cape coast and scrubland in the Karoo belt

WATER RESOURCES

Floods and droughts are both common in Southern Africa. Water scarcity is due to semi-aridity with low unreliable rainfall. Many rivers are dry during most parts of the year. In 1991 and 1992, Southern Africa, excluding Namibia, experienced the worst drought in living memory. In 2002, floods inundated crops, ruined forests and tree crops, destroyed villages and created a humanitarian crisis in Mozambique. River basin projects have been established to control floods and provide water. There are two major river basin projects – the Limpopo River Benchmark Basin and the Zambezi Basin.

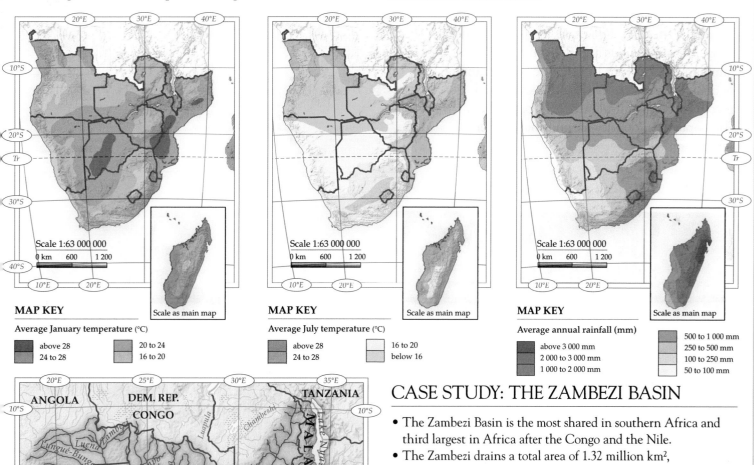

MAP KEY

Average January temperature (°C)

above 28	20 to 24
24 to 28	16 to 20

MAP KEY

Average July temperature (°C)

above 28	16 to 20
24 to 28	below 16

MAP KEY

Average annual rainfall (mm)

above 3 000 mm	500 to 1 000 mm
2 000 to 3 000 mm	250 to 500 mm
1 000 to 2 000 mm	100 to 250 mm
	50 to 100 mm

MAP KEY

— Zambezi river and tributaries

— other rivers

Scale 1:22 000 000

0 km   200   400   600

CASE STUDY: THE ZAMBEZI BASIN

- The Zambezi Basin is the most shared in southern Africa and third largest in Africa after the Congo and the Nile.
- The Zambezi drains a total area of 1.32 million km², stretching across eight countries – Angola, Botswana, Malawi, Mozambique, Namibia, Tanzania, Zambia and Zimbabwe.
- The Zambezi Basin takes up approximately 25 per cent of the total geographic area of the riparian countries, estimated at 5.6 million km²
- There are two large hydro-electric power stations on the Zambezi River. One is at Lake Kariba in Zimbabwe, the other is at Cahora Bassa Dam in Mozambique.
- The largest natural freshwater lake in the basin is Lake Malawi/Nyasa that covers 28 000 km² and is Africa's largest fresh water lake after Lake Victoria and Lake Tanganyika.

MINING AND ENERGY

South Africa is the world's sixth largest coal producer, producing 245.3 million tons of coal in 2002. Other minerals extracted are cobalt, gold, silver, gem-quality emeralds, diamonds and copper. The wealth of Zambia is based largely on mining in the rich copper belt.

THE COPPER BELT

For many Least Developed Countries, a substantial proportion of the country's export earnings is from the production and processing of primary commodities, such as copper. The Copper Belt, with mines that cover the towns around Ndola, Kitwe, Chingola, Luanshya and Mufulira, is among the richest in the world. Copper in the Copper Belt region is obtained by open-cast methods and shaft mining. The Zambian Copper Belt in its capacity, accounts for about 46 per cent of the production and reserves of the Central African Copper Belt. The population density around the Copper Belt is high.

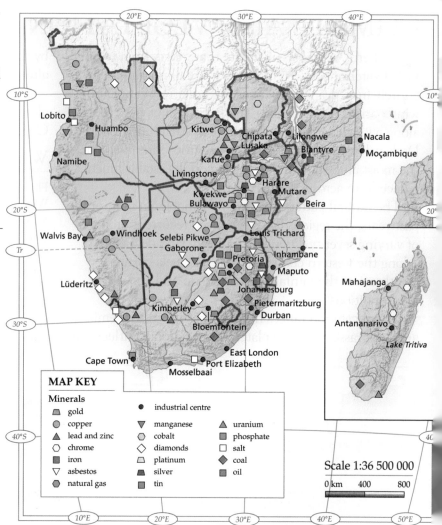

MAP KEY

Minerals

⬭ gold	⬤ industrial centre		
⬤ copper	▽ manganese	△ uranium	
△ lead and zinc	◓ cobalt	▢ phosphate	
◯ chrome	◇ diamonds	☐ salt	
⬤ iron	⬓ platinum	◆ coal	
▽ asbestos	⬛ silver	▢ oil	
⬡ natural gas	▪ tin		

Scale 1:36 500 000

0 km   400   800

Kitwe is the largest city in Zambia's Copperbelt Province

TOURISM AND WILDLIFE

Tourism is Southern Africa's fourth-largest industry, supporting some 700 hotels, 2800 guest-houses and bed and breakfast establishments and 10 000 restaurants. One in every nine jobs in the region is linked to tourism, and some 740 000 jobs in South Africa are created by the tourism economy.

The fastest growing segment of tourism in Southern Africa is ecological tourism (ecotourism), which includes nature photography, bird watching, botanical studies, snorkelling, hiking and mountaineering.

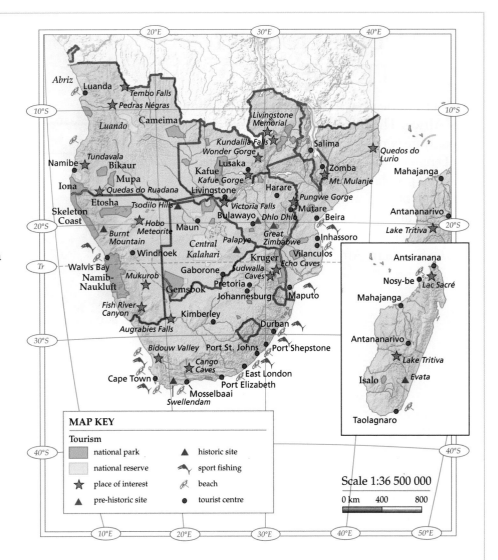

MAP KEY

Tourism

national park	▲ historic site
national reserve	🐟 sport fishing
⭐ place of interest	🦀 beach
▲ pre-historic site	● tourist centre

Scale 1:36 500 000

0 km 400 800

Victoria Falls

Kruger National Park

TRADE, INDUSTRY AND TRANSPORT

South Africa is the most industrialised country in Africa. The main industries include chemicals, food, transport equipment, iron and steel. The metal and engineering sector employs an estimated 325 000 people by over 900 companies.

Many other Southern African countries, such as Namibia and Botswana, have industrial development programmes in place, which are frequently reviewed by the Southern African Development Community.

Steam engine pulling trucks of mined ore to a processing plant in South Africa

MAP KEY

Communications
— major road
— minor road
— railway
⊕ international airport
⊕ major port

Settlements
■ capital city
○ other town

Industry
⚗ chemicals
⚙ engineering
🍶 food and drink processing
🧵 leather and textiles
🛢 oil refining
🚗 vehicle assembly

Scale 1:25 600 000
(projection: Lambert Azimuthal Equal Area)

0 km   400   800   1 200

AGRICULTURE

A large number of the population in Southern Africa are dependent on agriculture. There are many new developments and innovations in the sector. The countries are frequently affected by climate change. Among the new technologies is conservation agriculture, particularly for the subsistence farmers; others are vermiculture, and sustainable agriculture. Agriculture is centred around food security. Southern Africa grows maize on a large scale.

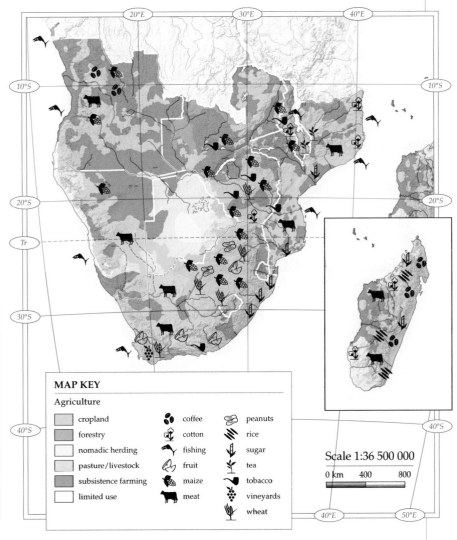

MAP KEY

Agriculture

cropland	
forestry	
nomadic herding	
pasture/livestock	
subsistence farming	
limited use	

- coffee
- cotton
- fishing
- fruit
- maize
- meat
- peanuts
- rice
- sugar
- tea
- tobacco
- vineyards
- wheat

Scale 1:36 500 000

0 km   400   800

Maize farm in Southern Africa

Sheep farming in Southern Africa

Vineyard in the Cape, South Africa

COUNTRIES AND RELIEF

Most of the African continent lies between the tropics of Cancer and Capricorn, and experiences high temperatures throughout the year. There is a great variation in precipitation characterised by high annual rainfall in the central tropical zone, and hot dry arid zones that form the greater part of North Africa and of the south western part of the southern Africa region. The inter-tropics account for most of the drainage, with big rivers and lakes in the Congo and in the Nile Basin of the central African region.

REGIONAL ORGANISATIONS, INDUSTRY AND TRADE

Most African countries have joined together with other countries to form economic organisations. These organisations are mainly established to promote regional economic co-operation through creation of common markets with free movement of goods and complete elimination of trade barriers. Some economic organisations also serve the purpose of ensuring regional political solidarity and peace.

COMESA (Common Market for Eastern and Southern Africa) established in 1994, is composed of 19 countries: Burundi, Comoros, Democratic Republic of Congo (DRC), Djibouti, Egypt, Eritrea, Ethiopia, Kenya, Libya, Madagascar, Malawi, Mauritius, Rwanda, Seychelles, Sudan, Swaziland, Uganda, Zambia and Zimbabwe.

ECCAS (Economic Community of Central African States) established in 1983, is composed of 11 countries: Angola, Burundi, Cameroon, Central African Republic (CAR), Chad, Congo, DRC, Equatorial Guinea, Gabon, Rwanda and São Tomé and Principe. The main purpose of the community is to form a common market with free movement of people, goods and services, but it has not been active since 1992 due to non-payment of fees by some member states.

ECOWAS (Economic Community of West African States) established in 1975, is composed of 15 countries: Benin, Burkina Faso, Cape Verde, Gambia, Ghana, Guinea, Guinea Bissau, Ivory Coast, Liberia, Mali, Niger, Nigeria, Senegal, Sierra Leone and Togo. The main purpose is to promote co-operation in economic, social and cultural fields and in the development of the region.

SADC (Southern African Development Community) established in 1980, is composed of 15 countries: Angola, Botswana, DRC, Lesotho, Madagascar, Malawi, Mauritius, Mozambique, Namibia, Seychelles, South Africa, Swaziland, Tanzania, Zambia and Zimbabwe. In addition to the promotion of economic integration and the elimination of trade barriers, SADC also acts as a political organisation that maintains solidarity and peace in the region.

EAC (East African Community) re-established in 1999, and formerly composed of three countries: Kenya, Tanzania and Uganda but now five countries including Rwanda and Burundi, which were integrated in 2007. The world's newest country, the Republic of Southern Sudan, is likely to join the bloc. The main purpose of the community is to form customs union, create a common market and eliminate trade barriers for sustainable development and security in the region.

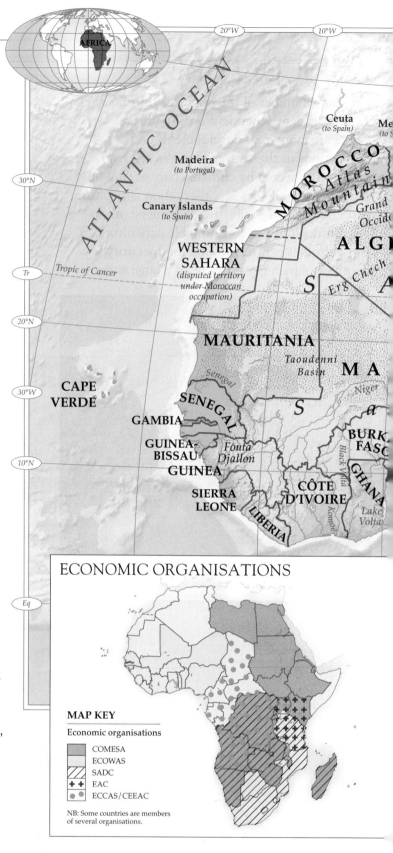

ECONOMIC ORGANISATIONS

MAP KEY

Economic organisations

- COMESA
- ECOWAS
- SADC
- ++ EAC
- ●● ECCAS/CEEAC

NB: Some countries are members of several organisations.

AU (African Union): formerly known as OAU (Organization of African Unity) but changed names and objectives in September 1999. Composed of 53 African states, the main objectives include the achievement of greater unity and solidarity between the African countries and the peoples of Africa; defence of the sovereignty, territorial integrity and independence of its member states; accelerating the political and socio-economic integration of the continent; promoting and defending African common positions on issues of interest to the continent and its peoples; encouraging international co-operation, taking due account of the Charter of the United Nations and the Universal Declaration of Human Rights; and promoting peace, security and stability on the continent.

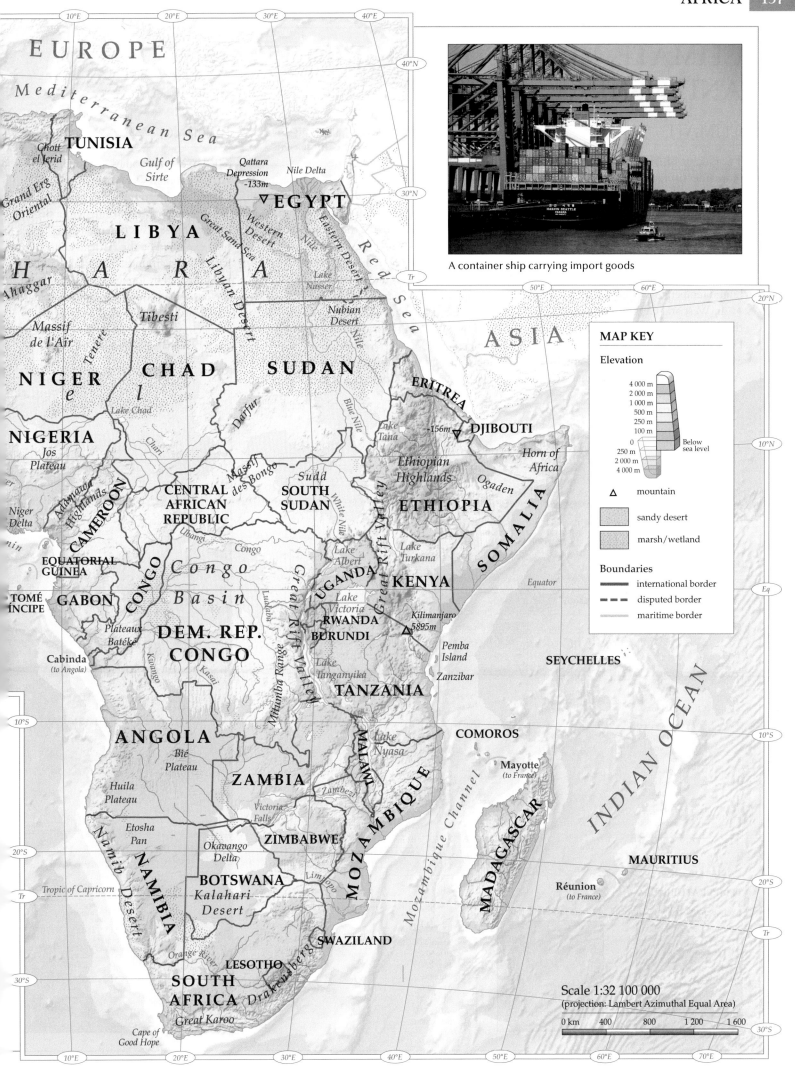

EUROPE

Mediterranean Sea

*Chott
el Jerid* **TUNISIA**

*Gulf of
Sirte*

*Qattara
Depression
-133m*

Nile Delta

▽ **EGYPT**

L I B Y A

*Grand Erg
Oriental*

Great Sand Sea

*Western
Desert*

Libyan Desert

Nile

Eastern Desert

40°N

30°N

S A H A R A

Ahaggar

*Massif
de l'Air*

Tibesti

*Lake
Nasser*

*Nubian
Desert*

Red Sea

A container ship carrying import goods

N I G E R

C H A D

Ténéré

Air

Lake Chad

Darfur

S U D A N

Blue Nile

ERITREA

Nile

ASIA

20°N

NIGERIA

*Jos
Plateau*

Chari

*Massif
des Bongo*

Sudd

**SOUTH
SUDAN**

*Lake
Tana*

-156m ▽ **DJIBOUTI**

*Ethiopian
Highlands*

*Horn of
Africa*

10°N

*Niger
Delta*

*Adamawa
Highlands*

**CENTRAL
AFRICAN
REPUBLIC**

Ubangi

White Nile

ETHIOPIA

Ogaden

MAP KEY

Elevation

4 000 m
2 000 m
1 000 m
500 m
250 m
100 m
0
250 m
2 000 m
4 000 m

Below
sea level

CAMEROON

**EQUATORIAL
GUINEA**

Congo

*Congo
Basin*

*Lake
Albert*

Great Rift Valley

*Lake
Turkana*

SOMALIA

△ mountain

**TOMÉ
ÍNCIPE**

GABON

CONGO

UGANDA

*Lake
Victoria*

KENYA

Equator

sandy desert

marsh/wetland

Eq

*Plateaux
Batéké*

**DEM. REP.
CONGO**

Lualaba

RWANDA

BURUNDI

*Kilimanjaro
5895m* △

Boundaries

international border

*Cabinda
(to Angola)*

Kwango

Kasai

Great Rift Valley

Mitumba Range

*Pemba
Island*

SEYCHELLES

disputed border

maritime border

*Lake
Tanganyika*

TANZANIA

Zanzibar

10°S

ANGOLA

*Bié
Plateau*

COMOROS

INDIAN OCEAN

*Huíla
Plateau*

ZAMBIA

*Lake
Nyasa*

MALAWI

*Mayotte
(to France)*

*Etosha
Pan*

*Okavango
Delta*

Zambezi

*Victoria
Falls*

ZIMBABWE

MOZAMBIQUE

Mozambique Channel

MADAGASCAR

MAURITIUS

20°S

NAMIBIA

Namib Desert

BOTSWANA

*Kalahari
Desert*

Limpopo

*Réunion
(to France)*

Tropic of Capricorn

SWAZILAND

Orange River

LESOTHO

Scale 1:32 100 000
(projection: Lambert Azimuthal Equal Area)

**SOUTH
AFRICA**

Drakensberg

Great Karoo

0 km   400   800   1 200   1 600

*Cape of
Good Hope*

30°S

CLIMATE, VEGETATION, AGRICULTURE AND FISHING

CLIMATE

The climate of Africa, as an average pattern of weather over a period of time, is generally uniform north and south of the Equator. However, climate is influenced by altitude above sea level. Regions around the Equator are the hottest.

Africa's climatic zones fall into three broad categories: humid equatorial, dry, and humid temperate Mediterranean.

• In West and Central Africa, along the Guinea Coast, in Gabon, Cameroon, Democratic Republic of the Congo, north-eastern Republic of the Congo and in Eastern Africa the climate is humid equatorial.

• North and south of the equator are the dry tropical regions, where the dry seasons are longer than the wet season.

• Further to the north the Sahel region stretches from east to west through Mali, Niger, Chad and Sudan, and borders the Sahara and, in the south, the Namib and Kalahari deserts. In the deserts, rainfall is extremely scarce and temperatures are very high during the day due to the lack of plants and moisture and very cold at night.

• The coastal regions of North Africa and the southern tip of Africa experience temperate or Mediterranean climate, including dry summers and wet winters, due to their proximity to the oceans.

FISHING

The large water bodies surrounding Africa – Indian Ocean, Atlantic Ocean, Mediterranean Sea and the Red Sea – form potential fishing grounds. Unfortunately, this potential is yet to be fully exploited by the African countries with fishing grounds. The fishing industry is dominated by foreign companies from the developed countries. Morocco, South Africa and Egypt are the leading fish producing countries in Africa. Egypt has the most developed fishing industry.

MAP KEY

Climate regions

- warm temperate
- mediterranean
- semi-arid
- arid
- tropical
- humid equatorial
- mountain

Local winds

→ cold wind
→ hot wind

Scale 1:78 280 000

0 km   1 000   2 000

TEMPERATURE

Average January temperature

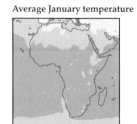

Average July temperature

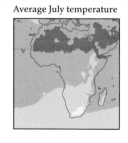

Temperature key

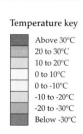

- Above 30°C
- 20 to 30°C
- 10 to 20°C
- 0 to 10°C
- 0 to -10°C
- -10 to -20°C
- -20 to -30°C
- Below -30°C

VEGETATION

The vegetation that will grow in an area is determined primarily by the climate and the type of soil. The variety of climate and soil conditions that occurs in Africa has produced a great diversity of plant species – each well adapted to and characteristic of the particular region in which it is found.

Plant communities in Africa include tropical rain forest, tropical deciduous forest and scrub, savanna, desert shrub and mountain vegetation. By comparing the map of natural vegetation with the climate map we can see that the plant communities or vegetation follow roughly the same pattern as the climates.

Most of Egypt relies on water from the River Nile for industrial and domestic use. The flat, fertile flood plains next to the river are used intensively for farming. The annual floods are now controlled upstream by the Aswan High Dam.

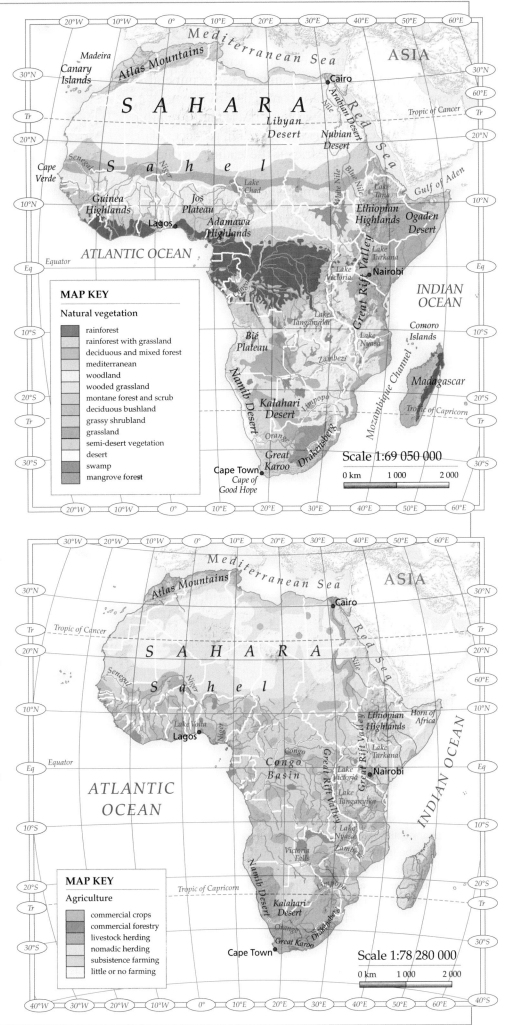

MAP KEY

Natural vegetation
- rainforest
- rainforest with grassland
- deciduous and mixed forest
- mediterranean
- woodland
- wooded grassland
- montane forest and scrub
- deciduous bushland
- grassy shrubland
- grassland
- semi-desert vegetation
- desert
- swamp
- mangrove forest

Scale 1:69 050 000

0 km   1 000   2 000

AGRICULTURE

Crop farming and livestock keeping in Africa is influenced by the different agro-climatic zones prevailing in the continent. Subsistence and commercial farming are dominant in most parts of the continent, while pastoralism is common in the Horn of Africa. Despite its semi-arid and arid conditions, the continent is known for large scale plantation agriculture. For example, Africa is the leading producer of cocoa in the world. Most of the cocoa is produced in West Africa, with Ghana and Côte d'Ivoire being the leading producers.

MAP KEY

Agriculture
- commercial crops
- commercial forestry
- livestock herding
- nomadic herding
- subsistence farming
- little or no farming

Scale 1:78 280 000

0 km   1 000   2 000

MINING AND ENERGY

Africa is rich in mineral and energy resources. Extracting and processing a range of mineral resources is an important contributor to the continent's economy. Nigeria is the leading producer of oil in Africa, Zambia is the leading producer of copper, while South Africa is the leading producer of gold. Unfortunately, the presence of mineral and energy resources in countries such as Nigeria (oil) and Sierra Leone (diamonds) has led to internal conflicts and wars over the resources.

Energy oil well, Hassi, Messaoud, Algeria

MINERAL RESOURCES

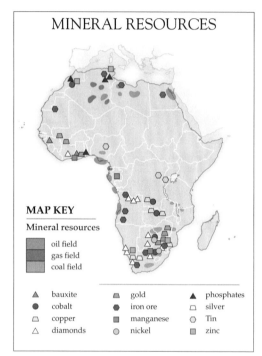

MAP KEY

Mineral resources

▬	oil field
▬	gas field
▬	coal field

▲	bauxite	◢	gold	▲	phosphates
●	cobalt	⬢	iron ore	△	silver
⬠	copper	■	manganese	○	Tin
△	diamonds	●	nickel	■	zinc

AFRICA'S HYDRO-ELECTRIC POWER POTENTIAL

The rivers of Africa have a hydro-electric power potential greater than that of any other single continent in the world, except Asia. African countries have harnessed this potential through a number of hydro-electric power projects such as Kariba in Zimbabwe and Zambia, Aswan in Egypt, Akosombo in Ghana, Kainji in Nigeria, Cahora Bassa in Mozambique, Seven Forks in Kenya and Owen Falls in Uganda. With the effects of climate change, a number of countries are presently exploiting the use of wind, geothermal and nuclear power to generate electricity.

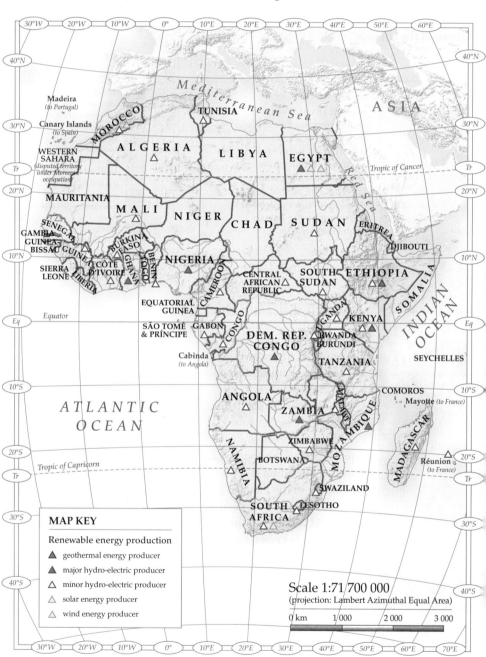

MAP KEY

Renewable energy production

▲	geothermal energy producer
▲	major hydro-electric producer
△	minor hydro-electric producer
△	solar energy producer
△	wind energy producer

Scale 1:71 700 000
(projection: Lambert Azimuthal Equal Area)

0 km   1 000   2 000   3 000

AFRICA'S RENEWABLE ENERGY PRODUCTION

The potential for Africa's geothermal resources is concentrated in the Great African Rift Valley. Despite this potential, only Kenya, Ethiopia and Zambia have geothermal power stations. From the map above, other sources of renewable energy resources can be identified as wind, solar and hydroelectricity.

POPULATION

Africa is the second largest continent after Asia, but its population is just over a sixth of the world's population. Most of Africa's population lives in areas with a reliable water supply, in wetter tropical countries. Nigeria has the largest population in Africa with an estimated population of 170 million and ranks eighth on the list of world's most populated countries, while the least populated individual country in Africa is the Seychelles, with an estimated population of around 84 000. Namibia and the Islamic Republic of Mauritania are the least densely populated countries in Africa with 2.9 people/km^2 and 3.0 people/km^2 respectively and Mauritius is the most densely populated country in Africa with 631.53 people/km^2. Cairo in Egypt ranks first in Africa and eleventh worldwide as the largest urban area with 19.9 million.

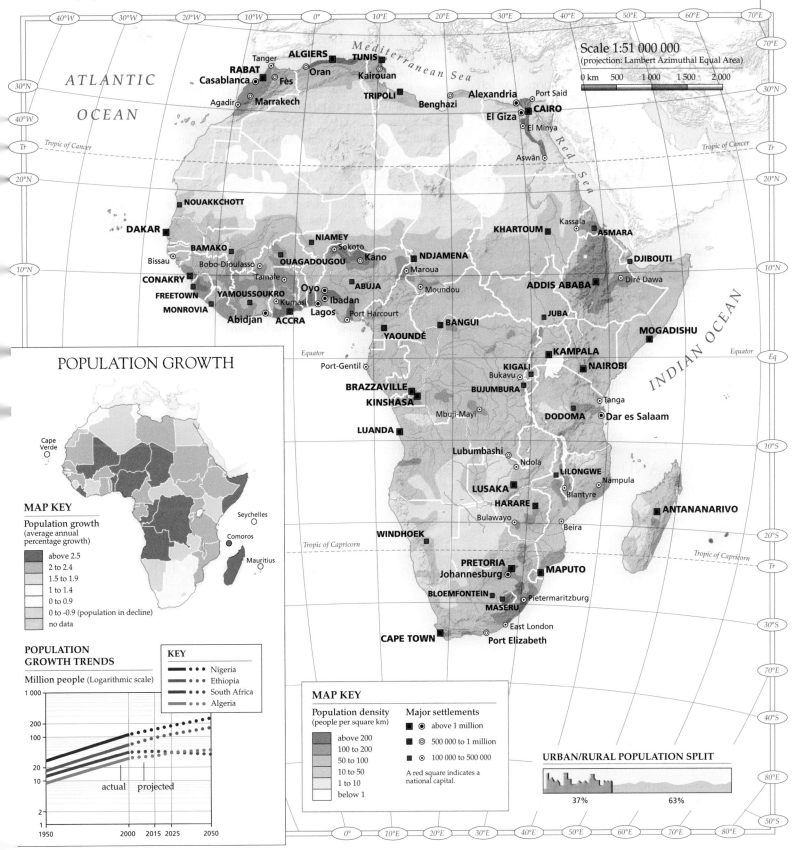

Scale 1:51 000 000
(projection: Lambert Azimuthal Equal Area)

0 km   500   1 000   1 500   2 000

POPULATION GROWTH

MAP KEY

Population growth
(average annual percentage growth)

- above 2.5
- 2 to 2.4
- 1.5 to 1.9
- 1 to 1.4
- 0 to 0.9
- 0 to -0.9 (population in decline)
- no data

POPULATION GROWTH TRENDS

Million people (Logarithmic scale)

KEY
- • • • Nigeria
- • • • Ethiopia
- • • • South Africa
- • • • Algeria

1 000
200
100
20
10
2
1

actual   projected

1950   2000   2015 2025   2050

MAP KEY

Population density
(people per square km)

- above 200
- 100 to 200
- 50 to 100
- 10 to 50
- 1 to 10
- below 1

Major settlements

- ■ ⊙ above 1 million
- ■ ⊙ 500 000 to 1 million
- ■ ⊙ 100 000 to 500 000

A red square indicates a national capital.

URBAN/RURAL POPULATION SPLIT

37%   63%

TRANSPORT AND TRADE

Transport networks in Africa consist of roads, railway lines, air and water. As engines of economic integration, transport infrastructure and service facilities constitute a precondition for facilitating trade and the movement of goods and persons. The increasing volume of imports and exports has not been accompanied by a similar increase in the rate of development of the transport systems of Africa. This, together with the challenges of globalisation, has left Africa trailing significantly behind in the development of regional trade, particularly because of the lack of reliable and adequate transport.

TRADE

In general, apart from a few emerging countries such as the South Africa, Egypt, Nigeria and Kenya, the industrial sector in Africa is not well developed. Most others countries' industrial sectors are still dominated by the primary sector although the current focus is to move as fast as possible into secondary, tertiary and quaternary sectors. Most African countries depend on imported commodities, which negatively affect their balance of trade, because expenditure on imported goods outweighs by far the income generated from exports.

EXPORTS AND IMPORTS

The main imported commodities are machinery and equipment, chemicals, petroleum products, scientific instruments and foodstuffs.

The main exported commodities are palm oil, gold and diamonds, oil, cocoa, timber and precious metals.

MARITIME TRANSPORT

Sea ports are fundamental outlets of international trade for both coastal and land-locked countries. Sea transport has a significant cost advantage over surface transport for dry and liquid bulk cargoes or containerised cargo.

The importance of maritime transport emanates from the fact that over 90 per cent of the world international trade transits through ports. Maritime transport is even more dominant in Africa as it accounts for 92 to 97 per cent of Africa's international trade. However, poorly maintained port infrastructure and inefficient operations remain major bottlenecks for African trade.

AIR TRANSPORT

In 2007, Africa had about 4000 airports and airfields of which only 20 per cent had paved runways. The vast majority of airports serve only smaller aircrafts for domestic services. A significant number of Africa's airports do not meet ICAO standards and recommended practices.

Runways, taxiways, parking spaces and passenger and freight terminals, as well as cargo handling and electro-mechanical equipment, are in such a poor condition that they require major rehabilitation and upgrading.

RAIL TRANSPORT

Railways are the most cost-effective mode of transport for moving bulk cargo for long distances over land. The railways in Africa carry only 1 per cent of the global railway passenger traffic and 2 per cent of the goods traffic. Railway connectivity is very low.

SUB-SAHARAN AFRICA'S IMPORTS				
Country	2005 ($ billions)	2005 (% Market share)	2006 ($ billions)	2006 (% Market share)
China	13.4	7.8	19.0	8.9
Germany	11.7	6.8	13.0	6.1
United States	10.3	6.0	12.1	5.6
France	10.8	6.3	11.3	5.3
United Kingdom	8.1	4.7	8.9	4.1
Japan	6.3	3.6	7.2	3.3
Italy	4.8	2.8	5.5	2.6
Spain	2.4	1.4	2.7	1.3
Total EU	54.7	31.7	62.3	29.0

SUB-SAHARAN AFRICA'S EXPORTS				
Country	2005 ($ billions)	2005 (% Market share)	2006 ($ billions)	2006 (% Market share)
United States	52.4	29.6	61.5	29.5
China	19.3	10.9	26.3	12.6
United Kingdom	12.6	7.1	13.0	6.2
Japan	9.4	5.3	12.5	6.0
Spain	9.3	5.2	10.8	5.2
France	8.6	4.9	9.2	4.4
Germany	7.1	4.0	8.5	4.1
Italy	6.3	3.6	7.4	3.6
Total EU	61.2	34.6	66.7	32.0

ENVIRONMENT

Africa has a wide range of terrestrial, aquatic, atmospheric and human environments. The terrestrial or land environment consists of natural ecosystems and built-up areas. The aquatic or water environment is composed of marine and coastal ecosystems, inland fresh water and saline lakes and a network of periodic and permanent rivers. The interaction between land, water and the atmosphere leads to Africa's rich biodiversity.

MAJOR ENVIRONMENTAL CONCERNS

The major environmental concerns in Africa include:

1. Loss of forests and forest land
2. Loss of wetlands and dwindling water resources
3. Loss of biodiversity
4. Population increase and urbanisation
5. Over exploitation and utilisation of natural resources
6. Pollution and environmental degradation
7. Climate-change and its potential impacts
8. Poverty versus environmental conservation

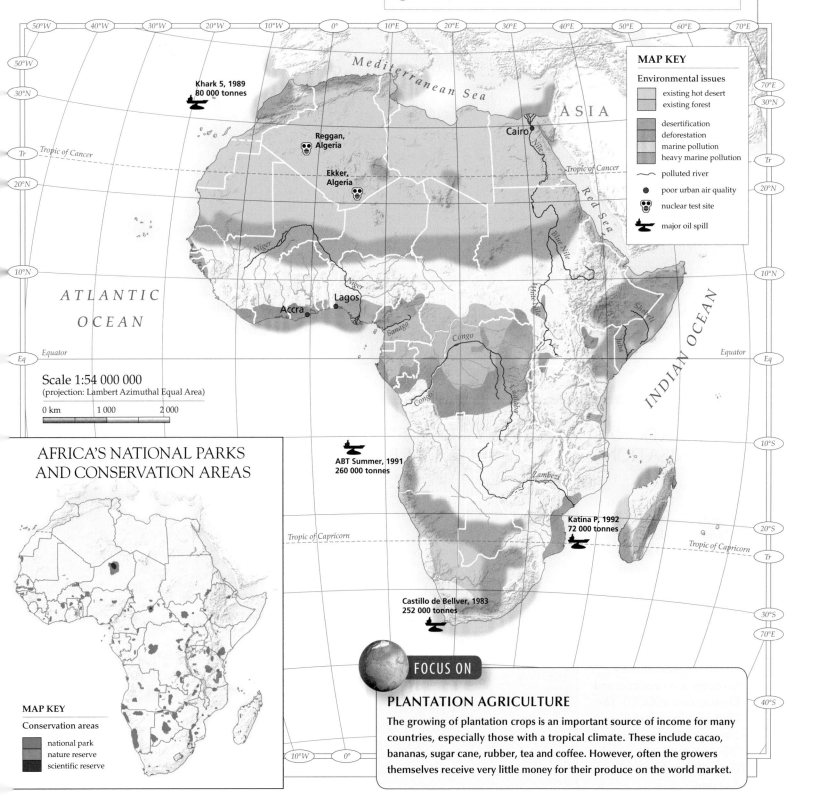

Khark 5, 1989
80 000 tonnes

Reggan,
Algeria

Ekker,
Algeria

Cairo

ABT Summer, 1991
260 000 tonnes

Katina P, 1992
72 000 tonnes

Castillo de Bellver, 1983
252 000 tonnes

Scale 1:54 000 000
(projection: Lambert Azimuthal Equal Area)

0 km   1 000   2 000

MAP KEY

Environmental issues

- existing hot desert
- existing forest
- desertification
- deforestation
- marine pollution
- heavy marine pollution
- polluted river
- poor urban air quality
- nuclear test site
- major oil spill

AFRICA'S NATIONAL PARKS AND CONSERVATION AREAS

MAP KEY

Conservation areas

- national park
- nature reserve
- scientific reserve

FOCUS ON

PLANTATION AGRICULTURE

The growing of plantation crops is an important source of income for many countries, especially those with a tropical climate. These include cacao, bananas, sugar cane, rubber, tea and coffee. However, often the growers themselves receive very little money for their produce on the world market.

COUNTRIES AND RELIEF

The world's third largest continent, North America, is made up of Canada, Mexico, the United States and the offshore islands of the Caribbean. It can be divided into a number of distinctive physical regions. The major mountains of the Western Cordillera in the west give way to the Great Plains in central Canada and the USA, drained by the Mississippi River into the Gulf of Mexico.

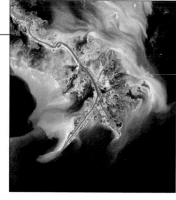

This satellite image shows the Mississippi River draining into the Gulf of Mexico. The Mississippi is 3779 km long and its drainage basin covers 2 979 000 km². The light blue areas in this photograph are sediments, which the river picks up and carries along as it flows towards the sea.

INTERNATIONAL ORGANISATIONS

The United States of America (USA) is known as a 'superpower' and is highly influential in global politics. It is a member of several international organisations including: the G8 countries; NATO; The North American Free Trade Agreement (NAFTA); Organisation of American States (OAS) and the Organisation for Economic Co-operation and Development (OECD). The USA has often carried out interventionist policies in other countries, for example, in the Afghanistan and Iraq wars.

Scale 1:47 400 000
(projection: Lambert Azimuthal Equal Area)

0 km   500   1 000   1 500

MAP KEY

Elevation

4 000 m
2 000 m
1 000 m
500 m
250 m
100 m
0
250 m
2 000 m
4 000 m
Below sea level

△ mountain
⌂ volcano
▽ depression

Plate boundaries

— constructive
—△— destructive
- - - conservative
····· uncertain

Settlements

■ over 1 million
■ 500 000 to 1 million
■ 100 000 to 500 000
■ 50 000 to 100 000
■ under 50 000

A red square indicates a national or administrative capital.

Boundaries

— international border
— maritime border

CLIMATE AND VEGETATION

Much of Canada, the USA and the Caribbean is rich farmland producing a range of crops and livestock. There are, however, large parts of the continent that are desert, mountain and ice, which are largely unproductive. Both Canada and the USA have a great variety of natural resources, providing a base for industrial activity and economic development.

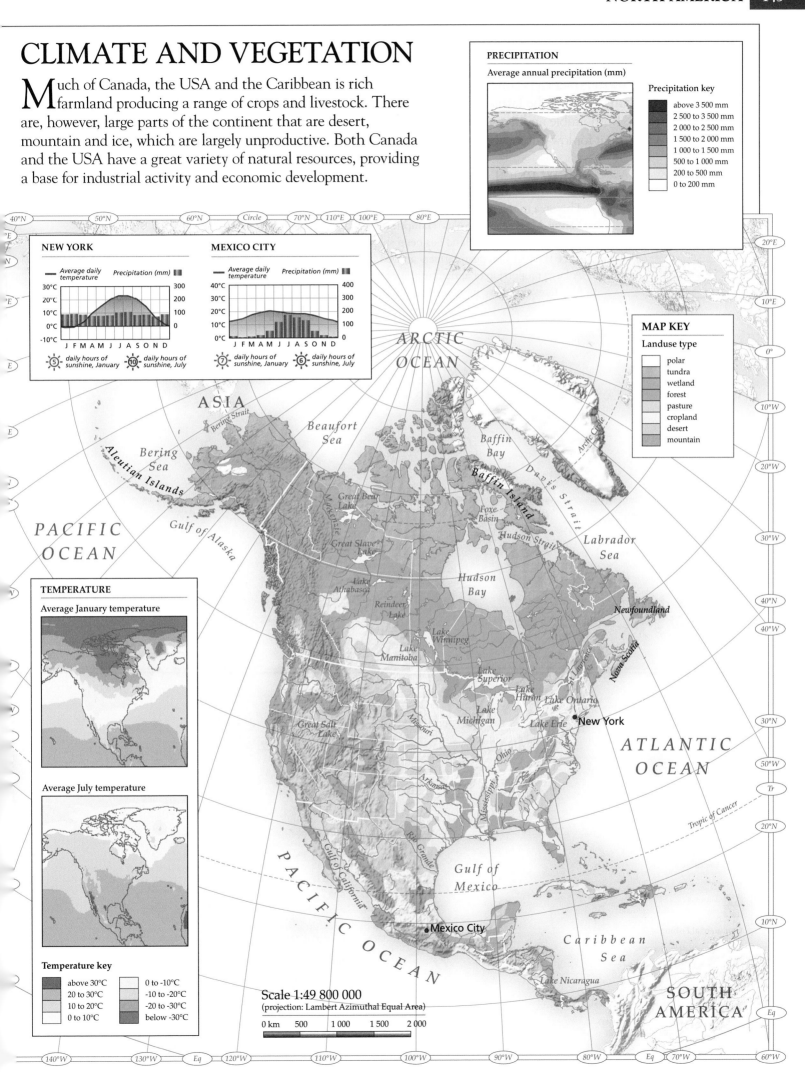

PRECIPITATION
Average annual precipitation (mm)

Precipitation key
- above 3 500 mm
- 2 500 to 3 500 mm
- 2 000 to 2 500 mm
- 1 500 to 2 000 mm
- 1 000 to 1 500 mm
- 500 to 1 000 mm
- 200 to 500 mm
- 0 to 200 mm

NEW YORK
— Average daily temperature
Precipitation (mm)
30°C / 20°C / 10°C / 0°C / -10°C
300 / 200 / 100 / 0
J F M A M J J A S O N D
daily hours of sunshine, January — 5
daily hours of sunshine, July — 10

MEXICO CITY
— Average daily temperature
Precipitation (mm)
40°C / 30°C / 20°C / 10°C / 0°C
400 / 300 / 200 / 100 / 0
J F M A M J J A S O N D
daily hours of sunshine, January — 7
daily hours of sunshine, July — 6

MAP KEY
Landuse type
- polar
- tundra
- wetland
- forest
- pasture
- cropland
- desert
- mountain

TEMPERATURE
Average January temperature

Average July temperature

Temperature key
- above 30°C
- 20 to 30°C
- 10 to 20°C
- 0 to 10°C
- 0 to -10°C
- -10 to -20°C
- -20 to -30°C
- below -30°C

Scale 1:49 800 000
(projection: Lambert Azimuthal Equal Area)

0 km   500   1 000   1 500   2 000

AGRICULTURE, LIVESTOCK, FORESTRY AND FISHING

Agriculture in North America is concentrated in the central plains. Most of the farms are large and highly mechanised. Both arable and livestock farming are based on a low-input-for-low-output model.

From the 1990s, genetically modified (GM) crops were grown. In the USA, soya beans are increasingly the most commonly grown GM food. Abundant natural resources provide a base for the forestry and fishing industries.

NEW ENGLAND, USA

This area in the northeast of the USA encompasses six states: Connecticut, Maine, Massachusetts, New Hampshire, Rhode Island and Vermont. The landscape of New England has been shaped by grain and dairy production since the first European farmers arrived in the early seventeenth century. A large proportion of agricultural income is generated from exports to other US states that have more service-based economies.

MAP KEY

Agriculture

- shifting cultivation
- subsistence - mixed
- commercial - grain
- commercial - mixed
- specialised - market gardening
- extensive livestock rearing
- intensive livestock rearing
- dairying
- nomadic herding
- limited use

Forestry

- softwood
- mixed softwood & hardwood

Commercial Fishing

- commercial fishing areas

Scale 1:50 000 000
(projection: Lambert Azimuthal Equal Area)

0 km   500   1 000   1 500   2 000

FORESTRY IN CANADA

Forest covers 45 per cent of Canada's land area and the country is the world's biggest exporter of timber. Canada contains 10 per cent of the world's total forest cover, including over 30 per cent of global boreal forest and 20 per cent of global temperate rainforest.

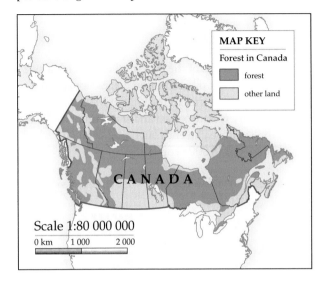

MAP KEY

Forest in Canada

- forest
- other land

CANADA

Scale 1:80 000 000

0 km   1 000   2 000

This area of forest, near Vancouver, British Columbia, is being clear-cut: all the trees in one area have been felled for timber.

BRITISH COLUMBIA, CANADA

With the Pacific Ocean at its western border, and possessing over 27 000 km of coastline, British Columbia has a well-established fishing industry. Sheltered bays and clean water provide an ideal environment for finfish and shellfish aquaculture. The largest agricultural export from British Columbia is farmed salmon. A favourable climate enables farmers to grow a wide variety of crops including grain, oilseed, fruit and vines. Livestock production is equally important and agriculture is an expanding industry in the province.

CANADA

BRITISH COLUMBIA

AGRICULTURAL PRODUCTION IN BRITISH COLUMBIA, 2002	
Commodity	**Total production**
Wheat ('000 tonnes)	34.7
Hay ('000 tonnes)	1428.8
Livestock (number of animals slaughtered) Cattle Sheep	50 800 77 100
Milk ('000 litres)	596 319
Egg production ('000 dozen)	67 561
Fish and fish products ('000 tonnes)	293.3

SOUTHERN CALIFORNIA, USA

The Californian coast enjoys a moderate Mediterranean climate cooled by sea breezes, whilst inland the valley landscape is much drier and hotter. Farms are smaller in size than the national average but produce high-value products. Along the coast, avocados, citrus fruits, peaches, vegetables and flowers are grown, whilst in the valleys, farmers grow alfalfa, cotton, citrus, dates, rice and winter vegetables. Farmers need expensive irrigation systems but because water is precious they must be careful how they use it.

UNITED STATES OF AMERICA

CALIFORNIA

Because rainfall in California is low, farmers have to pipe in water to spray onto their fields.

MINING

The USA has an abundance of natural resources, including oil. The 2001 Energy Plan aimed at stepping up the oil exploration and output, thus reducing the need for imports.

The large boat in the centre of this picture is laden with mineral ore. It is leaving Duluth Harbor on the south east of Lake Superior, the largest of the Great Lakes.

CANADA

Canada is a country with an enormous wealth of natural resources. Its minerals play a key role in Canada's transformation into an urban industrial economy. Alberta, British Colombia, Quebec and Saskatchewan are the principal mining regions.

MEXICO

Mexico is one of the largest oil exporters outside OPEC. Most oil production comes from offshore drilling platforms in the Gulf of Mexico. The industry is state owned and state run by PEMEX, the world's eighteenth largest oil company, which employs 138 000 people.

MAP KEY

Mineral resources

- coal field
- natural gas field
- oil field

- bauxite
- copper
- gold
- iron
- lead
- nickel
- phosphates
- silver
- uranium

Scale 1:49 000 000
projection: Lambert Azimuthal Equal Area

0 km   500   1 000   1 500   2 000

TRANSPORT AND COMMUNICATIONS

The Great Lakes, a chain of five large freshwater lakes across northern America, form the largest lake group in the world – covering an area of 246 048 km² (95 000 square miles). The lakes remain a significant transportation route for iron ore, steel, petroleum, grain, American automobiles and much more.

North America has a well connected network of railways, highways, waterways and air transport.

North America has several television networks, both state owned and private. There is a wide range of broadcasting stations and several newspapers are in circulation. 98 per cent of homes have internet access.

View of the Rocky Mountains, Banff National Park, Canada

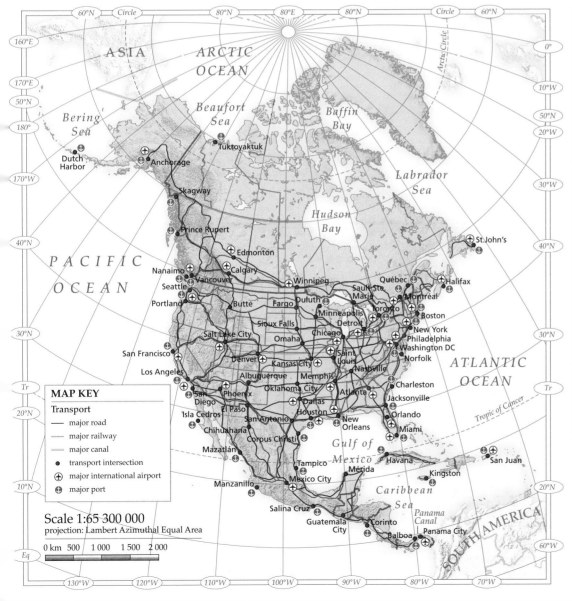

MAP KEY

Transport

— major road
— major railway
— major canal
● transport intersection
⊕ major international airport
⊕ major port

Scale 1:65 300 000
projection: Lambert Azimuthal Equal Area

0 km 500   1 000   1 500   2 000

California Los Angeles interchange

INDUSTRY AND TRADE

Canada and the United States are among the most wealthy and industrialised nations in the world. Mexico now has the ninth largest economy since becoming a member of OECD and a part of NAFTA – an agreement between Canada, the United States and Mexico, to eliminate tariffs on goods traded between themselves.

THE TENNESSEE VALLEY

The Tennessee Valley is an example of an area where high-technology industries have concentrated to produce a 'hot-spot' for research and technology.

UNITED STATES OF AMERICA
Tennessee Valley

The Oak Ridge National Laboratory, Tennessee, is concerned with a wide-ranging programme of science and technology research. Here we can see the Oak Ridge nuclear installation, Y-12, where nuclear weapons are developed.

MAP KEY

Industry

- ✈ aerospace
- ♭ brewing
- 🚗 car / vehicle manufacturing
- ♭ chemicals
- ♠ defence
- ⚡ electronics
- ⚙ engineering
- 🎥 film industry
- Ⓢ finance
- 🍴 food processing
- 💻 hi-tech industry
- 🚃 iron & steel
- ✎ pharmaceuticals
- 📖 printing & publishing
- ☢ research & development
- ⚓ shipbuilding
- ↓ sugar processing
- ⵌ textiles
- 🌲 timber processing
- ➴ tobacco processing
- ▪ coal
- ▲ oil
- ▲ gas
- ● industrial city

Scale 1:49 000 000
projection: Lambert Azimuthal Equal Area

0 km   500   1 000   1 500   2 000

POPULATION

N orth America has one of the largest populations in the world, with the USA having approximately 311 million people, and cities having 'city limits' of 600 000 people. The conurbations along the east and west coasts of the USA are amongst the most densely populated anywhere.

IMMIGRATION

Most Canadians are descendants of immigrants from Britain, France, Ireland and other European countries. There are over 100 different ethnic groups in Canada. In the USA, an immigration boom peaked in the early 1990s, with many new arrivals from Latin America and Asia. Today nearly 50 per cent of the population in the USA is of Latin American origin, and Spanish is very widely spoken, especially in the southern states.

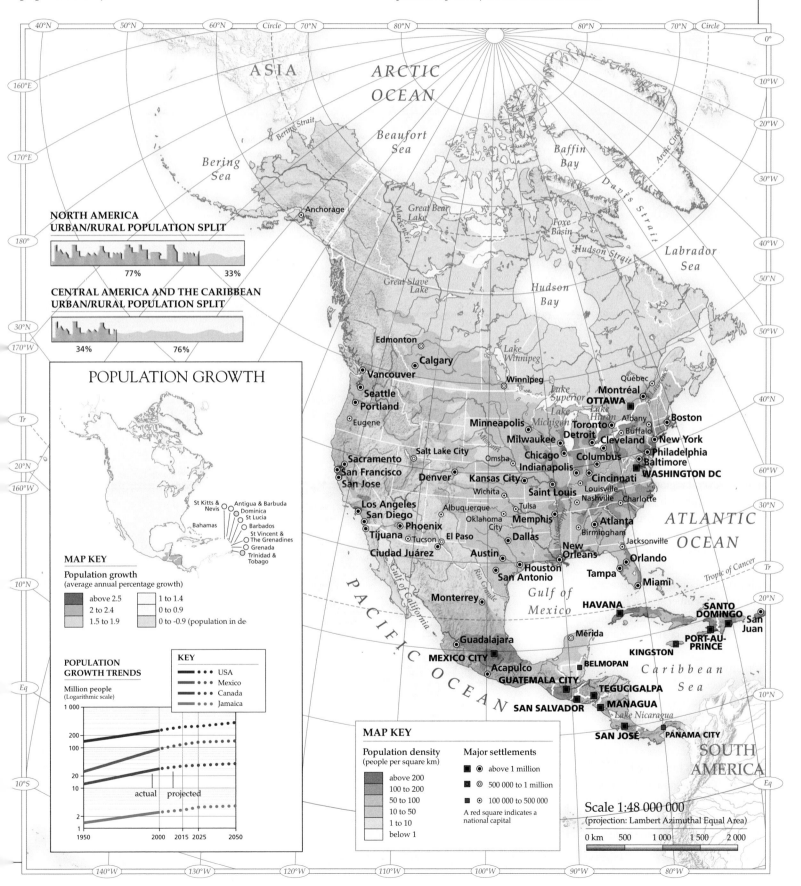

NORTH AMERICA URBAN/RURAL POPULATION SPLIT
77%   33%

CENTRAL AMERICA AND THE CARIBBEAN URBAN/RURAL POPULATION SPLIT
34%   76%

POPULATION GROWTH

St Kitts & Nevis
Antigua & Barbuda
Dominica
St Lucia
Barbados
St Vincent & The Grenadines
Grenada
Trinidad & Tobago
Bahamas

MAP KEY
Population growth
(average annual percentage growth)
- above 2.5
- 2 to 2.4
- 1.5 to 1.9
- 1 to 1.4
- 0 to 0.9
- 0 to -0.9 (population in de

POPULATION GROWTH TRENDS
Million people
(Logarithmic scale)

KEY
- USA
- Mexico
- Canada
- Jamaica

1 000
200
100
20
10
2
actual   projected
1950   2000 2015 2025 2050

MAP KEY

Population density
(people per square km)
- above 200
- 100 to 200
- 50 to 100
- 10 to 50
- 1 to 10
- below 1

Major settlements
- ■ ⦿ above 1 million
- ▪ ◉ 500 000 to 1 million
- ▪ ⊙ 100 000 to 500 000

A red square indicates a national capital

Scale 1:48 000 000
(projection: Lambert Azimuthal Equal Area)

0 km   500   1 000   1 500   2 000

COUNTRIES AND RELIEF

South America, the fourth largest continent in the world, is made up of 12 countries. The continent stretches from 12 degrees north of the Equator to Cape Hope, 56 degrees south. Brazil makes up half the total area of South America.

RELIEF

The Amazon Basin and the Andes mountain range dominate the physical landscape of the continent. South America hosts the world's highest water fall (Angel Falls), the largest river by volume (Amazon River), the longest mountain range (Andes), and the driest place on earth (Atacama Desert in Chile).

REGIONAL ORGANISATIONS

There are several regional organisations in South America. Three of them are Mercosur, Organization of American States and Latin America Integrated Association.

- Mercosur encourages free trade among its member states, Brazil, Argentina, Uruguay and Paraguay. Chile and Bolivia are associate members.
- Organization of American States encourages social and economic growth of the developing countries of Latin America with aid from developed countries, except Venezuela.
- Latin America Integrated Association encourages free trade and its member states are all North and South American countries except Mexico and Venezuela.

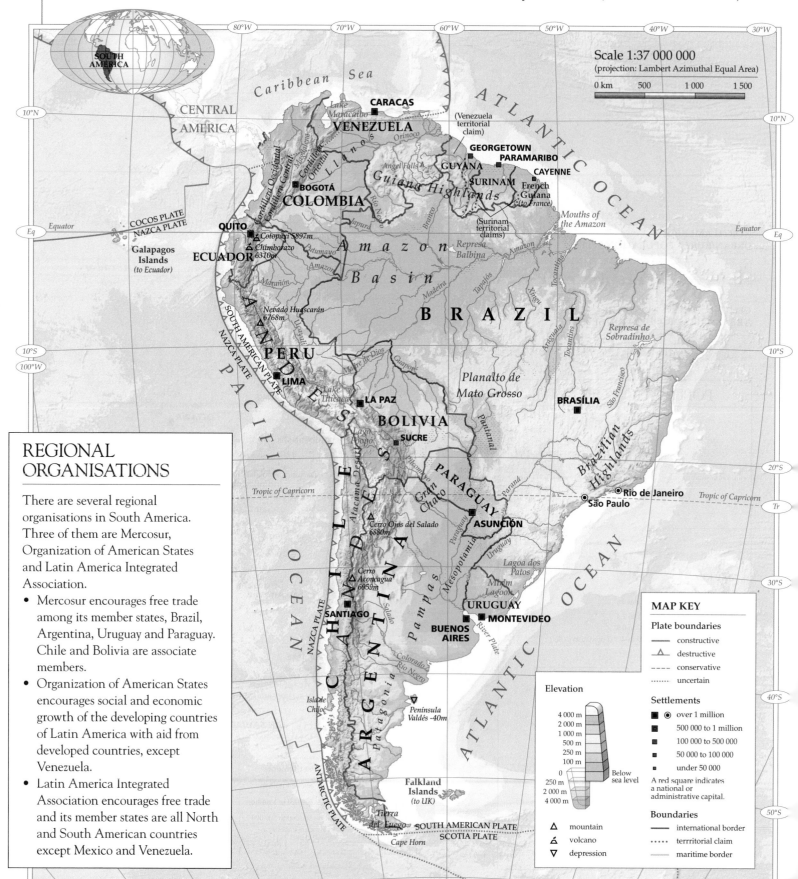

Scale 1:37 000 000
(projection: Lambert Azimuthal Equal Area)

0 km   500   1 000   1 500

MAP KEY

Plate boundaries
— constructive
△ destructive
- - - conservative
······ uncertain

Settlements
■ ⊙ over 1 million
■ 500 000 to 1 million
■ 100 000 to 500 000
■ 50 000 to 100 000
▪ under 50 000
A red square indicates a national or administrative capital.

Elevation
4 000 m
2 000 m
1 000 m
500 m
250 m
100 m
0
250 m
2 000 m
4 000 m
Below sea level

△ mountain
⌃ volcano
▽ depression

Boundaries
— international border
······ terrritorial claim
— maritime border

CLIMATE AND VEGETATION

South America is predominantly wet and hot. However, the continent has varied climatic conditions due to its large size, geographical location, ocean currents and winds. Tropical climate is dominant to the north, highland climate along the Pacific Ocean, and arid and semi-arid conditions to the south. A unique feature about South America's climate is the periodic El Niño rains that affect the drier parts of the continent.

VEGETATION

The vegetation types in South America are largely determined by the continent's climatic zones. Tropical rain forests dominate the northern parts, especially in the Amazon Basin. Drier regions are dominated by grasslands and savanna vegetation.

ENVIRONMENT AND BIODIVERSITY

South America has a wide range of ecosystems and is renowned for its richness in biodiversity. The Amazon rainforest in Brazil is the largest tropical rainforest. It hosts the largest collection of animal and plant species in the world. Most of the ecosystems have been protected because of their ecological importance. Unfortunately, vast tracts of rainforest have been destroyed for farming and other development activities.

Napo Wildlife Center, Yasuni National Park, Amazon Forest, Ecuador

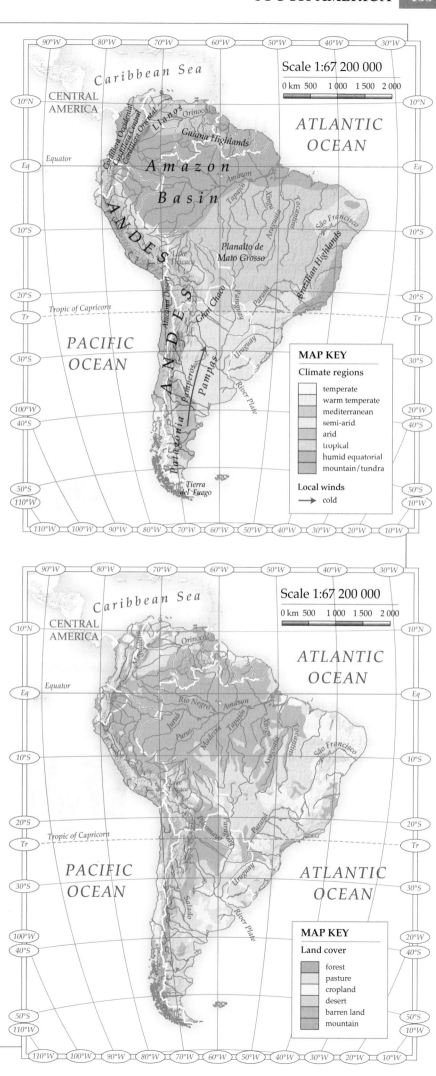

Scale 1:67 200 000

0 km 500   1 000   1 500   2 000

MAP KEY

Climate regions

- temperate
- warm temperate
- mediterranean
- semi-arid
- arid
- tropical
- humid equatorial
- mountain/tundra

Local winds

→ cold

Scale 1:67 200 000

0 km 500   1 000   1 500   2 000

MAP KEY

Land cover

- forest
- pasture
- cropland
- desert
- barren land
- mountain

AGRICULTURE, LIVESTOCK AND FISHING

Agriculture is an important sector of South America's economy. The continent has a variety of crop, livestock and fish products. Coffee is the most important tropical crop, produced mainly in the highlands of Brazil and in central and western Columbia. Other important crops include cacao in Brazil and Colombia, soya beans in Brazil, sugar cane and cotton in Peru, wool and hides in Uruguay and Argentina. Beef farming for export is important in Argentina, Uruguay, Paraguay and Colombia, while large scale fishing is concentrated in Peru, Chile, Guyana, Ecuador and Brazil.

LIVESTOCK PRODUCTION IN ARGENTINA

Cattle and sheep rearing are undertaken on the temperate grassland (pampas) – cattle rearing to the north and sheep rearing to the south west. The major products are beef, mutton, cooking fat and cheese. Livestock production in Argentina is successful because of favourable climatic conditions, the presence of extensive pampas, good transportation networks, adequate capital and good storage facilities, availability of markets, both locally and abroad, better cattle and sheep breeds, and a favourable land tenure system. Argentina, Brazil and Australia are the largest exporters of beef in the world.

MAP KEY

Livestock production

- pasture land
- cattle
- sheep
- cattle/meat packing
- o major conurbation

COFFEE PRODUCTION IN BRAZIL

Brazil started growing coffee in 1870 and produces about one-third of the world's coffee requirements. Brazil is the world's largest coffee producer, with about 27 000 km² of coffee plantations. Coffee is grown in Minas Gerais, São Paulo and Parana states. São Paolo is the market centre and Santos the export exit. Coffee production is successful in Brazil because of its favourable climate, good terrain and transport infrastructure, availability of labour and favourable land tenure.

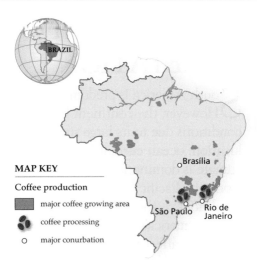

MAP KEY

Coffee production

- major coffee growing area
- coffee processing
- o major conurbation

Coffee plantation in Brazil

Beef farming in Argentina

FISHING IN PERU

Fish farming in Peru is most common in the Amazon, its tributaries and in a large number of ox-bow lakes. Fish farming is thriving in the Amazon due to abundant supplies of warm water, generally available pond inputs, and easily obtainable fingerlings (small fish). Fishing is the most important source of protein, income and livelihood in the Amazon Basin. Integrated aquaculture in the Amazon Basin is one way of protecting and conserving the rainforest ecosystem.

MINING AND ENERGY

South America has a variety of mineral and energy resources. The region's main mineral resources are gold, silver, copper, iron ore, tin and petroleum, largely localised in some countries. Uruguay and Paraguay are particularly devoid of mineral wealth. In terms of energy resources, large quantities of oil and natural gas are located in Venezuela while Brazil is known for hydro-electric power generation and production.

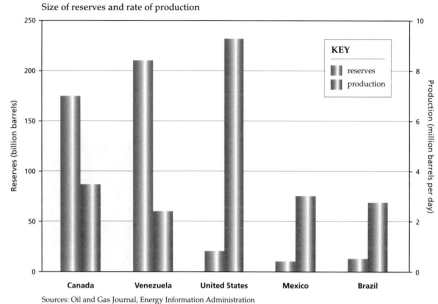

WESTERN HEMISPHERE PROVEN OIL RESERVES (2011) AND PRODUCTION (2010)

Size of reserves and rate of production

KEY
- reserves
- production

Sources: Oil and Gas Journal, Energy Information Administration

MAP KEY

Crude oil in Venezuela

- oil fields
- oil refinery
- ○ major settlement

CRUDE OIL IN VENEZUELA

South America is a crude oil producing continent. Most of the crude oil is produced in Venezuela. The Orinoco River in Venezuela has one of the largest reserves of heavy oil in the world, estimated at 297 billion barrels in 2011.

HYDRO-ELECTRIC POWER IN BRAZIL

Brazil is the largest producer of hydro-electric power in South America. About 20 per cent of the production comes from the Itaipu Dam. The dam is the largest operating hydroelectric facility in terms of annual generating capacity – generating 94.7 TWh in 2008 and 91.6 TWh in 2009. The dam, located on the border of Brazil and Paraguay, is now competing with China's Three Gorges Dam in terms of electricity generation.

Itaipu Dam

COUNTRIES

The breakup of the Soviet Union between 1989 and 1991 ended the political division of Eastern and Western Europe. This greatly changed the map of Europe, creating a number of newly independent countries and democracies. European countries have a history of forming alliances among themselves and beyond, for example NATO, the Warsaw Pact and the European Union.

European Parliament, Strasbourg, Bas-Rhin, France

MAP KEY

Settlements

■ over 1 million

■ 500 000 to 1 million

■ 100 000 to 500 000

■ 50 000 to 100 000

■ below 50 000

A red square indicates a national capital.

Boundaries

— international border

××× ceasefire line

Scale 1:25 300 000
(Projection: Lambert Azimuthal Equal Area)

0 km 250 500 750 1 000

ATLANTIC OCEAN

EUROPE

REYKJAVÍK
ICELAND

Arctic Circle

Norwegian Sea

Faeroe Islands (to Denmark)

Shetland Islands

Outer Hebrides

Scotland

Northern Ireland

IRELAND UNITED
DUBLIN Isle of Man (to UK)
KINGDOM
Wales England
Thames
LONDON

English Channel
Channel Islands (to UK)

Bay of Biscay

FRANCE

PORTUGAL

LISBON

MADRID

SPAIN

Gibraltar (to UK)
Ceuta (to Spain)
Melilla (to Spain)

Balearic Islands

Corsica

Sardinia

Mediterranean Sea

AFRICA

North Sea

DENMARK
COPENHAGEN

NETHERLANDS
AMSTERDAM
THE HAGUE
BELGIUM
BRUSSELS
Rhine
LUXEMBOURG
LUXEMBOURG
PARIS
Seine
Loire

BERN
SWITZERLAND
LIECHTENSTEIN
Po
MONACO

ANDORRA
ANDORRA LA VELLA

NORWAY

OSLO

SWEDEN

STOCKHOLM

FINLAND

HELSINKI

TALLINN
ESTONIA

Baltic Sea
Gulf of Bothnia

LATVIA
RĪGA

LITHUANIA
VILNIUS
RUSS. FED. (Kaliningrad)

White Sea

Northern Dvina

RUSSIAN FEDERATION

Volga

MOSCOW

MINSK
BELARUS

POLAND
BERLIN
WARSAW
Vistula

GERMANY
PRAGUE
CZECH REPUBLIC
VIENNA
AUSTRIA
BRATISLAVA
SLOVAKIA
BUDAPEST
HUNGARY
LJUBLJANA
SLOVENIA
ZAGREB
CROATIA
ITALY
SAN MARINO
BOSNIA & HERZEGOVINA
SARAJEVO
VATICAN CITY
ROME

KIEV

UKRAINE

CHIŞINĂU
MOLDOVA

ROMANIA
BUCHAREST

BELGRADE
SERBIA
Danube

MONTENEGRO
PODGORICA
KOSOVO (disputed)
PRIŠTINË
SKOPJE
MACEDONIA
TIRANA
ALBANIA

BULGARIA
SOFIA

Sea of Azov

Black Sea

TURKEY

GREECE
ATHENS

Tyrrhenian Sea

Sicily

Ionian Sea

MALTA
VALLETTA

Aegean Sea

Crete

ASIA

TURKEY

TURKISH REPUBLIC OF NORTHERN CYPRUS
(recognised only by Turkey)

CYPRUS NICOSIA

RELIEF

Europe is classed as a continent, although it is part of the Asian land mass. It has a wide range of landscape and scenery. The northern Europe plain is an area of unbroken lowland stretching for 4000 km across central and Eastern Europe, bordered to the south by the Alps and the Pyrenees and eroded plateau or massifs. To the north are the older mountains of Scandinavia and northern Britain.

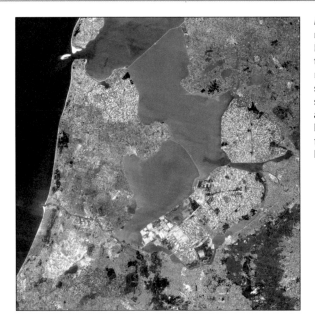

Much of the northwest of the Netherlands around the IJsselmeer is reclaimed land below sea level. A complex system of sea walls and dykes has been built to protect it from being flooded by the North Sea.

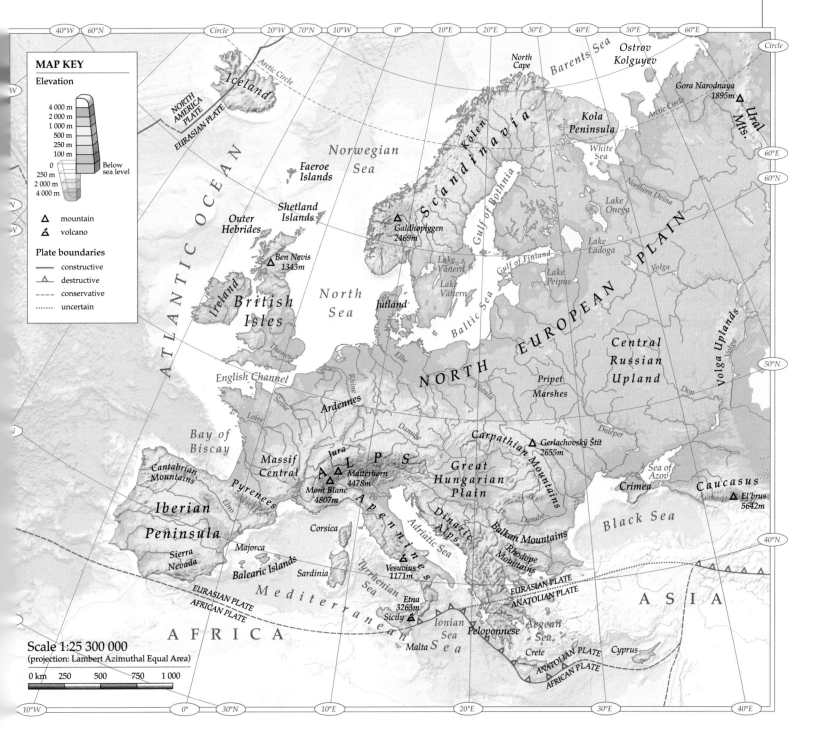

MAP KEY

Elevation

4 000 m	
2 000 m	
1 000 m	
500 m	
250 m	
100 m	
0	Below sea level
250 m	
2 000 m	
4 000 m	

△ mountain

◮ volcano

Plate boundaries

—— constructive

—△— destructive

- - - conservative

····· uncertain

Iceland

NORTH AMERICA PLATE

EURASIAN PLATE

Arctic Circle

ATLANTIC OCEAN

Faeroe Islands

Shetland Islands

Outer Hebrides

Ben Nevis 1343m

Ireland

British Isles

Thames

English Channel

Norwegian Sea

North Sea

Jutland

Scandinavia

Kölen

Galdhøpiggen 2469m

North Cape

Barents Sea

Ostrov Kolguyev

Gora Narodnaya 1895m

Ural Mts.

Kola Peninsula

White Sea

Gulf of Bothnia

Lake Onega

Northern Dvina

Lake Ladoga

Lake Vänern

Lake Vättern

Gulf of Finland

Lake Peipus

Baltic Sea

NORTH EUROPEAN PLAIN

Volga

Central Russian Upland

Volga Uplands

Volga

Elbe

Vistula

Pripet Marshes

Don

Dnieper

Bay of Biscay

Loire

Seine

Rhine

Ardennes

Danube

Carpathian Mountains

Gerlachovský Štít 2655m

Sea of Azov

Crimea

Caucasus

El'brus 5642m

Cantabrian Mountains

Pyrenees

Massif Central

Jura

ALPS

Matterhorn 4478m

Mont Blanc 4807m

Great Hungarian Plain

Dinaric Alps

Danube

Balkan Mountains

Rhodope Mountains

Black Sea

Iberian Peninsula

Ebro

Sierra Nevada

Corsica

Majorca

Balearic Islands

Sardinia

Apennines

Adriatic Sea

Vesuvius 1171m

Tyrrhenian Sea

EURASIAN PLATE

AFRICAN PLATE

Mediterranean Sea

AFRICA

Etna 3263m

Sicily

Malta

Ionian Sea

Peloponnese

Aegean Sea

Crete

EURASIAN PLATE

ANATOLIAN PLATE

ASIA

ANATOLIAN PLATE

AFRICAN PLATE

Cyprus

Scale 1:25 300 000
(projection: Lambert Azimuthal Equal Area)

0 km	250	500	750	1 000

CLIMATE AND VEGETATION

Land use across Europe varies greatly. Lowland regions tend to be more densely populated, with highly industrialised areas and intensive arable land and livestock farming. Coniferous forests are found in the mountainous regions, especially across Scandinavia in the north and in the Alps and Pyrenees where the climate is colder and wetter.

REYKJAVIK

ARCHANGEL

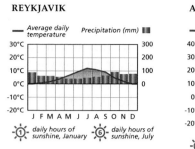

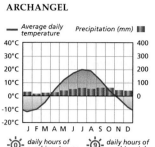

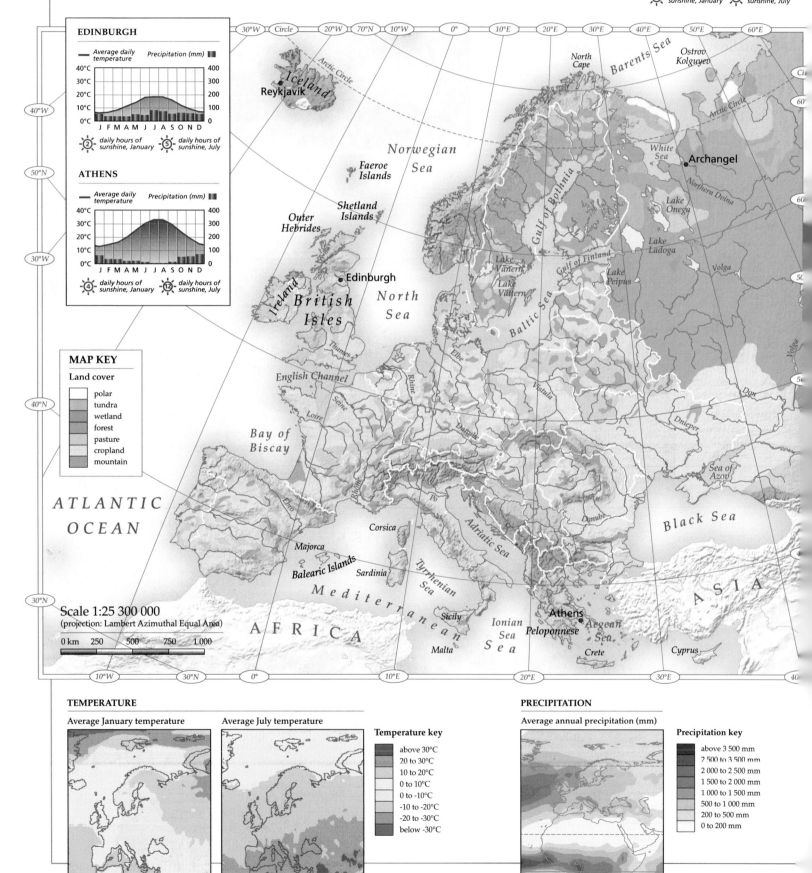

EDINBURGH

— Average daily temperature   Precipitation (mm)

daily hours of sunshine, January ②   daily hours of sunshine, July ⑤

ATHENS

— Average daily temperature   Precipitation (mm)

daily hours of sunshine, January ④   daily hours of sunshine, July ⑫

MAP KEY

Land cover
- polar
- tundra
- wetland
- forest
- pasture
- cropland
- mountain

Scale 1:25 300 000
(projection: Lambert Azimuthal Equal Area)

0 km   250   500   750   1 000

TEMPERATURE

Average January temperature

Average July temperature

Temperature key
- above 30°C
- 20 to 30°C
- 10 to 20°C
- 0 to 10°C
- 0 to -10°C
- -10 to -20°C
- -20 to -30°C
- below -30°C

PRECIPITATION

Average annual precipitation (mm)

Precipitation key
- above 3 500 mm
- 2 500 to 3 500 mm
- 2 000 to 2 500 mm
- 1 500 to 2 000 mm
- 1 000 to 1 500 mm
- 500 to 1 000 mm
- 200 to 500 mm
- 0 to 200 mm

TRANSPORT, COMMUNICATION AND TOURISM

Transport and communication are essential for a vigorous economic growth that creates jobs, and links people and markets to create wealth. Information technology and broadcasting have an ever increasing impact on the daily life of Europeans through modern communication systems. Transport and communication links across Europe and between Europe and the rest of the world are extremely well developed, especially the train system that links the whole of Europe. The price of air travel within Europe has dropped substantially over the last 15 years, so that more people than ever are able to travel to other countries for their holidays. Europe's largest airport is London Heathrow, in the United Kingdom. It is also the world's busiest airport.

TOURIST REVENUE

European revenue from international tourism, 2000 to 2003 (billion Euro)

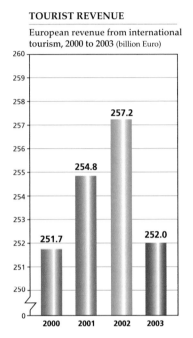

Year	Revenue
2000	251.7
2001	254.8
2002	257.2
2003	252.0

TOURISM

Tourism has more than doubled in Europe in the last 25 years, due partly to a remarkable revolution in transport and communication networks, increased standards of living and favourable economic factors that allow people to save for holidays. Europe has impressive scenery such as the Swiss Alps, a cultural heritage and historical and architectural areas of interest that attract many tourists. Tourism in Europe targets the summer season, when coastal areas are particularly popular places to visit. Europe has become a favoured tourist destination for people from East Asian countries such as China and Japan.

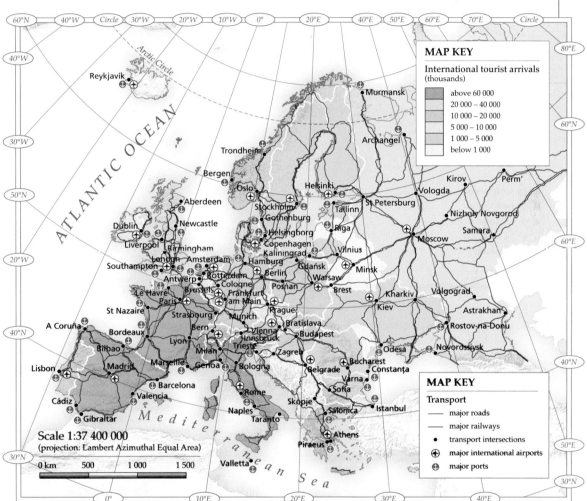

MAP KEY

International tourist arrivals (thousands)

- above 60 000
- 20 000 – 40 000
- 10 000 – 20 000
- 5 000 – 10 000
- 1 000 – 5 000
- below 1 000

MAP KEY

Transport

- —— major roads
- —— major railways
- • transport intersections
- ⊕ major international airports
- ⊕ major ports

Scale 1:37 400 000
(projection: Lambert Azimuthal Equal Area)

0 km   500   1 000   1 500

Foreign tourists are often attracted by snowy mountain resorts such as the one shown here.

POPULATION

Seventy-three per cent of Europe's population of 738 600 000 live in urban areas. There are also many rural settlements in the more isolated fringes and mountainous regions of the continent. Europe's population accounts for slightly more than 13 per cent of the world population and the population of the continent has grown. However, its growth has not come close to the pace of Asia or Africa. If demographic trends keep their pace,

Europe's contribution to world population may decline to around 7 per cent in 2050. Falling birth rates, mostly in Eastern and Central Europe, and high life expectancy in most European states, result in an ageing and declining population. This will therefore be a challenge for many European economies, political and social institutions. Northern and Western Europe have generally stronger growth than their Southern and Eastern counterparts.

MAP KEY

Population density
(people per square km)

- above 200
- 100 to 200
- 50 to 100
- 10 to 50
- 1 to 10
- 0 to 1

Major settlements

- ■ ◉ above 1 million
- ■ ◎ 500 000 to 1 million
- ■ ◦ below 500 000

A red square indicates a national capital.

Scale 1:25 300 000
(projection: Lambert Azimuthal Equal Area)

0 km   250   500   750   1 000

POPULATION IN SWEDEN

The Swedish population is mostly urban. Sweden has a low birth rate with fewer than two children born. However, the demographic profile of Sweden has changed significantly as a result of immigration since the 1970s.

- Population: 9 316 256 (31 August 2009)
- Annual population growth rate: 0.158% (2010)
- Net migration rate: 1.66 migrant(s)/1000 population (2010)
- Total fertility rate: 1.94 children born/woman (2010)
- Infant mortality rate: 2.75 deaths/1000 live births (2010)

- Life expectancy at birth: 80.86 years
  Male: 78.59 years; Female: 83.26 years (2010)

SWEDEN: URBAN/RURAL POPULATION SPLIT

83%   27%

SWEDEN: POPULATION AGE BREAKDOWN

MALES Age FEMALES

80+
60–79
40–59
20–39
0–19

12 10 8 6 4 2 0   0 2 4 6 8 10 12
Percentage of population by age group

MINING, INDUSTRY AND TRADE

Europe is not a major producer of metals, compared with other continents. However, Europe is home to some of the world's largest mining companies such as Anglo American, Rio Tinto and BHP Billiton. Base metals and gold are produced in Ireland, Spain, Portugal, Romania, Turkey, Sweden and Finland. Cyprus is well known for its base-metal deposits on Troodos. Turkey has a great potential for base metal and gold deposits, and is an established chromite producer. Coal is a major European product, with Germany and Poland being major producers.

Europe leads the world in terms of industrial diversity, output and the number of people employed in the sector. European industries are characterised by a high degree of technological proficiency and highly mechanised operations. The industrial belt is not continuous but extends from Britain, through north-east France and Belgium to the Rhineland of Germany and Silesia. Other main industrial areas are found in northern Italy, on the Swiss plateau, in central Sweden and in large cities of Europe such as Paris, London, Berlin and Milan.

The European Union is an important economic, political and legislative body as well as an important trade bloc. However, most European countries have trade links with African and Asian countries, especially China.

Barcelona Harbour, Cantabria, Spain

Scale 1:25 300 000
(projection: Lambert Azimuthal Equal Area)

0 km 250 500 750 1 000

AGRICULTURE, LIVESTOCK AND FISHING

Land use is influenced by topography, climate, level of development, accessibility and population size, density and distribution. Land use in Europe is dominated by agriculture, mainly under cereal production. European agriculture is fully mechanised and, across Europe, only 4 per cent of agricultural land is farmed organically. However, more farms become organic every year. In Sweden, for example, 20 per cent of farms are organic.

Forestry and fishing form important components of land use, especially among Scandinavian countries, while mining, industry, transport, human settlement and communication also present major land use activities.

DAIRY FARMING IN DENMARK

The Danish climate and soils provide optimum conditions for dairy farming. The climate is mild, rainfall is evenly distributed throughout the year and the soil is fertile. Despite the northerly location, spring and summer temperatures are high enough to promote lush grass growth.

DENMARK

MAP KEY

Land use type

- commercial farming, mainly grains
- commercial farming, mixed crops and livestock
- dairy farming
- intensive livestock rearing
- extensive livestock rearing
- specialised plantation and market gardening
- softwood forestry
- mixed softwood and hardwood forestry
- mountainous region
- sparsely populated region
- industrial region

Scale 1:25 300 000
(projection: Lambert Azimuthal Equal Area)

0 km 250 500 750 1 000

Since the 1960s, traditional Danish cattle breeds such as the Red Danish have been replaced by high-yielding foreign bloodlines like Dutch Holsteins and Friesians.

FARMING IN THE RHINELAND, GERMANY

Farmland accounts for just under 30 per cent of land use in the German Rhineland. Crops, including grain, potatoes, sugar beet, fruit and tobacco are grown along the floodplain of the River Rhine. Large-scale commercial farms are increasingly replacing small-scale enterprises in the Rhineland. The area also contains some of Germany's most successful wine producers.

Oilseed rape, with its distinctive yellow flowers, is just one of the crops that are grown successfully in the Rhineland.

DAIRY FARMING IN DENMARK

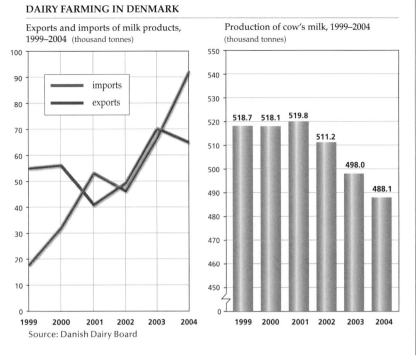

Exports and imports of milk products, 1999–2004 (thousand tonnes)

Production of cow's milk, 1999–2004 (thousand tonnes)

Source: Danish Dairy Board

MAP KEY

Settlements
- ◉ over 1 million
- ◎ 500 000 – 1 million
- ⊙ 100 000 – 500 000

Boundaries
- ▬ international border

Transport
- ═ major road
- ─ other road
- ─ railway
- ✈ airport

COUNTRIES

Asia is made up of 49 countries, many emerging from the break up of the USSR in 1991. In the west, the continent is separated from Europe by the Ural Mountains and Turkey. On the eastern edge are the island nations of Japan, Indonesia and the Philippines. The northern regions of the Russian Federation reach beyond the Arctic Circle, whilst Indonesia in the south lies across the Equator.

INTERNATIONAL ORGANISATIONS

ORGANISATION	AIM
Asian Development Bank (ADB)	To encourage regional development
Asia-Pacific Economic Cooperation (APEC)	To promote regional economic co-operation
Association of South-East Asian Nations (ASEAN)	To promote economic, social and cultural co-operation
Colombo Plan (CP)	To encourage economic and social development
Mekong River Commission	An accord on the sustainable development of the Mekong River Basin
Shanghai Cooperation Organisation: Members (SCO)	To promote security and co-operation (formerly the Shanghai Five)

MAP KEY

International organisations

- Asian Development Bank (ADB)
- Asia-Pacific Economic Cooperation (APEC)
- Association of South-East Asian Nations (ASEAN)
- Colombo Plan (CP)
- Mekong River Commission
- Shanghai Cooperation Organization: Members (SCO)

Maldives

Singapore

Scale 1:56 000 000
(projection: Lambert Azimuthal Equal Area)

0 km   500   1 000   1 500   2 000   2 500

MAP KEY

Settlements

- ■ over 1 million
- ■ 500 000 to 1 million
- ■ 100 000 to 500 000
- ▪ 50 000 to 100 000
- ▪ under 50 000

A red square indicates a national capital.

Boundaries

- ——— international border
- – – – disputed border
- ✕✕✕ ceasefire line
- ·········· territorial claim
- ——— maritime border

RELIEF

Asia is the world's largest continent. Geologically, the mountains and plateaux of the north are much older than the landscapes in the south. The south has the world's highest and youngest fold mountain range, the Himalayas. These are still rising as the Indo-Australian tectonic plate pushes against the Eurasian plate.

PHYSICAL FACTFILE

1 HIGHEST POINT: Mount Everest, Himalayas 8850 metres above sea level

2 LOWEST POINT: Dead Sea Shore, 417 metres below sea level

3 LARGEST LAKE: Caspian Sea, 371 000 km²

— **LONGEST RIVER:** Yangtze, 6300 km

— **LENGTH OF COASTLINE:** 422 698 km

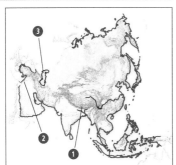

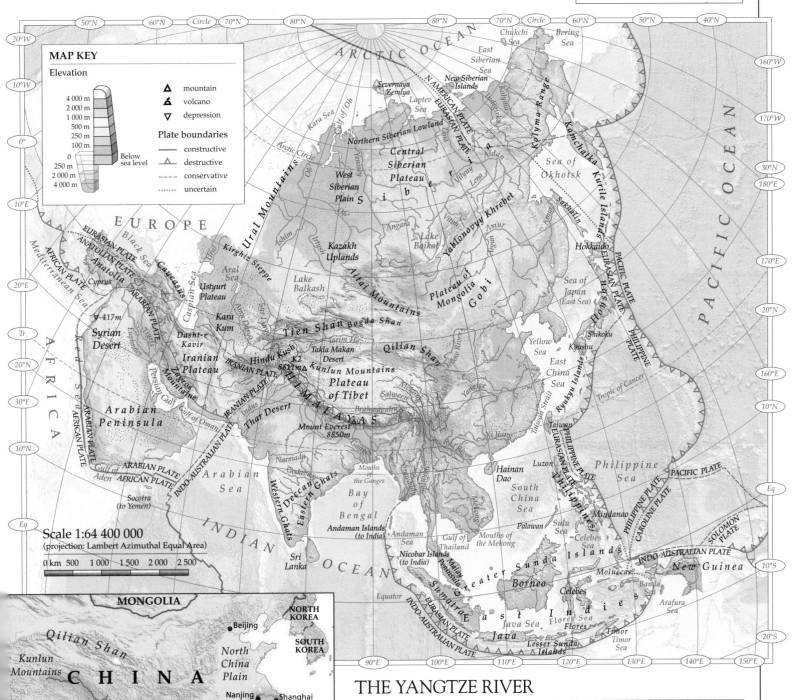

Scale 1:64 400 000
(projection: Lambert Azimuthal Equal Area)

0 km 500 1 000 1 500 2 000 2 500

MAP KEY

Elevation

4 000 m
2 000 m
1 000 m
500 m
250 m
100 m
0
250 m — Below sea level
2 000 m
4 000 m

△ mountain
⚲ volcano
▽ depression

Plate boundaries
—— constructive
△△ destructive
– – – conservative
········· uncertain

THE YANGTZE RIVER

The Yangtze is China's longest river: it flows 5526 km from its source in the Kunlun Mountains to its mouth at the East China Sea. The river is navigable by ocean-going vessels for about 1000 km and steamers can travel as far as Yichang, 1600 km from the sea. In addition to its importance as a transportation network, the Yangtze irrigates one of China's chief rice-growing areas.

CLIMATE AND LAND USE

Asia has all natural vegetation types due to the diversity of climatic types. In fact, almost every known major climatic type and its corresponding vegetation occurs in Asia.

Indonesia, Malaysia and parts of Sri Lanka have an equatorial type of climate. Hence the vegetation grows abundantly and rapidly, creating an impenetrable evergreen rain forest.

The monsoon climate has summer rain and a dry winter. Due to this dry winter, the forests here are less dense than those in the equatorial region.

Central and southwest Asia have a desert type of climate, consisting of hot summers and cool winters, with scanty or hardly any rainfall. Due to this lack of moisture, the vegetation consists of tough grass, thorny bushes and bulbous plants.

Parts of Turkey, Syria, Lebanon and Israel have a Mediterranean type of climate, which consists of hot, dry summers followed by mild, wet winters. In order to adapt to the hot, dry summers, the vegetation found in these areas is made up of trees and shrubs that have small deep roots.

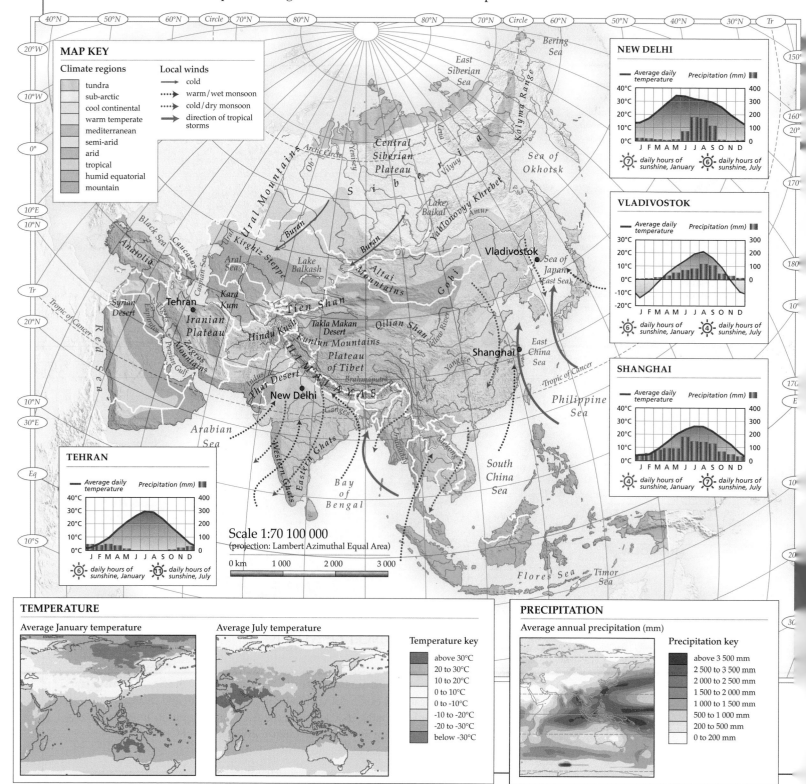

AGRICULTURE, LIVESTOCK AND FISHING

Rapidly increasing demand for livestock products, together with the changes in international trade, is placing pressure on Asia's livestock sector to expand and adapt. There is a shift in livestock functions and species, and a shift in agro-ecological and geographical zones, involving structural and technological changes.

Traditionally, livestock is taken to be an asset, which provides petty cash when the need arises and has an insurance function. However, these traditional functions of livestock are gradually being replaced by financial functions, as remote rural areas start to enter the monetary economy.

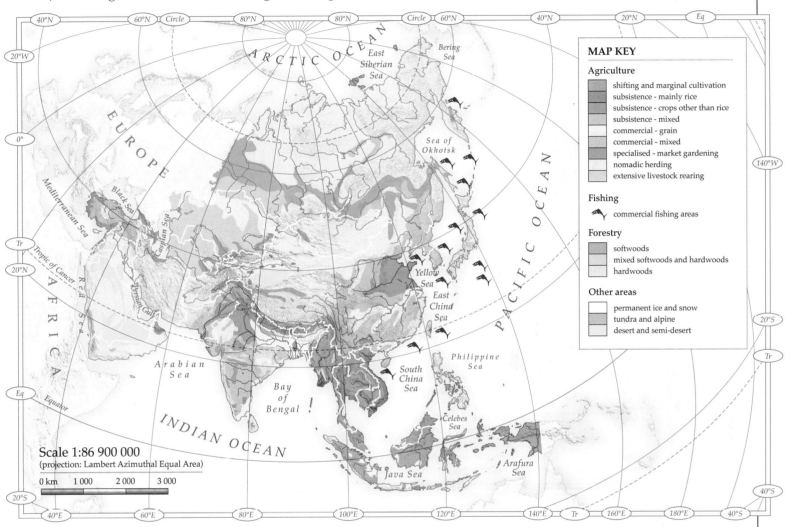

Scale 1:86 900 000
(projection: Lambert Azimuthal Equal Area)

0 km   1 000   2 000   3 000

MAP KEY

Agriculture
- shifting and marginal cultivation
- subsistence - mainly rice
- subsistence - crops other than rice
- subsistence - mixed
- commercial - grain
- commercial - mixed
- specialised - market gardening
- nomadic herding
- extensive livestock rearing

Fishing
- commercial fishing areas

Forestry
- softwoods
- mixed softwoods and hardwoods
- hardwoods

Other areas
- permanent ice and snow
- tundra and alpine
- desert and semi-desert

JAPAN: FORESTRY AND FISHING

Some 67 per cent of the total land area of Japan is woodland, 40 per cent of which contains softwoods. About 56 per cent of the forest area is privately owned. Although Japan ranks high in world production of timber, the steadily increasing domestic demand for lumber requires the country to import more than 70 per cent of its needs.

Fish is a food staple for the Japanese and is second in importance only to rice. Consequently, fishing is one of the most important industries, both for the domestic and export markets. The Japanese fishing fleet is one of the world's largest, and the annual catch is the second largest in the world behind China. Production from deep-sea fisheries has declined from past levels, due in part to fishing limitations imposed by other nations in waters near their shores. Japan is among the world's few remaining whaling countries, although it has abided by an international ban on most whaling since 1986.

Source : The Census of Agriculture and Forestry, Statistics and Information Department, Ministry of Agriculture, Forestry and Fisheries, Japan.

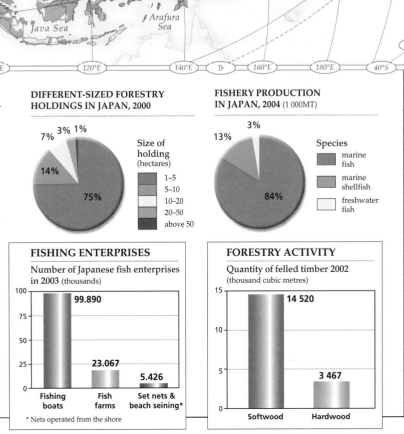

DIFFERENT-SIZED FORESTRY HOLDINGS IN JAPAN, 2000

7% 3% 1%
14%
75%

Size of holding (hectares)
- 1–5
- 5–10
- 10–20
- 20–50
- above 50

FISHERY PRODUCTION IN JAPAN, 2004 (1 000MT)

3%
13%
84%

Species
- marine fish
- marine shellfish
- freshwater fish

FISHING ENTERPRISES

Number of Japanese fish enterprises in 2003 (thousands)

- Fishing boats: 99.890
- Fish farms: 23.067
- Set nets & beach seining*: 5.426

* Nets operated from the shore

FORESTRY ACTIVITY

Quantity of felled timber 2002 (thousand cubic metres)

- Softwood: 14 520
- Hardwood: 3 467

MINING AND ENERGY

Mining is an important activity in most Asian countries, and it is a major export industry. Manganese is mined in India, tin in Malaysia, Thailand and Indonesia, and chromium ore in the Philippines. The most important mineral export, however, is petroleum, with Asian outputs accounting for about half the world's total. Southwest Asia contains the world's largest reserves of oil outside Russia, and most of the production is exported. Coal-mining is important in China – which contributes about 30 per cent to the world's total coal output – and in central and eastern Siberia, north-eastern India, Iran and Turkey.

Two-thirds of the world's crude oil supply originates in the Middle East. The main producer is Saudi Arabia, which produces a quarter of all crude oil sold worldwide – amounting to 7 million barrels per day in 1993. Iraq, Iran, United Arab Emirates and Kuwait are all significant oil producers too. As a consequence of this concentration of the oil industry, world oil prices are strongly affected by events in the Middle East, such as the American invasion of Iraq in 2003.

ENERGY

Petroleum-rich southwest Asia has few other sources for energy. India has immense hydroelectric potential, and about half the electricity generated there comes from waterpower. Nonetheless, much of the energy consumed in rural India continues to be derived from the burning of dung and brushwood. Both China and Japan have shown that small-scale hydroelectric plants can be effective providers of energy to small towns and rural areas.

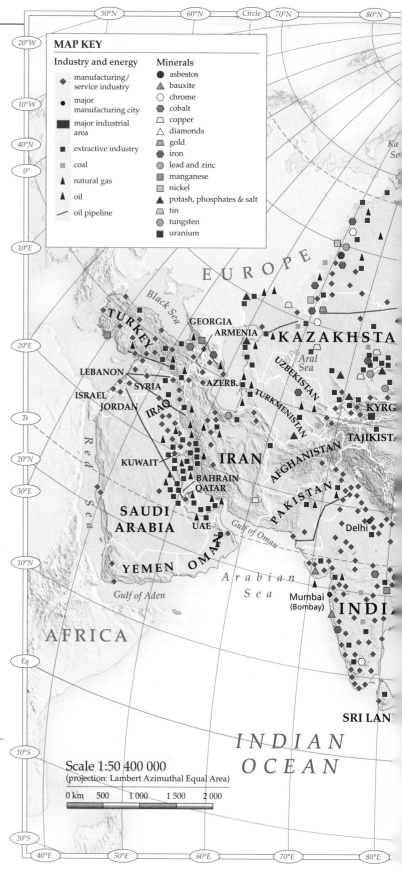

MAP KEY

Industry and energy
- manufacturing/service industry
- major manufacturing city
- major industrial area
- extractive industry
- coal
- natural gas
- oil
- oil pipeline

Minerals
- asbestos
- bauxite
- chrome
- cobalt
- copper
- diamonds
- gold
- iron
- lead and zinc
- manganese
- nickel
- potash, phosphates & salt
- tin
- tungsten
- uranium

Scale 1:50 400 000
(projection: Lambert Azimuthal Equal Area)

0 km   500   1 000   1 500   2 000

SOURCE OF ELECTRICITY IN SELECTED ASIAN COUNTRIES

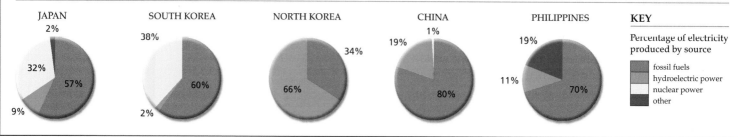

JAPAN
2%
32%
9%
57%

SOUTH KOREA
38%
2%
60%

NORTH KOREA
34%
66%

CHINA
1%
19%
80%

PHILIPPINES
19%
11%
70%

KEY
Percentage of electricity produced by source
- fossil fuels
- hydroelectric power
- nuclear power
- other

INDUSTRY AND TRADE

Asia's manufacturing capacity is unevenly spread, but growing quickly. Japan has a highly diversified industrial sector, constituting about one quarter of the labour force. China, Russia and India also have large manufacturing centres. In China, manufacturing employs some 27 per cent of the workforce. It is concentrated in Liaoning province in the northeast part of the country and in Shanghai's port cities of Tianjin, Qingdao and Wuhan.

High-tech industry is well-developed in South Korea. During the 1990s, the government initiated the growth of industries such as electronics by providing cheap state credit to emerging companies and encouraging foreign investment. The well-educated workforce provided an additional incentive to businesses. The principal centres for the electronics industry are Seoul and Inch'on in the north, and Masan and Busan in the south. Here a designer is working on the design of a new vacuum cleaner.

TRADE

Japan, S. Korea, Malaysia, China and India are the emerging economies that have increasing trade worldwide.

They have a huge demand for commodities such as coal and copper from Africa. In turn, Africa purchases such items as automobiles, electronic items, machinery and foodstuffs. Africa has the resources that Asia needs. It has an historic opportunity to transform its development, as Asia has begun to look at Africa as a market of high growth potential.

Trade between Asia and Africa, which together account for three-quarters of the world's 7 billion people, rose more than 400 per cent from 2001 to 2010.

African-Asian trade and investment flows are unlikely to abate for the foreseeable future. This reflects the underlying circular trend of the explosion in commerce between emerging markets. China is also investing in African projects such as roads, ports and power plants. Direct investment by China into Africa rose from $490 million in 2003 to $9.33 billion by the end of 2009 and reached $127 billion in 2010.

These new cars are lined up in a harbour in Tokyo, Japan, ready to be exported worldwide. Japan is the world leader in high-tech and automobile industries and Japanese companies have now established manufacturing plants in countries as far away as the UK. The growth of the car industry has flourished because of the high standard of research in Japan and the ability of Japanese scientists to develop ideas that have originated abroad.

TRANSPORT, COMMUNICATION AND TRADE

The major countries of Asia continue to rely heavily, and in some areas almost exclusively, on railways for both freight and passenger transportation. Passenger traffic on most systems is particularly heavy because of rapidly increasing populations and the comparative absence of modern highways. Asian railways still have the problem of finding funds for modernisation and development. Some countries, such as Japan, South Korea, Thailand and Malaysia, have done a spectacular job of keeping their railroads up to date since the heavy damage inflicted during World War II. Other railways in the region, such as those in Bangladesh, Pakistan, Vietnam and Cambodia, have fallen into a state of serious neglect through inattention, war or both.

TRADE: HONG KONG

Hong Kong is a former British colony that was taken back under Chinese sovereignty in 1997. In contrast to much of the Chinese mainland, Hong Kong is a thriving metropolis. The island has a capitalist economy that has remained untouched by communist China.

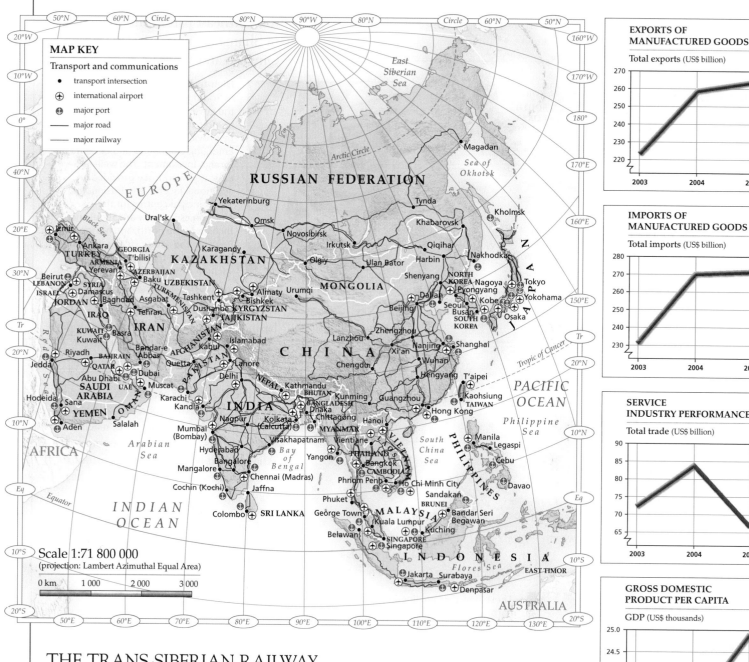

Scale 1:71 800 000
(projection: Lambert Azimuthal Equal Area)

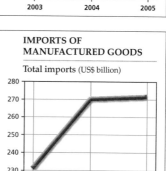

EXPORTS OF MANUFACTURED GOODS

Total exports (US$ billion)

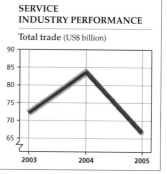

IMPORTS OF MANUFACTURED GOODS

Total imports (US$ billion)

SERVICE INDUSTRY PERFORMANCE

Total trade (US$ billion)

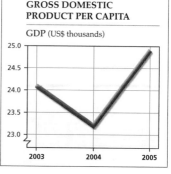

GROSS DOMESTIC PRODUCT PER CAPITA

GDP (US$ thousands)

THE TRANS-SIBERIAN RAILWAY

It takes at least six days to travel the entire length of the famous Trans-Siberian railway, which is more than 9000 km long. The line begins in Moscow, crosses the Ural Mountains, continues through Siberia and Mongolia and ends in Vladivostok on the eastern coast of Russia. The railway was built a hundred years ago and remains an important transport link.

POPULATION

China and India account for just under 40 per cent of the total world population, with over a billion people in each country. Many parts of Asia, such as Japan, have very high population densities, whilst the sub-arctic north and desert and mountain interiors of the continent have very few people.

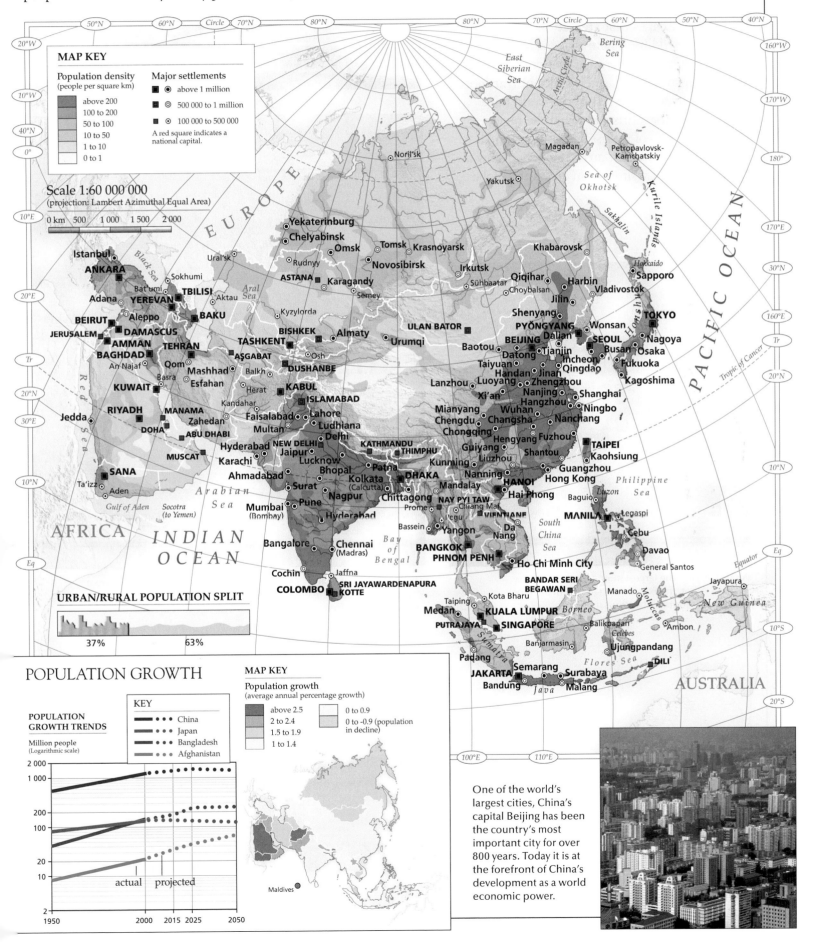

MAP KEY

Population density
(people per square km)

above 200
100 to 200
50 to 100
10 to 50
1 to 10
0 to 1

Major settlements

■ ⊙ above 1 million
◼ ◎ 500 000 to 1 million
▪ ⊙ 100 000 to 500 000

A red square indicates a national capital.

Scale 1:60 000 000
(projection: Lambert Azimuthal Equal Area)

0 km 500 1 000 1 500 2 000

URBAN/RURAL POPULATION SPLIT

37%   63%

POPULATION GROWTH

MAP KEY

Population growth
(average annual percentage growth)

above 2.5
2 to 2.4
1.5 to 1.9
1 to 1.4
0 to 0.9
0 to -0.9 (population in decline)

KEY

••• China
••• Japan
••• Bangladesh
••• Afghanistan

POPULATION GROWTH TRENDS

Million people
(Logarithmic scale)

2 000
1 000
200
100
20
10
2

1950   2000 2015 2025   2050

actual   projected

Maldives

One of the world's largest cities, China's capital Beijing has been the country's most important city for over 800 years. Today it is at the forefront of China's development as a world economic power.

TOURISM

Travelling through Asia is an opportunity to see the most diverse and beautiful landscapes in the world. There are a variety of tourist attractions such as the beaches, and natural landscapes that are rich in mountains, forests and wildlife. There is also a huge diversity of cultural heritage that provides splendid historical treasures. Efficient transport connections with the rest of the world have made it easy for tourists to reach the region.

Asia is a hub of tourist destinations and a large number of tourist attractions that draw a large number of visitors from across the globe each year.

Summer Palace – The residence of erstwhile rulers of China, this tourist attraction was first built in 1153.

Potala Palace – The largest monumental structure in Lhasa, Tibet, the Potala Palace is one of the most sought-after tourist attractions in Asia.

The Great Wall of China – One of the Wonders of the World, the Great Wall of China is the greatest architectural marvel of Asia. It is counted among the most frequently visited tourist attractions in Asia.

Red Fort – This elegant construction in northern India was built by the Mughal emperor, Shah Jahan as the royal residence and the seat of the royal throne.

Malaysia Beaches – The pristine beaches of Malaysia impress visitors with their beauty.

Mount Fuji – The highest peak in Japan, this revered volcano is among the most frequently visited tourist attractions.

Taj Mahal – Another Wonder of the World, this architectural splendour is known as 'poetry in stone'. People come to India in large numbers to have a glimpse of this tourist attraction.

COUNTRIES AND RELIEF

Australasia and Oceania region include the following countries: Australia, Fiji Island, French Polynesia, Guam, Kiribati, Marshall Islands, Micronesia, Nauru, New Caledonia, New Zealand, Palau, Papua New Guinea, Samoa, Solomon Islands, Tonga, Tuvalu and Vanuatu. Australia, is the biggest of them. It is an island continent lying between the Indian and Pacific Oceans. Its varied landscape includes tropical rainforest, the desert of the arid 'red centre', snow-capped mountains, pastoral land and beaches. Famous natural features in the continent include Uluru (formerly Ayers Rock) and the Great Barrier Reef.

Uluru is a huge red sandstone monolith – the second largest in the world. It is a sacred place to the Aboriginal population.

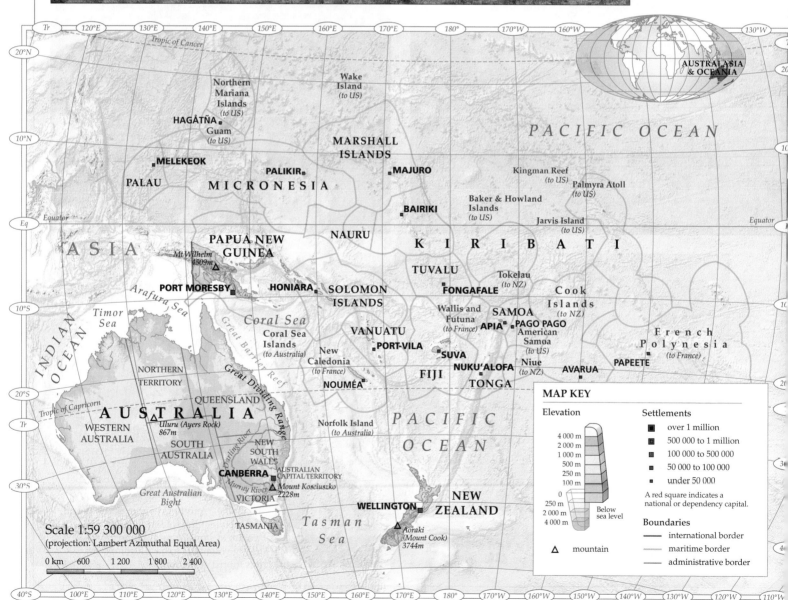

Scale 1:59 300 000
(projection: Lambert Azimuthal Equal Area)

0 km 600 1 200 1 800 2 400

MAP KEY

Elevation

4 000 m
2 000 m
1 000 m
500 m
250 m
100 m
0
250 m
2 000 m
4 000 m
Below sea level

△ mountain

Settlements

■ over 1 million
■ 500 000 to 1 million
■ 100 000 to 500 000
■ 50 000 to 100 000
▪ under 50 000

A red square indicates a national or dependency capital.

Boundaries

— international border
— maritime border
— administrative border

CLIMATE AND VEGETATION

Although it is largely dry, Australia has a wide range of climatic regions. The interior, west and south are arid and semi-arid, and very hot in summer. Central desert temperatures reach about 50°C. The north, around Darwin and Cape York Peninsula, are hot all the year but humid during the summer monsoon. Only the east and the southwest near Perth are temperate.

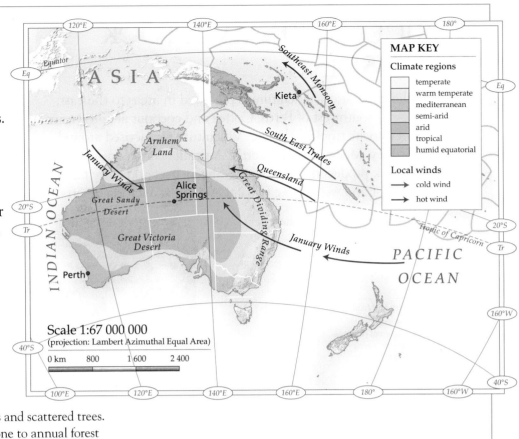

MAP KEY

Climate regions
- temperate
- warm temperate
- mediterranean
- semi-arid
- arid
- tropical
- humid equatorial

Local winds
- → cold wind
- → hot wind

Scale 1:67 000 000
(projection: Lambert Azimuthal Equal Area)

0 km   800   1 600   2 400

VEGETATION

Most of Australia is dominated by desert and savannah vegetation. The desert vegetation has a variety of shrubs and smaller plants. The savannah vegetation is composed of dense grass and scattered trees. The dry climatic conditions make Australia prone to annual forest fires. Forests are found along the east and north coastlines.

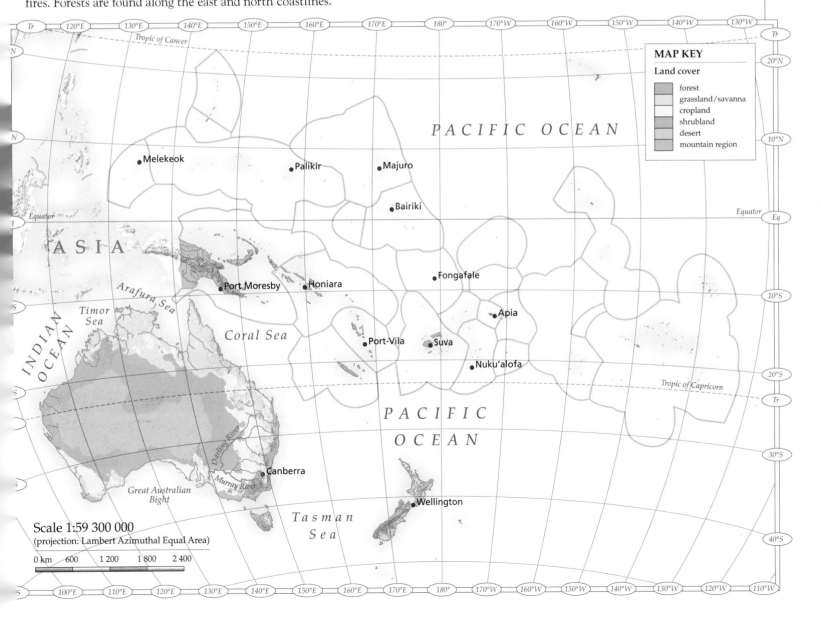

MAP KEY

Land cover
- forest
- grassland/savanna
- cropland
- shrubland
- desert
- mountain region

Scale 1:59 300 000
(projection: Lambert Azimuthal Equal Area)

0 km   600   1 200   1 800   2 400

AGRICULTURE, LIVESTOCK AND FISHING

In Australia, plantation agriculture is practised in areas to the east, southeast and southwest of Perth. Coffee and coconut are grown in Papua New Guinea's tropical climate. Viticulture is practised around Brisbane, Sydney, Melbourne and Perth. Australia is also one of the leading livestock producers in the world. Sheep, beef and dairy farms are found to the east and west of the Gibson and Great Victoria deserts.

FISHING

Fishing is a major occupation of many inhabitants of Australia and its neighbouring archipelagoes. Fishing takes place along the entire coastline. Marine reserve areas of Australia are larger than the country itself. A distinct feature of Australian waters is the presence of different species of sharks, habitating at the bottom of a continental slope or shelf. Most sharks can be caught by commercial and recreational fishers.

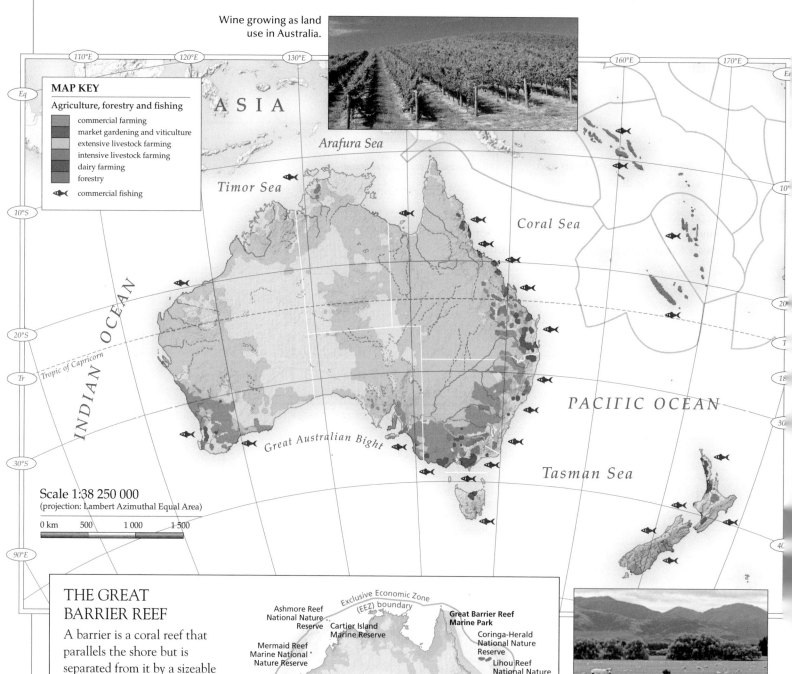

Wine growing as land use in Australia.

MAP KEY

Agriculture, forestry and fishing

- commercial farming
- market gardening and viticulture
- extensive livestock farming
- intensive livestock farming
- dairy farming
- forestry
- commercial fishing

Scale 1:38 250 000
(projection: Lambert Azimuthal Equal Area)

0 km   500   1 000   1 500

THE GREAT BARRIER REEF

A barrier is a coral reef that parallels the shore but is separated from it by a sizeable lagoon. The world's largest barrier reef is the Great Barrier Reef off the coast of Queensland, Australia. The Australian Great Barrier Reef is at risk due to rising sea temperatures. To protect the reef from environmental damage, fishing was banned in 2004 on 30 per cent of the reef area.

Exclusive Economic Zone (EEZ) boundary

Ashmore Reef National Nature Reserve
Cartier Island Marine Reserve
Mermaid Reef Marine National Nature Reserve
Ningaloo Marine Park
Great Barrier Reef Marine Park
Coringa-Herald National Nature Reserve
Lihou Reef National Nature Reserve
Elizabeth and Middleton Reefs Marine National Nature Reserve
Solitary Island Marine Reserve
Lord Howe Island Marine Park
Great Australian Bight Marine Park
Tasmanian Seamounts Marine Reserve

MAP KEY

- Marine Park
- Marine Reserve
- Exclusive Economic Zone boundary

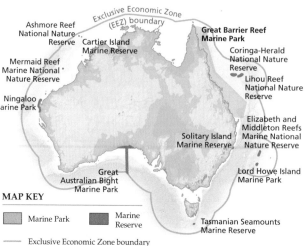

Farming is a major part of New Zealand's economy. Sheep, beef, dairy and poultry products are major exports. Other agricultural products are cereals, fruits and vegetables. In New Zealand, forests are found on the Southern Alps on the South Island, and to the north of the North Island.

MINING AND ENERGY

Australia is one of the major mining regions of the world. It has a wide range of valuable deposits of mineral resources ranging from oil and natural gas to iron-ore, gold and nickel. Most mines in the region are opencast mines. Despite the fact that mining underpins the region's wealth, environmental concerns need to be taken into consideration to build a sustainable mining industry. The major sources of energy in Australia include coal, oil and natural gas, geothermal energy and hydropower. Australia has significant wind and solar resources, and limited large hydro resources because of its low rainfall.

Sulphur, which will be used to process the nickel extracted at this mine in western Australia.

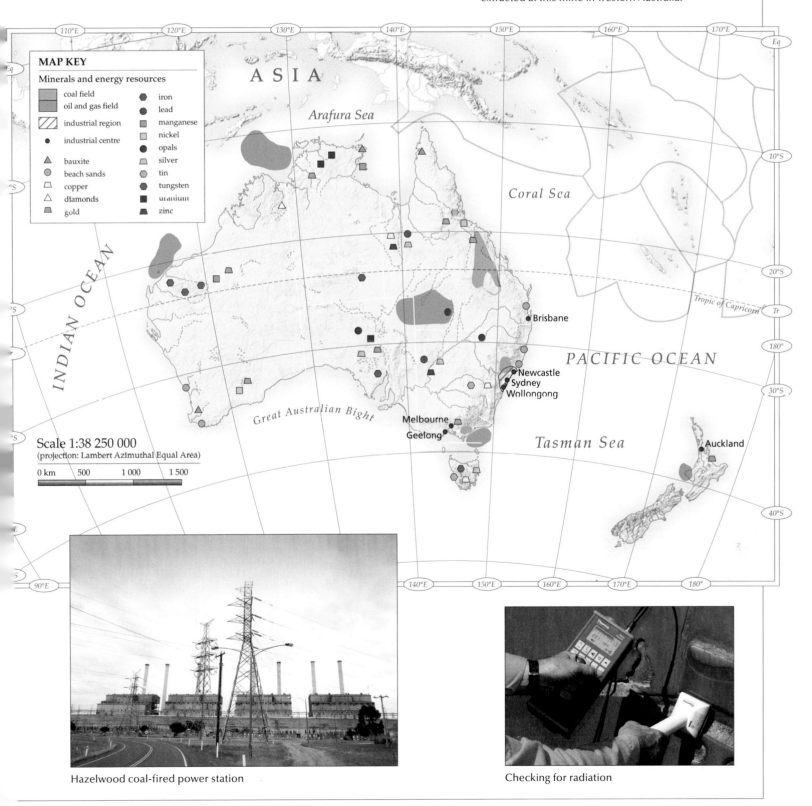

MAP KEY

Minerals and energy resources

- coal field
- oil and gas field
- industrial region
- • industrial centre
- ▲ bauxite
- ● beach sands
- ⬠ copper
- △ diamonds
- ⬡ gold
- ◆ iron
- ■ lead
- ■ manganese
- □ nickel
- ● opals
- ◻ silver
- ◒ tin
- ⬡ tungsten
- ■ uranium
- ▬ zinc

ASIA

Arafura Sea

Coral Sea

INDIAN OCEAN

Tropic of Capricorn

PACIFIC OCEAN

Brisbane

Newcastle
Sydney
Wollongong

Great Australian Bight

Melbourne
Geelong

Tasman Sea

Auckland

Scale 1:38 250 000
(projection: Lambert Azimuthal Equal Area)

0 km   500   1 000   1 500

Hazelwood coal-fired power station

Checking for radiation

INDUSTRY, TRADE AND TRANSPORT

Australia's industrial base is composed of manufacturing, electronics, metallurgy, computers, brewing and chemical manufacturing. Other industries include tourism and agro-based and forest-related industries. The region has a highly developed transport network consisting of roads, railways and airports.

Coal mining in Australia

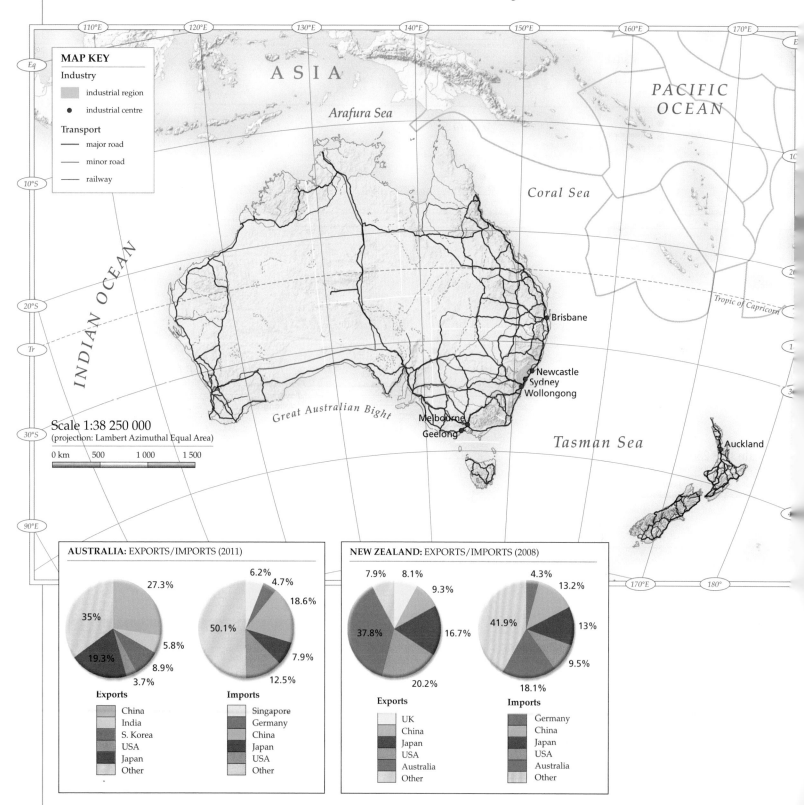

MAP KEY

Industry

▨ industrial region

● industrial centre

Transport

—— major road

—— minor road

—— railway

Scale 1:38 250 000
(projection: Lambert Azimuthal Equal Area)

0 km   500   1 000   1 500

AUSTRALIA: EXPORTS/IMPORTS (2011)

Exports: 27.3%, 35%, 5.8%, 19.3%, 8.9%, 3.7%

Imports: 6.2%, 4.7%, 18.6%, 50.1%, 7.9%, 12.5%

Exports
- China
- India
- S. Korea
- USA
- Japan
- Other

Imports
- Singapore
- Germany
- China
- Japan
- USA
- Other

NEW ZEALAND: EXPORTS/IMPORTS (2008)

Exports: 7.9%, 8.1%, 9.3%, 37.8%, 16.7%, 20.2%

Imports: 4.3%, 13.2%, 41.9%, 13%, 9.5%, 18.1%

Exports
- UK
- China
- Japan
- USA
- Australia
- Other

Imports
- Germany
- China
- Japan
- USA
- Australia
- Other

POPULATION

The region consists of many smaller countries with populations of between 10 000 and 500 000. Australia is the biggest country with over 22 million people, followed by Papua New Guinea (6.9 million) and New Zealand (4.4 million).

Source: 2011 World Population Data Sheet

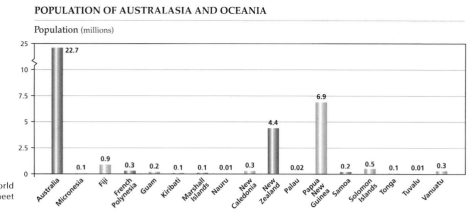

POPULATION OF AUSTRALASIA AND OCEANIA

Population (millions)

Country	Population
Australia	22.7
Micronesia	0.1
Fiji	0.9
French Polynesia	0.3
Guam	0.2
Kiribati	0.1
Marshall Islands	0.1
Nauru	0.01
New Caledonia	0.3
New Zealand	4.4
Palau	0.02
Papua New Guinea	6.9
Samoa	0.2
Solomon Islands	0.5
Tonga	0.1
Tuvalu	0.01
Vanuatu	0.3

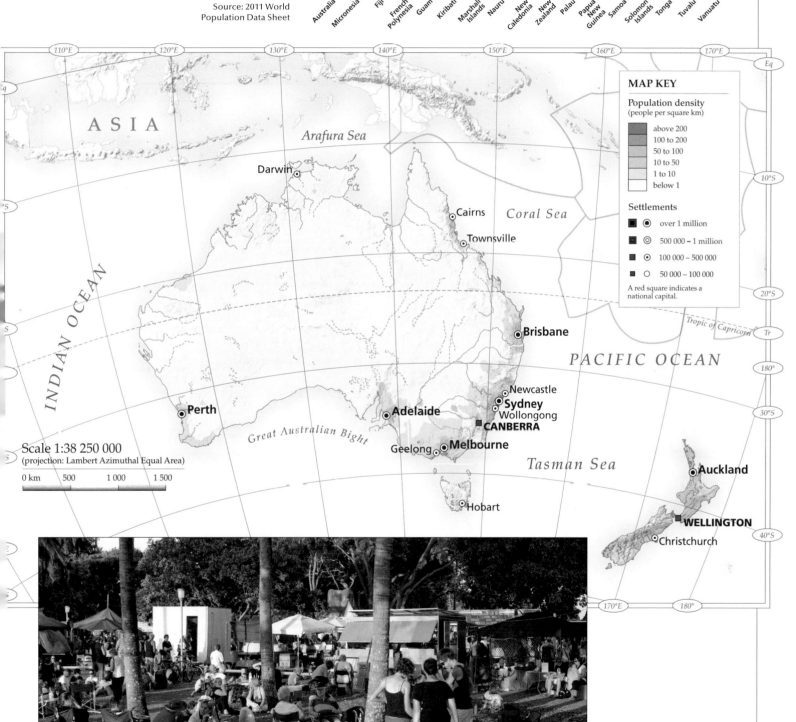

MAP KEY

Population density
(people per square km)

above 200
100 to 200
50 to 100
10 to 50
1 to 10
below 1

Settlements

over 1 million
500 000 – 1 million
100 000 – 500 000
50 000 – 100 000

A red square indicates a national capital.

Scale 1:38 250 000
(projection: Lambert Azimuthal Equal Area)

0 km   500   1 000   1 500

People picnicing at Mindil Beach Markets, Darwin, Australia

ARARCTIC

The Arctic Ocean forms the area around the North Pole. The ocean is covered by ice much of the year and is enclosed by the northern landmasses of North America, the Russian Federation, Greenland and Northern Europe. The Arctic Ocean has an area of 14 million km² and an average depth of 4665 m. The Arctic is the world's smallest ocean. Recent observations are that the Arctic sea ice has melted to a degree, certainly not experienced in at least 8000 years.

Greenland, the world's largest island, is almost completely covered by a massive ice sheet. Located on the edge of the Arctic Ocean, it is a self-governing part of Denmark with a population of under 60 000.

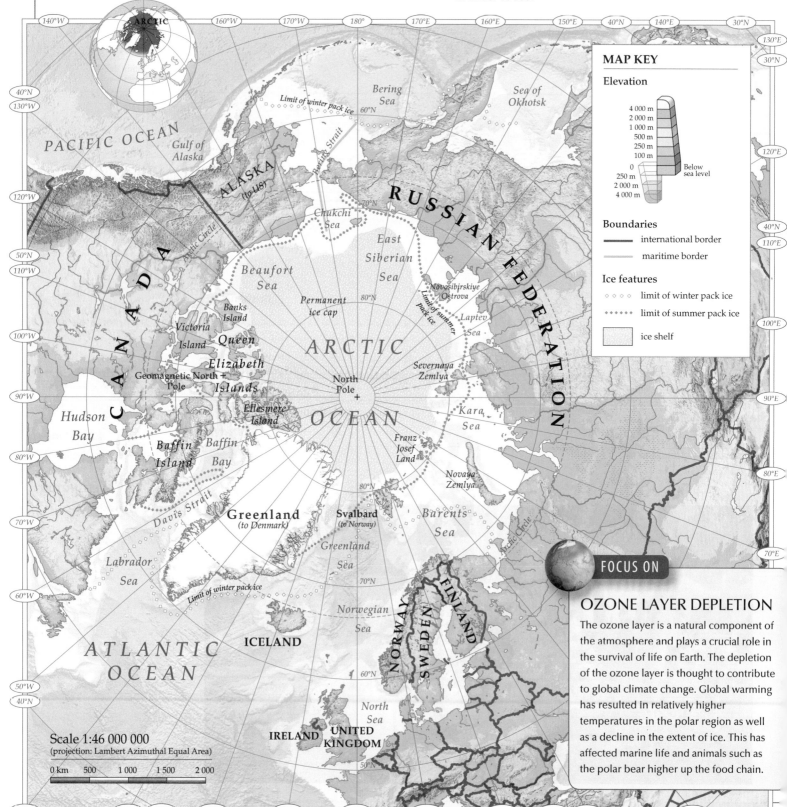

MAP KEY

Elevation

4 000 m
2 000 m
1 000 m
500 m
250 m
100 m
0
250 m
2 000 m
4 000 m
Below sea level

Boundaries

—— international border
—— maritime border

Ice features

◇ ◇ ◇ ◇ limit of winter pack ice
✦ ✦ ✦ ✦ limit of summer pack ice

☐ ice shelf

Scale 1:46 000 000
(projection: Lambert Azimuthal Equal Area)

0 km   500   1 000   1 500   2 000

FOCUS ON

OZONE LAYER DEPLETION

The ozone layer is a natural component of the atmosphere and plays a crucial role in the survival of life on Earth. The depletion of the ozone layer is thought to contribute to global climate change. Global warming has resulted in relatively higher temperatures in the polar region as well as a decline in the extent of ice. This has affected marine life and animals such as the polar bear higher up the food chain.

ANTARCTICA

Antarctica is the fifth largest continent in the world with an area of 14 million km². It is entirely covered by ice, which is about 2000 m thick. Despite having extreme physical conditions, Antarctica faces a number of environmental problems. Human activity, tourism, mining and fishing are major threats to the continent. Enforcement of international agreements has encouraged environmental sustainability in the region.

The ice caps that cover the Antarctic landmass are often several kilometres thick. They contain 70 per cent of all the fresh water in the world.

MAP KEY

ice cap

sea depth
- 0
- 250 m
- 2 000 m
- 4 000 m

△ mountain

⌂ volcano

● research station

◇◇◇ limit of winter pack ice

•••• limit of summer pack ice

▭ ice shelf

Scale 1:28 250 000
(projection: Lambert Azimuthal Equal Area)

0 km | 500 | 1 000 | 1 500

COUNTRIES

Today there are almost 200 separate countries in the world. National borders are influenced by physical features such as natural resources and the terrain, and by human factors such as ethnicity, culture, language, and religion. Straight-line borders often indicate former colonial rule. Whilst many countries have had the same borders for a long time, others are still disputing theirs.

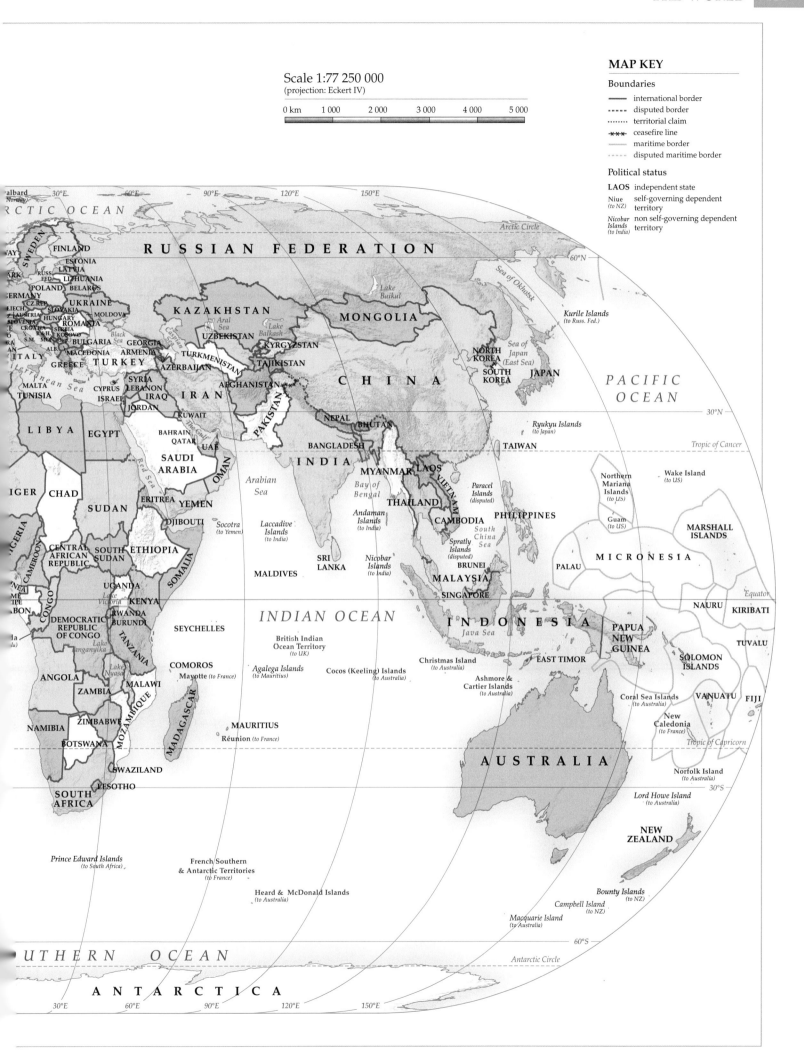

Scale 1:77 250 000
(projection: Eckert IV)

0 km   1 000   2 000   3 000   4 000   5 000

MAP KEY

Boundaries

——————— international border

- - - - - disputed border

·········· territorial claim

✕✕✕ ceasefire line

——————— maritime border

- - - - - disputed maritime border

Political status

LAOS independent state

Niue
(to NZ) self-governing dependent
territory

*Nicobar
Islands*
(to India) non self-governing dependent
territory

RELIEF

Approximately 70 per cent of the Earth is covered by water. The Pacific Ocean is the largest in the world and covers about a third of the globe.

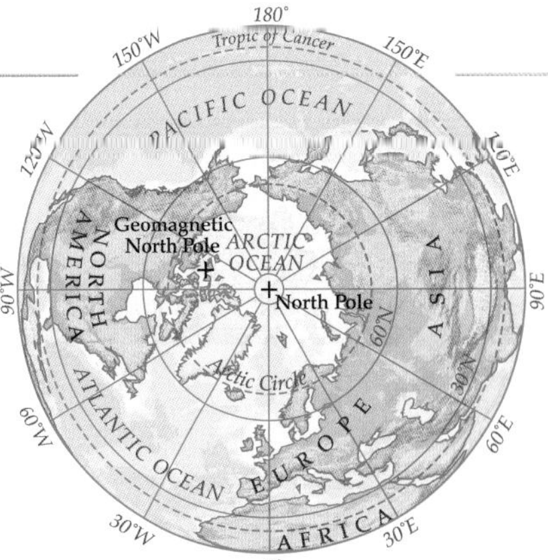
180°
Tropic of Cancer
150°W
150°E
120°W
120°E
PACIFIC OCEAN
NORTH AMERICA
Geomagnetic North Pole
ARCTIC OCEAN
North Pole
ASIA
90°W
90°E
60°N
30°N
Arctic Circle
ATLANTIC OCEAN
EUROPE
AFRICA
60°W
60°E
30°W
30°E
0°

NORTH POLE

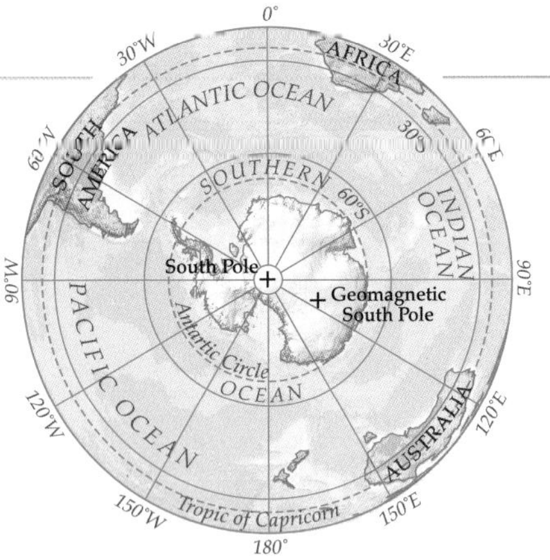
0°
30°W
30°E
AFRICA
ATLANTIC OCEAN
SOUTH AMERICA
60°N
30°S
60°E
SOUTHERN
60°S
INDIAN OCEAN
South Pole
Geomagnetic South Pole
90°W
90°E
PACIFIC OCEAN
Antarctic Circle
OCEAN
120°W
120°E
AUSTRALIA
150°W
150°E
Tropic of Capricorn
180°

SOUTH POLE

MAP KEY

Elevation

4 000 m
2 000 m
1 000 m
500 m
250 m
100 m
0
250 m
2 000 m
4 000 m
Below sea level

sandy desert

marsh/wetland

△ mountain

▽ depression

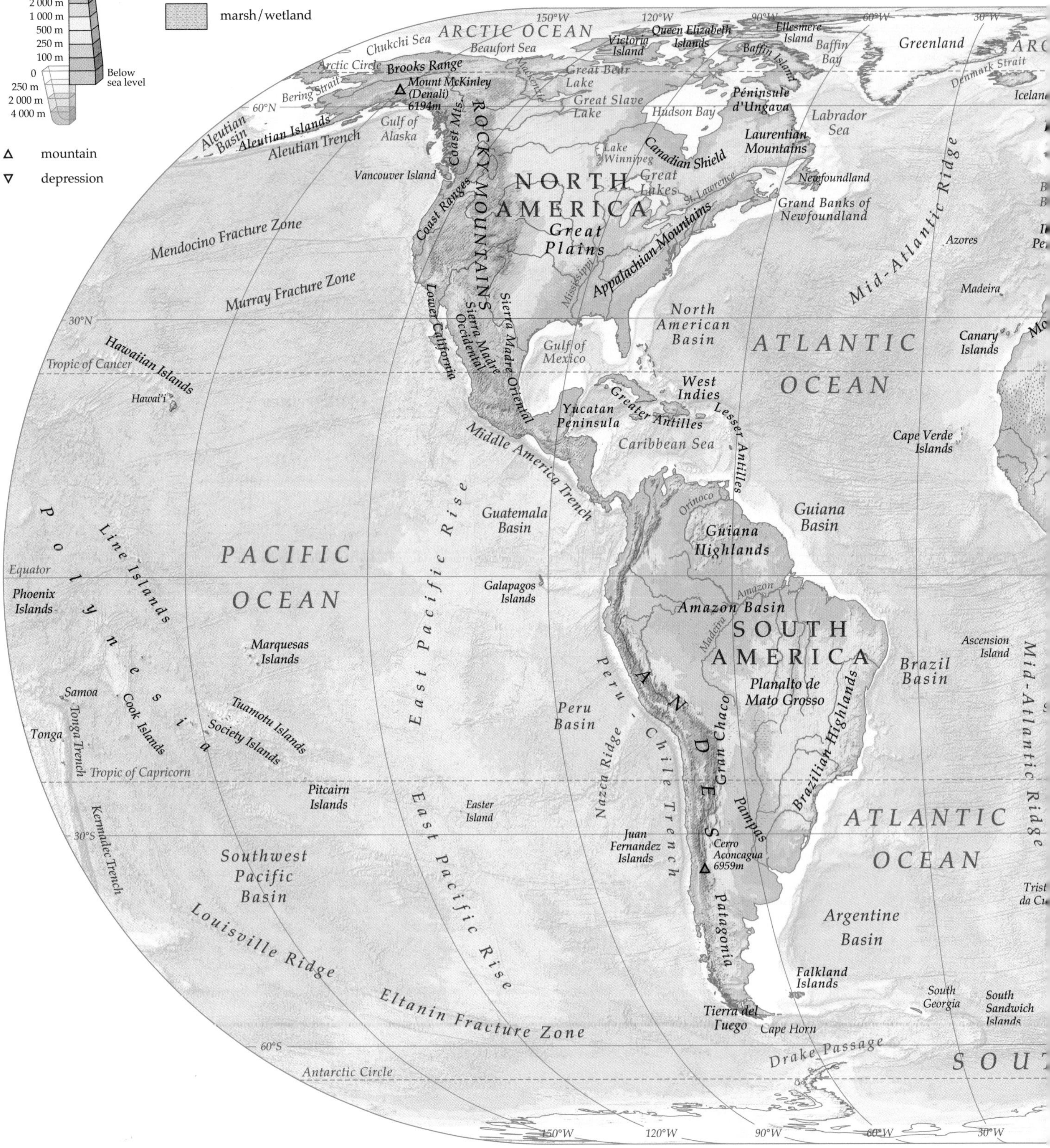
150°W
120°W
90°W
60°W
30°W
ARCTIC OCEAN
Chukchi Sea
Beaufort Sea
Victoria Island
Queen Elizabeth Islands
Ellesmere Island
Baffin Island
Baffin Bay
Greenland
Denmark Strait
Iceland
Arctic Circle
Brooks Range
Mount McKinley (Denali) 6194m
Bering Strait
Great Bear Lake
Great Slave Lake
Mackenzie
Hudson Bay
Péninsule d'Ungava
Labrador Sea
60°N
Aleutian Basin
Aleutian Islands
Aleutian Trench
Gulf of Alaska
Coast Mts
ROCKY MOUNTAINS
Lake Winnipeg
Canadian Shield
Laurentian Mountains
Vancouver Island
NORTH AMERICA
Great Lakes
St Lawrence
Newfoundland
Grand Banks of Newfoundland
Coast Ranges
Great Plains
Appalachian Mountains
Mid-Atlantic Ridge
Azores
Mendocino Fracture Zone
Murray Fracture Zone
Mississippi
Madeira
30°N
Lower California
Sierra Madre Occidental
Sierra Madre Oriental
North American Basin
ATLANTIC OCEAN
Canary Islands
Hawaiian Islands
Tropic of Cancer
Hawai'i
Gulf of Mexico
West Indies
Greater Antilles
Lesser Antilles
Yucatan Peninsula
Caribbean Sea
Cape Verde Islands
Middle America Trench
Orinoco
Guatemala Basin
Guiana Highlands
Guiana Basin
Polynesia
Line Islands
PACIFIC OCEAN
East Pacific Rise
Equator
Phoenix Islands
Galapagos Islands
Amazon
Amazon Basin
SOUTH AMERICA
Madeira
Ascension Island
Marquesas Islands
Brazil Basin
Mid-Atlantic Ridge
Planalto de Mato Grosso
Brazilian Highlands
Samoa
Cook Islands
Tuamotu Islands
Society Islands
Peru Basin
Peru-Chile Trench
ANDES
Gran Chaco
Tonga
Tonga Trench
Nazca Ridge
Tropic of Capricorn
Pitcairn Islands
Easter Island
Pampas
ATLANTIC OCEAN
Kermadec Trench
30°S
Juan Fernandez Islands
Cerro Aconcagua 6959m
Southwest Pacific Basin
Patagonia
Argentine Basin
Louisville Ridge
Falkland Islands
South Georgia
South Sandwich Islands
Eltanin Fracture Zone
Tierra del Fuego
Cape Horn
Drake Passage
60°S
Antarctic Circle

PHYSICAL FACTFILE

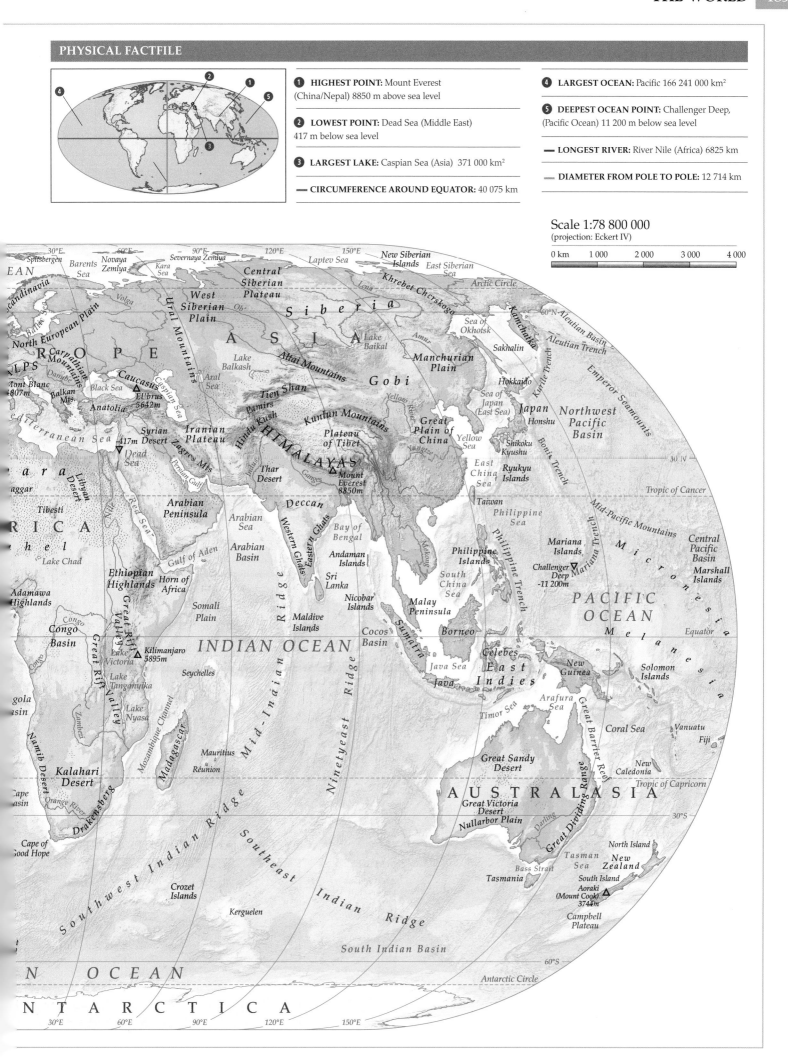

1 HIGHEST POINT: Mount Everest (China/Nepal) 8850 m above sea level

2 LOWEST POINT: Dead Sea (Middle East) 417 m below sea level

3 LARGEST LAKE: Caspian Sea (Asia) 371 000 km²

— **CIRCUMFERENCE AROUND EQUATOR:** 40 075 km

4 LARGEST OCEAN: Pacific 166 241 000 km²

5 DEEPEST OCEAN POINT: Challenger Deep, (Pacific Ocean) 11 200 m below sea level

— **LONGEST RIVER:** River Nile (Africa) 6825 km

— **DIAMETER FROM POLE TO POLE:** 12 714 km

Scale 1:78 800 000
(projection: Eckert IV)

0 km   1 000   2 000   3 000   4 000

CLIMATE

The world's atmospheric systems are driven by the energy of the Sun. The distribution of this energy, and therefore variations in climate across the world, depend upon distance from the Equator (latitude), height above sea level (altitude), winds, ocean currents and distance from the sea. Tropical climates along the Equator are separated from the two polar regions by a large temperate zone.

In the last decade there have been extreme weather conditions due to climate change. These include heat waves, tornadoes, hurricanes, severe drought, and extreme flooding.

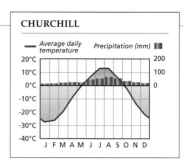

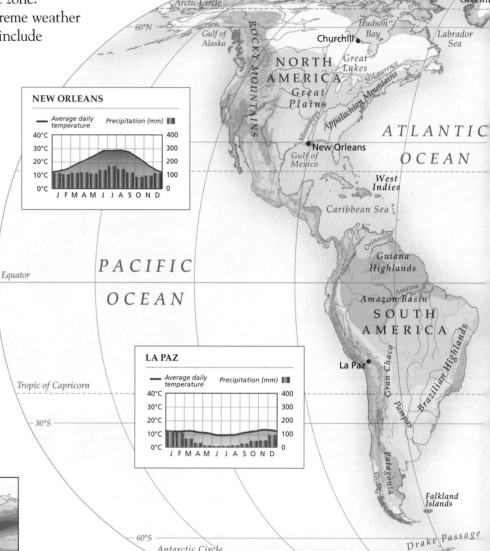

MAP KEY

Climate regions

- polar
- tundra
- sub-arctic
- cool continental
- temperate
- warm temperate
- mediterranean
- semi-arid
- arid
- tropical
- humid equatorial
- mountain

Scale 1:102 000 000
(projection: Eckert IV)

0 km 1 000 2 000 3 000 4 000 5 000

PRECIPITATION

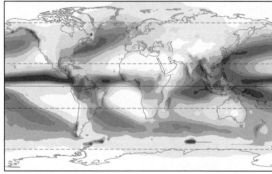

MAP KEY

Average annual precipitation (mm)

- above 3 500 mm
- 2 500 to 3 500 mm
- 2 000 to 2 500 mm
- 1 500 to 2 000 mm
- 1 000 to 1 500 mm
- 500 to 1 000 mm
- 200 to 500 mm
- 0 to 200 mm

AVERAGE JANUARY TEMPERATURE

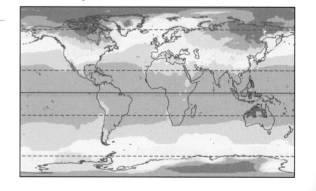

MAP KEY

Average January temperature

- above 30 °C
- 20 to 30 °C
- 10 to 20 °C
- 0 to 10 °C
- -10 to 0 °C
- -20 to -10 °C
- -30 to -20 °C
- below -30 °C

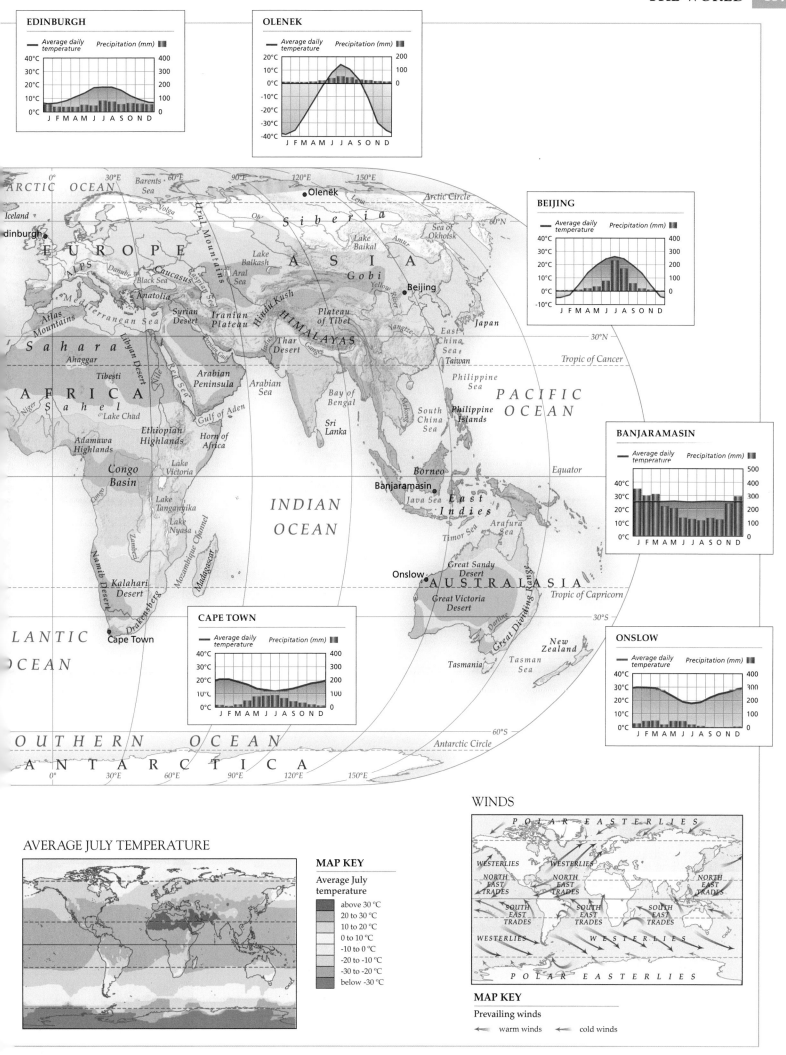

EDINBURGH

Average daily temperature — Precipitation (mm)

40°C 30°C 20°C 10°C 0°C — 400 300 200 100 0
J F M A M J J A S O N D

OLENEK

Average daily temperature — Precipitation (mm)

20°C 10°C 0°C -10°C -20°C -30°C -40°C — 200 100 0
J F M A M J J A S O N D

BEIJING

Average daily temperature — Precipitation (mm)

40°C 30°C 20°C 10°C 0°C -10°C — 400 300 200 100 0
J F M A M J J A S O N D

BANJARAMASIN

Average daily temperature — Precipitation (mm)

40°C 30°C 20°C 10°C 0°C — 500 400 300 200 100 0
J F M A M J J A S O N D

CAPE TOWN

Average daily temperature — Precipitation (mm)

40°C 30°C 20°C 10°C 0°C — 400 300 200 100 0
J F M A M J J A S O N D

ONSLOW

Average daily temperature — Precipitation (mm)

40°C 30°C 20°C 10°C 0°C — 400 300 200 100 0
J F M A M J J A S O N D

ARCTIC OCEAN
Barents Sea
Iceland
Edinburgh
EUROPE
ALPS
Danube
Black Sea
Caucasus
Anatolia
Mediterranean Sea
Atlas Mountains
Sahara
Ahaggar
Tibesti
AFRICA
Sahel
Niger
Lake Chad
Adamawa Highlands
Congo Basin
Congo
Lake Victoria
Lake Tanganyika
Lake Nyasa
Zambezi
Namib Desert
Kalahari Desert
Drakensberg
Cape Town
ATLANTIC OCEAN
SOUTHERN OCEAN
ANTARCTICA

Volga
Ural Mountains
Ob'
Siberia
Olenëk
Lena
Arctic Circle
Sea of Okhotsk
60°N
Lake Balkash
Aral Sea
Caspian Sea
Lake Baikal
Amur
ASIA
Gobi
Yellow River
Beijing
Persian Gulf
Syrian Desert
Iranian Plateau
Hindu Kush
HIMALAYAS
Plateau of Tibet
Yangtze
Japan
East China Sea
Taiwan
30°N
Tropic of Cancer
Red Sea
Arabian Peninsula
Gulf of Aden
Ethiopian Highlands
Horn of Africa
Nile
Ganges
Thar Desert
Arabian Sea
Bay of Bengal
Sri Lanka
Philippine Sea
PACIFIC OCEAN
Philippine Islands
South China Sea
Mekong
Borneo
Banjaramasin
Java Sea
East Indies
Equator
INDIAN OCEAN
Arafura Sea
Timor Sea
Onslow
Great Sandy Desert
AUSTRALASIA
Great Victoria Desert
Tropic of Capricorn
Great Dividing Range
Darling
New Zealand
Tasman Sea
Tasmania
30°S
60°S
Antarctic Circle

0° 30°E 60°E 90°E 120°E 150°E
0° 30°E 60°E 90°E 120°E 150°E

AVERAGE JULY TEMPERATURE

MAP KEY

Average July temperature

- above 30 °C
- 20 to 30 °C
- 10 to 20 °C
- 0 to 10 °C
- -10 to 0 °C
- -20 to -10 °C
- -30 to -20 °C
- below -30 °C

WINDS

POLAR EASTERLIES
WESTERLIES WESTERLIES
NORTH EAST TRADES NORTH EAST TRADES NORTH EAST TRADES
SOUTH EAST TRADES SOUTH EAST TRADES SOUTH EAST TRADES
WESTERLIES WESTERLIES
POLAR EASTERLIES

MAP KEY

Prevailing winds

⟵ warm winds   ⟵ cold winds

ENVIRONMENT

The world can be divided into a number of major biomes. These are regions with a specific combination of natural vegetation, animals, climates, soils and landscapes, which combine to give each its unique character. Some biomes have a far greater plant and animal biodiversity than others and many are under threat from human activity.

Tundra on Clavering Island, North East Greenland National Park, Greenland

Scale 1:108 000 000
(projection: Eckert IV)

0 km 1 000 2 000 3 000 4 000 5 000 6 000

MAP KEY

World biomes

- polar
- tundra
- coniferous forest
- deciduous forest
- temperate grassland
- mediterranean
- savanna
- tropical forest
- hot desert
- cold desert
- mountain

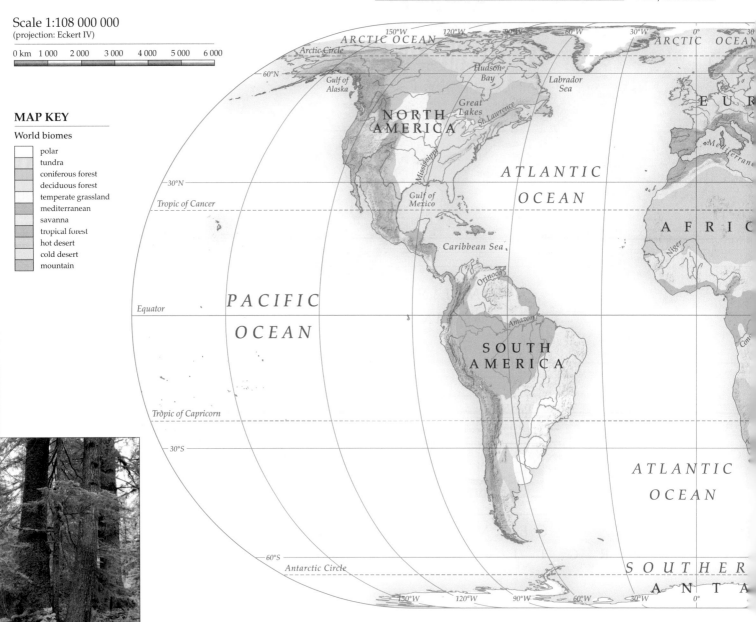

Coniferous forest, West Coast, British Columbia, Canada

Savanna in the Serengeti, Tanzania

Tropical rainforest in the Gambia, Africa

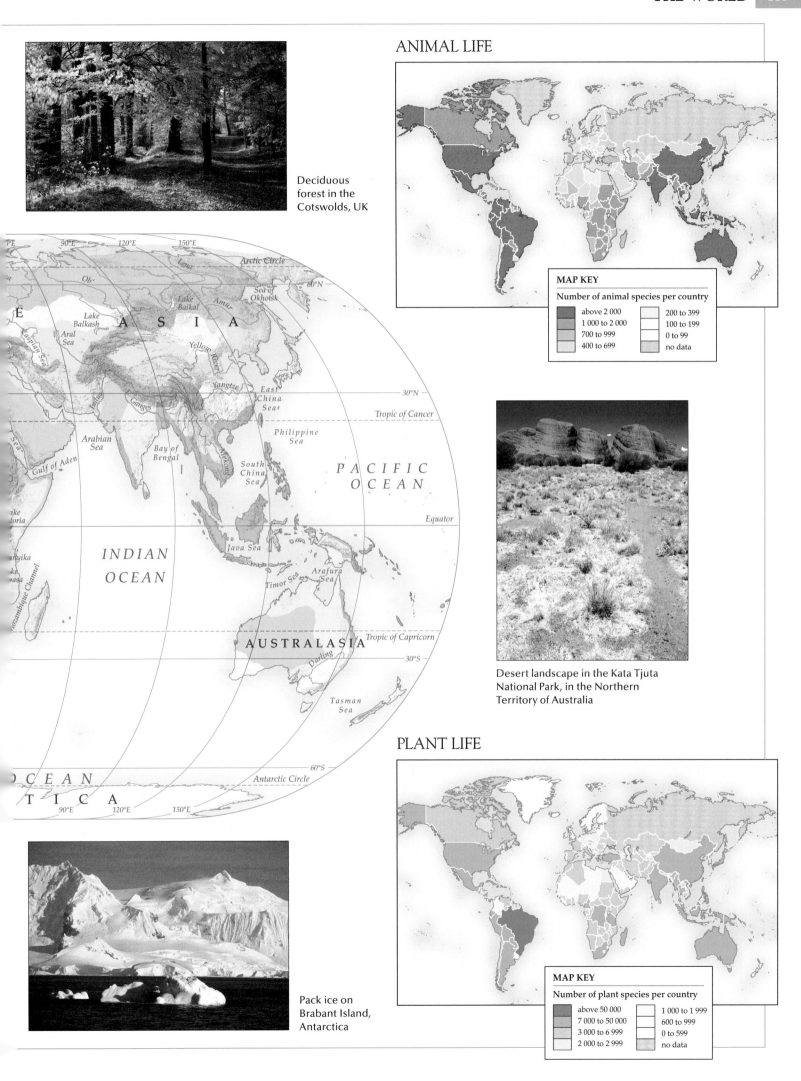

Deciduous forest in the Cotswolds, UK

ANIMAL LIFE

MAP KEY

Number of animal species per country

- above 2 000
- 1 000 to 2 000
- 700 to 999
- 400 to 699
- 200 to 399
- 100 to 199
- 0 to 99
- no data

Desert landscape in the Kata Tjuta National Park, in the Northern Territory of Australia

Pack ice on Brabant Island, Antarctica

PLANT LIFE

MAP KEY

Number of plant species per country

- above 50 000
- 7 000 to 50 000
- 3 000 to 6 999
- 2 000 to 2 999
- 1 000 to 1 999
- 600 to 999
- 0 to 599
- no data

TIME ZONES

The world is subdivided into 24 time zones. The time zones have a width of 15 degrees longitude each, measured east and west, starting from the Greenwich Prime Meridian (GPM) at 0 degree longitude. Each time zone has a uniform standard time in which the same clock time always corresponds to the same portion of the day as the Earth rotates. This means all areas or cities located within the same time zone can keep exactly the same time. The 180 degrees east of the GPM up to the International Date Line, which is located in the mid-Pacific Ocean, are divided into 12 time zones (+), and similarly those on the west into 12 time zones (-). As one moves east of the prime meridian, every time zone is ahead of the previous one by one hour. For instance, if it is mid-day in London, it will be 1:00 pm in Cameroon, which lies 15 degrees east longitude, 2:00 pm in Uganda, Rwanda and Burundi, and 3:00 pm in Addis Ababa, Nairobi and Dar es Salaam. This means people travelling to the east have to adjust their watch accordingly. On the other hand, time zones move back by one hour every

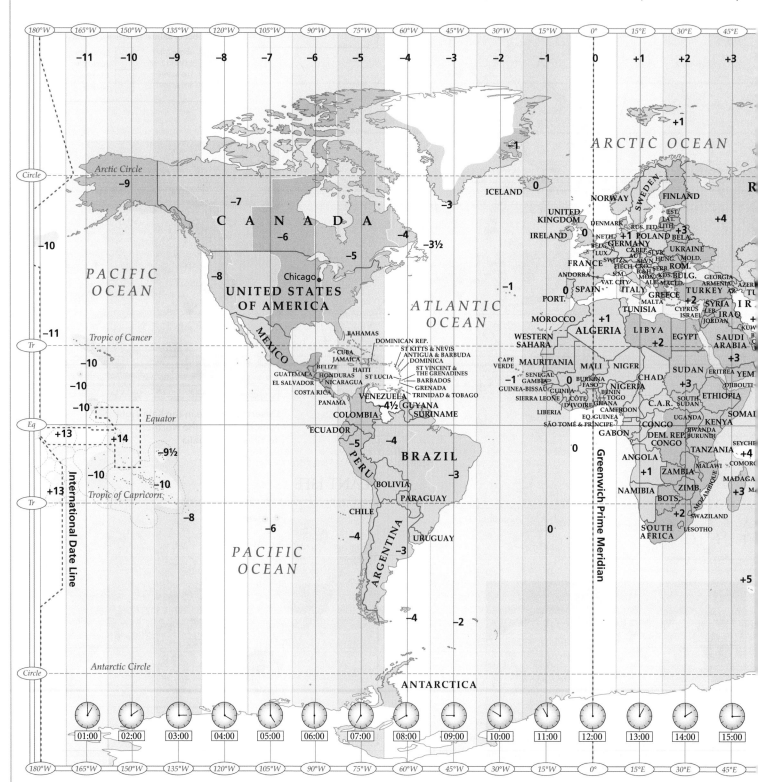

15 degrees movement to the west of the GPM. This means when it is midday in London (GPM), it is 8:00am in Brazil, which is 60 degrees west of London (GPM).

Some countries, however, do not strictly follow these 24 time zones. Iceland, for instance does not adopt the time zone that corresponds to its longitude. Others, like India, have adopted half-hour time zones by combining two neighbouring time zones. Some other countries also put the clocks forward by one hour (daylight saving) in order to have a longer period in the evening.

EXERCISE 15

Steps to follow: First identify the longitudinal location of the places or cities mentioned in the question, that is Tokyo and Chicago.

Divide the number of longitudes that each place or city is away from the GPM or London by 15 to find out the number of hours that each city is away from London either to the east or west.

If the city in question is east of London, the calculated number of hours is added to that of London; if it is to the west, the calculated time is subtracted from that of London.

QUESTIONS

1. What are the times in Tokyo and Chicago when it is 12:00 noon in London?

2. What is the time in Kigali when it is 9:00am in the morning in Addis Ababa?

ANSWERS

1. The time in Tokyo is found by dividing 140 degrees east by 15 = 9:30 hrs. Add this to 12:00 noon = 9:30pm

   The time in Chicago is found by dividing 90 degrees west by 15 = 6 hrs. Subtract this from 12:00 noon = 6:00am

2. The time in Kigali is found by subtracting 30 degrees E of Kigali from nearly 39E = 9 degrees west of Addis. When the difference is a little less or more than 15 degrees, it is up to the country to decide to which time zone it belongs. Rwanda preferred to be one hour behind Addis. It means the time in Kigali will be 8:00am.

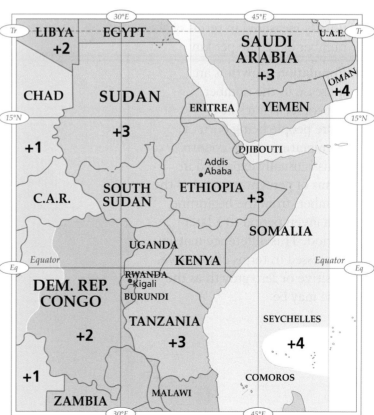

POPULATION

The current world population is about 7 billion, of which 60.8 per cent is found in Asia, 13 per cent in Africa, 12 per cent in Europe, 8 per cent in North America, 5.7 per cent in South America and 0.5 per cent in Australasia. The average population growth ranges from 0.9 per cent in Eurasia and North America to over 2.5 per cent in most parts of Africa and the Middle East. Most of the African population lives in rural areas, but worldwide the number of people that now live in towns and cities is the same as in the countryside.

There has been a tremendous increase in urbanisation which has occurred more among less developed economies since the 1950s. Pressure on land area has constantly increased, mainly as a result of high population density and growth. This has had a negative impact on the environment and ecosystems, as wetlands and other natural habitats have been encroached on.

- **Urbanisation** is the increase over time in the population of cities, in relation to the region's rural population, and is caused by movement of people from rural areas to urban areas.

- **Population density** is defined as the number of people in relation to the area they occupy, usually measured in terms of the number of people per km^2.

- **Population growth** is an increase in the number of people, as a result of more people being born or immigrating into a country. This is usually expressed in terms of percentage rates of the numbers from the beginning of a given period to a later period. This difference may be expressed in terms of negative, positive or zero growth as the case may be.

MEGA-CITIES

The world is becoming increasingly more urbanised and it is predicted that two-thirds of the world's population will live in cities by the year 2030. Today's cities are extremely populated and the term mega-city is used to describe a city with more than 10 million inhabitants. By 2011, there were 25 mega-cities in the world (16 of which are in Asia). These mega-cities were home to more than 300 million people, generated 18% of the world's GDP and were responsible for 10% of global carbon emissions. The number of mega-cities is expected to grow in the next decade.

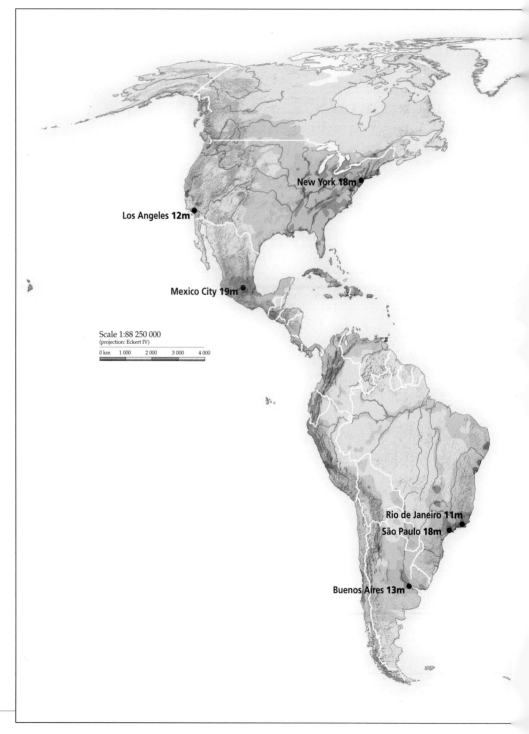

New York 18m

Los Angeles 12m

Mexico City 19m

Scale 1:88 250 000
(projection: Eckert IV)

0 km   1 000   2 000   3 000   4 000

Rio de Janeiro 11m

São Paulo 18m

Buenos Aires 13m

POPULATION GROWTH

POPULATION GROWTH FORECAST

Billions of people

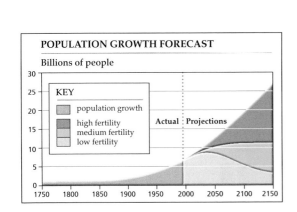

KEY
- population growth
- high fertility
- medium fertility
- low fertility

Actual | Projections

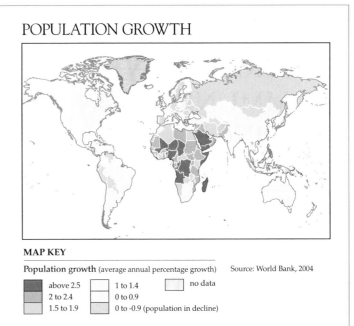

MAP KEY

Population growth (average annual percentage growth)   Source: World Bank, 2004

- above 2.5
- 2 to 2.4
- 1.5 to 1.9
- 1 to 1.4
- 0 to 0.9
- 0 to -0.9 (population in decline)
- no data

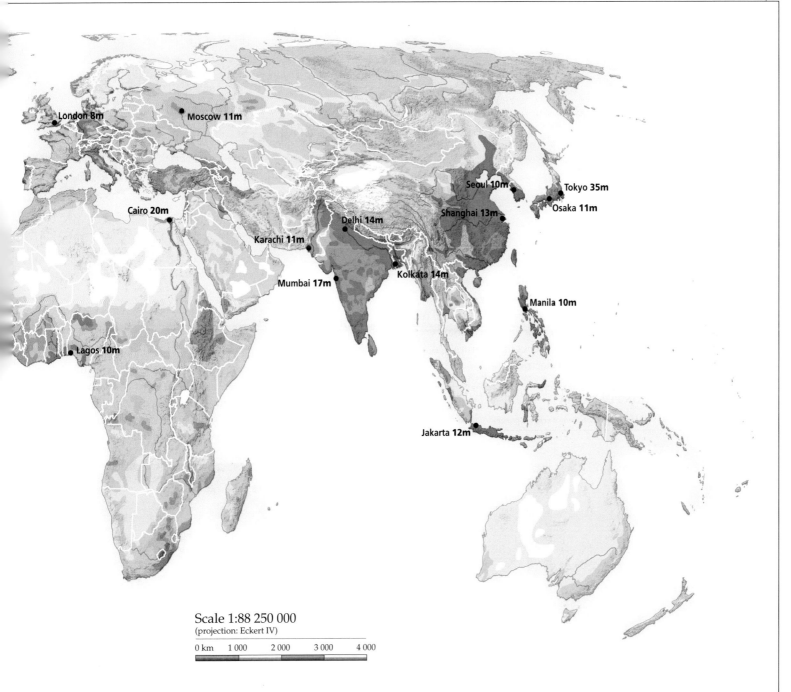

London 8m
Moscow 11m
Seoul 10m
Tokyo 35m
Osaka 11m
Cairo 20m
Shanghai 13m
Delhi 14m
Karachi 11m
Kolkata 14m
Mumbai 17m
Manila 10m
Lagos 10m
Jakarta 12m

Scale 1:88 250 000
(projection: Eckert IV)

0 km   1 000   2 000   3 000   4 000

MINING, ENERGY, INFORMATION AND COMMUNICATION TECHNOLOGY

Energy sources may be renewable or non-renewable. Renewable energy sources are continuous. They include solar, hydroelectricity, wind, geothermal, biomass fuel wood, ocean thermal energy and wave power. Non-renewable energy sources are drawn from finite resources; they include coal, oil and natural gas. These fossil fuels are becoming depleted but consumption is increasing in the developing countries and there is need to develop alternative sources of energy.

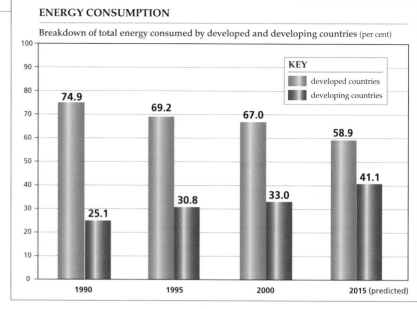

ENERGY CONSUMPTION

Breakdown of total energy consumed by developed and developing countries (per cent)

KEY
- developed countries
- developing countries

Year	Developed	Developing
1990	74.9	25.1
1995	69.2	30.8
2000	67.0	33.0
2015 (predicted)	58.9	41.1

WORLD PRIMARY ENERGY SUPPLY

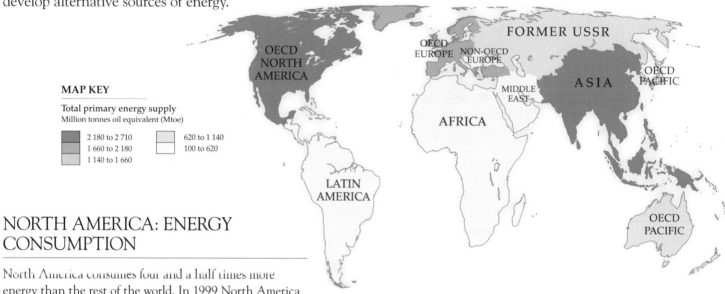

MAP KEY

Total primary energy supply
Million tonnes oil equivalent (Mtoe)

- 2 180 to 2 710
- 1 660 to 2 180
- 1 140 to 1 660
- 620 to 1 140
- 100 to 620

NORTH AMERICA: ENERGY CONSUMPTION

North America consumes four and a half times more energy than the rest of the world. In 1999 North America consumed most of the world's energy demand, which included oil, natural gas, coal and electricity. North America also accounts for 19 per cent of the oil production, 31 per cent of natural gas, 25 per cent of coal and 32 per cent of electricity.

ENERGY CONSUMPTION PER CAPITA

North America versus World (million British thermal units per person)

KEY
- North America
- World

Year	North America	World
1980	284	62
1990	280	64
1999	282	62
2010 (predicted)	311	71

BIOFUELS

In search of clean energy that does not pollute the environment, there has been development of biofuels from plants like jatropha and sugarcane, which can produce oil that can be added to diesel to reduce carbon emissions. This development poses another danger because it takes up land that should be used for producing food crops, resulting into famine.

Jatropha plant

OIL PRODUCTION AROUND THE WORLD

NORTH AMERICA

EUROPE

ASIA

AFRICA

SOUTH AMERICA

AUSTRALASIA

MAP KEY

Oil reserves

▨ oil reserve

WHO HAS THE OIL

New countries have discovered oil and are at different stages of exploration and development. These include Ghana, Equatorial Guinea, Uganda and Zanzibar.

INFORMATION AND COMMUNICATION TECHNOLOGY

The world has moved from the era of industrialisation, which was the engine for development, to an era of information society that is now the drive for growth and development.

Some manufacturing industries have been relocated in the developing countries like India, Indonesia and China. Some jobs are also outsourced to other countries and carried out through the Internet.

Information technology includes telecommunication like mobile phones, the Internet, digitalisation, fibre-optic cables and broadband. There are numerous innovations in the use of mobile phones to access and send money, text messages, pay bills, view the Internet and use email. Weather and agriculture trade information is received in real time, anywhere and at anytime where there is a network. In September 2011, Africa became the world's second most connected region in terms of mobile subscriptions. There are over 616 million mobile phone subscribers in Africa.

INTERNET

The internet is becoming increasingly accessible and used in Africa. There are 1.3 million internet users in Kenya. The internet is being used to aid learning in schools, delivering education courses, teleconferencing, Skype, social networks like Facebook, e-commerce for buying and selling products and even e-government. In developing countries, there are initiatives to make the internet more affordable through fibre-optic cables and broadband.

New technologies are developed everyday, replacing older technology such as telegraphs and the use of the post office.

Satellite dish on top of a roof

Inside an Internet café in Africa

ECONOMY

The world economy is usually assessed on countries' gross domestic product (GDP) and on associated per capita income. There are four sectors of an economy: the primary sector, which mainly involves the production of raw materials; the secondary sector, which is concerned with manufacturing; the tertiary sector, which involves service industries; and the quaternary sector, a relatively new sector concerned with intellectual services. This is basically a knowledge-based part of the economy which includes special services such as information generation and sharing, information technology, consultation, education, research and development, financial planning, and other knowledge-based services such as the entertainment industry.

The strength of the four sectors is a strong indicator of how economically developed a country is. Less developed countries usually have a larger primary sector and a poorly developed secondary sector, while more economically developed countries have highly developed secondary, tertiary and quaternary sectors and only a small proportion of the population is involved in modern agriculture.

The world economy has recently faced financial crisis and this has negatively affected developing countries in terms of demand for their exports and also reduced foreign aid. High levels of corruption in many developing countries have also had a negative impact on individual countries' economic growth.

PRIMARY SECTOR

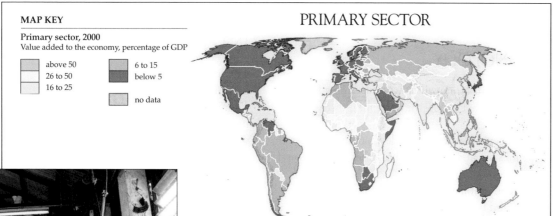

MAP KEY

Primary sector, 2000
Value added to the economy, percentage of GDP

above 50	6 to 15
26 to 50	below 5
16 to 25	no data

NORTH AMERICA (2009)

Sector	USA	Mexico	Jamaica
Primary (% of GDP)	1.2	3.9	5.8
Secondary (% of GDP)	22.1	32.8	29.5
Tertiary (% of GDP)	76.7	63.4	64.7

Sheep shearing in Australia

Bread loaves on production line

SECONDARY SECTOR

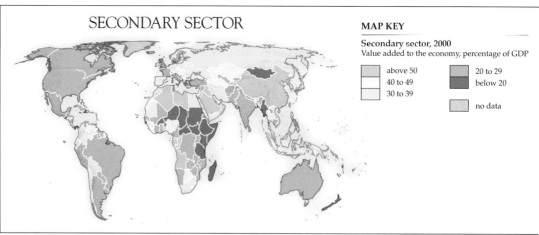

MAP KEY

Secondary sector, 2000
Value added to the economy, percentage of GDP

above 50	20 to 29
40 to 49	below 20
30 to 39	no data

TERTIARY SECTOR

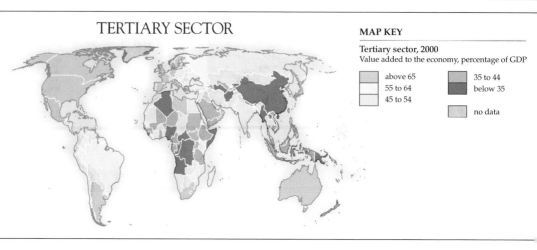

MAP KEY

Tertiary sector, 2000
Value added to the economy, percentage of GDP

above 65	35 to 44
55 to 64	below 35
45 to 54	no data

WORLD GDP

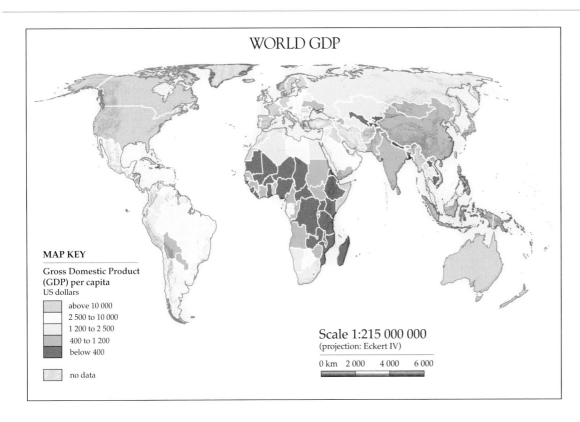

MAP KEY

Gross Domestic Product
(GDP) per capita
US dollars

- above 10 000
- 2 500 to 10 000
- 1 200 to 2 500
- 400 to 1 200
- below 400

- no data

Scale 1:215 000 000
(projection: Eckert IV)

0 km   2 000   4 000   6 000

EUROPE (2009)			
Sector	Norway	UK	Albania
Primary (% of GDP)	2.6	0.7	20.7
Secondary (% of GDP)	39.7	21.4	19.7
Tertiary (% of GDP)	57.7	77.8	59.6

AFRICA (2009)			
Sector	Algeria	S. Africa	Malawi
Primary (% of GDP)	12	2.5	30.3
Secondary (% of GDP)	56.5	31.6	16.7
Tertiary (% of GDP)	31.5	65.9	53

SOUTH AMERICA (2009)			
Sector	Argentina	Brazil	Bolivia
Primary (% of GDP)	10	5.5	10
Secondary (% of GDP)	30.7	27.5	40
Tertiary (% of GDP)	59.2	67	50

GROSS DOMESTIC PRODUCT (GDP)

Gross Domestic Product (GDP) normally refers to the market value of all final goods and services produced within a country in a given period. In some cases GDP is defined differently depending on the country's approach. Definitions of GDP may take a production approach, income approach or expenditure approach as countries may decide for themselves.

NEWLY INDUSTRIALISED COUNTRIES

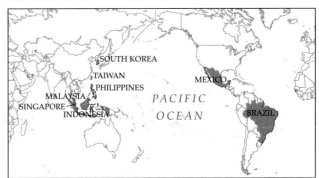

ASIA (2009)			
Sector	Japan	China	Bangladesh
Primary (% of GDP)	1.2	10.1	18.4
Secondary (% of GDP)	27.3	46.8	28.6
Tertiary (% of GDP)	71.6	43.1	53

MAJOR TRADE BLOCS

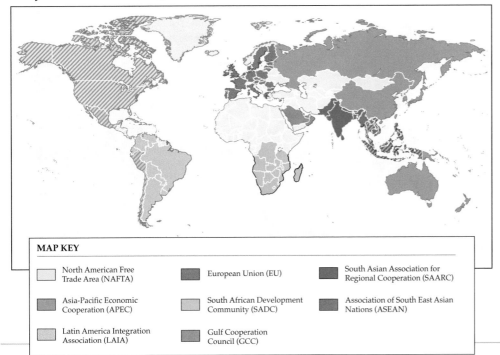

MAP KEY

- North American Free Trade Area (NAFTA)
- Asia-Pacific Economic Cooperation (APEC)
- Latin America Integration Association (LAIA)
- European Union (EU)
- South African Development Community (SADC)
- Gulf Cooperation Council (GCC)
- South Asian Association for Regional Cooperation (SAARC)
- Association of South East Asian Nations (ASEAN)

AUSTRALASIA AND OCEANIA (2009)			
Sector	Australia	Fiji	New Zealand
Primary (% of GDP)	4	12	4.8
Secondary (% of GDP)	24.6	20.2	24.5
Tertiary (% of GDP)	71.4	67.7	70.7

INDUSTRIALISATION AND POLLUTION

Industrialisation is considered to be the engine of development. For example, development in countries such as China and Indonesia has been driven by the rapid growth of industries like the mining of metal ores. Chemicals, mineral fuels and petroleum products are among the top five commodities that are exported from countries such as Singapore. Singapore exports its chemicals to the following countries: USA, Canada, India, China, Malaysia and Indonesia.

NEWLY INDUSTRIALISED AND INDUSTRIALISING COUNTRIES

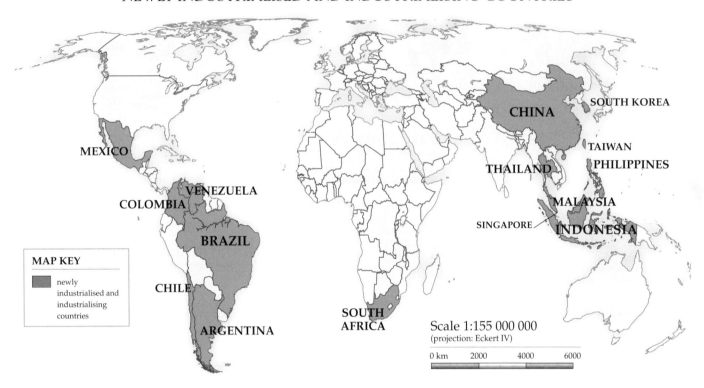

MAP KEY

newly industrialised and industrialising countries

Scale 1:155 000 000
(projection: Eckert IV)

0 km   2000   4000   6000

POLLUTION

The world is faced by a problem of different types of pollution. Pollution is contaminating air, water bodies and land. Air pollution has led to a build-up of greenhouse gases in the atmosphere. In the seas and oceans, major oil spills threaten marine wildlife and fisheries. Toxic contaminants are also choking fresh water bodies. Agricultural and industrial waste, litter and improper garbage disposal are major contributors to soil contamination.

Water and air pollution have negative effects on human health. Noise is a common type of pollution whose sources range from traffic in major cities, construction works and some industries. Exposure to noise pollution can result in permanent hearing damage. Because of increasing pollution, laws and regulations have been put in place to control it. Cleaner production processes and reduction of carbon emissions are being promoted.

A municipal dump ground in Hafani, India

Liquid manure being pumped into a river near Rotterdam, Holland

MARINE POLLUTION

As well as being subject to climate change, the Earth is under threat from pollution. This map (below left) shows the extent of marine pollution. Such pollution can originate from air pollution, shipping, dumping of toxic substances and, most frequently, run-off from sewers, cities and agricultural activity.

Fort Portal waste composting site

Barrels filled with nuclear waste

MARINE POLLUTION

NORTH AMERICA

EUROPE

ASIA

AFRICA

SOUTH AMERICA

AUSTRALASIA

MAP KEY

Marine pollution

Areas of severe coastal pollution (very concentrated pollution, for all or part of the year, seriously affecting marine life and ecosystems)

Areas of resistant coastal pollution (long term, though not necessarily severe, pollution)

ACID RAIN

A form of pollution; acid rain causes considerable damage to trees, buildings, river systems and oceans. It results mostly from the burning of fossil fuels that releases emissions of sulphur and nitrogen. These emissions combine with water vapour, and oxygen in the atmosphere.

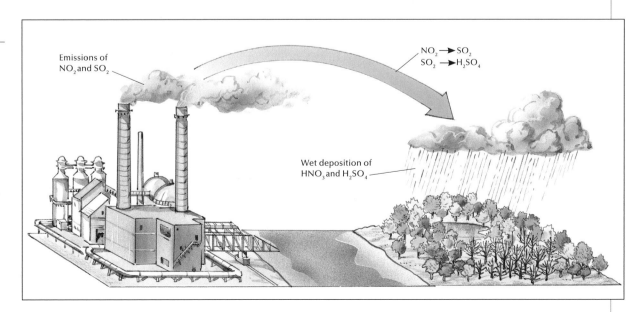

Emissions of NO_2 and SO_2

$NO_2 \rightarrow SO_2$
$SO_2 \rightarrow H_2SO_4$

Wet deposition of HNO_3 and H_2SO_4

CLIMATE CHANGE AND THE ENVIRONMENT

Global warming is the continuous heating up of the Earth as a result of the emission of greenhouse gases into the atmosphere.

EVIDENCE OF GLOBAL WARMING

There is growing evidence that human-induced global warming is threatening the Earth with disaster. Some of the manifestations of global warming are as follows:

- Since the beginning of the 20th century, the Earth's mean surface temperature has increased by 0.6°C.
- Experience, in 1998, of the strongest El Niño phenomenon to date.
- Global sea level has risen about three times faster over the past 100 years compared with the previous 3000 years.
- The Arctic ice peak has lost about 40 per cent of its thickness over the past four decades. Its polar ice is declining at 9 per cent per decade.
- The increasing desertification of areas near the great deserts such as the Sahara.
- Shifts in climate leading to change in range and behaviour of certain plants and animals.

CAUSES OF GLOBAL WARMING

- It is generally agreed that global warming results primarily from human activities that release heat-trapping gases and particles into the air.
- Industrialisation continues to emit heat trapping gases such as carbon dioxide (CO_2), chlorofluorocarbons (CFCs), methane, nitrous oxide and hydroflourocarbons (HFCs) into the atmosphere. Less developed countries are at a greater danger because they do not have the financial wherewithal and engineering expertise to limit gas emissions from industries.
- The increasing global energy needs and the resultant burning of fossil fuels is accelerating global warming and increasing atmospheric carbon dioxide concentrations. In the USA, coal-burning plants – the largest source of CO_2 pollution – produce 2.5 billion tonnes of CO_2 annually.
- The increasing deforestation and wetland drainage for settlement, fuel and agriculture.

TACKLING GLOBAL WARMING

- To reduce the emission of heat-trapping gases, such as CO_2, methane, CFC and nitrous oxides, there is a need to cut consumption of fossil fuels even though developing countries are constrained by inadequate finances to do this. It is essential to use cost effective technologies that emit fewer fumes, and appliances that conserve energy.
- Countries meet every year to negotiate and lay strategies to mitigate climate change. These strategies include 2005 Kyoto Protocol, 2009 Copenhagen, 2010 Cancun and 2011 Durban, South Africa.
- The climate change fund is support to be provided to developing countries for mitigation measures.

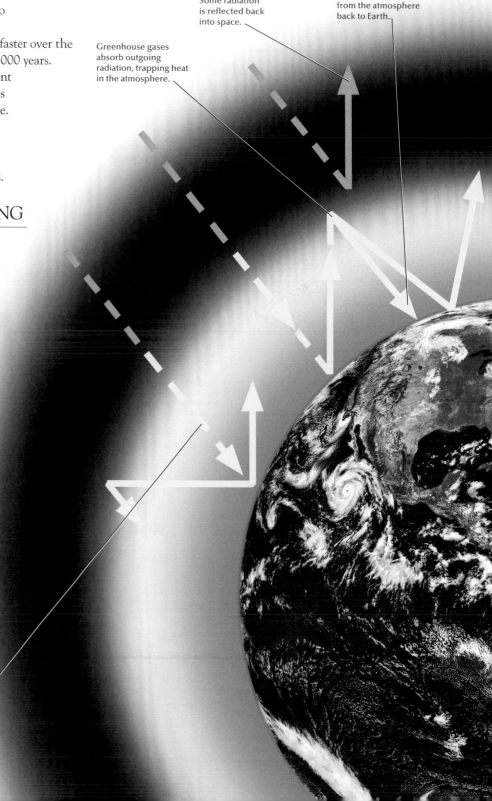

Some radiation is reflected back into space.

Radiation is re-emitted from the atmosphere back to Earth.

Greenhouse gases absorb outgoing radiation, trapping heat in the atmosphere.

Greenhouse gases allow sufficient solar radiation through to warm the Earth's surface.

BIODIVERSITY

Biodiversity is the number of different species found within a defined area, or ecosystem. Ecosystem diversity takes in the broad differences between ecosystem types, and the diversity of habitats and ecological processes occurring within each ecosystem type. Humanity derives all of its food and many medicines and industrial products from the wild and domesticated components of biological diversity. Biotic resources also serve recreation and tourism and underpin the ecosystems that provide us with many services. While the benefits of such resources are considerable, the value of biological diversity is not restricted to these. The enormous diversity of life in itself is of crucial value, probably giving greater resilience to ecosystems and organisms. Biodiversity also has important social and cultural values.

Human impact such as over-exploitation of the land, climate change and the introduction of 'invasive' new species are all contributing to a huge worldwide reduction in biodiversity. Worldwide, over 140 species of birds, animals and marine life are threatened with extinction; and between 1990 and 2000, 8.9 million hectares of forest were destroyed every year.

Part of the ecosystem

TACKLING BIODIVERSITY

- Conventions were set up and signed between countries in honour of biodiversity, as highlighted below:
  - Countries of the world signed a Convention on Biological Diversity (CBD), because of the importance of biodiversity.
  - The Convention on International Trade in Endangered Species of Wild Fauna and Flora (CITES) was drawn up, because of the trade in endangered species.
- There are also laws and agreements to prevent species from over exploitation and extinction, for example the International Whaling Agreements.
- There are international organisations that support the conservation of biodiversity, such as:
  - WWF – World Wide Fund for Nature.
  - IUCN – The International Union for Conservation of Nature. There are many national and local organisations that promote conservation work, including wildlife clubs in schools.

VEGETATION: PROTECTION OF WATER RESOURCES

Natural vegetation cover in water catchments helps to maintain hydrological cycles, regulating and stabilising water runoff, and acting as a buffer against extreme events such as flood and drought. Vegetation removal results in siltation of catchment waterways, loss of water yield and quality, and degradation of aquatic habitat, among other things. Vegetation also helps to regulate underground water tables, preventing dry land salinity, which affects vast areas of Australia's agricultural lands, at great cost to the community. Wetlands and forests act as water purifying systems, while mangroves trap silt, reducing impacts on marine ecosystems.

VEGETATION: SOIL FORMATION AND PROTECTION

Biological diversity helps in the formation and maintenance of soil structure and the retention of moisture and nutrient levels. The loss of biological diversity through clearing of vegetation has contributed to the salinisation of soils, leaching of nutrients, laterisation of minerals and accelerated erosion of topsoil, reducing the land's productivity. Trees, on the other hand, lower the water table and remove deposited salt from the upper soil horizons. Soil protection by maintenance of biological diversity can preserve the productive capacity of the soil, prevent landslides, safeguard coastlines and riverbanks, and prevent the degradation of coral reefs, and freshwater and coastal fisheries, by siltation.

VEGETATION: CONTRIBUTION TO CLIMATE STABILITY

Vegetation influences climate at the macro and micro levels. Growing evidence suggests that undisturbed forest helps to maintain the rainfall in its immediate vicinity by recycling water vapour at a steady rate back into the atmosphere, and through the canopy's effect in promoting atmospheric turbulence. At smaller scales, vegetation has a moderating influence on local climates and may create quite specific microclimates. Some organisms are dependent on such microclimates for their existence.

SUSTAINABLE DEVELOPMENT

Sustainable development is development that meets the needs of the present generation without compromising the ability of future generations to meet their own needs. Rapid population growth has put pressure on the world's resources and affected quality of life. There is increased famine, hunger and poverty and natural disasters. The third United Nations Conference on Sustainable Development was held in June 2012 in Rio de Janeiro in Brazil after 20 years to review the progress made. While countries of the world have made efforts encourage sustainable development, there are emerging challenges like climate change and natural disasters that hamper progress.

ORGANISATIONS

There are many Non Governmental Organisations (NGOs) that promote sustainable development. OXFAM, for example, advocates for justice in development. Others are active in the conservation of natural resources, such as the World Wide Fund for Nature (WWF), and the International Union for Conservation of Nature (IUCN).

For development to be sustainable, it must not destroy the environment through degradation and pollution. Society must be at the centre of development. Production must not exploit people. Profits should be made without exploiting people or the environment. Sustainable use of resource areas, using more resources that do not pollute the environment, include solar energy and biogas. Unsustainable use of energy is the excessive use of biomass, for example, charcoal which leads to deforestation.

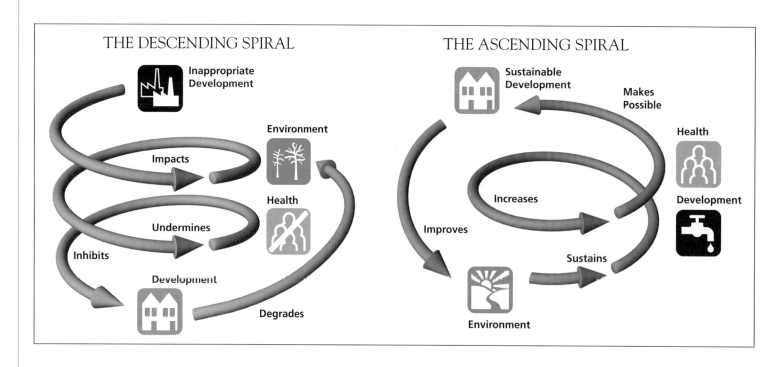

A built-up water well in Africa

Solar power farm

MILLENNIUM DEVELOPMENT GOALS

Governments at the United Nations Millennium Summit in 2000 agreed the following goals – and set quantifiable targets to be achieved by 2015.

1. Eradicate extreme poverty and hunger
2. Achieve universal primary education
3. Promote gender equality and empower women
4. Reduce child mortality
5. Improve maternal health
6. Combat HIV/AIDS, malaria and other diseases
7. Ensure environmental sustainability
8. Develop a global partnership for development

UN Secretary-General, Ban Ki-moon

THE UNITED NATIONS DEVELOPMENT PROGRAMME

The United Nations Development Programme (UNDP) co-ordinates the implementation of the MDG and provides national performance updates. Many international and national organisations promote different aspects of the MDGs. In East Africa, different countries have made progress in some of the goal areas. In 2010, according to the report on the status of the MDGs in the East African Community, it was noted that all the states had made strides in attaining over 90 per cent enrolment in primary education. Uganda had made good progress with 7.5 million children enrolled in primary school. Kenya and Rwanda had registered success in gender equity, where the ratio of boys and girls in schools was equal. The inequality in tertiary institutions still persists. All states made progress in reducing child mortality.

UN Headquarters

GLOBALISATION

Globalisation refers to the way the world's economy is being united through removal of trade barriers and import quotas. It is becoming increasingly easy to get goods and services from different parts of the world. This has been facilitated through communication, transportation and trade, foreign investment, migration and the spread of technology like mobile phones and the internet. Apart from economic integration, there is also social integration through sports like the World Cup and military support among others. Globalisation may also be accountable for such negative effects like loss of local cultures, adoption of foreign cultures and international conflicts.

2010 World Cup in Cape Town, South Africa.

ACCESS TO WATER

During the past century, while world population has tripled, the use of water has increased sixfold. Some rivers that formerly reached the sea no longer do so; all of the water is diverted before it reaches the river's mouth. 70 per cent of the world's freshwater supply is devoted to agriculture.

Half the world's wetlands have disappeared in the same period. Many important aquifers are being depleted, and water tables in many parts of the world are dropping at an alarming rate. World water use is projected to increase by about 50 per cent in the next 30 years.

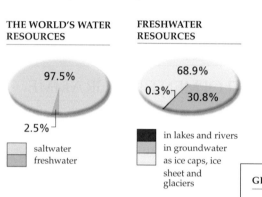

THE WORLD'S WATER RESOURCES

97.5%

2.5%

saltwater
freshwater

FRESHWATER RESOURCES

68.9%

0.3%

30.8%

in lakes and rivers
in groundwater
as ice caps, ice sheet and glaciers

In Africa alone, 40 billion hours are used every year to fetch and carry water – mainly by women and children. Having good local supplies, like this well in The Gambia, saves time and enables children to attend school and women to do other work.

SAFE WATER

It is estimated that, by 2025, 4 billion people, half the world's population at that time, will live under conditions of severe water stress, with conditions particularly severe in Africa, the Middle East and South Asia.

Water that is safe to drink remains as central to survival as to improving the lives of the poor. Currently, an estimated 1.1 billion people lack access to safe water, 2.6 billion are without adequate sanitation, and more than 4 billion do not have their wastewater treated to any degree.

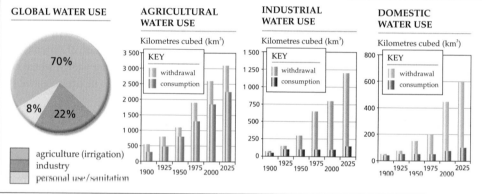

GLOBAL WATER USE

70%

8%   22%

agriculture (irrigation)
industry
personal use/sanitation

AGRICULTURAL WATER USE

Kilometres cubed (km³)

KEY
withdrawal
consumption

3 500
3 000
2 500
2 000
1 500
1 000
500
0

1900 1925 1950 1975 2000 2025

INDUSTRIAL WATER USE

Kilometres cubed (km³)

KEY
withdrawal
consumption

1 500
1 250
1 000
750
500
250
0

1900 1925 1950 1975 2000 2025

DOMESTIC WATER USE

Kilometres cubed (km³)

KEY
withdrawal
consumption

800
600
400
200
0

1900 1925 1950 1975 2000 2025

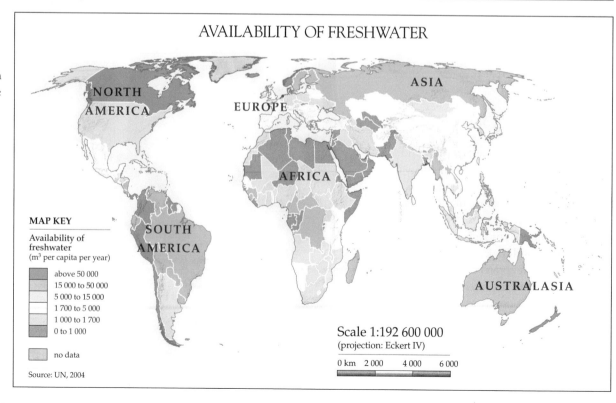

AVAILABILITY OF FRESHWATER

NORTH AMERICA

SOUTH AMERICA

EUROPE

ASIA

AFRICA

AUSTRALASIA

MAP KEY

Availability of freshwater
(m³ per capita per year)

above 50 000
15 000 to 50 000
5 000 to 15 000
1 700 to 5 000
1 000 to 1 700
0 to 1 000

no data

Source: UN, 2004

Scale 1:192 600 000
(projection: Eckert IV)

0 km   2 000   4 000   6 000

ACCESS TO CLEAN WATER BY COUNTRY

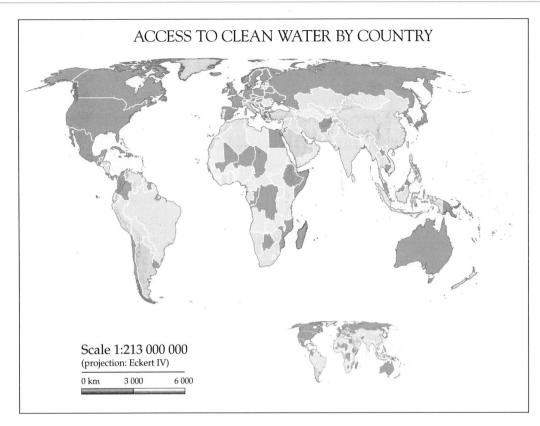

Scale 1:213 000 000
(projection: Eckert IV)

0 km   3 000   6 000

THE URBAN AND RURAL DIVIDE

Despite the world's population being almost equally divided between urban and rural dwellers, the vast majority without access to water and sanitation live in rural areas. Seven out of ten people without basic sanitation are rural inhabitants and more than eight out of ten people without access to improved drinking water sources live in rural areas.

Unsafe water, sanitation and hygiene claim the lives of an estimated 1.5 million children under the age of five each year. Lack of access to water, sanitation and hygiene affects the health, security, livelihood and quality of life for children, severely affecting women and girls first and foremost. They are much more likely than men and boys to be the ones burdened with collecting drinking water.

WATER STRESS IN 1995

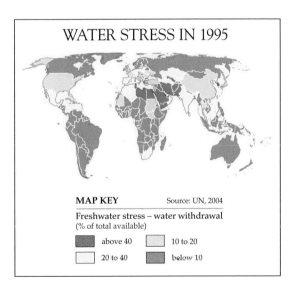

MAP KEY   Source: UN, 2004

Freshwater stress – water withdrawal
(% of total available)

| | above 40 | | 10 to 20 |
| | 20 to 40 | | below 10 |

PREDICTED WATER STRESS IN 2025

Water shortages are the most extreme in Africa and the Middle East, and the hardest hit are nations along the Gulf.

The 2011 Water Stress Index calculates the ratio of domestic, industrial and agricultural water consumption against renewable supplies of water from precipitation, rivers and groundwater. Of the 17 countries designated as being at 'extreme risk', Bahrain, Qatar and Saudi Arabia are the countries most likely to experience a major interruption to their water supply.

It is noted that rapid economic growth and a building boom in oil-rich Gulf States such as the United Arab Emirates have exacerbated existing water shortages, in addition to increasing the demand for water among their growing populations.

PREDICTED WATER STRESS IN 2025

MAP KEY   Source: UN, 2004

Freshwater stress – water withdrawal
(% of total available)

| | above 40 | | 10 to 20 |
| | 20 to 40 | | below 10 |

Bottled drinking water from the Middle East. In many places, bottled water is the only safe, clean source of drinking water.

HIV AND AIDS

One of the major human health challenges facing the world today is the HIV/AIDS epidemic. Little was known about HIV/AIDS until the 1980s. Although the epidemic has stabilised, the number of people infected, affected, suffering and dying from the disease is still high, especially in sub-Saharan Africa. Globally, it is estimated that 34 million people were living with HIV at the end of 2010. There were about 2.7 million new HIV infections and 1.8 million AIDS-related deaths. The fight against HIV/AIDS has been intensified globally, nationally and locally with various initiatives and support. Globally, there is the Global Fund and the World Health Organization's Global Programme on AIDS (WHO/GPA).

WHAT IS HIV/AIDS?

HIV (Human Immunodeficiency Virus) is the retrovirus that causes AIDS (Acquired Immunodeficiency Syndrome). The disease progressively weakens the body's immune system leading to non-resistance to even minor infections – and therefore a life threatening situation. However, it is possible to be HIV positive for many years without becoming ill. The HIV virus is carried in blood, sexual fluids and breast milk, and is passed on when these enter another person's body. There is no cure for HIV/AIDS yet. However, life-prolonging anti-retroviral (ARV) treatments exist. Efforts to find a vaccine for the virus have been going on over the years.

2010 REGIONAL HIV STATISTICS

	People living with HIV	New HIV infections	AIDS-related deaths
Sub-Saharan Africa	22.9 million	1.9 million	1.2 million
Middle East and North Africa	470 000	59 000	35 000
South and South-East Asia	4.0 million	270 000	250 000
East Asia	790 000	88 000	56 000
Oceania	54 000	3300	1600
Latin America	1.5 million	100 000	67 000
Caribbean	200 000	12 000	9 000
Eastern Europe and Central Asia	1.5 million	160 000	90 000
Western and Central Europe	840 000	30 000	9 900
North America	1.3 million	58 000	20 000

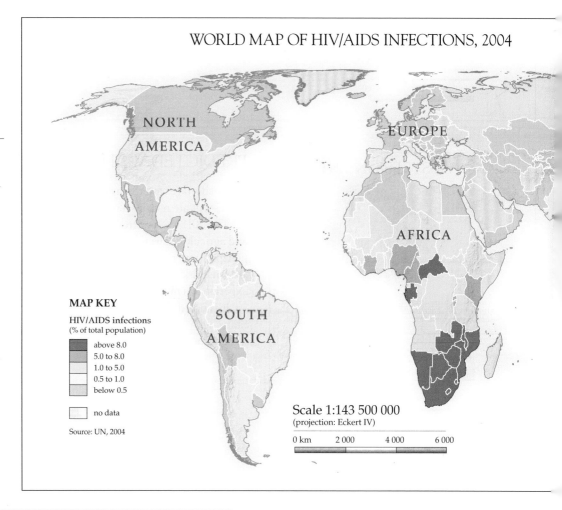

WORLD MAP OF HIV/AIDS INFECTIONS, 2004

MAP KEY

HIV/AIDS infections
(% of total population)

- above 8.0
- 5.0 to 8.0
- 1.0 to 5.0
- 0.5 to 1.0
- below 0.5

- no data

Source: UN, 2004

Scale 1:143 500 000
(projection: Eckert IV)

0 km   2 000   4 000   6 000

USEFUL DEFINITIONS

Epidemic	Widespread and severe outbreak of a disease in an area, region, country or continent.
Virus	An infection or disease caused by an infected particle that multiplies in the cells of the host organism. There are two kinds of viruses: DNA (Deoxyribonucleic acid) and RNA (Ribonucleic acid).
Retrovirus	An RNA virus that inserts a DNA copy of its genome into the host cell, e.g. HIV.
DNA	DNA is the genetic base of cells and organisms.

SPREAD OF HIV/AIDS

When the HIV virus was first named, it mainly affected intravenous drug users and male homosexuals, the majority of whom were in developed countries. Nowadays, HIV/AIDS is largely spread through unprotected sex, especially among the young and those with multiple sexual partners. HIV/AIDS can also be transmitted from mother to child through breast-feeding or through blood.

Tents of the Organisation for Social Services for AIDS, Tigray, Ethiopia

HIV/AIDS IN SUB-SAHARAN AFRICA

Sub-Saharan Africa continues to suffer disproportionately from the global HIV/AIDS epidemic. HIV prevalence is highest in Southern Africa, which otherwise leads other sub-Saharan countries in many health indicators. Estimates suggest that the epidemic has stabilised – often at very high levels – in much of sub-Saharan Africa, where an estimated 22 million people are living with HIV/AIDS. This accounts for 67 per cent of all people living with HIV worldwide. In 2008, more than half of people with HIV in sub-Saharan Africa were found in four countries: South Africa (5.5 million), Nigeria (2.9 million), Zimbabwe (1.7 million) and Tanzania (1.4 million). Young people, particularly young women, are especially vulnerable to HIV/AIDS.

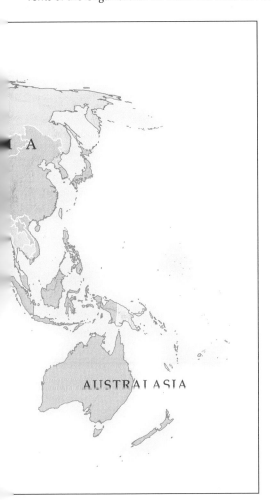

PERCENT OF ADULT POPULATION AGED 15 TO 49 WITH HIV/AIDS, SELECTED AFRICAN COUNTRIES (2009)

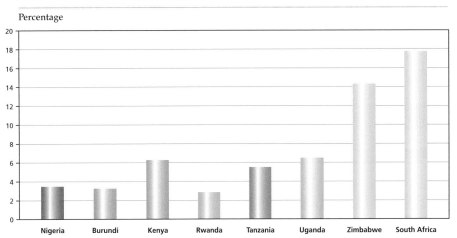

Source: 2011 World Population Data Sheet, Population Reference Bureau, WashingtonDC

WIDER IMPACTS

HIV/AIDS has a far wider impact than just on the health of individuals. These are:

- An increase in orphans and child-headed households.
- Loss of household livelihoods and income through illness or death.
- Burden on women, children, grand parents and relatives.
- High expenditures on HIV/AIDS related health care.
- Loss of national human resource and workforce through illness and death.
- Impact on national economy and social service infrastructure.

EFFECTIVE STRATEGIES

Fighting and reducing the HIV/AIDS epidemic calls for effective strategies globally, nationally and locally, including:

- Involvement of all stakeholders and a multi-sectoral approach.
- Comprehensive and integrated interventions.
- Focusing on both HIV prevention and reproductive health services for women living with HIV.

- Building the capacity and empowering communities to prevent, respond to and mitigate the impacts of HIV/AIDS.
- Preventive measures focusing on education, awareness, care and support.
- Accessible and affordable health care and anti-retroviral therapy.
- Special focus and measures on vulnerable and high risk population and groups.
- Enhanced and continuous HIV/AIDS

testing and counselling.
- Adoption of supportive (rather than discriminatory) legal frameworks and policies.
- Prevention of mother-to-child transmission.
- Positive behavioural change.

	GENERAL FACTS					POPULATION	
Country	Capital City	Land area (km²)	Main language spoken		Unit of currency	Population (2011)	Popula density
AFRICA							
Algeria	Algiers	2381741	Arabic, French and Berber		Dinar	35980193	
Angola	Luanda	1246700	Portuguese		Kwanza	19618432	
Benin	Porto-Novo	110622	French, Fon and Yoruba		CFA Franc	9099922	
Botswana	Gaborone	566730	Setswana, Kalanga, Sekgalagadi, English, other		Pula	2030738	
Burkina Faso	Ouagadougou	273800	French,		CFA Franc	16967845	
Burundi	Bujumbura	25680	Kirundi, French, Swahili		Franc	8575172	
Cameroon	Yaoundé	472710	English, French		CFA Franc	20030362	
Cape Verde	Praia	4033	Portuguese, Crioulo		Escudo	500585	
Central African Republic	Bangui	622984	French, Sangho		CFA Franc	4486837	
Chad	N'Djamena	1259200	French, Arabic, Sara r		CFA Franc	11525496	
Comoros	Moroni	1862	Arabic, French, Shikomoro		Franc	753943	
Congo Democratic Republic of the	Kinshasha	2267048	French, Lingala and Monokutuba		Franc	67757577	
Congo, Republic of the	Brazzaville	341500	French, Lingala, Kingwana, Kikongo, Tshiluba		CFA Franc	4139748	
Côte D'Ivoire	Yamoussoukro	318003	French		CFA Franc	20152894	
Djibouti	Djibouti	23180	French, Arabic, Somali, Afar		Franc	905564	
Egypt	Cairo	995450	Arabic, English and French		Pound	82536770	
Equatorial Guinea	Malabo	28051	Spanish, Fang, Bubi		CFA Franc	720213	
Eritrea	Asmara	101000	Tigrinya, Arabic, English, Tigre, Kunama, Afar		Nakfa	5415280	
Ethiopia	Addis Ababa	1000000	Amarigna, Oromigna, Tigrigna, Somaligna, Guaragigna, Sidamigna, Hadiyigna, English, Arabic		Birr	84734262	
Gabon	Libreville	257667	French, Fang, Myene, Nzebi, Bapounou, Bandjabi		CFA Franc	1534262	
Gambia	Banjul	10000	English, Mandinka, Wolof, Fula		Dalasi	1776103	
Ghana	Accra	227533	Asante, Ewe, Fante, Boron, Dagomba, Dangme, Dagarte, Akyem, Ga, Akuapem ,		Cedi	24965816	
Guinea-Bissau	Bissau	28120	Portuguese, Crioulo		CFA Franc	1547061	
Guinea	Conakry	245717	French		Franc	10221808	
Kenya	Nairobi	569140	English, Kiswahili		Shilling	41609728	
Lesotho	Maseru	30355	Sesotho, English, Zulu, Xhosa		Loti	2193843	
Liberia	Monrovia	96320	English		Dollar	4128572	
Libya	Tripoli	1759540	Arabic, Italian, English		Dinar	6422772	
Madagascar	Antananarivo	581540	French, Malagasy, English		Franc	21315135	
Malawi	Lilongwe	94080	English, Chichewa		Kwacha	15380888	
Mali	Bamko	1220190	French, Bambara		CFA Franc	15839538	
Mauritania	Nouakchott	1030700	Arabic, Pulaar, Soninke, Wolof, French, Hassaniya		Ouguiya	3541540	
Mauritius	Port Louis	2030	Creole, Bhojpuri, French, English		Rupee	1286051	
Morocco	Rabat	446300	Arabic, Berber, French		Dirham	32272974	
Mozambique	Maputo	786380	Emakhuwa, Portuguese, Cisena, Elomwe, E		Metical	23929708	
Namibia	Windhoek	823290	English, Afrikaans, German		Dollar	2324004	
Niger	Niamey	1266700	French, Hausa, Djerma		CFA Franc	16068994	
Nigeria	Abuja	910768	English, Hausa, Yoruba, Igbo Fulani		Naira	162470737	
Rwanda	Kigali	24668	Kinyarwanda, French, English, Kiswahili		Franc	10942950	
São Tomé and Prinncipe	São Tomé	964	Portuguese		Dobra	168526	
Senegal	Dakar	192530	French, Wolof, Pulaar, Jola, Mandinka		CFA Franc	12767556	
Seychelles	Victoria	455	Creole, English		Rupee	86000	
Sierra Leone	Freetown	71620	English, Mende, Krio		Leone	5997486	
Somalia	Mogadishu	627337	Somali, Arabic, Italian, English		Shilling	9556873	
South Africa	Tshwane/Cape Town/ Bloemfontein	1214470	Isizulu, Isixhosa, Afrikaans, English		Rand	50586757	
Sudan	Khartoum	2506000	Arabic, English		Dinar	34318385	
South Sudan	Juba	619745	English, Arabic, Dinka		Pound	10314021	
Swaziland	Mbabane	17204	English, Siswati		Lilangeni	1067773	
Tanzania	Dodoma	885800	Kiswahili, English		Shilling	46218486	
Togo	Lomé	54385	French, Ewe, Mina		CFA Franc	6154813	
Tunisia	Tunis	155360	Arabic, French		Dinar	10673800	

- = no data avaiable   CFA = Communauté Financiére Africaine
Source: World Bank Development Indicators, 2005; CIA World Factbook, 2006; Human Development Report, 2005

Birth rate per 1000 population (2010)	Death rate per 1000 population (2010)	Life expectancy at birth (years) Male	Female	HEALTH & EDUCATION Infant Mortality (death per 1000 live births: 2011 estimated)	Adult Literacy Male	Female	ECONOMIC DEVELOPMENT Annual electricity consumption (1 000 000000 kwh) 2011	TECHNOLOGY DEVELOPMENT Mobile telephones (million)	Internet users (million)
12.5	4.9	75	72	31	79.6	60.1	33.94	35.62	5.04
15.1	20.5	53	50	98	82.7	58.1	3.75	9.49	2.90
16.5	11.2	59	55	73	55.2	30.3	0.79	7.77	0.32
18.7	14.1	51	54	36	84	84.9	2.98	2.90	0.14
19.2	14.4	57	55	93	29.4	15.2	0.68	7.68	0.51
19.9	15.6	53	50	88	72.9	61.8	0.27	1.24	0.10
20.5	14.4	54	51	84	84	67.8	5.20	10.49	1.00
21.3	4.7	78	71	29	89.3	79.4	0.24	0.40	0.16
21.7	18.1	51	48	106	69.3	43.2	0.15	1.12	0.10
22.3	15.4	52	49	99	45	24.2	0.09	3.67	0.22
22.9	6.5	63	60	63	80.2	69.7	0.05	0.22	0.04
25.2	18.1	51	47	112	76.9	57	6.67	15.67	0.81
27	11.4	59	57	61	89.6	78.4	0.58	3.88	0.23
27.1	15.4	58	55	86	65.2	46.6	3.94	17.42	0.44
28.4	11.3	60	57	73	78	58.4	0.26	0.19	0.06
28.7	5.6	76	72	19	80.3	63.5	123.45	83.43	29.40
28.7	14.8	53	50	81	97.1	90.6	0.09	0.43	0.04
29.9	9.2	64	60	42	78.7	57.5	0.26	0.24	0.34
29.9	13	62	58	68	50.3	35.1	3.72	14.13	0.93
30	11.7	64	62	54	91.9	84.9	1.36	1.80	0.12
30.3	10.4	60	58	57	60	40.4	0.20	1.58	0.19
31	9.3	66	64	50	73.2	61.2	6.32	21.17	3.52
31.9	18.4	50	47	81	68.2	40.6	0.07	0.40	0.04
32.7	11.9	56	53	92	52	30	0.86	4.50	0.13
33	11.8	59	57	55	90.6	84.2	5.82	26.98	11.65
33.3	19.2	48	50	65	83.3	95.6	0.24	1.05	0.09
34.4	18.3	59	56	74	64.8	56.8	0.31	2.03	0.12
34.5	4.1	78	73	13	95.6	82.7	26.12	10.00	1.09
34.6	9.7	69	65	43	67.4	61.8	1.03	8.16	0.40
34.6	14.8	55	55	58	81.1	68.5	1.56	3.66	0.31
34.9	14.7	53	51	99	43.4	20.4	0.46	10.82	0.32
35.7	7.9	61	57	75	64.9	51.2	0.51	3.28	0.16
35.9	7	77	70	13	90.9	86.2	2.23	1.29	0.46
35.9	5.8	75	70	30	68.9	43.9	23.90	36.55	16.46
36.3	19.8	52	50	92	70.8	42.8	10.36	7.86	1.03
36.5	12.4	63	62	29	89	88.5	3.53	2.44	0.28
36.9	13.8	56	55	73	42.9	15.1	0.62	4.34	0.21
36.9	16.8	53	52	88	72.1	50.4	18.617	95.17	46.19
37.4	17.2	57	54	59	74.8	67.5	0.24		0.77
37.6	7.5	66	64	53	92.2	77.9	0.38	0.12	0.03
37.6	9	61	59	50	51.1	29.1	2.373	9.35	2.23
38.3	6.9	78	68	12	91.4	92.3	0.24	0.13	0.04
39.3	28.1	49	48	114	46.9	24.4	0.54	2.14	0.01
39.9	16.6	53	50	108	49.7	25.8	0.3	0.66	0.12
40.6	17	54	53	41	87	85.7	223.52	64.00	10.59
41	10.1	64	60	66	71.8	50.5	4.854	25.11	8.48
42.1	21.2	61	62	66	40	16	-	-	-
42.4	21.2	49	50	55	82.6	80.8	1.2	0.77	0.22
43	12.9	54	52	50	77.6	62.2	3.729	25.67	5.55
43.4	10.1	59	56	66	83.4	46.9	0.654	3.10	0.22
43.9	5.6	77	73	14	76.8	65.3	13.689	12.39	4.14

Country	Capital City	Land area (km²)	Main language spoken	Unit of currency	Population (2011)	Population density (k
GENERAL FACTS					**POPULATION**	
Uganda	Kampala	197100	English, Luganda, Luo, Swahili	Shilling	34509205	
Western Sahara [1]	Laâyoune	266000	French, Arabic, Sara r	Tala	513000	
Zambia	Lusaka	743398	Bemba, Chewa, English	Kwacha	13474959	
Zimbabwe	Harare	386847	English, Shona, Sindebele	Dollar	12754378	
NORTH AMERICA						
Antigua and Barbuda	Saint John's	442.6	English, Local Dialects	East Caribbean dollar	89612	
Bahamas [The]	Nassau	10010	English, Creole	Dollar	347176	
Barbados	Bridgetown	431	English	Dollar	273925	
Belize	Belmopan	22806	Spanish, Creole, Mayan, English, Garifuna, German, other	Dollar	356600	
Canada	Ottawa	9093507	English, French	Dollar	34482779	
Cuba	Havana	109820	Spanish, English	Peso	4726575	
Costa Rica	San José	51060	Spanish	East Caribbean dollar	11253665	
Dominica	Roseau	751	English, French Patois	Peso	67675	
Dominican-Republic	Santo Domingo	48320	Spanish	Peso	10056181	
El Salvador	San Salvador	20721	Spanish, Nahua (Amerindians)	US Dollar	6227491	
Greenland (Kalaallit Nunaat)	Nuuk	2166086	Greenlandic, Danish, English	Danish Krone	56744	
Grenada	Saint-George's	344	English, French	East Caribbean dollar	104890	
Guatemala	Guatemala City	107159	Spanish, Amerindian	Queztal, US Dollar	14757316	
Haiti	Port-au-Prince	27560	French, Creole	Gourde	10123787	
Honduras	Tegucigalpa	111890	Spanish, Amerindian	Lempira	7754687	
Jamaica	Kingston	10831	English, English Patois	Jamaican dollar	2709300	
Mexico	Mexico City	1943945	Spanish, Spanish and indigenous languages	Peso	114793341	
Nicaragua	Managua	119990	Spanish, Miskito	Córdoba	5869859	
Panama	Panama City	74340	Spanish, English	Balboa; U.S. dollar	3571185	
Saint Kitts-and Nevis		261	English	East Caribbean dollar	53051	
Saint Lucia	Castries	606	English, French	East Caribbean dollar	176000	
Saint Vincent and the Grenadines	Kingstown	389	English, French patois	East Caribbean dollar	109365	
Trinidad and Tobago	Port-of-Spain	5128	English, Caribbean Hindustani, French, Spanish, Chinese	Dollar	1346350	
United States of America	Washington D.C.	9158960	English, Spanish, other Indo-European, other	Dollar	311591917	
SOUTH AMERICA						
Argentina	Buenos Aires	2736690	Spanish, Italian, English, German, French	Peso	40764561	
Bolivia	LaPaz and Sucre	1083301	Spanish, Quechua, Aymara, foreign languages, other	Boliviano	10088108	
Brazil	Brasília	8459417	Portuguese, other	Real	196655014	
Chile	Santiago	743812	Spanish, Mapudungun, German, English	Peso	17269525	
Colombia	Bogotá	1038700	Spanish	Peso	46927125	
Ecuador	Quito	276841	Spanish, Amerindian (Quechua)	U.S. dollar	14666055	
Guyana	Georgetown	196849	English, Amerindian, Creole, Caribbean Hindustani, Urdu	Guyanese dollar	756040	
Paraguay	Asunción	397302	Spanish, Guarani	Guaraní	6568290	
Peru	Lima	1279996	Spanish, Quechua, Aymara, Ashaninka, other (native languages), other	Nuevo sol	29399817	
Suriname	Paramaribo	156000	Dutch, English, Sranang Tongo (Surinamese(Taki-Taki), Caribbean Hindustani (a dialect of Hindi), Javanese	Dollar	529419	
Uruguay	Montevideo	175015	Spanish, Portunol, Brazilero	Peso	3368595	
Venezuela	Caracas	882050	Spanish, other	Bolivar	29278000	
EUROPE						
Albania	Tirana	27398	Albanian, Greek, Vlach, Romani, Slavic	Lek	3215988	
Andorra		468	Catalan (official), French, Castilian, Portuguese	Euro	86165	
Austria	Vienna	82445	German, Turkish, Serbian, Croatian (, Slovene, and Hungarian	Euro	8419000	
Belarus	Minsk	202900	Belarusian, Russian, other	Ruble	9473000	
Belgium	Brussels	30278	Dutch, French, German, Dutch and French	Euro	11008000	
Bosnia and Herzegovina	Sarajevo	51187	Bosnian (official), Croatian (official), Serbian	Marka	3752228	
Bulgaria	Sofia	108489	Bulgarian, Turkis, Roma, other	Lev	7476000	
Croatia	Zagreb	55974	Croatian, Serbian, other	Kuna	4407000	
Cyrpus	Nicosia	9241	Greek, Turkish, English	Euro	1116564	
Czech Republic	Prague	77247	Czech, Slovak, other	Koruna	10546000	

- = no data avaiable

Source: World Bank Development Indicators, 2005; CIA World Factbook, 2006; Human Development Report, 2005   [1]Disputed territory under Moroccan occupation

h rate 1000 ulation 0)	Death rate per 1000 population (2010)	Life expectancy at birth (years)		Infant Mortality (death per 1000 live births: 2011 estimated)	Adult Literacy		Annual electricity consumption (1 000 000 000 kwh) 2011	Mobile users (million)	Internet users (million)
		Male	Female		Male	Female			
44.5	13.4	55	54	63	81	57.7	1.95	16.70	4.49
45	5.8	70	66	59			0.08		
46.5	18.8	50	49	69	86.8	74.8	8.08	8.16	1.55
47.7	17.9	53	54	51	94.2	87.2	12.801	9.20	2.00
16.2	5.7	75	73	7			0.11	0.16	0.07
15.2	6.1	79	73	14	94.7	96.5	1.91	0.30	0.23
10.9	7	80	74	17	99.7	99.7	0.95	0.35	0.20
24	3.8	78	75	14	76.7	77.1	0.20	0.20	0.04
11.3	7.4	83	79	5	99	99	521.85	25.86	28.51
15.3	4.1	82	77	9	99.8	99.8	15.18	1.32	2.61
9.6	7.6	81	77	5	94.7	95.1	8.32	4.36	1.99
18.27	8	78	74	11	94	94	0.08	0.11	0.03
20.9	5.9	77	71	22	86.8	87.2	13.31	8.77	3.57
20	5.9	77	68	14	82.8	79.6	5.21	7.84	1.10
14.6	8.2	72	67	9	96	96	0.18	0.12	0.03
19.3	8.3	70	67	25	75.4	63.3	7.69	20.72	1.73
31.5	5.7	75	68	70	54.8	51.2	0.35	4.20	0.84
25.7	9.2	64	61	20	79.8	80.2	5.05	8.06	1.23
25.8	5.6	76	71	20	84.1	91.6	5.13	2.97	0.87
17.9	7.1	76	71	14	86.9	85.3	217.66	94.57	41.50
18.5	4.8	80	75	23	67.2	67.8	2.62	4.82	0.62
22.8	4.7	77	71	17	92.5	91.2	6.01	7.28	1.52
19.1	5	79	74	7	98	98	0.12	0.08	0.04
18.02	8.3	71	68	14	89.5	90.6	0.31	0.22	0.07
16.9	6.6	78	72	19	96	96	0.12	0.13	0.05
16.4	6.8	75	70	24	99.1	98	7.57	1.83	0.74
14.3	8.1	74	67	7	99	99	3961.56	331.60	243.78
13.7	8.2	81	76	7			0.11	0.16	0.07
16.8	7.7	80	72	12	100	99	110.52	55.00	19.45
25.8	7.6	69	65	42	98	87	5.46	8.35	3.03
15	6.3	77	71	17	90	90	426.34	242.23	88.49
14	3.4	82	76	8	na	na	55.67	22.40	9.31
18.9	5.5	78	70	17	93	93	47.80	46.20	18.96
19.8	5.1	79	73	18	92	90	15.91	15.33	4.61
17.4	8.4	73	67	25	92	91	0.69	0.52	0.24
23.7	5.5	75	71	21	96	93	6.70	6.53	1.57
19.6	6.1	77	72	15	95	85	32.67	32.46	10.73
17.8	6.9	74	68	27	95	94	1.44	0.95	0.17
14.5	9.2	81	74	9	98	99	8.93	4.76	1.74
19.8	5.1	78	72	16	95	95	89.45	28.78	11.84
12.8	5.9	80	74	16	99.2	98.3	5.578	3.10	1.58
9.26	6.5	85	80	3	100	100	0.599	0.07	0.07
8.6	9.4	84	78	4	98	98	66.457	13.02	6.71
11.2	14.7	76	65	4	99.8	99.5	31.36	10.69	3.79
11.4	10	83	77	4	99	99	85.325	12.54	8.39
8.2	9.5	78	73	8	99.4	96.5	10.802	3.17	2.25
10	14.8	77	70	11	98.7	98	33.381	10.48	3.80
9.8	12.1	80	73	5	99.5	98.2	16.44	5.12	3.11
11.5	7.5	82	78	3	98.9	96.3	5.038	1.09	0.64
10.9	10.9	81	75	3	99	99	64.119	12.81	7.69

GENERAL FACTS					POPULATION	
Country	Capital City	Land area (km²)	Main language spoken	Unit of currency	Population (2011)	Population density (k
Denmark	Copenhagen	42434	Danish, Faroese, Greenlandic, German	Krone	5574000	
Estonia	Taillin	42388	Estonian, Russian, other	Euro	1340000	
Finland	Helsinki	303815	Finnish, Swedish, other	Euro	5387000	
France	Paris	640427	French, other (Provencal, Breton, Alsatian, Corsican, Catalan, Basque, Flemish)	Euro	65436552	
Germany	Berlin	348672	German	Euro	81726000	
Greece	Athens	130647	Greek, other (English and French)	Euro	11304000	
Hungary	Budapest	89608	Hungarian, other	Forint	9971000	
Iceland	Reykjavík	100250	Icelandic, English, Nordic, German	Króna	319000	
Ireland	Dublin	68883	English, Irish (Gaelic or Gaeilge)	Euro	4487000	
Italy	Rome	294140	Italian, German, French, Slovene	Euro	60770000	
Kosovo	Pristina	10910	Albanians, Serbian, Bosnian, Turkish, Roma	Euro	1794303	
Latvia	Riga	62249	Latvian, Russian, Lithuanian and other	Lats	2220000	
Liechtenstein	Vaduz	160	German	Swiss franc	36304	
Lithuania	Vilnus	62680	Lithuanian, Russian, Polish, other	Litas	3203000	
Luxembourg	Luxembourg	2586	Luxembourgish, German, French	Euro	517000	
Macedonia	Skopje	25433	Macedonian	Denar	2063893	
Malta	Valetta	316	Maltese, English	Lira	419000	1
Moldova	Chişinău	32891	Moldovan, Russian, Gaguaz	Leu	3559000	
Monaco	Monaco	2	French, Engish, Italian, Monegasque	Euro	35427	17
Montenegro	Podgorica	13452	Serbian, Hungarian, Bosniak, Romany (Gypsy), other	Euro	632261	
Netherlands	Amsterdam	33893	Dutch, Frisian	Euro	16696000	
Norway	Oslo	304282	Bokmal Norwegian, Nynorsk Norwegian, other	Krone	4952000	
Poland	Warsaw	304255	Polish, other	Zloty	38216000	
Portugal	Lisbon	91470	Portuguese, Mirandese	Euro	10637000	
Romaina	Bucharest	229891	Romanian, (Hungarian, Romany, other	Leu	21390000	
Russian Federation	Moscow	16377742	Russian, other	Ruble	141930000	
San Marino		61			31735	
Serbia	Belgrade	88246	Serbian, Hungarian, Bosniak, Romany (Gypsy)	Serbian Dinar	7261000	
Slovakia	Bratislava	48105	Slovak, Hungarian, Roma, Ukrainian, other	Koruna	5440000	
Slovenia	Ljubljana	20151	Slovenian, Serbo-Croatian, other or unspecified, Italian, Hungarian	Slovenian Dinar	2052000	
Spain	Madrid	498980	Castilian Spanish, Catalan, Galician, Basque	Euro	46235000	
Sweden	Stockholm	410335	Swedish, other (small Sami- and Finnish-speaking minorities)	Krona	9453000	
Switzerland	Berne	39997	German, French, Italian, Serbo-Croatian, Albanian, Portuguese, Spanish, English, Romansch, other	Swiss franc	7907000	
Ukraine	Kiev	579330	Ukrainian, Russian, other	Hryvna	45706100	
United Kingdom	London	241930	English	Pound	62641000	
Vatican City	Vatican City	0.44	Euro	Euro	832	
ASIA²						
Afghanistan	Kabul	652230	Afghan Persian or Dari, Pashto, Turkic, ...other	Afghanistan	35320445	
Armenia	Yerevan	28,203	Armenian, Yezidi, Russian	Drams	3100236	
Azerbaijan	Baku	82,629	Azeri, Lezgi, Russian, Armenian	Manats	9168000	
Bahrain	Manama	765	Arabic, English, Farsi, Urdu	Dinar	1323535	
Bangladesh	Dacca	130168	Bangla (Bengali), English	Taka (BDT)	150493658	
Bhutan	Thimpu	38394	Sharchhopka, Dzongkha, Lhotshamkha, other	Ngultrum, indian rupee	738267	
Brunei	Bandar Seri Begawan	5265	Malay, English, Chinese	Brunei Dollar (BND)	405938	
Cambodia	Phnom Penh	176515	Khmer, French, English	Riel	14305183	
China	Beijing	9569901	Chinese or Mandarin, Yue (Cantonese), Wu (Shanghainese), Minbei (Fuzhou), Minnan (Hokkien-Taiwanese), Xiang, Gan, Hakka dialects, other	Yuan	1344130000	
East Timor	Dili	14874	Tetum, Portuguese, Indonesian, English	US Dollars	1175880	
Georgia	Tbilisi	69700	Georgian, Russian, Armenian, Azeri, other	Lari	4486000	
India	New Delhi	2973193	Hindi, Bengali, Telugu, Marathi, Tamil, Urdu, Gujarati, Kannada, Malayalam, Oriya, Punjabi, Assamese, Maithili	Rupee	1241491960	
Indonesia	Jakarta	1811569	Bahasa Indonesia, modified form of Malay, English, Dutch, other local dialects	Rupiah	242325638	

- = no data avaiable

Source: World Bank Development Indicators, 2005; CIA World Factbook, 2006; Human Development Report, 2005   ²Russian Federation can be found in the Europe section

h rate 1000 ulation 0)	Death rate per 1000 population (2010)	Life expectancy at birth (years)		Infant Mortality (death per 1000 live births: 2011 estimated)	Adult Literacy		Annual electricity consumption (1 000 000000 kwh) 2011	Mobile telephones (million)	Internet users (million)
		Male	Female		Male	Female			
11.3	10.3	81	77	3	99	99	34.5	7.05	5.02
12.1	14.3	80	70	4	99.8	99.8	7.975	1.86	1.03
11.4	9.7	83	77	2	100	100	81.373	8.94	4.81
12.4	8.9	85	78	3	99	99	483.324	66.30	50.24
8.7	10.7	83	78	3	99	99	555.188	108.70	68.19
10.1	9.9	83	78	3	97.8	94.2	62.509	12.13	6.04
10.1	13.2	78	71	5	99.2	99	37.817	11.69	5.88
14.7	6.2	84	80	2	99	99	16.326	0.34	0.31
15.6	7	83	78	3	99	99	26.905	4.91	3.48
9.1	10.5	85	79	3	98.8	98	317.248	92.30	34.53
11	7	71	67	-	97	88	5.674	0.56	
11	13.6	79	69	8	99.8	99.8	6.482	2.31	1.61
10.7	6.7	84	77	2	100	100	N/A	0.04	0.03
10.8	12.3	78	67	5	99.7	99.7	11.457	5.00	2.15
11.8	8.7	83	76	2	100	100	7.18	0.76	0.47
10.5	9.2	77	72	10	98.7	95.9	7.079	2.15	1.17
10.3	8.72	82	78	5	91.7	93.9	1.828	0.52	0.29
12.1	12.6	73	66	16	99.1	98.1	3.63	3.71	1.35
6.8	8.5	83	79	3	99	99	-	0.03	0.03
12	8.6	83	79	7	99.4	97.4	4.1	1.17	0.25
10.8	9.1	81	72	4	99	99	113.988	19.84	15.38
12.3	10	83	77	3	100	100	113.715	5.75	4.63
10.9	10.6	78	71	5	99.7	99.4	136.996	49.20	24.85
8.8	12.4	75	63	3	96.9	93.6	51.191	12.28	5.91
10.3	16.2	77	72	11	98.5	97.4	48.69	23.40	9.44
11.8	8	94	86	9	99.7	99.5	870.331	256.12	69.99
11	11.6	77	73	2	97	95	-	0.035	0.02
11	9.6	86	80	6	99.2	96.7	30.926	10.18	3.43
10.7	10	80	72	7	99.7	99.6	26.685	5.98	4.07
9.9	9.9	83	76	2	99.7	99.7	12.449	2.17	1.47
10.6	8.8	85	79	4	98.5	97	275.743	53.07	31.40
12	10.1	84	80	2	99	99	131.497	11.19	8.59
10	8.1	85	80	4	99	99	62.114	10.02	6.56
10.9	16.4	75	64	11	99.8	99.6	147.392	55.57	13.83
12.1	9.9	82	78	5	99	99	351.804	81.61	51.18
0	na	na	na	na	100	100	5.578	3.10	0.00
42.3	19.9	49	49	103	43.1	12.6	0.23	17.56	1.62
15	9.6	77	71	18	99.7	99.4	4.78	3.21	0.47
19.5	7.6	74	68	39	99.9	99.7	14.50	10.12	4.65
17.9	3.2	76	75	9	96.1	91.6	10.78	1.69	1.02
19.5	7.5	70	69	38	61.3	52.2	37.00	85.00	7.52
19.6	7.2	70	66	44	60	34	0.18	0.48	0.16
18.2	2.8	81	76	6	95.2	90.2	3.39	0.44	0.23
21.6	9	65	62	43	84.7	64.1	1.83	10.00	0.44
11.9	7.1	76	72	16	96	88.5	3503.40	986.25	516.12
37.6	5.86	70	65	46	-	-	0.07	0.61	0.01
11.5	11.8	77	71	20	99.8	99.7	6.99	4.43	1.58
21.3	8.2	68	64	48	73.4	47.8	689.54	893.86	125.02
17.4	6.3	72	68	27	94	86.8	140.11	236.80	43.62

GENERAL FACTS					POPULATION	
Country	Capital City	Land area (km²)	Main language spoken	Unit of currency	Population (2011)	Population density (k...
Iran	Teheran	1531595	Persian, Azeri Turkic and Turkic dialects, Kurdish, Gilaki and Mazandarani, Luri, Balochi, Arabic, other	Rial	74798599	
Iraq	Baghdad	437367	Arabic, Kurdish, Turkoman, Assyrian (Neo-Aramaic), Armenian	Dinar	32961959	
Israel	Jerusalem	20330	Hebrew, Arabic, English	Shekel	7765700	3
Japan	Tokyo	364485	Japanese	Yen	127817277	3
Jordan	Amman	88802	Arabic, English	Dinar	6181000	
Kazakhstan	Astana	2699700	Kazakh (Qazaq), Russian	Tenge	16558459	
Kyrgyzstan	Bishkek	191801	Kyrgyz, Uzbek, Russian, Dungun	Som	2818042	
Kuwait	Kuwait City	17818	Arabic (official), English	Dinar	5507000	
Laos	Vientiane	230800	Lao (official), French, English	Kip	6288037	
Lebanon	Beirut	10230	Arabic, French, English, Armenian	Pound	4259405	
Malaysia	Kuala Lumpur	329613	Bahasa Malaysia, English, Chinese, Tamil, Telugu, Malayalam, Panjabi, Thai	Ringgit	28859154	
Maldives	Male	298	Dhivehi, English	Rufiyaa	320081	1
Mongolia	Ulan Bator	1553556	Khalkha Mongol, Turkic, Russian	Togrog Tugrik	2800114	
Myanmar [Burma]	Naypyidaw	653508	Burmese	Kyat	48336763	
Nepal	Kathmandu	143351	Nepali, Maithali, Bhojpuri, Tharu (Dagaura/Rana), Tamang, Newar, Magar, Awadhi, other	Rupee	30485798	
North Korea	Pyongyang	120500	Korean	Won	24451285	
Oman	Muscat	309500	Arabic, English, Baluchi, Urdu, Indian dialects	Rial	2846145	
Pakistan	Islamabad	856692	Punjabi, Sindhi, Saraiki (a Punjabi variant), Pashtu, Urdu, Balochi, Hindko, Brahui, English, Burushaski, other	Rupee	176745364	
Philippines	Manila	298170	Filipino, and English, other	Peso	94852030	
Qatar	Doha	11586	Arabic, English	Rial	1870041	
Saudi Arabia	Riyadh	2149690	Arabic	Riyal	28082541	
Singapore	Singapore	687	Mandarin, English, Malay, Hokkien, Cantonese, Teochew, Tamil, other	Dollar	5183700	7
South Korea	Seoul	100210	Korean, English	Won	49779000	
Sri Lanka	Colombo	62732	Sinhala, Tamil, other	Rupee	20869000	
Syria	Damascus	183630	Arabic, Kurdish, Armenian, Aramaic, Circassian; French, English	Pound	20820311	
Taiwan	Taipei	32260	Mandarin Chinese, Taiwanese, Hakka	Dollar	23174528	
Tajikistan	Dushanbe	141510	Tajik, Russian	somoni	6976958	
Thailand	Bangkok	510890	Thai, English, ethnic and other (regional dialects)	Baht	69518555	
Turkey	Ankara	769632	Togrog Tugrik		73639596	
Turkmenistan	Aşhgabat	469930	Turkmen, Russian, Uzbek, other	Manat	5105301	
U.A.E.	Abu Dhabi	83600	Arabic, Persian, English, Hindi, Urdu	Dirham	7890924	
Uzbekistan	Tashkent	425400	Uzbek, Russian, Tajik, other	Soum	29341200	
Vietnam	Hanoi	310070	Vietnamese, English, French, Chinese, and Khmer, mountain area languages (Mon-Khmer and Malayo-Polynesian)	Dong	87840000	
Yemen	Sanaa	527968	Arabic	Rial	24799880	
AUSTRALIA AND ITS NEIGHBOURS						
Australia	Canberra	7682300	English	Dollar	22620600	
Fiji	Suva	18274	English, Fijan, Hindustani	Dollar	868406	
Kiribati	Tarawa	811	I-kiribati, English	Australian Dollar	101093	
Marshall Islands	Majuro	181	Marshallese	US Dollar	54816	
Micronesia, federated states of	Palikir	702	English, Trukese, Pohnpeian, Yapese, Kosrean, Ulithian, Woleaian, Nukuoro	US Dollar	111542	
Nauru	Yaren District	21	Nauruan, English	Australian Dollar	9322	
New zealand	Wellington	262443	English, Maori	Dollar	4405200	
Palau	Ngerulmud.	459	Palauan	US Dollar	20609	
Papua New Guinea	Port Moresby	452860	Tok Pisin, English, Hiri Motu, Other (indigenous languages)	Kina	7013829	
Samoa	Apia	2821	Samoan, English	Tala	183874	
solomon Islands	Honiara	27986	Melanesian Pidgin, English	Dollar	552267	
Tonga	Nuku'alofa	717	Tongan, English	Pa'anga	104509	
Tuvalu	Funafuti	26	Tuvaluan, English, Samoan, Kiribati	Australian dollar	9847	
Vanuatu	Port Vila	12189	English, Bislama, French	Vatu	245619	

– = no data avaiable

Source: World Bank Development Indicators, 2005; CIA World Factbook, 2006; Human Development Report, 2005

Birth rate per 1000 population (2010)	Death rate per 1000 population (2010)	Life expectancy at birth (years)		HEALTH & EDUCATION	Adult Literacy		ECONOMIC DEVELOPMENT	TECHNOLOGY DEVELOPMENT	
				Infant Mortality (death per 1000 live births: 2011 estimated)			Annual electricity consumption (1 000 000000 kwh) 2011	Mobile telephones (million)	Internet users (million)
		Male	Female		Male	Female			
16.2	5.4	75	72	22	83.5	70.4	163.65	56.04	15.71
34.1	9.1	73	68	31	86	70.6	33.22	25.52	1.63
20.5	5.5	84	80	4	98.5	95.9	49.46	9.20	5.29
8.5	9	87	80	2	99	99	997.40	129.87	100.60
23.7	3.9	75	72	18	95.8	89.2	12.49	7.48	2.21
20.6	10.1	73	62	29	99.8	99.3	71.59	23.10	7.29
17.4	1.9	76	74	10	94.4	91	43.60	4.40	2.09
24	8.1	72	64	33	99.3	98.1	7.46	5.65	1.08
21.8	7.1	69	66	42	83	63	2.23	5.48	0.57
14.9	7	75	71	19	93.1	82.2	13.14	3.35	2.21
19.8	4.5	77	73	5	92	85.4	101.00	36.66	17.60
16.5	5.7	79	76	14	93	94.7	0.05	0.53	0.11
22.7	6.6	73	65	26	96.9	97.9	3.83	2.94	0.56
16.7	9.7	68	64	50	93.9	86.4	4.94	1.24	0.47
23.2	7.7	70	68	41	73	48.3	2.68	13.35	2.74
14.2	9.12	67	61	26	99	99	17.76	1.00	
16.9	2.7	76	71	8	86.8	73.5	15.52	4.81	1.94
26.3	7.1	67	65	70	68.6	40.3	76.61	108.89	15.91
24.5	4.8	73	66	23	92.5	92.7	54.42	87.26	27.51
11.6	2.4	78	79	7	96.5	95.4	23.04	2.30	1.61
21.4	3.7	76	73	15	90.4	81.3	199.12	53.71	13.34
9.5	5.3	84	79	2	96.6	88.6	39.65	7.76	3.89
9.9	6.83	84	77	4	99.2	96.6	437.73	52.51	40.55
17	7.2	78	72	14	92.5	90	8.44	18.32	3.16
21.9	3.4	78	74	14	86	73.6	31.32	13.12	4.67
0.9	7.12	83	76	5	96.1	96.1	220.80	27.84	16.15
27.7	6.4	71	65	11	98.8	99.6	13.47	6.32	0.91
11.5	8.5	78	71	14	94.9	90.5	140.49	78.67	16.48
16.9	5.9	75	71	14	95.3	79.6	165.09	65.32	31.00
21.7	8.2	69	61	41	99.3	98.3	12.18	3.51	0.26
12.3	1.4	78	76	6	76.1	81.7	79.54	11.73	5.52
20.8	6.7	72	66	44	99.6	99	45.43	25.44	8.38
15.9	5.1	77	73	19	96.1	92	78.93	127.32	31.14
37.2	7.4	68	65	57	81.2	46.8	5.11	11.67	3.70
13.5	7.1	84	80	4	99	99	243.96	24.49	17.86
20.6	6.6	72	67	15	95.5	91.9	0.87	0.73	0.24
26.6	7.3	63	59	39	-	-	0.02	0.01	0.01
28.1	4.3	71	67	22	93.6	93.7	-	0.00	0.00
24.2	4.3	70	68	34	91	88	0.18	0.03	0.02
27	5.6	57	55	32	-	-	0.03	0.01	0.00
14.3	7.1	83	79	5	99	99	40.34	4.82	3.80
10.7	7.9	72	66	15	93	90	107.90	0.02	0.00
29	9.6	66	61	47	63.4	50.9	2.76	1.91	0.14
23.7	5.4	76	70	17	99.6	99.7	0.10	0.17	0.01
30.4	7.2	70	67	23	-	-	0.07	0.27	0.03
25.7	4.8	75	70	13	98.8	99	0.04	0.06	0.03
23.3	9.1	65	62	27	-	-	0.04	0.00	0.00
28.7	7.2	74	70	12			0.04	0.29	0.02

HOW TO USE THIS INDEX

To find a place in the atlas first look up the name in the index. Next to the name you will see a page number and a latitude and longitude, e.g. **Maseru 104** 29°21'S 27°35'E. This reference is used to find the exact position of a place on the surface of the earth.

- First, take note of the page number, latitude and longitude.
- Next go to that page and find the appropriate map.
- Using the numbers and grid on the map trace imaginary lines across from 29°S and up from 27°E.

You will find **Maseru** where these two lines intersect.

To pinpoint locations latitudes and longitudes are broken down into degrees and minutes, one degree being divided into 60 minutes. So for example 27°30'E is a line halfway between 27°E and 28°E. This method is used to accurately locate the position of point symbols such as towns or mountains.

For more information about latitude and longitude, see page 6.

◆ Country • ● Country capital • ◇ Dependent territory • ○ Dependent territory capital • ◆ Administrative region • ▲ Mountain • ▲ Mountain range • ⣿ Volcano • ⌁ River • ⊚ Lake • ⊠ Reservoir

◆ Country ● Country capital ◇ Dependent territory ◎ Dependent territory capital ◈ Administrative region ▲ Mountain ▲ Mountain range ☆ Volcano ✍ River ◎ Lake ◙ Reservoir

◆ Country   ● Country capital   ◇ Dependent territory   ○ Dependent territory capital   ◈ Administrative region   ▲ Mountain   ▲ Mountain range   ☒ Volcano   ⌁ River   ⊙ Lake   ☒ Reservoir

◆ Country   ● Country capital   ◇ Dependent territory   ○ Dependent territory capital   ◆ Administrative region   ▲ Mountain   ▲ Mountain range   ☒ Volcano   ⚃ River   ◎ Lake   ◙ Reservoir

Picture credits
The publisher would like to thank the following for their kind permission to reproduce their photographs:

(Key: b-bottom; c-centre; l-left; r-right; t-top)

Beatrice Adimola: 199 (fort portal); **Alamy Images**: 22t, 22b, 23t, 24b, 25tr, 28l, 28-29c, 34cl, 36bl, 37tr, 41tl, 41r, 45c, 45b, 48t, 49tr, 50c, 51tl, 51tr, 56tr, 57br, 59br, 60c, 60cl, 61tr, 61br, 62tl, 64bl, 66bl, 67bl, 68l, 69cr, 69br, 71br, 72bl, 72br, 73cr, 73bl, 74br, 77bc, 78tr, 79t, 79b, 81cr, 81b, 82c, 82cl, 82bl, 83 (apartments), 83 (Dry lands), 83 (Flooded Farmland), 83 (slash and burn), 83 (Tanganyika), 83 (Terraced farming), 83bc, 84t, 86bc, 87cr, 91tr, 93b, 96tr, 97cr, 97b, 99bl, 100tr, 101tr, 101br, 102tl, 103tl, 103tr, 104tr,105tr, 105br, 109tr, 109b, 110bl, 110br, 111bl, 113cl, 115t, 116tr, 117t, 117b, 118bl, 119tr, 120bl, 120br, 121cl, 122tr, 124cr, 125cl, 125cr, 125br, 126br, 127bl, 128br, 129bl, 130tr, 132b, 133bl, 133br, 134tr, 135cl, 135bl, 135br, 137tr, 140tr, 147tr, 147bl, 148tc, 149tr, 149br, 153bl, 154t, 154b, 155br, 156tr, 159br, 161tr, 163bl, 171br, 172t, 172l, 172bl, 172-173c, 173t, 173c, 173b, 174t, 176br, 177bl, 177br, 178tr, 178tr, 179bl, 181t, 194br, 195bl, 195br, 196cl, 196bl, 199cr, 199br, 201cl, 202br, 203tr, 203bl, 203br, 207tl; **Art Directors and TRIP Photo Library**: 112tr; **Brian J. McMorrow**: 90tr; **Corbis**: 19t, 21bl,29tl, 31c, 40tr, 42tl, 44b, 65tr, 75t, 85tr, 86tr, 86cr, 86br, 87br, 97tl, 105bl, 111cl, 115bl, 115br, 124b, 138-139bc, 169c, 169bl, 176tl, 188bl,

189cr, 189bl, 202bl, 204tr; **Getty Images**: 11c, 11r, 35r, 43bl, 48r, 56bl, 66br, 74tr, 82bc, 83bl, 109cl, 177tr, 198br, 205br; **Glow Images**: 11tc, 24t; **Photo courtesy Google UK**: 20tl, 20br; **Nature Picture Library**: 189tl; **Reuters**: 26bl; **Rex Features**: 162-163tc, 199tl; **Robert Harding World Imagery**: 55tr, 67br; **Science Photo Library Ltd**: 107cr, 110tr, 144tr, 150tc, 188t, 188bc, 188br; **Shutterstock.com**: 29br, 36t, 50t, 62t, 74t, 88t, 102tr; **Wikimedia Commons**: 50l, 74cr, 86bl; **Wikimedia Foundation Inc**: 59tr; **World Pictures / Photoshot Holdings**: 180tr

Cover images: Front: **Shutterstock.com**; Back: **Planetary Visions**

In some instances we have been unable to trace the owners of copyright material, and we would appreciate any information that would enable us to do so.

All other images © Dorling Kindersley.
For further information see www.dkimages.com

Picture Research by: Iman Naciri

DK EDUCATION
Cartographer: Ed Merritt

Pearson Education
Edinburgh Gate
Harlow
Essex
CM20 2JE
England and Associated Companies throughout the World
This edition © Pearson Education Limited 2013
The rights of Beatrice Adimola, Tsegay Asgele, Charles Gahima, Joseph S Mmbando and Samuel Owuor to be identified as the authors of this Work have been asserted by them in accordance with the Copyright, Designs and Patents Act of 1988.

ISBN: 978 1 408 29944 9

First published in 2006
Second Edition © Pearson Education 2007
Third Edition © Pearson Education 2013

Reprinted with corrections 2013 and 2014

Printed in Slovakia by Neografia

20

IMP 10 9 8 7 6

Maps, design and compilation © Dorling Kindersley Limited 2013

This atlas has been produced in collaboration with the Geographical Association, who offered advice on the structure and content.